WILLARD Z. PARK'S
ETHNOGRAPHIC NOTES

Willard Z. Park at Pyramid Lake Reservation, 1960. Photograph by Susan Park.

Number 114 1989

WILLARD Z. PARK'S ETHNOGRAPHIC NOTES ON THE NORTHERN PAIUTE OF WESTERN NEVADA, 1933-1940
VOLUME 1

Compiled and Edited
by
Catherine S. Fowler

University of Utah
Anthropological Papers
University of Utah Press
Salt Lake City, Utah

∞ The paper in this book meets the standards for
permanence and durability established by the
Committee on Production Guidelines for Book Longevity
of the Council on Library Resources

Cover: Twining a tule duck-egg collecting bag. Drawing by Susan Lohse

To Harry Sampson (d. 1970), who
always had a deep and sincere
interest in the history and
culture of his people.

Contents

Illustrations

Preface

The untimely death of Willard Z. Park in 1965 left unpublished his vast accumulation of Northern Paiute ethnographic notes made between 1933 and 1940. In the early 1970s, Park's widow, Susan, herself an ethnographer and fully aware of the value of her husband's data, kindly turned the material over to me for editing and publication. Since that time, I have worked on segments of them as time permitted, and especially on a sabbatical leave from the University of Nevada, Reno, in 1977–78. During that year, I also traveled to several U.S. museums to study the collections Park had made of Northern Paiute material culture, as well as other comparative collections. The National Science Foundation kindly supported this travel and supplemented my salary during that year (BNS 77-1348).

Park's data are so numerous that trying to fit them into a single volume proved unworkable. Thus, the present volume contains roughly half of the total number of sections that will ultimately appear. Those included in volume 1 are Territory and Intergroup Relationships, Subsistence, Material Culture, Houses, Clothing and Adornment, Transportation, Dogs and Horses, Medicines, and Political Organization. Volume 2 will contain Social Organization (Kinship and Marriage), the Life Cycle (Birth, Child Rearing, Puberty, Death), Religion, Shamanism, Miscellaneous Beliefs and Customs, Games and Amusements, Tobacco and Smoking, Music and Dance, and Myths and Tales. These sections are arranged according to the paradigm of cultural description of Park's day, and one that is still a useful scheme for presenting descriptive data.

Many people are owed debts of thanks and appreciation for aiding me through the years with this work. To Susan Park and the Park children, Nancy Jane and Henry, who have waited so long to see the material in print, I owe a special debt of gratitude for allowing me to work on the project. To the various museum personnel (curators and staff), I am also indebted for making my visits pleasant as well as rewarding. These include, at the American Museum of Natural History, Dr. David Hurst Thomas and Anibal Rodriguez; at the Field Museum of Natural History, Phyllis Rabineau; at the Lowie Museum of Anthropology, University of California, Berkeley, Frank Norick and Lawrence E. Dawson; at the Milwaukee Public Museum, Phil Sidoff and Susan Otto; at the Museum of the American Indian, Heye Foundation, Dr. James G. E. Smith and Brenda Holland; at the National Museum of Natural History, Smithsonian Institution, Drs. Clifford Evans and Betty J. Meggars; and at the Peabody Museum of Archaeology and Ethnology, Harvard University, Dr. Ian Brown, Sally Bond, and Barbara Isaac. Dr. Sven Liljeblad, at the University of Nevada, Reno, as always has answered my endless questions with great interest and enthusiasm, and allowed me *carte blanche* with his lexical files. His expertise in matters of Northern Paiute linguistics and ethnology is unequalled, and I have profited much from all of our discussions.

Joyce E. Bath checked Park's typescript notes against the original field notebooks, and was a delightful assistant in studies at the Peabody Museum and the Lowie Museum. Line drawings of artifacts and persons were skillfully made by Susan Lohse. Patricia DeBunch drafted the maps and drew Figures 12c, 25a, and 25b. Photographic prints of artifacts, except where provided by museums (Peabody Museum; some from Milwaukee Public Museum), were made by Maribeth Hamby and Gary Yarbrough. Ella Kleiner typed portions of the manuscript.

Finally, I wish to acknowledge the contributions of my husband, Don, as willing discussant, supporter, and uncomplaining artifact photographer. His encouragement and patience with a project too long in the doing is much appreciated.

CSF
February, 1987

Abbreviations

AMNH	American Museum of Natural History, New York
FM	Field Museum of Natural History, Chicago
LMA	Lowie Museum of Anthropology, University of California, Berkeley
MPM	Milwaukee Public Museum, Milwaukee
MAI	Museum of the American Indian, Heye Foundation, New York
NAA-SI	National Anthropological Archives, Smithsonian Institution, Washington, D.C.
NMNH	National Museum of Natural History, Smithsonian Institution, Washington, D.C.
PM	Peabody Museum of Archaeology and Ethnology, Harvard University, Cambridge

PARK'S CONSULTANTS

See further discussion of these people and places in the section on Park's Consultants in the Introduction.

AC,LG-F	Annie Cushman, Lizzie Gibbon — Fallon
AC-WR	Annie Cowell — Walker River
AD-R	Annie Downington — Reno
AD-WR	Annie Dick — Walker River
AM-PL	Abraham Mahwee — Pyramid Lake
BB-PL	Billy Biscuit — Pyramid Lake
BF-PL	Billy Frazer — Pyramid Lake
BR-L,PL	Billy Roberts — Lovelock, Pyramid Lake
CW-PL	Charlie Winnemucca — Pyramid Lake
DL-WR	Daisy Lopez — Walker River
DM-PL	Dick Mahwee — Pyramid Lake
GK-WR	George Knerim — Walker River
HS-D	Harry Sampson — Dayton
HW-Y	Henry Williams — Yerington
JB-PL	Jigger Bob — Pyramid Lake
JC-WR	Johnnie Cleveland — Walker River
JG-PL	Joe Green — Pyramid Lake
JH-PL	Jane Holbrook — Pyramid Lake
JN-R,PL	Johnnie Newman — Reno, Pyramid Lake
JO-PL	Jackson Overton — Pyramid Lake
JS-R	Juanita Sampson — Reno
LA-PL	Louie Anthony — Pyramid Lake
MS-R	Maud Sampson — Reno
ND-HL	Nick Downington — Honey Lake
RP-WR	Rosie Plummer — Walker River
TM-WR,Y	Tom Mitchell — Walker River, Reno

Introduction

WILLARD Z. PARK

The materials presented herein are the result of field investigations by Willard Zerbe Park among the Northern Paiute people of western Nevada between the years 1933 and 1940. Park focussed primarily on the pre- and immediately post-contact ethnography of the people at Pyramid Lake, Walker River, Honey Lake, Dayton, and Yerington, although his notes also contain accounts concerning life at Lovelock, Reno, and, to a lesser degree, Fallon-Stillwater. Roughly 27 people spoke with him, giving him information on all aspects of early lifeways (see Park's Consultants, below). For the most part, they were elderly people, although Park's involvement with Harry Sampson—then a young man but a person with a deep and sincere interest in the old ways and one who over the next few years prodded Park through letters to finish his work—was an exception. This volume is dedicated to Mr. Sampson, as I am sure would have been Park's wish.

Park began his Northern Paiute field work in the summer of 1933, after having completed an A.B. degree in anthropology and a year's graduate study at the University of California, Berkeley. While at Berkeley, Park had been introduced to the ethnography of the Great Basin by Alfred L. Kroeber, Robert H. Lowie, and Edward W. Gifford, all pioneers in ethnographic description in the region. According to Park's widow, Susan, herself an undergraduate anthropology major at Berkeley at the time, it was Lowie who convinced Park to study in western Nevada. Lowie had done his own preliminary field reconnaissance among the people at Pyramid Lake and Fallon in 1914, while making artifact collections for the American Museum of Natural History (Lowie 1924). He had also worked among the adjacent Washoe in 1926 (Lowie 1939). Park's first field season, of approximately two months' duration, was quite successful, netting him roughly 600 pages of raw data. Most of the data were on general cultural description, following roughly the paradigm of the day: material culture, subsistence, housing, clothing, political organization, social organization, religion, mythology, etc.

In the fall of 1933, Park entered graduate school at Yale, at the suggestion of fellow Berkeley graduate W. W. Hill, who had also enrolled. There Park came under the influence of Edward Sapir. Sapir's own interest in the Great Basin had come through his work with Tony Tillohash, from whom Sapir acquired the data for his Southern Paiute grammar, texts, and lexicon (Sapir 1930–31). Sapir's interests in culture and personality would influence Park's subsequent lines of inquiry into these aspects of Northern Paiute life (to be summarized in vol. 2 of this work). Sapir's courses in linguistics, never favorites of Park's, were probably also responsible for a shift in his transcription of Northern Paiute lexical data in later field seasons (see Appendix).

But although Park had a good deal of contact with Sapir at Yale, it was Leslie Spier who apparently provided more guidance in field studies. Spier seemingly read with care the results of Park's first field season, making several marginal notes on Park's typed excerpts (Spier's hand kindly indentified by Robert C. Euler, 1983). Spier's own interests in the region were likewise keen, as in the preparation of his Havasupai ethnography he made frequent reference to comparative data from the Great Basin (Spier 1928). Spier's marginal notes and queries on Park's MSS, and undoubtedly verbal comments as well, clearly set the stage for some of the lines of inquiry Park would pursue in later field seasons.

Park returned to western Nevada for more field work in the summers of 1934 and 1935, while still pursuing graduate studies at Yale. In 1936, he completed his doctoral dissertation on shamanism in western North America while an instructor in anthropology at Northwestern University. The dissertation, in which his Northern Paiute data were prominently featured, also contains the comparative perspective so important to Spier and others of the day.

Park's decision to focus on shamanism for the dissertation had been at the suggestion of Sapir and Spier. In 1934, he published a short paper on the topic in the *American Anthropologist*. At that time, shamanism was a little-known topic in the Great Basin. Isabel Kelly (1932) had written on it briefly in her monograph of the Surprise Valley Paiute. Julian Steward (1933) had also treated the topic briefly in his Owens Valley Paiute ethnography. Spier (1928) had provided data for the adjacent Havasupai, and others had given notes for various groups in California.

But the topic was hardly well known for the region. Park's data on shamanism went beyond descriptive aspects, probing the motivations behind this system of thought. He presented biographical data from several individuals interviewed as to their sources of power, their doctoring experiences, and, in some cases, their failures in maintaining the powers that had once been theirs. Park's dissertation, later published by Northwestern University (Park 1938a) in revised form, has remained required reading in the field of shamanism and a classic in Great Basin studies.

Park's other published contributions to Northern Paiute and Great Basin anthropology were completed while he taught anthropology, first at Northwestern University (1935–1938), and then at the University of Oklahoma (1938–1942). At Oklahoma, Park also served as Chair of the Department of Anthropology and Sociology (Murdock 1966:136). In 1937, Park published a brief article on cases of Northern Paiute polyandry as part of an exchange between himself and Omer Stewart (1937) and Julian Steward (1936), who had also heard reports of the practice among the Northern Paiute and Western Shoshone. He likewise took the lead in a series of short articles on territorial boundaries and group identity for the Basin, with his own contribution on the Northern Paiute of western Nevada, whom he saw as a somewhat distinct entity within the distribution of Northern Paiute speech, and whom he called the Paviotso (fig. 1). Park's use of this term parallels a suggestion made by John Wesley Powell in 1873 (Powell and Ingalls 1873). The term is the anglicized version of the Western Shoshone term for the people of west-central Nevada (*pa.piocco* [Miller 1972:125]), and has been bandied about in the literature for some years. Park's application of the term to groups in western Nevada follows rather closely the extent of its application by the Western Shoshone, an application not necessarily followed by Park's colleagues. Largely because of inconsistencies in its use, as well as its somewhat derogatory implications, the term has generally gone out of favor today (Fowler and Goddard 1986). Northern Paiute, a designation not without its own problems, is now preferred.

In 1941, Park contributed a paper titled "Cultural Succession in the Great Basin" to a festschrift honoring the memory of Edward Sapir. It was to be his last published report from his field studies, which by now had been expanded to include brief field trips in the summers of 1939 and 1940. In this paper, Park attempted to reconstruct the purpose and distribution of dance forms in the Great Basin, including the Circle Dance and Hunchback or Clown Dance, and to compare these to more recent introductions such as the Bear Dance. As in his dissertation, he relied heavily on a comparative-historical approach, which would have pleased not only one of the volume editors, Leslie Spier, but also the

volume's honoree, Sapir. Park's paper again serves as an important landmark in the interpretation of aspects of Great Basin culture, then still largely the focus of description rather than synthesis (but see Steward 1938 for an exception).

During the summers of 1937 and 1941, Park made field reconnaissances and studies among the Kaguba, a group in the Sierra Nevada de Santa Marta in Colombia. He published data on the group and region in the *Handbook of South American Indians*, edited by Julian Steward (Park 1946). But Park's remaining years would take him away from anthropological field work and teaching and into other facets of the field. United States involvement in World War II led Park to move to Washington. From 1942 to 1944 he served in various capacities in the office of Nelson A. Rockefeller, Coordinator of Inter-American Affairs. While associated with that office, he was responsible for a massive project involving the systematic survey of Latin American census and demographic data, and also helped to coordinate efforts to assemble and organize ethnographic and other social-science data for Latin America for the Strategic Index of the Americas at Yale University (Murdock 1966:136). From this post Park entered the United Nations Relief and Rehabilitation Administration (UNRRA), serving as Chief of the Coordination staff in the Foreign Economic Administration (1944–45) and as Chief of the UNRRA mission to Ethiopia (1945–47) (Murdock 1966:136). When UNRRA was dissolved, Park returned to Washington and went into private business. He and his family returned to Ethiopia in 1955, making it their home and business address until 1962. While there, Park also served as a lecturer at University College of Addis Ababa, where he introduced the first courses in anthropology (Murdock 1966: 136). He also facilitated the work of several young scholars who had come to study in the region.

Park returned to western Nevada in 1963 with the firm intention of editing and preparing his remaining Northern Paiute materials for publication. Based in Reno and at Sutcliffe, near Pyramid Lake, he inquired after and contacted various of the people he had once interviewed. He also began an extensive ethnohistoric bibliography of the Northern Paiute, focussing particular attention on descriptions of the lifeways of the people by trappers, explorers, emigrants, and early Indian agents. These data were undoubtedly intended to supplement his own extensive field observations. During this time Park was associated with the Desert Research Institute of the University of Nevada, Reno. Park also participated in the 1964 Great Basin Anthropological Conference in Reno, delivering a paper on Northern Paiute social organization. A sudden respiratory infection took his life in April, 1965, before he could complete his publication plans.

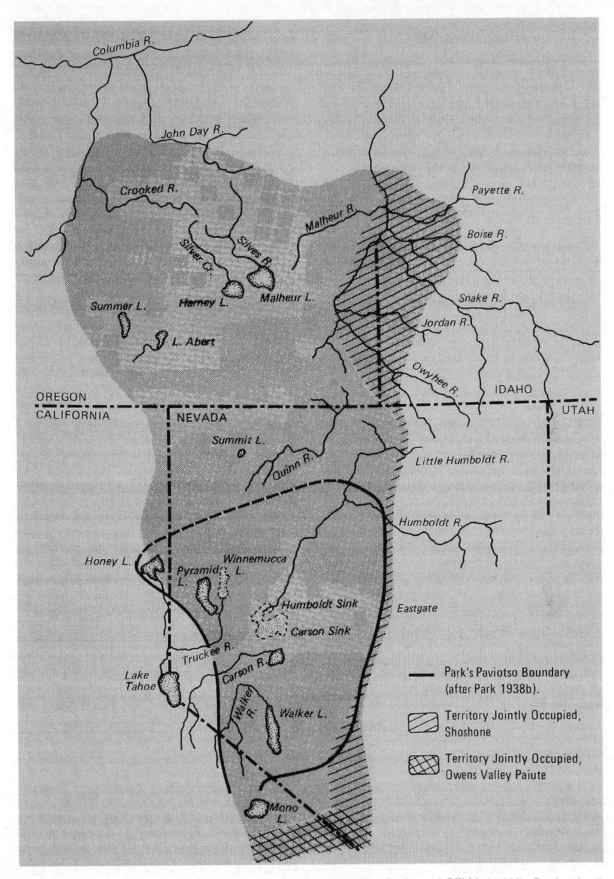

Figure 1. Maximal extent of Northern Paiute speech, *ca.* 1800–1830 (after Fowler and Liljeblad 1986). Drafted by Patricia DeBunch.

Park's legacy of ethnographic manuscripts on the Northern Paiute includes handwritten field notebooks of interviews with consultants and fully excerpted typescripts of these, arranged by subject. Data in the field notebooks are presented in a somewhat telegraphic style, suggesting that notes were taken during interviews rather than recorded afterwards. Data in the typescripts closely parallel those in the notebooks, retaining much of the flavor of the interviews, but also completing sentences in many instances. Occasionally the typescripts contain notes by Park to himself, indicating that he should ask an additional question on a subject, or perhaps compare this account with a specific previously published one that was either the same or different. There are few hints as to Park's actual field methods, beyond the occasional reference that indicated he might have shown people pictures of artifacts previously published, and a brief series of queries written in notebooks that were apparently to serve as particular lines of inquiry with particular persons. His personal files contain a questionnaire on musical instruments prepared by George Herzog and used in 1934, one on child care and development prepared by Robert Redfield and Melville Herskovits and used in 1934–35, and various trait lists, possibly as drawn up for the Culture Element Distribution Survey of the University of California, Berkeley (typed on the back of University of California, Berkeley, stationery). Susan Park conducted independent research among Northen Paiute women on childbirth and child rearing in 1934 and again in 1940. She also collected most of the genealogies and kinship terminologies. During part of the summer of 1933, while Park was working in western Nevada, Susan was concluding her own field investigations among the Hat Creek Atsugewi in adjacent California. She has recently published some of her Atsugewi notes (S. Park 1986). Mrs. Park's Northern Paiute data are to be included in volume 2 of Willard Park's materials, credited to her.

In all, Park's manuscript materials are credited as follows: for 1933, six field notebooks totalling roughly 600 pages; for 1934, 11 field notebooks with nearly 700 pages; for 1935, three notebooks with 275 pages; for 1939, one notebook with 50 pages; and for 1940, two notebooks with 75 pages. Typescripts from these notebooks total more than 2,000 pages. Typescripts and notebooks are retained by the Special Collections Department, Getchell Library, University of Nevada, Reno.

The procedure followed in editing the present volume for publication has been as follows: 1) All typescripts were checked against the original field notebooks for accuracy and thoroughness. Any discrepancies were noted. The assistance of Joyce E. Bath is gratefully acknowledged in this task. 2) Working from the typescripts, all accounts were compared for completeness and detail. Those giving the best account of a subject were chosen to be included, verbatim (with a few minor corrections) as they occur in the typescripts, with the consultants' initials and place of residence indicated. In cases where accounts differed, and these differences appeared to be the result of what might be significant individual and/or areal differences, more than one account was included. If the accounts differed only in minor points of detail, these points of disagreement were placed in the footnotes for each section. 3) Comparative published data, either affirming or contrasting with the accounts chosen, were then provided in footnotes. Most comparisons were made with monographs by Steward (1933) on the Owens Valley Paiute, Kelly (1932) on the Surprise Valley Paiute, and Riddell (1960) on the Honey Lake Paiute. Data from Omer Stewart's (1941) Culture Element Distribution Survey for the Northern Paiute were included, as well as other, more specialized accounts. 4) An introduction, summarizing the number of accounts Park received, something of the unifying themes they contain, and any obvious descrepancies, was then written for each section. These editorial comments appear in brackets, as do any other data added to the accounts themselves (e.g., botanical and zoological identifications, etc.). Park's transcriptions of Paiute lexical items remain as he had them in his original notes. Although it is clear that he changed transcription systems during the course of his field work, undoubtedly as he became more familiar with the language and probably also because of associations with Sapir, it was felt that these data should be preserved as they are, as they may contain valuable hints to usages now obsolete. The appendix, which represents efforts at retranscription and/or reconstruction of Park's lexicon, is provided for comparative purposes. As the reader will note, a certain percentage of Park's data have been lost to the present generation of speakers (1960s to 1980s). Thus his record provides valuable data of possible comparative interest.

The above procedures were deemed appropriate given that Park was prevented from synthesizing his own field data. With his greater familiarity with individuals, and with the circumstances under which the data were collected, he would probably have presented them differently. He would have undoubtedly added ethnohistoric materials, a job too large for the present undertaking. But in many senses, presenting the data as they are below, rather than synthesized, gives a certain perspective to Park's time in the field and field studies in general. Field data are made up of personal accounts from one's consultants. At a time when there is increased attention focussed on the nature of this collaboration, and also on how theoretical orientations can intrude between original data and monographic treatments of them (Clifford 1986), it can be refreshing to read materials largely in a raw state. Although Park's accounts are by no means verbatim (in some cases he worked with monolinguals and interpreters), they are close to contextual notes from conversations. A local Native American student once remarked to me on having read some of them that he liked them because "they sound like the old people talking." The ethnographer's bias and social science jargon have not intruded. Those who wish to take these data, rework them, and synthesize them within a theoretical framework, are welcome to do so. But as they stand, Park's materials provide exceedingly valuable additions to the ethnography of the region.

It is interesting to speculate as to what the impact of Park's data might have been on our knowledge of the region had they appeared in the 1930s or 1940s. Certainly a monograph on the western Nevada Northern Paiute by him would have stood alongside the now invaluable decriptive works of Kelly (1932) on the Surprise Valley Paiute and Steward (1933) on the Owens Valley Paiute, and would have filled the geographic gap between the two. It would also have added flesh to the trait lists of Omer Stewart (1941), themselves valuable sources for this central but as yet uncovered area of Northern Paiute territory. It may have been that given that various Basin ethnographers such as Steward, Kelly, and Stewart certainly knew of Park's field studies, they and others felt less urgency in filling the gap. But it is also possible that this ethnographic oversight was due as well to factors of interest and the lack of sufficient anthropological students to cover all areas in the region.

For whatever reason or reasons, however, the oversight has been significant. If they serve no other purpose, Park's data will at last document the richness of the lake and riverine subsistence regimes of the Pyramid Lake and Walker River Northern Paiute. Although suggested in the archaelogy (Heizer and Napton 1970), their ethnographic significance has not been fully realized until recent years (Speth 1969; Fowler and Bath 1981; Follett 1982). The significance of this type of adaptation has also been largely ignored in comparative theoretical treatments of the ethnography of the region as a whole (Steward 1938; 1955).

Park's data also document and enlarge upon our knowledge of other aspects of subsistence, such as large game hunting, small mammal trapping, waterfowl collection, and native plant harvesting. The data on clothing, manufactures, and housing, along with the material culture collections made by Park for various museums, also go a long way toward a definition of the material aspects of Northern Paiute life. Data on social and political organization, child rearing, puberty, birth and death, belief systems, dances, games, and mythology also add immeasurably to the data base for the region. Only those on shamanism will appear familiar, but here, too, Park's original notes contain more than he was able to use in his monograph. These, as well as a host of other points of detail, should make the Park data important to ethnographers, archaeologists, and linguists for many years to come. Northern Paiute people should be able to benefit as well from the many things Park records, now fading from memory even among the most elderly.

THE COLLECTIONS

Park made material culture collections for the Peabody Museum of Archaeology and Ethnology of Harvard University and the American Museum of Natural History during the 1934 and 1935 field seasons. He also deposited a few pieces at the Lowie Museum of Anthropology of the University of California, Berkeley, in 1934. Park's collections for the Peabody, accessions 34–114–10 and 35–120–10, total 112 pieces. Accession 34–62 at the American Museum has 59 pieces. Park's Lowie Museum collection, accession 500 CG, has five pieces. The two large collections also contain roughly 20 photographs each (duplicate sets).

The collections contain a good cross-section of materials that would have been available in the 1930s. They are particularly rich in basketry, but hunting implements, clothing, ornaments, games, and ritual materials are also well represented. Some specimens are models—fish harpoons, net shuttles, fish traps, arrows, hair combs, etc. But Park's notes that accompany the collections generally make it clear when specimens are models rather than functional items. Provenience by area is recorded (e.g., Pyramid Lake, Walker Lake, etc.), but makers are not named.

That Park's collection is heaviest in models of fishing gear is particularly interesting. His predecessors in field collecting, Stephen Powers in 1876, Robert Lowie in 1914, Samuel Barrett in 1916, and Mark Harrington in 1924, had been able to obtain functional items in this subsistence category: nets, harpoons, traps, spears, hooks and lines, etc. But by the early 1930s there were apparently no more of these items remaining. Previous collectors may, in fact, have bought the last. Although a few people continued to fish for trout, cui-ui, and other species in the 1930s, the former glory of the Pyramid Lake and Walker Lake fisheries had been largely destroyed. Roughly 75 years of overexploitation, upstream water diversion, and stream pollution and erosion had taken their toll. What Park learned of pre- and immediately post-contact fishing was largely from the collective memory of his consultants rather than from direct observation. People still remembered how to construct items of fishing technology from the past, but by this time had changed emphases and their own gear to accommodate new conditions. Similarly disfunctional and out of use was game hunting technology involving bows, arrows and arrow making, and quivers. Field collections were likewise difficult to obtain in this category other than models. The careful use of well-documented museum collections, including those of Park and his predecessors, can tell us a great deal about the history of changes in various aspects of culture such as subsistence (Fowler and Fowler 1981).

Insofar as possible, illustrations for this volume have been chosen from the specimens that Park collected for museums and from his photographs. Other illustrations have been added, either when a particular item mentioned in the ethnographies was not available in Park's collections, or when one from another collection was either in better condition or was a functional piece. Some of Park's models are illustrated, however. Captions for illustrations come from Park's notes as well as other sources.

PARK'S CONSULTANTS

Park's notes contain various brief biographical sketches of the Northern Paiute individuals with whom he worked, as well as some data on the types of information obtained from each person and his assessment of the consultant's expertise. Sometime after his field work, probably in the 1950s in connection with testimony for the Northern Paiute Claims Case (Park n.d.), Park prepared a brief manuscript summarizing these data on several of the individuals. The following is essentially as he wrote it, with a few additions and corrections. Home communities of the consultants follow each person's initials and are coded as follows: PL, Pyramid Lake; WR, Walker River, HL, Honey Lake; L, Lovelock; D, Dayton; Y, Yerington; F, Fallon; and R, Reno. The individuals included in his manuscript are those from whom Park received most of his data. Following his manuscript, biographical notes taken by him on several other individuals with whom he worked are added. The initials and community abbreviations used here are the same as those used in the remainder of this volume. Thus, each person's account is properly credited, and the community from which he/she comes identified. Variation in accounts may be regionally significant in some cases. In others, it may be the result of individual differences or knowledge. Park's own preface to the brief biographical sketches also defines something of the field circumstances under which the data—with variations—were obtained.

Park: Each particular account is credited to an individual [data for the Claims Case (Park n.d.) were so presented], but in the majority of interviews, bystanders participated in discussing the question asked by the ethnographer and frequently corrected or revised the answer of the account given by the principal individual. Often the group of bystanders numbered five or six people and frequently discussion lasted as long as ten minutes before the interpreter gave rendering of the answer to the question that had been put to the individual.

The Paviotso Indians took a good deal of interest in these interviews and made a serious effort to give a careful answer to questions put to them. Unfortunately, due to the ethnographer's lack of knowledge of the Northern Paiute language, it was not possible to record these various discussions and the opinions expressed during such discussions by the several bystanders. Thus, in the majority of cases, the statements have been subject to correction or addition of information by other Northern Paiute people.

ND-HL. Nick Downington was in his youth associated with the Honey Lake band. During the latter 20 or 25 years of his life, he lived in the Indian Colony near Reno [Reno-Sparks Colony]. Nick Downington was an extremely rich source of information and as he spoke very little English, all of his interests were in the aboriginal culture of the Northern Paiute. He was ably assisted in most of the interviews by his wife, Annie Downington [AD-R]. Annie Downington was the daughter of Johnson Sides, one of the last of the outstanding Northern Paiute chiefs. Johnson Sides's Paiute name was translated as "Peacemaker." [AD was born near Carson city, but lived most of her life in the Reno-Sparks Colony.]

Nick Downington was between 75 and 80 years of age in 1933 [AD was also in her eighties]. Both were interviewed extensively on each field trip from 1933 to 1940. Nick Downington died several years ago [d. 1937; Park continued to interview AD in 1939 and 1940]. A brief autobiographical account of Nick Downington follows.

ND-HL: I was born near Doyle, California. There were no white people there then. One white man settled in Long Valley when I was a boy. He had a ranch. My father built fences for him.

When I was young we lived in a house made of willows and tule. We did not stay there all year. In the spring, as soon as things were green, we moved across Long Valley Creek to Red Rock (about 30 miles northwest of Reno). We moved around looking for food.

In September we built the house (*nobi*) in preparation for the winter. We rarely used the same house for two winters. When I was a boy we always stayed in Long Valley or Honey Lake Valley with the *wadatukad* for the winter. When I was about ten, we lived near the present site of Reno one winter. The only place where we could cross the Truckee River was at the site of the present bridge near the county asylum [Nevada Mental Health Institute, east Glendale Avenue, Sparks].

In the winter we hunted deer. The snow was deep and the deer came down from the mountains. A hunter could get close to them. We used the seeds that we had gathered in the summer. Sometimes Washoes wintered

Figure 2. Some of Park's consultants. a (top left). George Knerim. b (top middle). Rosie Plummer. c (top right). Annie Cowell (a.k.a. Annie Dick). d (bottom left). Harry Sampson. e (bottom middle). Nick Downington. f (bottom right). Joe Green. Photographs by Willard Z. Park, 1934.

with us near Doyle. There were three or four houses of Washoes at Reno the winter I stayed there.

I spent a winter near Carson City when I was young. A sister was born that winter. There were no whites there then.

In the winter the women stayed in camp. The men were out hunting all the time. The only time the women got away from the camp was in the summer when they went out to dig roots and gather seeds. In case of death during the winter the house was burned and the family moved to a new camp. This was the only time we moved camp in the winter.

The only time of the year that we went to Pyramid Lake was when the *kuyui* fish were running. The only fish that we caught in Honey Lake were suckers. They lived in shallow water where the river emptied into the lake. I stayed around Honey Lake Valley until I was about twenty years old.

When the little green shoots started to come up in the spring we moved camp. If we had spent the winter at Reno, we went to Pyramid Lake in the spring. Sometimes there were a few Washoes or Shoshones there in the spring.

When I was a boy I had no clothes. One time some White people gave me a man's shirt. That was all the clothing I had. I put it on and tied a string around my waist. My father cut off the tops of some boots he got from some White people and made moccasins for me with the tops.

Our parents cut our hair when we were children. They left several small bunches, one in front and one on top of the head. I do not know why they did that. It looked funny. When I was old enough we made bows and arrows to shoot birds. The boys played with the girls when they were young. We played that we were holding a pow-wow.

HS-D. Harry Sampson was born near Virginia City. He married Nick Downington's daughter, Juanita [*JS-R*], and he and his wife lived with her parents. Harry Sampson was particularly well versed in the Northern Paiute language and spoke good English. He could read and write with a facility rather unusual for a Northern Paiute of his generation [Harry Sampson had graduated from Stewart Indian School, Carson City]. He was utilized extensively as an interpreter, not only when working with ND but with a number of other Northern Paiute individuals. Harry Sampson was very much interested in the aboriginal culture and became much a student of it in his own right. He was careful and very cooperative in all his work.

JG-PL. Joe Green, of the Pyramid Lake band, was about 60 in 1933. He was born at Gold Hill near Virginia City and moved to Wadsworth when he was still a little boy. At that time his family lived in an aboriginal

tule house. He spoke English sufficiently well to make an interpreter unnecessary. Joe Green had a very rich knowledge of aboriginal culture and made an excellent collaborator. As he was very nearly blind, his interests pretty largely centered around the past.

In his youth, Joe Green had visited, as was the custom of the Northern Paiute, all of the other bands and was well acquainted with the Paviotso in other groups in Western Nevada. Joe Green was well liked and highly respected among the members of his group at Pyramid Lake and exercised some influence among them.

GK-WR. George Knerim was born at Schurz at Walker Lake. He was nearly 60 years old in 1933. In his youth he had worked for a German family by the name of Knerim in the Yerington Valley [Mason Valley]. George Knerim was a man of considerable influence amoung the people of Schurz. Although he was generally accepted as a chief by them, he "has never been elected officially by a big meeting of the Indians held to choose a head man as was done in the old days." [He was a strong proponent of Indian rights in the 1920s and 1930s (Johnson 1975).]

George Knerim reported that his mother died when he was a baby, "while I was in the basket." He was brought up by his grandmother. He was close to his uncle, Captain Sam, who was one of the chiefs in the early reservation days.

George Knerim was an excellent source, careful in his replies and quick to state that he did not know when he could not give an answer to a question. He did not seem to have much information about other Northern Paiute bands as he had not traveled as much as other Paviotso had.

HW-Y. Henry Williams was born near Sweetwater. His parents were identified with the Sweetwater group. He had lived in Schurz for about 25 years [by 1933]. His wife, who helped him with the information, was born in Yerington.

In 1933, Henry Williams was a little past 50. He had spent some time prior to this in Lovelock, where he had gone to accompany his father. It is reported that Henry Williams died in the winter of 1933–1934.

RP-WR. Rosie Plummer was a shaman on the Walker River Reservation. She was born in that region and was between 60 and 65 years old in 1933. Her sister-in-law, Annie Cowell [*AC-WR*], who was about five years older, was almost always present at the interviews and assisted Rosie Plummer in giving information. Rosie Plummer spoke almost no English. Daisy Lopez [*DL-WR*], her daughter, acted as interpreter. Daisy Lopez was very intelligent and sympathetic to the work being done. She had an unusually good command of English in addition to a far better knowledge of the Paviotso language than is usual among the younger generation. Moreover,

Daisy Lopez had been constantly with her mother except for the few years spent at school and consequently was well informed on a great deal of the aboriginal culture.

BR-L, PL. Billy Roberts was born at Nixon and was about 70 years old in 1933. At that time he was healthy, alert and made an intelligent source. He was thoroughly familiar with many of the aboriginal customs and had actively participated in a number of practices in his youth. His father had been a shaman.

Billy Roberts was one of the individuals who made a distinction between the Northern Paiute of Humboldt Lake and those of Walker Lake. He had lived and traveled in the Lovelock area and many of his comments relate to practices in that vicinity.

JO-PL. Jackson Overton was identified with the Pyramid Lake band, although he did not state where he was born. He was in his 70s when interviewed in 1933. Jackson Overton was far from cooperative, and evidently resented efforts to pry into aboriginal conditions. [Park noted: "This may have been precipitated by criticisms of his participation by others in the community."] He was often impatient at questions and frequently responded by stating that he did not know.

JC-WR. Johnnie Cleveland lived on the Walker River Reservation in 1933. At that time he was between 60 and 65. He was born in the vicinity of Virginia City. Johnnie Cleveland had a good knowledge of aboriginal hunting and fishing activities and was the source of some information on the material culture of the Northern Paiute; but beyond that his information was scanty.

AM-PL. Abraham Mahwee claimed to be a chief on the Pyramid Lake Reservation, but his claim to chieftainship was not always substantiated by others. He was between 80 and 90 when interviewed in 1933. He was born in the vicinity of Pyramid Lake. Although not especially knowledgeable, he was the source of a certain amount of information which was corroborated by bystanders to the interviews.

JB-PL. Jigger Bob was born around Fort Bidwell. His father was from Pyramid Lake and his mother from Gerlach. In his youth the family usually wintered at Nixon [Pyramid Lake]. In 1933, Jigger Bob claimed to be more than 100 years old. He certainly was aged and was beginning to be a little difficult to work with as his mind wandered. However, with the collaboration of his wife, he was the source of considerable information. He was very good on material culture.

At the time that he was interviewed in 1933, Jigger Bob was living with his wife in the hills on the southwestern side of Pyramid Lake. He and his wife had lived in such isolated camps for many years. In his youth, Jigger Bob had traveled extensively among the Northern Paiute bands in western Nevada and eastern California. He apparently regarded himself as a wandering cowboy in that earlier period.

[The following brief biographical sketches on the remainder of his consultants are taken largely verbatim from Park's notes.]

BB-PL. Billy Biscuit was interviewed at Pyramid Lake where he had lived most of his life. Billy Biscuit was past 70 in 1933. He stated that he was three or four years old at the time the Paiutes and the Whites fought a battle near Pyramid Lake [Pyramid Lake War, 1860].

Billy Biscuit was born near Silver City. He was an excellent source of information, particularly on material culture. He was old enough to have attended as a young man one of the dances held by Jack Wilson [Wovoka] at Schurz in about 1890, and gave an excellent eyewitness account of this manifestation of the Ghost Dance movement.

AC, LG-F. Annie Cushman was born on the Grimes Ranch on the Carson River. Lizzie Gibbon was born on the Cushman Ranch. Annie Cushman and her husband always lived with and belonged to the Carson Sink band. Lizzie Gibbon and her family likewise. Both were in their 60s in 1934. They had an extremely limited command of English, and both were very suspicious and quite reserved. This attitude was typical of all the Paiutes living at Fallon; but perhaps the people living at the sub-agency at Stillwater, fifteen minutes east of Fallon might be different if a good interpreter could be found. The attitude at Fallon was in striking contrast to the friendliness and willingness, as well as interest displayed at Pyramid Lake and Walker River. Only a limited amount of data was secured from Annie Cushman and Lizzie Gibbon.

BF-PL. Billy Frazer was in his late 50s when interviewed in 1933. He was born near Pyramid Lake and his father and grandfather belonged to the Pyramid Lake band. He had lived around Pyramid Lake all his life. [His father was Jigger Bob's brother, and he and Jigger Bob used to travel together.]

Billy Frazer was an excellent source for myths, and he had a wonderful sense of humor and a racy style in telling stories. He was genial and liked to talk. The interpreter was Teddy Jim of Nixon.

JH-PL. Jane Holbrook was about 80 in 1934. She was born near Pyramid Lake and had always been associated with the Pyramid Lake band. Jane Holbrook was completely crippled in the lower legs, but moved with great agility. She had a great sense of humor and was an unusually able source of information.

DM-PL. Dick Mahwee was born at Pyramid Lake. He was about 60 when first interviewed in 1933. Dick Mahwee was an outstanding source of information. He had spent several months in 1914 at the University of

California Museum of Anthropology in San Francisco, acting as an informant in linguistic studies [see Natches 1923]. Subsequently Dick Mahwee became a shaman and was recognized in the years 1933–1935 as one of the ablest shamans at Pyramid Lake.

TM-WR, Y. Tom Mitchell was born near Wellington. He was about 90 years old in 1934. He belonged to the Walker River band. He was a shaman who had practiced for many years.

He was very feeble. His nephew, Joe Green, said that as he got physically weaker, Tom Mitchell's shamanistic power was gradually leaving him and his son who was taking over his power was becoming a more powerful shaman.

Tom Mitchell was quite willing to talk but tired easily. He knew a great deal more than was given in the short time that I had to work with him. His son and son-in-law acted as interpreters. Their command of English was extremely poor and they were sullen and suspicious. To some questions I could get a bare negative or affirmative statement which they refused to explain. Questions that they did not understand or could not think of the Paiute words for they simply refused to bother with. Added to these difficulties the six or eight people who gathered around precluded all attempts to go into Tom Mitchell's personal shamanistic experiences as well as inhibited both the interpreters and Tom Mitchell.

JN-R, PL. Johnnie Newman was born in Winnemucca Valley, southwest of Pyramid Lake. He has lived in Reno most of his life. He was about 70 years old in 1940. He used to live at the spring at the northwest end of Winnemucca Valley. They hunted deer and rabbits in the valley and got sunflower seeds and other seeds in the mountains. They lived there in the valley in the summer and went to Pyramid Lake in the spring for fish. In the fall they went to the range east of Gardnerville and around Virginia City for pinenuts. In the winter they stayed around Nixon fishing. There were usually ten or more families scattered at the various springs in Winnemucca Valley into the summer.

CW-PL. Charlie Winnemucca is the grandson of Chief Winnemucca [Old Winnemucca]. He was born near Granite Mountain north of Winnemucca Lake. He was in his late 50s in 1933. He spent his summers near Granite Mountain and in the winter moved south to Antelope Springs. They had hard times as the snow was very deep. In the summer they had many seeds and roots. There was no fishing in Lake Winnemucca. There was no lake there during the Chief's [Winnemucca's] time; it was a swamp with tules.

MS-R. Maud Sampson was born in Reno and was 27 in 1934. She does not know where her parents were born, but perhaps it was at Pyramid Lake.

AD-WR. Annie Dick was near 90 when interviewed in 1933. She was born at Schurz. She was the source of several mythological tales as well as general information. She was interviewed with Rosie Plummer, Daisy Lopez acting as interpreter.

LA-PL. [Only Louie Anthony's group affiliation, Pyramid Lake, is recorded. He was the source of some historical tales.]

ENVIRONMENT

The area covered by Park's ethnographic inquiries is part of the larger physiographic/hydrographic Great Basin, a region characterized by basin and range topography and interior drainage (Fenneman 1931). Overall, this region is semi-arid, being characterized by low annual precipitation and high evaporation. Flora and fauna are conditioned by these climatic regimes as well as by the varied topography so that diversity is high but overall numbers are low (Harper 1986.) Thus, a system of broad-based hunting, gathering and fishing was not only characteristic in aboriginal times of the people Park studied but also was practicable.

More specifically, Park's area of ethnographic concentration ranged from the Honey Lake basin of northeastern California on the north, to and through much of west-central Nevada (Pyramid Lake, Carson River, Walker River basins) as far south as Walker Lake. Much of this area falls in the immediate rain shadow of the Sierra Nevada, which rises dramatically on its western edge as much as 4,000 to 6,000 ft above its 4,000-ft base. The Sierra effectively prevents precipitation from reaching much of the area, so that averages of 2 to 5 in. of moisture fall annually on the valley floors, with 5 to 15 in. on intervening ranges (Brown 1960.) However, the Sierra itself, which may receive 70 in. annually, provides water to most of the area's streams and rivers in the form of runoff. Without it Pyramid Lake, Walker Lake, and Carson Lake would suffer severe declines or cease to exist.

The plant geography of this portion of western Nevada-northeastern California is divided into two primary vegetation sections, the Lahontan basin section and the Reno section (fig. 3; Cronquist et al. 1972). In the Lahontan section, which covers the Honey Lake, Pyramid Lake, and Walker Lake basins and the Humboldt and Carson sinks, the typical Great Basin basin and range topography is altered, so that mountain ranges are smaller and are separated by broader and more irregularly shaped basins (Cronquist et al. 1972:87). Much of the area is playa or playa remnant and alluvial flat. Soils are salty in and near playas and may also be so at higher elevations. Base elevation averages around 3,000 ft above sea level, with summits of ranges around 6,000 ft. During

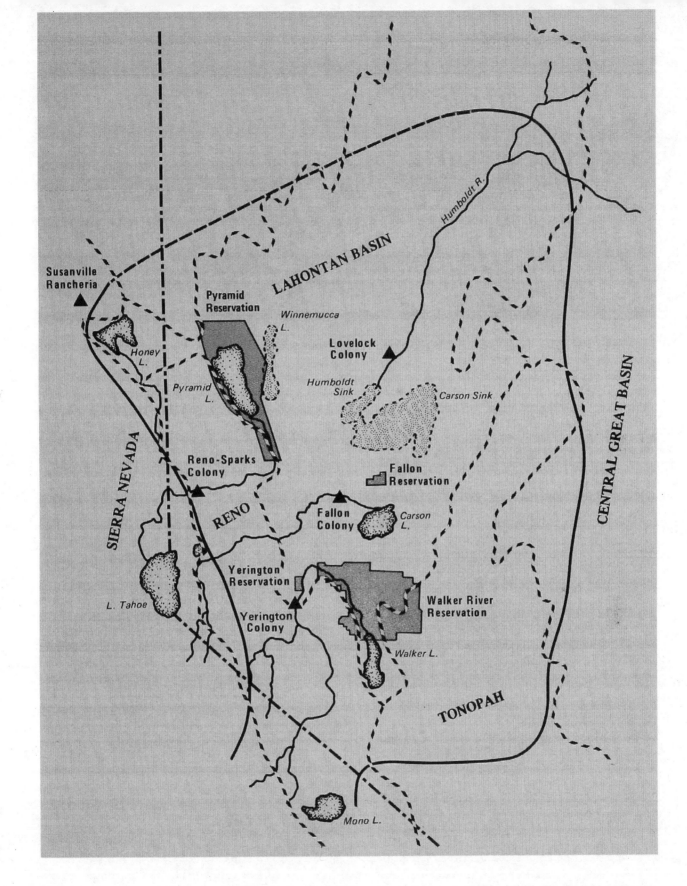

Figure 3. Western Great Basin plant geography; Northern Paiute reservations and colonies. Drafted by Patricia DeBunch.

Figure 4. Lower Truckee River with riparian vegetation and fields, Pyramid Lake Reservation. Photograph by S. A. Barrett, 1916. Milwaukee Public Museum photograph.

the Pleistocene, much of the area was covered by Lake Lahontan, which cut terraces on intervening ranges and deposited clay, sand, and gravel bars along their slopes (Morrison 1964).

Rather than the more characteristic sagebrush association that typifies much of the rest of the Great Basin, the Lahontan section is more commonly dominated by the little greasewood-shadscale (*Sarcobatus baileyi–Atriplex confertifolia*) association. These low-growing woody shrubs are widely spaced over much of the best-drained of the Lahontan soils. Playa margins support big greasewood (*Sarcobatus vermiculatus*), pickleweed (*Allenrolfea occidentalis*), quail bush (*Atriplex lentiformus*), samphire (*Salicornia europaea*), iodine weed or seepweed (*Suaeda depressa*), saltgrass (*Distichlis spicata*), and others. Rabbitbrush (*Chrysothamnus nauseosus*) and horsebrush (*Tetrademia canescens, T. spinosa*) may be on sandy areas away from the playas, while Nevada dalea (*Psorothamnus polyadenius*) dominates dunes (Lott and McCormick n.d.; Cronquist et al. 1972:90). Indian ricegrass (*Oryzopsis hymenoides*), a significant economic resource for the Northern Paiute, is also common in sandy areas.

Streams flowing into the Lahontan section from the Sierra (Truckee, Carson, Walker rivers) have gallery forests of cottonwood (*Populus fremontii*) and also support various species of willow (*Salix* spp.; fig. 4). Marsh plants that may occur where streams slow or spread out include American bulrush (*Scirpus americanus*), tule bulrush (*S. acutus*), alkali bulrush (*S. maritimus*), cattail (*Typha domingensis*) and a variety of rushes (*Juncus* spp.).

Some areas support the sagebrush (*Artemesia tridentata*) association, especially where fresh water is close to the surface (Cronquist et al. 1972:90). Grasses such as Great Basin wild rye (*Elymus cinereus*), wheat grass

(*Agropyron* spp.), love grass (*Eragrostis* spp.) and barnyard grass (*Echinochloa crusgalli* [introduced]), along with Indian ricegrass, also occur in this community. Most persist at higher elevations as well, where Utah juniper (*Juniperus osteosperma*) forms sparse to open stands. Singleleaf pinyon (*Pinus monophylla*) is rare to absent here, with all reserves occuring south of the Humboldt River. The vegetative section to the east, called the Central Great Basin, does contain extensive pinyon reserves (Cronqust et al. 1972:93). However, only its most western edge is within Northern Paiute territory (fig. 3). The Tonopah section, south of the Lahontan Basin, is in many ways similar in flora to the Lahontan Basin, with shadscale, big sagebrush, and black sage (*Artemesia arbuscula* var. *nova*) as the principal dominants.

The Reno section is a narrow sector between the Lahontan section and the Sierra Nevada. It differs from the Lahontan section largely because of climatic factors produced through the proximity of the Sierra and also because of a slightly higher base elevation (4,200–4,400 ft above sea level; Cronquist et al. 1972:90). Although storms are normally blocked by the Sierra, a few come over the summit and add to the precipitation rate, which is near an average 8 to 10 in. in the valleys and 10 to 16 in. at higher elevations (Harper 1986:Figure 1). The sagebrush community is more characteristic here of valley floors, while the pinyon-juniper woodland is well developed on the ranges.

This section also has several high ranges such as the Pine Nut Mountains, with Mount Siegel at 9,450 ft, the Sweetwater Mountains, up to 11,712 ft, and the Wassuk Range, with Mount Grant at 11,239 ft (Cronquist et al. 1972:91). In addition to the pinyon-juniper woodland, the upper elevations of these ranges support Jeffrey pine

(*Pinus jeffreyi*) and ponderosa pine (*P. ponderosa*). Other Sierran trees occurring in the section are Sierran white fir (*Abies concolor* var. *lowiana*), Sierra lodgepole pine (*P. contorta* var. *murrayana*) and western white pine (*P. monticola*). Streamside and springside vegetation in the ranges includes chokecherry (*Prunus melanocarpa*), currants (*Ribes aureum, R. cereum*), elderberry (*Sambucus caerulea, S. racemosa*), silver buffalo berry (*Shepherdia argentea*), and others. Several desert parsleys (*Lomatium* spp.), yampa (*Perideridia bolanderi, P. gairdneri*), spring beauty (*Claytonia umbellata*) and bitterroot (*Lewisia rediviva*) occur on slopes of ranges or valley floors. Grasses include most of those in the Lahontan section that occur here in more abundance. Nevada bluegrass (*Poa nevadensis*), mat Muhly (*Muhlenbergia richardsonis*), and others are added, as are many plants of economic value.

The fauna of both the Lahontan and Reno vegetative sections is nowhere dense except in the marshes and lakes at breeding and nesting time for waterfowl and at times of fall and spring fish runs. Given that the region is on the Pacific flyway, many migrating species stop to feed and rest or nest in the lakes, streams, and marshes of the Lahontan section. Pyramid Lake supports the largest breeding colony in North America of White Pelican (*Pelecanus erythrorhynchos*), and the American Avocet (*Recurvivostra americana*) is likewise common throughout the area (Ryser 1985:7). Mallards (*Anus platyrhynchos*), Northern Pintails (*A. acuta*), Green-winged and Cinnamon Teal (*A. cerecca, A. cyanoptera*), the Redhead (*Aythya affinis*), Canvasback (*A. valisineria*), Canada Goose (*Branta canadensis*), American Coot (*Fulica americana*), and many more are resident or visitants. Fish occurring in abundance at times in Pyramid Lake and Walker Lake include Lahontan cutthroat (*Salmo clarki henshawi*), Tahoe sucker (*Catostomus tahoensis*), tui chub (*Gila bicolor obesus*) and cui-ui (*Chasmistes cuyus;* Pyramid Lake only.)

Large mammals are sparsely distributed in the Lahontan section but more common in the Reno section, where forage is better. Deer (*Odocoileus hemionus*), pronghorn (*Antilocapra americana*), and mountain sheep (*Ovis canadensis*) were the principal large game species, all of which were hunted for food and skins. All areas had smaller game, such as ground squirrels (*Spermophilus beecheyi, S. beldingi, S. lateralis, S. townsendii*), yellow-bellied marmot (*Marmota flaviventris*), woodrats (*Neotoma cinerea, N. lepida*), jackrabbits (*Lepus californicus, L. townsendii*), cottontail (*Sylvilagus nuttallii*), badger (*Taxidea taxus*), and others. Land birds included Sage Grouse (*Centrocercus urophasianus*), Mountain Quail (*Oreortyx pictus*), Mourning Dove (*Zenaida macroura*), and many more. Insect resources included the Mormon cricket (*Anabrus simplex*), white-lined sphinx moth (*Hyles lineata*), cicada (*Okanogodes* spp.), and others (see Subsistence, chap. 2).

Microhabitats were highly significant to Northern Paiute hunters and gatherers. Knowing where to find a particular species and at what time of the year conditioned collecting strategies as well as habitation. Although Park's ethnographies do not discuss the details of seasonal or daily rounds, the lists and descriptions of plants, animals, birds, fish, and insects taken often contain data from which these can be extrapolated. In all, the data on subsistence are among the richest Park collected.

HISTORY

The culture of the Northern Paiute peoples described here by Park is based on consultants' memories, clearest to roughly 1860–70. By that time several significant changes in aboriginal patterns had already occurred, owing primarily to Euro-American incursions beginning in the late 1820s and continuing through settlement in the 1850s to 1860s. The federal reservation system was also in place by this time, and thus significant reductions in the aboriginal range of families and groups and alterations in their aboriginal subsistence pursuits were in effect. Some changes in material culture had occurred as early as the 1820s with the introduction of the first Euro-American goods. Social and political features had undergone some alteration with the rise and fall of mounted predatory bands in the 1850s to 1870s and the changes in group size and headmanship that that entailed. Although Park was clearly directing his research efforts toward reconstructing pre-contact conditions for the region, in some cases the accounts he received show evidence of some of these historical conditions.

The late 1820s are the time of the first historical accounts of Northern Paiute peoples of the western Great Basin. In 1827, the trapper Jedediah Smith visited the Walker Lake area on one of his various traverses of the larger region (Brooks 1977). He describes encounters in the area with semisedentary fishermen, obviously in possession of a technology that approximates what Park describes, as well as a group of 20 to 30 horsemen in possession of Spanish blankets, buffalo robes, and knives. In 1829, trapper Peter Skene Ogden encountered a much larger ("upwards of 200") contingent of mounted people in the Humboldt Sink, also in possession of some Euro-American goods (Davies 1961: 153–54). It is thus clear that at least some aspects of horse-using lifeways, introduced into surrounding regions in the mid to late 1700s, were in effect at an early date (Fowler and Liljeblad 1986:455).

But it is equally clear that patterns not affected by the introduction of the horse also continued in the region much longer. In the 1830s, people at the Humboldt Sink and on the Carson River were described by the trapper-guide Zenas Leonard as subsisting "upon grass-seeds,

Figure 5. Reservation scenes, 1934. a (top). House with sun shade, Walker River. b (bottom). Compound with several houses, Pyramid Lake. Photographs by Willard Z. Park.

frogs, fish, &c" (Wagner 1904:166). John C. Fremont (1845:218) likewise visited a large village of fishermen near the mouth of the Truckee River at Pyramid Lake in 1843. He described the people as living quite well on the large trout they caught behind numerous weirs in the river. They were in possession of some Euro-American goods, however.

In the late 1840s and through the 1850s, much of western Nevada Northern Paiute territory came under the devastating impact of emigration brought about by the discovery of gold in California in 1848. During this period, thousands of persons and wagons and tens of thousands of livestock traversed the Overland Trail to California, leaving in their wake the destruction of veg-

etative resources and game and exhausted and fouled water supplies (G. Stewart 1962:231ff). These conditions were felt most heavily in the Humboldt-Truckee River basins and the Carson River basin (both with branches of the trail), but doubtless had more far-reaching impacts. The rise of mounted predatory bands of Northern Paiute, operating in various areas of western Nevada and well into Oregon, was a direct response to traverses and trespasses here as well as elsewhere (Steward and Wheeler-Voegelin 1974).

In 1859, gold and silver were discovered in the Virginia Range on the western edge of Northern Paiute territory in western Nevada, and emigrants flocked to the mines. Ranches were also established in most of the best-watered and fertile areas to feed the population. Scarcity of subsistence resources as well as other more deep-seated conflicts gave rise to the Pyramid Lake War of 1860 (Egan 1972) and additional conflicts and skirmishes for roughly another decade. Many groups throughout the area had been displaced or were feeling the direct effects of settlement within their region (Fowler and Liljeblad 1986:457). Agitation by local non-Indians ultimately led to the setting aside of federal lands at Pyramid Lake and Walker River in 1859 and the formal establishment of these reservations in 1874.

Although it was thought that these two large reservations would be sufficient to contain most of the Paiute people of western Nevada, and at various times through the 1870s people were encouraged to go there, this plan ultimately proved unworkable. Many Paiute families had already settled on ranches and near towns elsewhere in the area, where they were earning a living through labor exchange for food and goods and through wagework. Thus, well into the twentieth century smaller colonies and reservations continued to be established in the area: Fallon Reservation (Stillwater) in 1902; Lovelock Colony in 1910; Fallon Colony, Reno-Sparks Colony, and Yerington Colony in 1917; Susanville Reservation in 1923; and Yerington Reservation in 1936–41 (Clemmer

and Stewart 1986:532–33). Whether on the larger reservations or in colonies and towns, the Northern Paiute people faced a difficult period of adjustment from what had been aboriginal conditions to those of the present.

When Park worked with his consultants in the 1930s, he found them living for the most part on reserved lands (fig. 5). They were still following older ways to varying degrees (see Consultants, above, for his evaluations). The memories of most for the conditions of an earlier time were remarkably intact on many subjects. They were fragmentary on others. Undoubtedly Park could have extracted more, had he known then what another generation of Great Basin field workers and/or anthropological theoreticians now knows and finds of interest. But he cannot be faulted for not asking questions that today seem more pertinent. No field worker can record everything. The data he recorded are remarkably rich, and a testimony to the degree of his ability and involvement as well as to the tenacity of cultural memory present at that time. Data with the richness of detail that these possess could hardly be gathered today. However, some 50 years after he worked, some of the same aspects of cultural memory and cultural persistence are still present and are no less tenaciously guarded by the descendants of Park's consultants.

1

Territory and Intergroup Relationships

[In 1938, Park published a statement on the territorial distribution and nature of Paviotso subgroups in the *American Anthropologist* (Park 1938b). The following section of this chapter, titled "The Organization and Habitat of Paviotso Bands,"* is essentially as he wrote it. It is reproduced here largely because it represents his summary and synthesis of these data form his field notes and also outlines his thinking as to why he saw these particular groups in the western Great Basin as a distinct entity. When originally submitted, his article contained an additional section titled "Band Organization." This is presented here for the first time. After these two sections, Park's raw field data on territory, subgroupings, neighbors, intergroup relationships, and place names are added. Some of these data had been excerpted by Park under these headings; others were gleaned from his field notes and added to these sections or placed in others as deemed appropriate.]

THE ORGANIZATION AND HABITAT OF PAVIOTSO BANDS

The Shoshonean speaking people known as the Paviotso or Northern Paiute of western Nevada are grouped in five main, loosely organized, named, and localized bands. These groups and their locations are [fig.6]

A. *kuyuítükəd°* (*kuyuí*, a variety of fish [*Chasmistes cujus*] in Pyramid Lake; *tükəd°*, 'eater'). This band centers around Pyramid Lake, particularly near the mouth of the Truckee River.

B. *agaítükəd°* (*agaí*, 'trout'). The members of this group usually winter on the banks of Walker River close to the point at which it empties into Walker Lake.

C. *toítükəd°* (*toi*, 'tule').[1] Formerly this band lived along the Carson River; now living at Fallon and Stillwater.

D. *wadátükəd°* (*wadá*, small seeds harvested in abundance form a plant not identified [Pursh seepweed, *Suaeda depressa*], growing in Long Valley, California). Members of this group claimed Long Valley and the shores of Honey Lake in California as their winter home.

E. *hápuDtükəd°* (*hápuD*, meaning not known to informants, probably a food plant).[2] Members of this band usually wintered along the banks of the Humboldt River from the lake to the present site of Winnemucca.

In addition to these larger bands, smaller named groups that returned to certain localities each year were recognized. Thus the people formerly living in Winnemucca Valley, between the present site of Reno and Pyramid Lake, were known as *kamútükəd°* (*kamú*, 'rabbit'), while those who returned each year to a small lake east of Fallon were known as *ko.sípatükəd°* (*ko.sípa*, the seed of a grass commonly found in that vicinity).[3] It seems likely that these smaller bands were even less stable in membership than the larger groups listed above.

Boundaries separating the territories of the several bands listed here were not recognized. Members of one band frequently ranged in search of food in the locality of another group. Thus people wintering in the neighborhood of the present site of Fallon appeared each spring on the Walker River to join with members of that band in taking of trout during the annual run of these fish. In a similar fashion people from several bands came together each fall in one locality for the pinenut harvest. There

---

*Reproduced by permission of the American Anthropological Association from *American Anthropologist* 40:4, 1938. Not to be reproduced without written permission from the American Anthropological Association.

[1] The term *toi* should more properly be translated as 'cattail' (*Typha latifolia*; *T. domingensis*). This conforms to present-day usage. The common names "tule" and "cattail" are often con-

---

fused by people in the Great Basin, and sometimes used interchangeably.

[2] If a food, it remains unidentified. Elsewhere in his field notes, Park equates the term *hapuD* with Humboldt Lake (a place name). The compound 'Humboldt Lake eaters,' which would then involve a place name rather than a food, is idiomatic, as 'eaters' can be and often is equated more generally with a group of people; i.e., 'dwellers.'

[3] Park's *ko.sípa* is /kusi·pa/, 'dust [alkali] water,' the name for Carson Lake. Prior to the 1860s, the lake was a large body of water. A change in the course of the Carson River as well as upstream diversion led to its ultimate demise. A small group camped on the lake where Allen Creek (fresh water) entered it. In 1859, men were seen by explorer James H. Simpson (1876) in this vicinity with piles of drying fish.

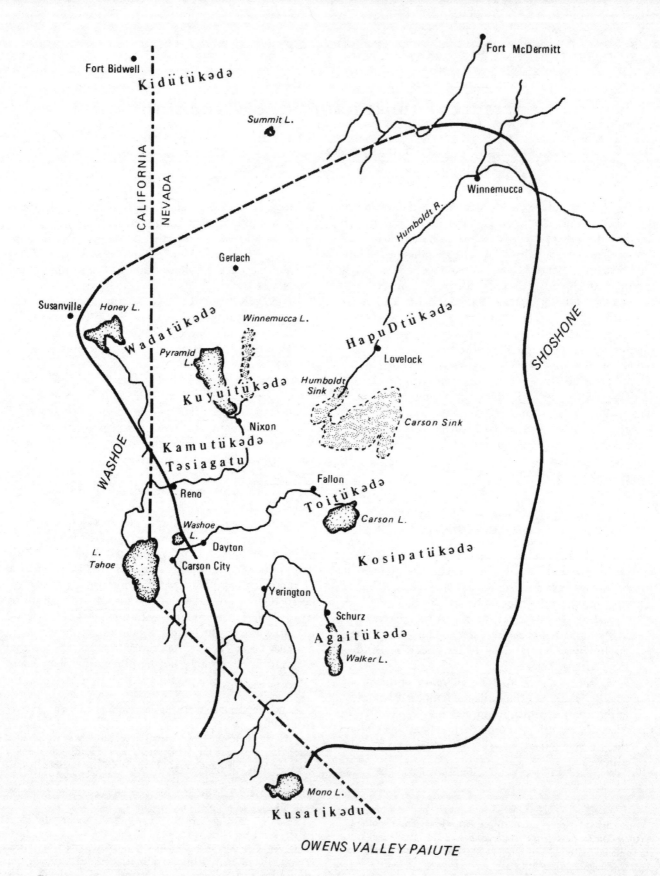

Figure 6. Names and locations of Paviotso subgroups (after Park 1938b; 1933–40). Drafted by Patricia DeBunch.

was, moreover, considerable shifting of population from one group to another. A family attached to one band often wintered with another group for several successive years. Family connections, friendships, the search for food, and perhaps the mere desire for a change seem to have motivated these inter-band moves. Certainly informants unanimously agreed that band territorial divisions did not exist, in fact were contrary to the Paviotso way of life.

In contrast to the above situation, fairly well defined boundaries marked off the territory of these five bands as a whole from the habitat of surrounding people. These lines, however, seem to have shifted from time to time. The penetration of Washoe Valley is a case in point. Usually the ridge of the hills to the east of the valley was regarded as the boundary between the Paviotso and Washo countries. Peaceful relations with the Washo and the need for game, however, might lead to hunting on the floor of the valley. Continued success and failure of the Washo to repulse the invasion brought more and more Paviotso into this heretofore alien territory. Several fatal clashes with the Washoes would result in the Paviotso withdrawing. For the following few years the Paviotso would confine themselves to the country set off by the old boundaries.

Similar penetration of foreign territory, both of the Washo and of the Shoshoni to the east, occured when the pine trees in the Paviotso habitat proved barren of nuts for a season or two. The invasion of the Paviotso country by Washo and Shoshoni from the same motivation suggests that a strip of territory on each side of the ridges, customarily constituting the formal boundaries, was exploited by whichever group arrived on the scene first.

It is noteworthy that no such territorial divisions existed between the Paviotso and their close linguistic and cultural relatives the Surprise Valley and Owens Valley Paiutes. Despite the recognized similarity in dialectic and custom to these California neighbors the Paviotso of Nevada regarded themselves as an entirely distinct group.[4] This attitude may be regarded as an incipient feeling of nationality. Although the Paviotso differentiate themselves in this fashion from their Northern Paiute neighbors they hold that even vague territorial boundaries never marked off their habitat form the territories of California Paiute. This situation is true only in respect to the several Northern Paiute groups. The boundaries separating the Northern Maidu and Pit River Indians from the Paviotso were well defined. Possibly they were more sharply drawn than those between their Shoshoni neighbors to the east as the Pit River people were the traditional enemies of the Paviotso while enmity towards the Northern Maidu seems to have been about equally intense.

The limits of territory claimed by the Paviotso in California differ somewhat from the tribal boundaries drawn up by Kroeber.[5] The western shores of Honey Lake are placed in Northeastern Maidu country and Long Valley between the lake and the California-Nevada state line is regarded as Washo. Informants, chiefly from Pyramid Lake were in general agreement that these landmarks were well within Paviotso territory. Only two informants belonging to the nearly extinct Honey Lake band could be found. Their testimony agreed substantially with that of Pyramid Lake people.[6]

The Paviotso boundary to the north was quite vaguely defined. A large part of the country between Pyramid and Summit Lakes is desert and nearly devoid of game and other usable resources. Consequently there was little interest in this area. This may in part explain the vagueness of Paviotso informants on the subject of the people who lived at Summit Lake and in the neighborhood of McDermitt. It is clear at any rate that relations with these Northern Paiute as well as those of Oregon were not as close as the ties that bound the Paviotso and the Surprise Valley People.

Territorial divisions to the east are fairly definite. Usually the ridges of hills are regarded as boundaries. These borders seem to have shifted back and forth in the same manner as those dividing the Paviotso and Washo lands. The border between Paviotso-Shoshoni territory supplied by Paviotso informants agrees substantially with that mapped by Steward [1937:fig. 1]. Information from the Paviotso would suggest, however, that the boundary swings somewhat more to the west in the neighborhood of the present site of Winnemucca.

The available evidence offers no clue as to the length of time the Paviotso have occupied the territory claimed by them just before they were confined to the reservations. Traditions that Pit River Indians once lived in the neighborhood of Lovelock have been recorded by several investigators (Loud and Harrington 1929; Steward 1937:626).[7] These tales cannot be taken as actual his-

---

[4] See Introduction for a discussion of this point.

[5] Park's note. He cites Kroeber (1925:plate 37).

[6] Long Valley and Honey Lake Valley appear to have been jointly occupied by Northern Paiute and Washoe, at least in historic times. Kroeber's (1925) Maidu boundary that excludes both from Honey Lake Valley proper is likely in error. Whether Honey Lake Valley was ever the exclusive area of any one of these three groups in pre-count times may never be known (d'Azevedo 1986).

[7] Park refers here to the numerous accounts of Northern Paiute encounters with the saidukaʔa, and their ultimate defeat by the Paiute. The name saidukaʔa 'under the tules (mats)' (Liljeblad 1982) is now equated generally with 'enemy,' and is variously applied to the Pit River groups (Achumawi, Atsugewi), Umatilla, etc.

tory without corroboratory evidence. There is a tendency in all Paviotso folklore to give a specific locality for each event. The account of Pit River Indians in the recent habitat of the Paviotso may then be no more than a reflection of this feature.

The relation of the archaeological material to the recent culture remains to be determined. It seems likely, however, that competent analysis may only show successive changes in material culture with little or no evidence of population movements.[8]

Similar vagueness of tribal locations is characteristic of the scanty data in the accounts of early Indian-White contacts in western Nevada. Careful sifting of the literature leads to the conclusion that in the first quarter of the 19th century the Paviotso habitat did not differ substantially from that claimed by the tribe at the opening of the reservation period.[9]

Band Organization

[The following section, titled "Band Organization," was originally submitted as part of the above manuscript. It was not printed with the article, and is given here in full because of the information it contains on Park's point of view of organizational principles and band differences.]

Membership in the Paviotso localized bands was extremely fluid. Individuals or families frequently shifted from one band to another and associated with the new group for an indefinite time. The frequency with which people moved from band to band is amply illustrated by genealogical evidence.

The Paviotso bands played only a minor role at the most in the social and political life of the tribe. Marriage was controlled by kinship, not by band membership. Private property such as the pine groves and fishing sites was in the hands of the family. People crossed band lines at all times to exploit the pine trees and the fishing sites inherited in the family and available equally to all members of that group regardless of temporary or permanent band affiliation or locality of residence. These statements are borne out both by genealogical material and numerous anecdotal accounts.

Likewise in communal undertakings, such as war, antelope, mudhen, and rabbit drives, and the seasonal dances, participation was open to all qualified Paviotso.

Of course most of the people engaging in any of these activities were drawn from those who happened to be living conveniently at hand. This involved, therefore, people largely of a more or less localized group. Nevertheless these events were not only open to members of other bands but were actually attended by families and individuals in substantial numbers from more distant localities.

In practice, then, as well as in theory the families that were the fundamental social and economic units in Paviotso life tended to form informal and unorganized aggregates in the localities of rich natural resources. The bonds among these families were not sufficiently strong to exclude or set off as outsiders similar kinship units from other localities.[10] Moreover, continued membership in a local group was determined by a number of factors: availability of resources from year to year, habit, interests, and kinship.

It is clear, therefore, that Paviotso families tended to come together in localities of rich food resources for only one to two seasons of the year. The seasonal association of families tended to persist year after year but changes were sufficiently numerous to keep the membership of any one group in a state of flux. These local groups derived names from one of the more abundant foods of the region in which they gathered annually. But sufficient organization and solidarity to set off such people from all others had not developed.

In view of the temporary nature of local residence it seems doubtful that the seasonal gatherings of families fall into the category of village groups. Certainly there was no village organization, nor was there a feeling of membership in such a unit. This would suggest that the Paviotso differ somewhat from other Northern Paiute (Steward 1937:631).[11]

It is evident that Paviotso political and social organization, above that of the basic family units, consists of a number of very loosely grouped, ever largely temporary, seasonally localized bands. Individuals are first and foremost Paviotso (*numa*) with a pronounced feeling of solidarity and recognizing a definitely delimited habitat. Within this group residence is shifted or is permanent largely in reponse to economic interests.

Correlated with the frequent changes of residence and participation in communal undertakings is the absence of marked ethnic differences between local groups. A detailed comparison of cultural data recorded from infor-

---

[8]The most detailed analysis of continuities-discontinuities in the archaeological record is that by Grosscup (1974). He reviews site survey and excavation data from western Nevada, some of which is indisputably Northern Paiute. He suggests that there may be continuity between that record and the archaeological Lovelock culture, a point still under discussion.

[9]See Stewart (1966) for extensive comparative mapping, generally substantiating this conclusion.

[10]Park argues here for a more fluid concept of groups than does Stewart (1939).

[11]Steward (1937) refers primarily to the situation in Owens Valley, south of the Northern Paiute. The nature of "villages" there is also open to question, as, with few exceptions, Steward did not define these in any detail (see also Steward 1933; 1938; 1970).

mants in the several localities suggests that significant differences in statements are not to be ascribed to local distinctions in culture. Exceptions to this do occur but generally the tribe [i.e., Paviotso] may be considered an ethnic unit.

In short then, the Paviotso may be regarded as an ethnically, politically, and socially distinct tribe, with a fairly well defined territory. Within the larger group local aggregates of families seasonally exploit the resources of particular regions in the Paviotso habitat. These informal bands are largely lacking in organization and a feeling of solidarity. Their existence is the result of interest in economic productions and kinship ties.

[The above account is based on Park's assessment as of 1938 of the aboriginal territory and subgroupings of the people he called "Paviotso." The following notes are the raw data on these topics in his field notes from which he drew some of these conclusions. He had undoubtedly read accounts by other ethnographers in the region (Barrett 1917; Kelly 1932; Lowie 1924, 1939; Steward 1933), and was likely aware of some of the historical and archaeological data. These helped to amplify the field notes. See also Warfare and Trade in chap. 9].

TERRITORY AND NEIGHBORS.

TM-WR, Y: The Shoshone lived around Austin and Smoke Valley. They came as far west as Eastgate [fig. 1]. The Shoshoni occupied the eastern side of the mountains just west of Fallon and the Paiute owned the western side of the mountains. The highest mountain in this range was called *waŋíhai*. The range was also known by this name [Stillwater Range].

In the old days the Paiutes did not fight the Shoshone (*təbənig*). The Paiutes could not understand Shoshonean.[12] Nowadays some of the Paiutes can talk their languages. A long time ago there was some trading done with the Shoshone. The Paiutes gave the Shoshone rabbit skins.

The Paiutes gathered pinenuts on the moutains west of Smith Valley. The Washoes occupied the western side of these mountains. Paiutes went into Washo country and Washoes came into the Paiute country. Fights resulted from these invasions. The valley in which Minden and Gardnerville are located was Washo country. The mountains to the east and the country around Virginia City belonged to the Paiutes. Carson Valley and Washoe Valley belonged to the Washoes.

JG-PL: Before the Whites came, there were no Paiutes or Washo around the present site of Reno.[13] The Paiutes from Pyramid Lake used to go through that country on their way to the pinenut country east of Gardnerville. Later when a store was built at Reno and the railroad came through there, some of the Washoes moved from around Gardnerville to Reno. In the old days it was not until the Paiutes got below Carson City that they would see any Washoes.[14]

The Washoes had the west side of the Pinenut mountains and the Paiutes had the east side. The Paiutes and the Washoes stayed away from each other in the Pinenut mountains. In the old days some of the Washoes would come to Pyramid Lake. They called the Washoes who visited them their cousins. They were not related to the Paiute, they just called them cousins. The Washoes did not stay long. I heard that the Washoes were sort of wild and liked to live where there were many trees. That is why they did not like to live down in the valleys.[15]

ND-HL: The Indians from Honey Lake used to go to the Pinenut Mountains east of Gardnerville and Minden for pinenuts.[16] The Paiutes occupied the eastern slope of the Pinenut Mountains and the Washo gathered nuts on the western slopes. The Paiute were on the east side of Washo Lake and the Washoes on the west. The Washoes lived around Washoe City, Birdeye [Verdi], Topaz, Sierra Valley (Loyalton is in Sierra Valley), and Gardnerville. A few of the Washo were friendly with the Paiutes and came to visit with them and to hunt, fish or gather seeds in the Paiute country. The whole band of Washoes never came into Paiute country. Some of the Washoes could talk a little Paiute. Some Digger and Pit River Indians could understand and talk some Paiute. None of the Paiutes could understand any of these languages.[17]

The Honey Lake band of Paiutes lived on both the west and east side of the lake. They used to go up around the eastern shores of Eagle Lake to get *yapa* but this was not their territory.[18] The Digger Indians (Maidu) lived

---

[12] The language in question is more properly called Shoshoni. Shoshon*ean* was a term used to designate several related Northern Uto-Aztecan languages: i.e., Plateau Shoshonean (Kroeber 1907).

[13] This seems a little doubtful, as the Washo were known to have fished extensively in the Truckee River, including in the Truckee Meadows (Downs 1966). It is possible, however, that this reference is to a time when emigrant traffic had cleared several valleys of aboriginal population concentrations.

[14] A permanent crossing was established at what was to become Reno in 1859, and the railroad arrived in 1868 (Angel 1881:634).

[15] This is clearly an ethnic stereotype, as the Washo spent the winters in low-lying, treeless valleys along the eastern Sierran front (d'Azevedo 1986).

[16] Elsewhere, ND implies that this was done in historic times after the introduction of the horse and wagon.

[17] It seems doubtful that some bilingualism did not occur across all of these borders. But, this may reflect a language attitude common to at least some speakers.

[18] Eagle Lake is within the territory of the Atsugewi (Garth 1978:236).

in the mountains as around Susanville. They did not come out into the valley. The Honey Lake Paiutes occupied Long Valley in California.

RP-WR: The Paiutes around Bishop, Independence and Big Pine are called *pit ənagwətə*. They do not speak the same language as the people on the Walker River reservation.[19]

Walker River people hunted as far south as Mina. The Shoshone came up around Tonopah. The Paiutes traveled east as far as Ione and Reese River for pinenuts and deer. People went on foot to the range west of the valley in which Ione is located. This range [Paradise Range?] was called *pabui wəyu'a*.

JG-PL, JO-PL, HS-D, BF-PL: Names of other tribes: *sai*, the Pit River Indians [Achumowi] lived around Likely and Alturas [California]. *izizawi* is another name for the people at Alturas because of their location. *manəts* is the Washoes; *takoni* are the Digger Indians [Maidu] around Susanville, and at Chico and Sacramento; *tugaisin* are the people around Sacramento [Miwok?].

BANDS, RANGES, AND INTERGROUP RELATIONSHIPS.

HS-D: The *kuyuitüka* are the fish-eaters of Pyramid Lake; the *agitüka*, the trout-eaters of Walker Lake and Walker River; the *toitüka*, the tule-eaters, lived along the Carson River in winter and now live at Fallon and Stillwater; the *wadatüka*, the *wada* (kind of seed) eaters are the Honey Lake Paiutes; the *kamutiküd*, the Winnemucca Valley rabbit-eaters (rabbits especially plentiful there).

JG-PL: The Paiute at Lovelock on the Humboldt were called *hapuDtukəd°*. They got ducks on the lake. There were only minnows in the river. These people got *sai, toy, wa.dá, su.nú*, and *wai* [see Vegetable Foods in chap. 2] around the lake. These people only ranged a little ways from Lovelock. There is no meaning for the word *hápuD*. These people ranged north about 25 mi. and east to pinenut mountains (RP does not know the name of these mountains [probably Clan Alpine Range]) and around to Humboldt Lake.

JN-R, PL: The band living in Winnemucca Valley is *təsiágatu (numa)*, "middle."[20] They lived at the springs in the northwest end of Winnemucca Valley. They hunted deer and rabbits in this valley. They got seeds in the

mountains—sunflower seeds and others. They lived there in summer, came to Pyramid Lake in the spring for fish and went for pinenuts in the fall—went to the range east of Gardnerville and around Virginia City. In the winter they were around Nixon fishing. There were ten or slightly more families scattered at various springs in the Winnemucca Valley.

RP-WR: The people around Mono Lake speak almost the same language as the Walker Lake people. The Mono Lake Paiutes are called *kusatikədu*. *kusa* is a small maggot-like insect [*Ephydra hians*] found on top of the water at Mono Lake. They are gathered by the *kusatikədu*, dried and boiled.

People at Walker River would visit Fallon and Yerington. A few might go to Wadsworth or Nixon for a big dance. Certain men from Schurz used to go up and help the people at Pyramid Lake when they were fighting the Pit River or Modocs [see Tales of War in chap. 9].

The Indians at Walker Lake and Pyramid Lake were better off than the Indians from other places. They always had plenty of trout to eat. The other Indians would hear about it and come for trout. [See Fishing in chap. 2.] They were starving and some of them never reached the lakes. Some of them got so hungry they ate their own children. The Indians came from Fallon and from around Bishop and even from further away. RP's mother has seen them arrive at Walker Lake. Some of then were so starved they could hardly walk.[21]

GK-WR: The Paiutes did not range south of the mountains around Hawthorne and Mina.[22] There was no boundary between the Walker Lake people and the Mono Lake people. They were the same kind of Indians. In the old days people went from Walker Lake to Mono Lake to hunt and get ducks. When I was a boy I saw people come from Mono Lake for fish. I saw them at Walker Lake every spring. [Park noted: "There does not seem to be any feeling that Mono Lake Paiutes were a separate people. At Walker Lake informants feel that

---

[19] The people of Owens Valley (Bishop, Big Pine, Independence, Lone Pine) speak dialects of the Mono language, closely related to Northern Paiute. Although the two are held to be distinct (Lamb 1958), sufficient data have not been analyzed to confirm the degree of separation.

[20] Stewart (1939) also recorded a group by this name in the region and termed them a separate "band." Park seems to have favored placing them, perhaps because of the small numbers and close ties, with the group at Pyramid Lake.

[21] *BR-L, PL* confirmed that people from Humboldt Lake and Humboldt River also went to Pyramid Lake to fish, often in a poor and weakened condition. Some died along the way. "The old people say that some might get some fish and eat so much that the next morning they would be dead. These people had gone without food so long that they ate enough to make them sick and they died." The same happened with people from Stillwater going to Walker Lake each spring. *HW-Y* confirmed traffic between Mono Lake and Walker Lake, with people coming from the former in the spring and summer to fish. They stayed all summer and then returned with dried fish to Mono Lake.

[22] Again, GK suggests some type of division between the Owens Valley Paiute and the Walker River Northern Paiute. He denies, however, any break between Walker River and Mono Lake People, the latter also speakers of Northern Paiute.

the Mono Lake people are just the same as the people at Walker Lake and that they came to Walker Lake or these people went to Mono Lake frequently. It is impossible to get any informant to indicate a boundary between the two groups. The idea seems strange to them."]

TM-WR, Y: The Paiutes on the Walker River ranged as far as Desert Creek and Topaz (Desert Creek is in Nevada, Topaz in California). Most of the Paiutes lived around Walker Lake in the old days. They all came to Schurz in the spring for fish. People came from Mina, Bridgeport, Mono Lake and Fallon for fish. In the old days a few of the people from around Walker Lake went to the country around Mono Lake for hunting or for gathering pinenuts.

JG-PL: In the old days the Paiutes hunted around Gerlach. In Granite Spring Valley there were many antelope and deer. On the mountains such as Limbo the mountain sheep were plentiful. The people from Pyramid Lake went on the other side of Gerlach to hunt around Granite Peak and the other mountains in the Granite Range.

Sometimes four or five camps would go around Granite Mountain in the spring to hunt deer and mountain sheep. Before they had horses, they never went beyond Granite Mountain. When they had horses they went on the other side of Granite Mountain. They went all the way to Fort Bidwell where there is timber. Fort Bidwell is called *yamoswait*. The people were called *kidütükəd°*.

People from around here did not hunt at Summit Lake before they had horses. Summit Lake is a long ways. These people speak the same language but they talk slower than we do. The people at Summit Lake are called *agaitukəd°*. The lake and the place was called *agaiBənu'na*.

JB-PL: The Indians would stay on both sides of the river around Nixon during the winter. Indians would be welcome from Reno, Susanville, etc. People from Walker River would come for *quiui*, mullet. The trout did not keep very well but they could dry mullet and it would keep a long time. People would come from everywhere to catch mullet, dry them and take the dried fish home.

CW-PL: CW's group spent the summers near Granite Mountain, north of Lake Winnemuca.[23] In the summer they moved south of Winnemucca, to Antelope Springs. They came down to Pyramid Lake during spawning time for *quiui* [April].

ND-HL: The Honey Lake people used to go to Summit Lake. Not all the band went on these trips. Just a few of them would make the trip. Some people even went into Idaho to visit the Bannocks. They walked all the way. Summit Lake people were called *agaipanúnawaitu*, 'trout lake people of that place.' The people from Pyramid and Honey lakes went to Summit Lake to visit friends. The people at Summit Lake were the same as the people at Pyramid and Honey lakes. They ate the same kind of food. The Paiute wintered along the Susan River. They also stayed north of the river near Litchfield and along the mountains southeast of the lake. The Digger Indians (Maidu) lived along and in the mountains around Susanville. They did not live around Honey Lake.

HS-D: Indians from around Reno and Virginia City would go to Honey Lake Valley in the Spring. Suckers and other fish would come up Long Valley Creek. In the summer they all went to Pyramid Lake.

AC, LG-F: The Paiutes lived on a lake near Douglas, called, *kosipa*. The Allen River flowed into the lake. Annie's family lived there a long time and when her husband died they came to Fallon. The people who lived on the lake at Cushman's Ranch were called *ko.sipatukədə*.[24]

Miscellaneous: ND-HL: The *zaputukuda* were westward [perhaps of Likely, California]. The *kazutukudə* are by Alturas (*kazu* is like *yapa* [*Perideridia* sp.]). The *tunuyutukad* are in Big Valley (*tunyu* is a root with black skin, about 6 in. long [*Lomatium* sp.]). *BF-PL.* Honey Lake Indians are called *sana*.

PLACE NAMES

[Park specifically collected place names from five individuals. None of the lists is lengthy, and each probably represents only a few that came readily to mind. The numbers key the locations of these names to figure 7. A few additional place names are scattered throughout the text.]

ND-HL: 1. *nawɔtunɔhopi*, valley where Deep Hole is located. 2. *wədəkatədə*, Granite Mountain. 3. *wadanunədu*, Honey Lake. 4. *wada*, Honey Lake Valley. 5. *sainunədu*, Washoe Lake. 6. *padi.kwa*, high mountains on east side of Pyramid Lake [Lake Range, Tohakam Peak]. 7. *tumuhabuno*, highest mountain on westside of Pyramid Lake [probably Virginia Peak]. 8. *pabagatüdü*, highest mountain near Jigger Bob's place [probably Tule Peak].[25]

HS-D: 9. *suhu*, Long Valley Creek and a spring not far from Carson City. 10. *kuyuinahukwa*, Truckee River.

---

[23] Park does not mention this group in his 1938 article (Park 1938b), and perhaps incorporates them into the Pyramid Lake group. There were undoubtedly many small groups with differing seasonal rounds in addition to the large groups that Park (1938b) and Stewart (1939) name.

[24] This term means literally 'dusty water eaters,' and is idiomatic based on analogy to other food-named groups. The principle of food naming was so common that such analogies occurred with some frequency.

[25] *JG-PL: pabikatud* is the largest mountain west of Sutcliffe. "It means mountains spread out wide." It is literally 'big sitter.'

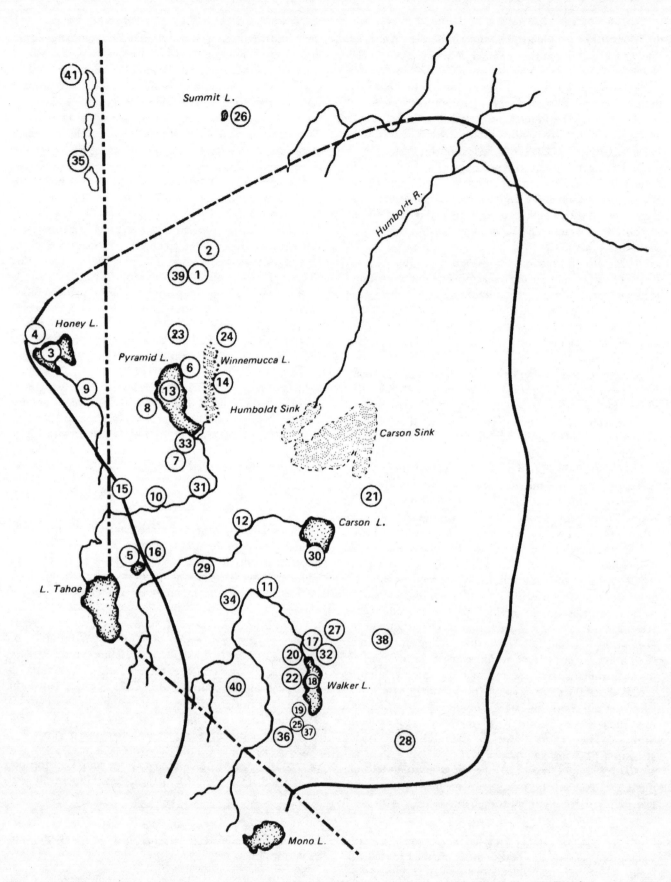

Figure 7. Locations and place names recorded by Willard Z. Park (1933–40). Drafted by Patricia DeBunch.

[8] **AP 114/UU**

11. *againahukwa*, Walker River. 12. *toinahukwa*, Carson River. 13. *kuyuipanünəd*, Pyramid Lake. 14. *izikuyuipanünəd*, Winnemucca Lake. 15. *akugaib*, Peavine Mountain, just northwest of Reno. 16. *patsunəkaib*, Sun Mountain at Virginia City [probably Mount Davidson].

GK-WR: 17. *agaitukəd*, Walker Lake Valley. 18. *panu.nədə*, Walker Lake (literally water standing in one place) [lake, pond]. 19. *kodəgwadə*, Mount Grant. 20. *ə.bə*, Black Mountains (literally, "many rocks"). 21. *waŋigodəgwa*, range of mountains east of Fallon [Stillwater Range]. The Paiutes went into these mountains for pinenuts. Most of the time they lived in the valley. All the springs on the Bald Mountain were named but GK has never heard a name for the mountain. Every spring and water hole in the Paiute country had a name. 22. *kaiba*, range of mountains west of Walker Lake [Wassuk Range].

TM-WR, Y: 11. *agai*, Walker River. 19. *kodəgwᵉ*, Mount Grant. Smith Valley was named but TM cannot remember the name.

RP-WR: The range west of the valley in which Ione is located is called *pabui wəyu'a* [Paradise Range?]. The range west of Walker Lake is not named.[26] There are names for the canyons which were claimed by the people who harvested the pinenuts in them. A person gave it a name from some feature of it, some green grass, willows, or something else which grew in it. The names became known, and other people referred to the canyons by these names.

Mount Grant was *kudəgwə* (19). People went to Mount Grant to get various medicines such as *sikəabu* [death camas, *Zigadenus venenosus, Z. paniculatus*], like onion, used for swellings; *kudagwabu* [unidentified], shaped like a parsnip and used to keep rattlesnakes away and for swelling; and *tsinibab* [unidentified], for sore throat. Many other kinds of medicines are also found on Mount Grant. Tobacco was also gathered there [see Medicines, chap. 8].

Miscellaneous: 23. *wakatudə*, Fox Mountain, north of Pyramid Lake [Pah-rum Peak?]. 24. *yanani'*, no meaning. This is Limbo Mountain southeast of Gerlach. 25. *aduponoki'i*, mountain near Hawthorne [Corey Peak?]. 26. *agaibənuna*, Summit Lake. 27. *asaka*, 'red tipped,' east of Schurz [Red Ridge in Cedar Hills]. 28. *huda*, cave near Lunning. 29. *hakwapa too*, cave near Fort Churchill. 30. *kosipa*, Allen River. 31. *pabahub*, Truckee River; 32. *osaba*, Double Springs. 33. *saiyatukəd*, Mudhen lake. [small marsh near Pyramid Lake]. 34. *tagwani*, mountain near Wobuska. [Carson Hill, Cleaver Peak?]. 35. *takakudawa*, mountain with obsidian near Eagleville. 36. *takatubi'i*, mountain with obsidian near Walker Lake [Mount Hicks?]. 37. *tonobi-duhaka*, mountain south of Hawthorne [Buller Mountain?]. 38. *tumə'əkwina'a*, mountains on east side of Walker Lake Reservation [Rawhide Peak and Black Eagle Hill?]. 39. *tunapiw*, 'antelope heart', 10 mi west of Deep Hole. 40. *uduhu'u*, Pine Grove stream. 41. *yamoswait*, Fort Bidwell.

TRAILS

JG-PL: There were well defined trails taking the shortest route to a place. There were trails going to such places as Carson Lake, Humboldt Lake, Walker River, etc. The trails were as straight as the topography of the country allowed. They followed the shortest but easiest route, turning aside for high ridges, etc. The trail to Walker Lake is called *agaibəə*; the Carson Lake trail, *toibəə*; Humboldt Lake trail, *hapudəbəə*; (Humboldt Lake, *hapudə*, Humboldt River, *hu.pə*. Fort Bidwell trail, *yamosəbəə*; (Fort Bidwell, literally 'big bend,' *yamosə*). Trails were open to everybody.

There were no special rest places along the trail.[27] People did not travel during the middle of the day. When people traveled, they got up early in the morning quite a while before sunrise, about three o'clock. They traveled until about ten o'clock when they stopped to rest until the day was cooler, say about four o'clock in the afternoon. These habits of travel applied in the late spring, summer, and fall when the days were hot. Travelers would rest or stop for the night any place along the trail.

If another person or party was met along the trail, they all stopped to talk. The first thing that was said was: *üdüta hada*, 'it is hot.' The reply would be, *aha, naüdüt puni hada*, 'yes, it is hot.' Afterwards one would ask, *hano'yu ükima*, 'where do you come from?'

GK-WR: There were trails to all the important places, e.g., a trail from Walker River to the Fallon district; to the south end of Walker Lake (to the general vicinity of Hawthorne); to Pyramid Lake, etc. These trails were direct as possible. "They made them shorter, they go right straight," but they followed the contours of the country; i.e., they avoided if possible climbing hills, etc. A trail was called *pɔɔ*. Roads are now called *pɔɔ*. The trails do not seem to have been named.

Resting and camping places were at springs. If a jug of water was carried, camp was made or a stop for rest was made at any convenient place along the trail. Aside from springs, there were no special resting or camping places. Trails were not owned. "Anybody could go along the trail."

---

[26] *GK-WR* gave the name as *kaiba*, (see No. 22), literally 'mountain/s,' rather than a specific name. This seems to confirm *RP*'s statement.

[27] There is no mention here of "doctor rocks," special places where travelers left offerings for a safe journey, good health, etc. (Wheat 1967:20).

2

Subsistence

[Park's data on subsistence are rich in the details of techniques for hunting large and small game, fishing, gathering and processing plant foods, taking waterfowl, and collecting insects. They clearly illustrate that there was a range of techniques applied in the region to a diverse, if not always predictable, resource base. Numerous individuals were interviewed with respect to these practices, often agreeing on techniques, but also occasionally suggesting alternative methods—predictable over a broad expanse of space and also over the range of species sought. Park's data add a great deal to what we know of Northern Paiute subsistence in particular, and, by extension, of Great Basin subsistence in general.]

SEASONAL AND DAILY ROUNDS

[Park's data are less complete on details of the seasonal and daily rounds. These are probably difficult aspects for individuals to reconstruct from memory, and are better observed and recorded firsthand. Park obtained only one reasonably full account on the seasonal round, and this specifically from a Walker River consultant. Notes on the daily round are also from Walker River respondents. Other comments on both subjects can be gleaned from the accounts of specific subsistence practices (see also Park's Consultants, ND-HL's autobiography in Introduction)].

RP-WR: Most of the people built their houses along the river for the winter. The people who camped along the river built their houses close to the river banks so it would be convenient for fishing. Fishing was done in the winter. If the river were frozen, fish were caught in nets through holes cut in the ice [see Fishing, below, for this and other techniques]. Men also hunted for deer and rabbits in the winter. The women stayed in camp. They ground seeds and made and repaired baskets. The women from nearby house groups got together and ground seeds together and played gambling games, especially *nubɔkɔi·ba* [basket dice; see Games in vol. 2]. The men gambled too. No dances were held during the winter. Dances started in the early spring and lasted through to late fall.

In the spring, the people living along the river moved back some distance from the banks because of the spring oods. They moved the frames of the houses but covered them with fresh matting. In the spring, in addition to fish, fresh tender green plants were gathered. There was very little hunting in the spring or summer. Most of the hunting was done in the late fall.

During the summer, the people scattered in groups in search of seeds. The men helped move the camp to the grounds where seeds are gathered and then returned to the river to fish. They carry the fresh fish to the camps where the women are.[1]

Roots of various kinds were dug in the fall.[2] Roots were ripe at about the same time as pinenuts. They go out for pinenuts about August. Pine cones are full at that time. They are knocked down with long poles and big piles of cones are made. About a month later the cones in the piles and those on the trees open up.

Some people may stay in the pinenut hills all winter and come down in the spring. The men leave the women on the mountains with the pinenuts and come back to their nets. The fish they catch are taken back to their camps in the hills.

(Vegetable food—seeds and roots—and fish seem to have been the most important in the diet. The women spent most of their time grinding seeds into meal. Meat seems to have been used to a much lesser degree than the seeds and fish. RP and AD say that seeds and fish were eaten every day, but there would be many days when they had no meat.)[3]

---

[1] These intriguing comments on house and camp movements seem to indicate a degree of winter sedentism and camp clustering followed by a breakup and dispersal—but with the men still tethered to the river and fishing. The same pattern was likely for Pyramid Lake, although Park's data are weaker there. In other Northern Paiute areas where fishing was not as important, winter sedentism and spring-summer dispersal seem to have worked the same for both sexes. Men might be absent hunting for some period of time.

[2] Far more roots were collected in spring and early summer than fall. This may be an error, or there may be some confusion based on the proper time to harvest White-introduced products.

[3] Park's summation of data from RP-WR and AD-WR to himself. The importance of fishing for this group, as well as for the people of Pyramid Lake, can hardly be denied.

People got up before sunrise. If people are in bed when the sun comes up, the rays of the sun get in them and they are lazy and sickly. After that, they cannot do much. Children are not allowed to stay in bed but must get up before sunrise.[4] Otherwise, they would be tired and lazy. It is also believed that a lazy man has his joints infected with small lice. They call him "father," and they tell him not to move. They say, "I am very comfortable, father. Don't move." This is a story that is told. They tell children this story. They tell the children not to listen to these lice in their joints so the children will jump up.

As soon as people get up, they wash their face, hands, and hair. They pray when they wash. The sun is asked to be good to them, not to hit them and make them lazy. The old people pray for the young ones as well as themselves. As soon as the women wash, they grind seeds and prepare food for the morning meal. If seeds had to be ground, a meal was not eaten upon arising, but food was ready about 10 or 11 o'clock in the morning. If only fish was to be eaten, it could be quickly roasted over a fire.

If the camp is near the river, the men get up before the women and go to the river to fish. If they are fishing with a weir, men take their turn on the platform, returning in time for the morning meal. After eating, men or women rest or gamble for a few hours before returning to the nets or starting to grind meal for the evening meal. The evening meal was eaten about sunset. Only two meals a day were eaten.

In the evening people visit around and tell stories. The children were taught the stories. The men sat around in groups by themselves and sang and told stories. While talking and singing, the men passed around a pipe and smoked. Men never smoked alone. When a pipe was smoked, it was cleaned, refilled and passed around again. The women did not smoke when they sat around and talked. The only women who smoked were those who were shamans. These women could smoke for pleasure if they liked. Other women smoked only when they attended a doctoring [see Tobacco and Smoking, and Shamanism, in vol. 2].

GK-WR: People would get up before sunrise, or just about sunrise. The women would start to grind the seeds, and if there was no wood, the men would go out and bring in some to cook the morning meal. The men sometimes helped the women grind the seeds in the morning. It took several hours of grinding before the meal was ready. The morning meal was eaten about 10 o'clock.

The evening meal was eaten about dark or after dark. Two meals a day were eaten.

The search for food was the main thing in life. We hunted and gathered seeds every day.[5] If we could get enough meat by hunting we would rest for a day or two. Seeds had to be saved for winter. We dried fish and stored it also. The fish were dried in a willow shade covered only on the sunny side. Seeds, meat and fish were kept in baskets. They were buried in baskets or in sacks woven from sagebrush bark. The cache was covered with willows and then dirt was put on top. [See also descriptions of subsistence items for additional data on storage.]

LARGE GAME HUNTING

[Hunting large game animals was an important activity for Northern Paiute men. They spent much of their time, particularly from fall through spring, trailing, stalking, and driving deer, antelope, mountain sheep, and, occasionally, bear, in order to provide meat for their camps. These large mammals were found in varying proportions throughout the district, with some areas being well known for a particular species while others were known for an accompanying scarcity or absence. It is very difficult at this point to estimate the differential potential for large game of Northern Paiute districts in the protohistoric period. But based on the accounts given here, deer and mountain sheep seem to have been more common in the Walker River district, and antelope in the Pyramid Lake region.

The data that follow are organized so as to first illustrate the primary techniques used for taking each large game species. These discussions are then followed by separate sections on butchering large game animals, cooking and eating them, and on some of the associated beliefs about hunting luck. One gets the feeling from reading the accounts that a measure of luck was indeed involved, particularly for taking deer and mountain sheep. There also appear to have been some individual and local variations in such matters as insuring hunting luck by properly disposing of various parts of the animal, making proper preparations for the hunt, etc. These should be kept in mind as the data are read.]

Deer Hunting

[The principal means for taking mule dear (*Odocoileus hemionus*) were by trailing, laying in wait, stalking, driv-

---

[4] According to Park, GK-WR seemed less adamant about adults and children rising before sunrise.

[5] GK-WR may be referring primarily to the summer season, while RP-WR's account of the daily round seems more characteristic of winter.

ing, and the use of pitfalls, corrals, and fire surrounds. Each technique displays some variation in the accounts given, probably owing to personal preferences as well as some regional variation. Most of the accounts involving the investment of time in semipermanent or permanent structures for deer hunting, such as corrals, blinds, and pits, come from the Walker River district. This is also the area where claims of ownership of such structures are made. It is difficult to judge at this point in time how meaningful these apparent differences are, but one suspects that they are representative of the more cohesive structure of the Walker River groups (Fowler and Liljeblad, 1986)].

HS-D: Female deer (and female antelope) were not hunted from May to October. Neither the males nor the females were hunted during the breeding season. The meat does not taste right.[6]

When the breeding season is at an end the bucks are all together. They separate from the does. The horns shed the outer coating and the hair of the deer is shed about August. About the latter part of September the horns resume their usual color. Hunting starts then.

The deer calve from the latter part of April to about the first of June. The calves are not killed for a couple of months.

The deer are good to eat now (end of May) but they are not hunted until August or September. Deer were more plentiful in the northern part of Washo country than anywhere else in the Paiute country.[7]

Trailing

JG-PL: Hunting deer by trailing them is called *maimwa*. Deer were trailed sometimes all day until they were tired and the hunter could approach close enough to shoot. Poison was used on deer arrows and it killed the deer quickly. Arrow poison can be made of deer blood [see Arrow Poison in chap. 3]. The blood was set in the sun and allowed to rot. This was then rubbed on the arrow heads. There was only one kind of deer in the Paiute country. That was the mule deer (*tuhu'ya*). They did not like timber and were out in the open country.

When two or three hunters were out trailing together fire was used to signal the others when one killed game. The one who killed the game built a fire and when the others saw the smoke they came. As each arrived he placed his hands on a part of the carcass. That was done on the part he wanted for his share.[8] The man who made the kill got the skin.

HS-D: Mule deer (*tuhuya*) were tracked and sometimes frightened off. The hunter then followed the game. By noon or at the end of the day the deer was so tired the hunter could get close to it for a good shot. Sneaking up on a deer to kill it is called *hoamai*. He used a poisoned arrow to shoot the deer. Then he would go home. Early the next day he would go back to the place and start tracking for the game would now be dead.

Around Reno deer were shot with arrows feathered with owl feathers instead of eagle feathers. There was a very slight noise when the bow is drawn if the arrows have eagle feathers. With owl feathers there is no noise.

HW-Y: A man who is not a shaman has his own dreams about antelope, deer and mountain sheep. Then the man goes out and finds the animal that he dreamed about very quickly. To go out alone after mountain sheep or deer is called *maimwa*.

Lying in Wait

ND-HL: In winter the deer are hunted by waiting by the trail at night.[9] A hunter may have to wait two or three nights. When he shoots a deer he does not follow at once for it is too dark. Early in the morning he starts out and trails the deer by the marks of blood on the trail. This hunting is called *togabaidua*. The hunter also may wait at night by a spring where the deer come to drink.

HS-D: Deer (*tuhuya*) were hunted at night. A man sat by a deer trail. He might have to wait there two or three nights before a deer came along. When he shot a deer he did not follow it that night. Early the next morning he started out to track the wounded deer. He used a poisoned arrow so the deer would die quickly.

GK-WR: Pits were dug along deer and mountain sheep trails from which the animals were shot when they came down to water.[10] The pits were 3 to 5 ft deep. A hunter would lie in wait during the day and sometimes at night. Brush was put around the hold to conceal it. The pit belonged to the man who dug it. The dirt was loosened with a sharpened stick and thrown out with the hands. GK says his uncles used to hunt this way on Mount

---

[6] Although most consultants stated this, some added the provision that they might be hunted any time if the camp were without food.

[7] Washoe country was, for the most part, mountainous and timbered. It also included on its western periphery several well-watered low valleys. The area was indeed a lusher deer habitat than some—but not all—parts of adjacent Northern Paiute territory.

[8] Various principles for the division of game apparently existed. In Owens Valley, where deer were more often hunted communally, Steward (1933:253) states that the leader usually took a larger—often double—share. The others received equal portions. Special leaders for deer hunts are not reported in Park's data.

[9] Kelly (1932:82) describes a case of this in Surprise Valley wherein a man waited near a brush fence he had constructed to channel the movements of the deer.

[10] Kelly (1932:82) also describes the use of pits as hiding places for waiting hunters. Smith (1913:226) also gives a historical account of hunting by this means.

Grant. The hole or pit is called *tuhiwi*. To sit there and wait to kill something is called *oituhawai katukwətə*. Hunting from a pit is thus designated.

Stalking

BF-PL: Deer were stalked (*tüa*) by putting on horns and a deerskin.[11] The hunter approached the deer from the direction in which the wind was blowing. He approached the deer bent over and walking with sticks in his hands to simulate walking on all fours. He threw up his head occasionally just as the deer tosses his head. The hunter made a noise like the deer chewing on grass. When he was quite close to the deer he shot with a bow and arrow.

In the mating season the hunter disguised himself as a buck. He approached several does. After he shot one doe the others ran off. The hunter ran in the opposite direction. Then they would turn and run with the buck. Then he stopped and pretended to eat grass. The does also start to eat. Gradually the hunter and does approached each other. When he came close enough he again shot one of them. This was repeated as long as it was possible. Sometimes a hunter got 3 or 4 does.

JG-PL: To stalk deer, a hunter puts on a deerskin and approaches the deer walking as the deer do. When the hunter approaches the deer he makes noises like deer. He must approach on the windward side. This is a dangerous way to hunt deer because when a strange buck appears it will always attack the stranger. The hunter has no way to protect himself and may be killed. Stalking deer was not often used in hunting because of the danger.

Pitfalls

HW-Y: Pits (*podiatu*) were dug on the deer trail.[12] They were deep enough so the deer could not get out. The pits were dug with a stick. The dirt was thrown out with the hands. The pits were covered with willow branches. When the deer came along, he stepped on the branches and fell into the pit. The hunter shot the deer with bow and arrow.

Corrals

TM-WR, Y: Deer were gotten by building a corral on the deer trails.[13] There were no wings to this corral. It was called *wadəgoəp*. Men were stationed along the trail at intervels to form the wings of the corral. Two men were stationed at the gate, one on each side. They waited until deer came along the trail and walked into the corral. Then the men forming the wings covered the gate so the deer could not get out. Sometimes 6 to 10 deer went into the corral at one time. Two of the best shots with bows and arrows went into the corral to shoot the deer. The men forming the wings were hidden behind rocks or trees. The corral on the deer trail was built in the fall. The deer came along the trail during the night.

Deer Drives[14]

ND-HL: Deer, antelope and mountain sheep are driven toward concealed hunters. The hunters who hide while the others drive are called *wagadu*. Those who drive the game are called *tunabonigə*. The drivers shout and make noises to drive the deer along. No dogs are used. The hunters who were hiding dug no trench nor built no shelter. They hid behind brush and did not move until the game came very close. Then they shot the game.

Not many people usually took part in this type of drive—perhaps two or three. ND knows of no prayers or special preparation for this drive. They just say the usual prayer in the morning [see Miscellaneous Beliefs About Hunting, below]. No attempt was made to drive a number of deer or antelope into the river or lake.

JG-PL: Sometimes three or four men go out hunting. One man tracked the deer and the others were hidden along the summit of a hill. When the man tracking came on a deer[15] it always ran toward the summit. The men hidden there shot it. These men divided the meat. The men who shot the deer got the skin and some of the meat. Nothing but the contents of the stomach was thrown away. This was dumped on the ground.

When I was a boy, I was with my parents at Granite Mountain near Gerlach. There were many deer there at that time. There were about eight men there. They were not all in my family. Since I was a boy, I did not hunt. My cousin was the only other boy. We went with the men. We stayed in camp while the men hunted. No women went on this hunting trip. There were just men. The men helped each other cook while they camped over there. The eight men killed about three deer a day. The meat was dried on racks [see Cooking and Eating Large Game, below]. When the meat was dry it was put in a gunny sack. I do not know what they stored dried meat in a long time ago. We were over there about two weeks. When they got through hunting we came back to Pyramid Lake.

---

[11] Stalking in disguises has a scattered distribution among the Northern Paiute according to Stewart (1941:366). Lowie (1924:197) affirms the use of such disguises, as do Steward (1933:252) for Owens Valley and Kelly (1932:81) for Surprise Valley. JG-PL denied to Park that such disguises were used.

[12] Kelly (1932:81) affirms this as an occasional Surprise Valley technique.

[13] Stewart (1941:366) also received information on this technique as did Curtis (1926:252). Simpson (1876:70) also gives an account of small corrals seen in Western Shoshone country in 1859.

---

[14] Communal drives for deer were not a common technique according to Stewart's (1941:366) element survey.

[15] This account perhaps indicates cooperative hunting rather than true driving.

Fire Surrounds

HS-D, ND-HL: A knoll or mountain, such as Peavine was surrounded by a number of Indians—not as many as took part in the antelope drive. Fires were built all the way around the mountain so the deer could not get out.[16] Then the hunters chased them inside the ring of fire and killed them with bows and arrows. This was done in August and September when the deer were fat. The circle of fire used in the deer hunt is called *kupidə* (or *kupidu*).

Lures and Calls

ND-HL: When hunting if a fawn is seen the hunter sneaks close to the fawn. A leaf from the tree, usually cottonwood or willow, is put between the teeth with the point of the leaf in the mouth.[17] The breath was drawn in sharply through the mouth. The sound was very similar to the call of the fawn. It attracted the attention of the fawn's mother or the buck. The mother or the buck often strays off to graze some distance away. The mother would run over to the fawn: "It thinks the baby is hungry" and then the hunter shoots it.

Antelope Hunting

[Antelope (pronghorn, *Antilocapra americana*) were hunted in many parts of Northern Paiute territory and at least seasonally were an important source of meat. They were usually hunted communally, with the hunts being under the direction of a man with specific powers over animals. Park received several excellent accounts of the rather elaborate procedure for the hunt, of which the following five are the most complete or most variant in details. It is clear that these hunts were attended by several specific requirements and procedures, making them one of the most ritualized of Northern Paiute events.]

ND-HL: March was the best time for the antelope drive (*tunágapɨ*).[18] Drives were held in early spring. In the fall the antelope are scattered. In the winter they come together in herds.

The usual place for antelope drives was at a knoll called *tuna piwə* (*tuna*, antelope; *piwə*, heart). This was just west (about 10 mi) of Deep Hole. Deep Hole is north of Pyramid Lake [fig. 6]. The people from Pyramid Lake also went to Deep Hole for the antelope drives. Drives were also held in Secret Valley, between Honey Lake and Horse Lake. ND's mother took part in three

or four drives in Secret Valley but ND has never seen one. The drives were not held in his time. His mother told him about the drives. The last drive was at the time his mother and father were married [1860s?].

When an antelope drive was to be held word was sent around and people from Pyramid Lake, Gerlach, Reno, Winnemucca Valley, Honey Lake and Long Valley would gather for the drive.[19] Sometimes a few people from Lovelock, Fallon and Walker Lake came to take part in the drive. But, as a rule, people from these bands did not take part in the drives at Pyramid Lake and Honey Lake.

When an antelope herd is seen, the chief of the antelope drive sets the date for the drive. The chief of the drive is a shaman. He is an antelope charmer. A place where there is a great deal of sagebrush is selected for the site of the corral. The people move out to the site and camp near it. That night, a dance is held. It is held before the fence is built. This dance is called *tunanugᵃ*. This dance lasts one night.[20] The antelope chief is leader of the dance.[21] The regular round dance was not danced. All the people dance. They do not hold hands. The hands are tightly closed and the arms flexed with the forearms held close and parallel to the body. ND does not know what step was danced. His mother told him about the dance, he has never seen it, but she did not tell him what the step was.[22] The antelope shaman does not wear an antelope skin or horns.[23] This dance is held where the corral is to be built the next day.

Music is provided by scraping on a piece of deer horn which has been wrapped with a bow string.[24] Another short piece of deer horn, such as the short piece

---

[19] About half of Park's informants on this topic stated that these hunts were limited to the local group although they occasionally attracted some visitors.

[20] Stewart (1941:367) reports that although one night's charming was usually sufficient, people noted that sometimes up to five nights might be required. Sarah Winnemucca Hopkins (1883:57) also suggested five days.

[21] BB-PL told Park that another man served as dance leader and that he furnished the music for the dance by playing on his bow string with an arrow. Yet another man also made music with a rasp.

[22] JG-PL stated that for the dance, men and women were in a line. In the dance, one foot was raised and stamped on the ground; then the other. ND and HS-D on another occasion stated that the dancers stood behind each other in a line; a wife or sister went behind a husband or brother. The movement of the dance was slow.

[23] DM-PL noted that the shaman had his hair fixed like antelope horns. Kelly's accounts (1932:85) from Surprise Valley informants include wearing of antelope horns and skins.

[24] LA-PL claimed that the true rasp was used to charm the antelope. This notched stick which was rubbed with another stick was called *küda*. Lowie (1924:304) also describes the use of a rasp. See also Stewart (1941:422).

---

[16] This technique is affirmed by Steward (1933:252) for Owens Valley and by Kelly (1932:82) for Surprise Valley. Riddell (1960:39) also discusses it for Honey Lake Valley.

[17] Substantially the same account was given by TM-WR,Y.

[18] The antelope drive was also given other names by Park's consultants, including *tunagadu* (HS-D); *tuna mahútwa* (DM-PL); *tanoə* (TM-WR,Y) and *nagəna* (BB-PL).

of horn that is used for chipping obsidian, is used to scrape across the wrapped horn. The horn was wrapped spirally. The horn was not hollowed out. The horn that was wrapped was about 8 in. long. Two bow strings tied end to end were wrapped in a spiral around the horn. The spirals were close together. The bowstrings were of sinew. Bowstrings were called *pagagwi*. The short piece that is rubbed over the horn is called *mókano*. The whole instrument is called *túkwiɔ́nugwino*.

Another instrument is made by rolling three or four blankets together, enough to make a roll about 1 ft in diameter. Some of the blankets would be of buckskin that had the hair scraped off. Some of the blankets were ones that had been tanned with the hair on. The roll was stuffed with rabbit skins or sagebrush bark. The roll was tied at each end with several wrappings of sinew. The horn wrapped with bowstrings was slipped under the lashings of the roll. The instrument was in front of one man who scraped with a piece of horn while the others sang. The player was called *tunakwiba* (*kwiba*, hitter). This instrument had the same name as the simple horn wrapped with bowstrings.[25]

This dance lasted half the night. The antelope shaman did not go into a trance during the dance.[26] After the older people stopped dancing about midnight, it is quiet for a while, then the young people, men and girls, come in and dance and make funny songs. This goes on until daylight. ND has not heard of dancers walking around to imitate the antelope [see below].

The chief tells the people not to have sexual intercourse before the drive. If people did it would spoil everything. Pregnant women or menstruating women do not go to the antelope drive or dance. They stay home and do not go to the camp made near the site selected for the corral.[27]

The next day a scout is sent out to find the herd. He returns to the camp in the afternoon and another man is sent out to watch the herd. During that time the antelope chief has had the people working at making rope from sagebrush bark. When the rope is made it is taken to the site that has been selected for the corral. This is a knoll of ground. The antelope chief walks ahead and falls down in a trance. Then all the people pile sagebrush on him.[28] The trance lasts about 10 minutes. When he comes to he shakes and it is hard for him to remain still. The brush is piled on him in the shape of one of the gate posts. This post is called *waisidupɔ* (old man).

From the place where they pile sagebrush on the antelope chief, they stretch the rope on piles of sagebrush around the knoll to form the corral (*koɔpɔ*). The sagebrush piled up to form the posts is piled upside down with the roots in the air. Between the piles of sagebrush strings with balls of sagebrush were suspended from the rope forming the fence. These were about 5 ft apart. The piles of brush were about 15 ft apart. There were about four balls of sagebrush suspended between each pair of piles. The leader led the way and showed the people where to put each pile of brush. The gate was ¼ mi across. It was 2 or 3 mi around the fence.[29] No wings ran out from the gate posts. The people spread out to form the wings of the corral.

The women formed the wings closest to the corral. They stood about 20 yds. apart. The corral was finished within a very short time. After the corral was built the people waited around until very early the next morning when they spread out to drive the antelope in.[30]

When the men get around in back of the herd they start the drive. They wave their blankets in the air to frighten the antelope on.[31] The women forming the fan-shaped wings of the corral wave blankets to keep the antelope from running out the side of the wings. The men do not carry bows and arrows. The antelope are very wild and the men do not come close enough to them to shoot. As the herd goes on towards the corral past the people forming the wings these people

---

[25] Sarah Winnemucca Hopkins (1883:55), whose father, Old Winnemucca, was an antelope shaman, also describes a similar instrument. Kelly (1932:83) notes that in Surprise Valley the bundle's cords were rubbed, "like a violin."

[26] There is a difference of opinion here among several of Park's consultants. Some felt that a trance state was achieved during the night's dancing, or during the next day (see ND, below). Others felt that the antelope were charmed without this special state.

[27] These prohibitions are general according to all consultants. Others added the following: BB-PL: People cannot lose anything or it will make a weak spot in the fence. The husbands of pregnant or menstruating women are also forbidden to take part in the dance or drive. JO-PL: If anyone at the drive needs to urinate, it must be done inside the corral. Otherwise the antelope would break down the fence. But DM-PL: The shaman warned the people not to defecate or urinate around the fence. They must go a long way away. ND-HL: Women who had just borne a child could not help in killing the antelope. They always bring bad luck. Stewart (1941:367) also

lists taboos against mentruating women, sexual intercourse just before the hunt, and the loss of objects.

[28] This practice was also given in an account recorded by Stewart (1941:423).

[29] Several different dimensions were given for these corrals. JB-PL also stated that the function of the rope was to keep the antelope in place. It was jerked when the antelope came near and the dangling objects would frighten them back to the center.

[30] ND stated on another occasion that if the corral were finished by noon, the antelope might be driven into it the same day. Other accounts also agree that driving takes place the same day.

[31] According to CW-PL, the drivers shout *husa, husa*, while chasing the antelope into the corral.

move in back of the herd and help drive it on. As soon as the herd has been driven into the corral, a fence is constructed across the opening.[32] Then the people scatter to their stations around the fence. The herd usually is driven into the corral in the later afternoon or evening. In the evening fires are built all the way around the corral. These fires are kept burning all night long.[33]

Early the next morning a runner goes into the corral. He carries a stick to drive the antelope.[34] He keeps the antelope moving. He drives the antelope until they are tired. He is the best runner in the band. He starts before sunrise. Usually by early afternoon the antelope are tired. Around Yerington, a dirt is gotten from a mountain called *whuwaits* (also name of the dirt) which is used to paralyze the antelope in the drive (*tɔbɔ* is the same thing.[35] This is also found at Yerington.) This dirt is put in a fire that is built in the corral. When the antelope smell the smoke of this fire they are paralyzed. They fall down and cannot get up. ND thinks this was only used around Yerington.

When the antelope are tired the runner gives the signal for the kill to begin. Before the runner gives the signal he gets close to a young antelope (male or female) about six months old. He kills this one with a bow and arrow. It is given to the antelope shaman who is chief of the drive.[36] Doing this brings good luck.

When the runner tells the people to come into the corral and kill the antelope, both men and women start killing. Whoever touches an antelope owns the skin no matter who kills it. For example if a woman touches an antelope but cannot kill it and has to ask a man to kill it or someone else unasked kills that animal, the skin belongs to the woman but the meat belongs to the one who killed the antelope. The heads of the antelope killed are not given to the chief of the drive.[37] When the antelope was skinned the body was cut in two. Women caught the blood in basket hats. They took out the intestines and filled them with blood and dried them. They did not stay to dry the meat. They took it home.

---

[32] Some say this is unnecessary (to have a gate), as the antelope are charmed and will therefore stay in the corral.

[33] LA-PL also stated that antelope killed near one of these fires belonged to the tender of the fire.

[34] HS-D stated that the instrument made of the stick with wrapped sinew and the bone scraper was used to keep the antelope running.

[35] *tubo* is a ferrous material but the identity of the other "dirt" is unknown [see Basketry in chap. 3].

[36] This is confirmed by BB-PL. Other patterns of killing are also followed, however (see below).

[37] Kelly (1932:86) received a statement to the effect that the heads were given to the shaman. He also wore the horns of those animals killed around his neck.

When the jawbones are cleaned of all the meat they are hung up on the sagebrush around the camp. The bladder (*si·nup'*) and the *abui'wi* (a small pear-shaped organ inky in color located by the liver) is put into a hole and covered up. The eyes are taken out and tied together and hung on trees or brush or buried with the bladder and *abui'wi*. They do not want the dogs or the coyotes to eat them. That is why they do this. At the time of the antelope drive the antelope have shed their horns so there are no horns to be disposed of.

The antelope meat is dried on racks in the shade. The racks (*wato·sai*) were made by putting two poles in the ground. These had crotches. A pole was put across these in the crotches and another tied across the upright poles about half way down. The meat, cut in strips, was hung on these cross poles. When the meat was dried it was stored on a rack built near the house. This rack (*pa·soni*) was made by putting four poles in the ground [see Houses, chap. 4]. These poles stood 7 or 8 ft high. The plan was rectangular. Two poles were put across between the uprights forming the long sides of the rectangle. Willow poles were put across these poles. These poles were close together. This was then covered with grass (*wiyab*). Then the dried meat was put on the grass and covered with 6 or 8 in. of grass or tule.

When the weather got warm enough, the antelope skins gotten in the drive were made into clothes so that when the people returned to Pyramid Lake for fishing they had new clothing. Other Paiutes knew that they had gone out for an antelope drive so that usually people from Fallon were waiting for them at Pyramid Lake. The Fallon people had red paint (*pi·jɔp*) which they exchanged for the old clothes of the people who had taken part in the antelope drive.

JG-PL: There is an antelope doctor. The spirit tells this doctor just what he must do. The shaman has the power to charm antelope.

The antelope shaman sends a man to look for antelope. When the man comes back and reports where he saw the herd of antelope, the shaman tells the people to make a corral (*koɔp*). The corral is about 150 ft in diameter. The fence is made by pulling up sagebrush which are placed together with the roots in the air. The entrance to the corral is about 15 ft wide. On one side of the entrance a wing runs out about 75 yds. On the other side which is toward a hill, the wing is about 50 ft long. It runs up to the hill. There is one of these corrals made of sagebrush near a mountain called Limbo about 15 mi from Gerlach.

The antelope doctor sets the date for the drive. He is going to charm the antelope during the night. He is going to take their minds away so they will not know what to do. He calls a meeting of men, women and children around a big fire. The shaman got up and sang but the people did not dance. They were sitting all the way around the fire and the shaman was by the fire.

During part of his singing he walked around the fire. He did not sing as long as the shamans do when doctoring. He sang a little while and then sat down and started another song. He sang only four or five songs. He sang four songs and then he sat down and talked. He said, "It looks like we are going to get these antelope. We have only one more song. If it looks as if we are going to get the antelope after that song I am going to tell you." Then he sang the last song and went around the fire and then he sat down. Then he told the people, "I think we have those antelope. They are coming and they do not go any place else. They are coming into our corral. I think we have them."

When the antelope shaman was singing he wore an antelope skin with the hair scraped off. He put this skin away and only wore it when he was doctoring. This skin was tanned. It was the skin of the young antelope. Sometimes I think it was male. That depends upon what his spirit tells him. Horns were not worn by the antelope shaman.

My (JG's) grandfather could charm antelope. My mother saw him charm antelope at Stillwater a long time ago. While he sang he moved his hand in front of him with his palm turned up. As he sang he closed his hand. Then he opened it and showed the people antelope hair. That was how he charmed the antelope.

The antelope doctor sings nearly half the night. That night he talks, prays and sings. When he is finished, he picks out two good runners to start early in the morning for the antelope. When these men found the antelope they were to drive them towards the corral. Then the doctoring was over. The people went home and these two men got ready to start early in the morning.

The camp was made several miles from the corral.[38] They did not want to make the camp close to the corral for the scent of the people would drive the antelope away. The doctoring for the antelope was held in the camp.

In the morning, the two men go out to drive in the antelope herd. The people are spread out fan-wise so the antelope will be driven into the corral. They stand about 4 or 5 ft apart. The gate of the corral is about 15 ft across. As soon as the antelope are in the corral the antelope doctor picks two or three men to kill them. They go into the corral with bows and arrows and kill the antelope.[39] When the antelope are killed the women

come and help carry the meat home. The women are not allowed around the drive.[40] The meat and skins are divided evenly among those who take part in the drive. The shaman does not get any larger share than the others.[41] His power told him how to get the antelope this way and if he takes a larger share than the others he will spoil his power.

The heads were not given to the shaman. Everybody got a share. When the head was roasted and all the meat taken off the head and the jaws were put in the middle of a clump of sagebrush. Sometimes the jaws and skull were put away together and sometimes they put the jaws in one clump and the skull in another. The eyes and brains were eaten. Mountain sheep and deer are preferred for their meat to antelope. These two have more fat with their meat. The fat is chopped up with the meat on a metate. The fat makes the meat taste better.

The corral is used year after year. The shaman owns the corral[42] [see Property in chap. 9]. He tells the people to fix up the corral. Other people cannot use it. Sometimes about 10 camps live together. All these people got in and helped make the corral. Just the men helped build the corral and drove the antelope. The women were at home in the camps.

These drives are usually held early in the fall or late in the summer. These drives may take place any time in spring, summer, or fall when the people get short of meat.

Antelope can be hunted with horses. When they are found in the valley the chief tells some of the men with horses to get ready because they are going to drive the antelope the next day. He stations men widely separated all around the valley. One man goes out to drive the antelope until he comes to one of the men stationed along the valley. Then this man on a fresh horse takes up the drive. The antelope will run only in the valley. They will not climb the hills. This drive was not used before horses were known to the Paiutes.[43] The antelope run too fast for men to drive them on foot. The antelope are driven until the early afternoon. The antelope may be driven around the valley three or four times. When the antelope are tired two or three men catch up to them and shoot them.

---

[38] People made their camp inside the corral the first night according to BB-PL.

[39] In some accounts, the shaman does all of the killing. According to CW-PL, the antelope were killed by twisting their necks. This was done after they were run until they were tired — in relay fashion if necessary.

[40] This differs from ND's account where women are regular participants in the drives. Other accounts (see below) also suggest that women do not participate.

[41] On another occasion, JG stated that the shaman got two or three skins and the other men who participated got one apiece.

[42] Ownership of corrals was also claimed for Walker River people by GK-WR and RP-WR.

[43] Horses were introduced ca. 1820s–1830s (Layton 1981: 133).

AP 114/UU [17]

JG has never heard of using a bow to make music in charming the antelope. He has also never heard of putting a row of flat rocks across the opening into the corral [see HW-Y below]. He also does not think that the antelope shaman goes into a trance. He dreams the night of the dance and in his dreams he finds out everything and he gets the antelope under control.

TM-WR, Y: When a herd of antelope was seen it was reported to the chief of the antelope drive. The next day the men went out to build a corral. The women did not help in building the corral. The day after the corral was built eight or ten men went out to drive in the antelope. The corral was about ¼ mi in diameter. Wings ran out from the gate. The wings were about ¼ mi long.

There was no dance the night before the antelope drive. The chief of the antelope drive had power over the antelope. When the antelope have been driven into the corral the gate is not closed because the antelope shaman has a song that he sings at the gate. Then he goes into the center of the corral with a bow and arrow. He continues to sing until he has killed all the antelope. He is the only one to kill the antelope.[44] The people who have taken part in the drive stay some distance away and watch the shaman shoot the antelope. When all the antelope are killed he shouts for the men and women to come to the corral.

The antelope are put in one camp and the chief of the drive divides them among the camps of those who took part in the drive. The antelope are divided evenly among the people. The chief of the drive takes the same share of skins and meat that he gives to the other people.

When the heads have been skinned they are roasted in pits. After the heads of the antelope have been roasted and the meat eaten the skull and bones of the head are hung in trees to bring good luck in the next hunt. The bones are left in the tree until the string tying them rots and lets the bones fall to the ground.[45] When the bones fall they are left on the ground. They are not put back on the tree.

The antelope shaman gets his power over the antelope in dreams just as the doctor treats sickness. His songs come to him in dreams.

The Walker River people usually had antelope drives in Smith Valley. There were no more antelope there [i.e., at Walker River]. Drives were held anytime in the year that a herd was found. The drive was called *ta·noə*. The corral was called *ko·duə* or *tətugap*.

---

[44] Again, accounts vary as to who kills the antelope. More often it seems that the shaman appointed others to do it.

[45] This seems to imply that the bones are bound together in bundles.

HW-Y: On the other side of Powder Valley there is an antelope corral (*koup*). The corral is made of cedar and pine branches. It is about 10 ft high and 200 yds in diameter. A single row of flat stones is placed across the entrance so the antelope cannot smell where the men have stepped. If this were not done the antelope would turn back. One man is stationed at the gate to close it when the antelope are driven in. Usually from 20 to 25 antelope are gotten in one drive. When they are in the corral they are shot with bow and arrow.

The head man of the drive is the owner of the corral. He divides the antelope that are killed. He gives the men who helped him one antelope and keeps two for himself. The antelope drive is held when the people go up in the hills for pinenuts [i.e., early fall]. Only men take part or are present at the antelope drive. Menstruating women cannot eat the meat. If they did it would hurt the hunters. This tabu applies to all meat. A dance is held for a single night following the antelope drive.

The man who is head of the drive is a shaman. He would dream about the antelope and the next day he called the men together to go out for the antelope. He could find them very quickly because he had dreamed about them. All the men taking part in the drive had their bodies and faces painted. None of the men taking part in the antelope drive wore a special costume, such as an antelope skin. There was no ceremony to charm the antelope. The dream that showed the shaman where the antelope were was called *nasiu*. The man who dreamed about the antelope was always a shaman.

RP-WR: One shaman who lived at Schurz had his own way of calling antelope. He is the only one who did it this way. He would tell the people that they would get some meat. He would play his bowstring with an arrow and sing to the music. He would have the people gather about noon. He would have them sit in the following order: an old woman sitting next to the shaman; then an old man next to her; then a woman not so old. This is continued in this order down to the children. He would play his bowstring and sing. Then he had the people pull up sagebrush and pile it roots up to form a corral. Then he had the people crawl around the circle of the corral on all fours like the antelope.[46] He sings while the others crawl around in imitation of the antelope. The old men came first and then the women, followed by the younger people. The people's faces were painted. The only clothing worn was a breechclout. The shaman is dressed in a loin cloth. After everyone had gone around the corral, they sat in a circle around the leader. He told them to watch him and he sang and played his bowstring. Little patches of antelope hair appeared on

---

[46] According to CW-PL, while the corral was being built, some people went into the corral and imitated the antelope by jumping around and making a noise like them.

his arms and body. Then the people saw dust in the distance as the antelope herd came towards them. The antelope are not afraid because they have been charmed. The shaman had charmed them and they did not know what they were doing. They follow the same path as the people who have been crawling around. The antelope charmer stops singing then. The antelope are driven into the corral. The charming lasts all night and the herd appears about noon the next day. The people start to kill the antelope as soon as they are driven into the corral. They had all the meat they wanted. If anything was wasted, it would bring bad luck. The intestines were buried in a cool place and sagebrush put over it. If a piece of this was dropped anyplace the antelope would know it and it would bring bad luck. They could not kill any more antelope. There was no dance following the killing. The people do not dance during the charming.

This shaman was not paid for charming the antelope. This shaman could also cure.[47] He was the one who doctored wounded people when the people got to fighting and wounded each other when they were out gathering seeds [see Shamanism in vol. 2]. Antelope gave this man his power in a dream. He gave him the songs that would attract the antelope. This man was the only antelope charmer known to RP.

Mountain Sheep Hunting

[There are very few data on the hunting of mountain sheep (bighorn sheep, *Ovis canadensis*) in Park's notes. From those that are present, one can extract trailing, snaring, and lying in wait as the principal techniques. Sheep were probably absent in some areas, although one cannot be sure from the notes. Fig. 43e is of a necklace of mountain sheep phalanges collected at Pyramid Lake in 1875 by Stephen Powers.]

HS-D: Moutain sheep (*koipa*) calve about the end of June or early July. They have a rutting period in January. They are usually hunted in the fall. A shortage of food will drive the people to hunt mountain sheep any time of the year. In December the males are together and they are found on the sunny side of the mountains. Mountain sheep are shot with bow and arrow. The skin was tanned. There used to be many mountain sheep on the ridges near Dayton.

TM-WR, Y: Sometimes fish nets were cut for mountain sheep snares.[48] A hole large enough for the moun-

tain sheep to get its head through was made in a fish net. The net was suspended from branches over the trail of the mountain sheep. The net was hung in such a way that the hole was in a position so the mountain sheep would put his head in it as he came along the trail. The corner of the net was tied to a heavy log. When the mountain sheep felt the net over his shoulders he dragged the log until he was choked to death.

JG-PL: JG's uncle told him of hiding by a water hole where mountain sheep came to drink. The mountain sheep approached and then ran away. This was repeated several times. After a while they got down to the water and started to drink. While they were drinking he shot the largest one. This was when he was living in the mountains below Schurz [Walker River Reservation]. Whenever he ran out of meat he went up and killed a mountain sheep this way. He stayed there by himself for four years. He was on his father's ranch down there.

GK-WR: Pits were dug on mountain sheep trails from which the animals were shot when they came to water [see GK-WR's account of deer hunting].

JG-PL: Mountain sheep were stalked. A man would wait on a deer trail at night for them to come along. He used owl feathers on his arrows so that it would not make any noise. He does not dress up in any kind of skin to stalk mountain sheep.

Bear Hunting

[Bears, probably mostly black bears [*Ursus americanus*] were apparently rare in most of Northern Paiute country in Western Nevada. Their hunting was considered dangerous and great deference was paid to them (see Mythology, in vol. 2)].

DM-PL: Bear were hunted around Fallon. Bark was scraped off a brush called *magu.tuhupi* [*Psorothamnus polydenius*]. The bark was burned in the fire to drive the bears away from camps. There were a great many bears around Stillwater and Fallon. The bear did not like the smell of the bark burning. When the bear was hunted several men chased the bear or let the bear chase one of them in relays. The others shot at the bear. When the bear was exhausted they killed it. When the bear was killed the heart was taken out. The tip was cut off and cut into small pieces. Each hunter ate a piece of the tip of the heart raw. It made him brave. The bear was not addressed when killed.[49]

---

[47] Apparently the ability to cure illness was not among the powers of all antelope shaman [see Shamans in vol. 2]. According to DM-PL, however, the antelope shaman was called *puhagɔm*, as were other shamans.

[48] Osborne and Riddell (1978) describe a cache of rope "deer snares" recovered from Owens Valley. The Field Museum of Natural History has two such snares cataloged as "moun-

tain sheep lassos" that were collected by J. H. Hudson in 1904. However, this technique was not mentioned to Steward (1933) nor to Stewart (1941).

[49] Kelly (1932:86) describes bear hunting as a winter pursuit in Surprise Valley. Steward (1933:253) states that Owens Valley people expressed fear of hunting bears because of their likeness to humans.

JG-PL: There were no bears in the country around Pyramid Lake. The bears live in the timber. The people at Pyramid Lake never went bear hunting.

Butchering Large Game

ND-HL: After a deer or antelope is killed it is carried home. The fore and hind legs are tied together. The deer is bled and the intestines are taken out before the carcass is carried home [see Disposal of Parts of Large Game, below]. The skin is stripped back a few inches from the hooves and with this the hind and forelegs are tied and this skin formed a tumpline which came around the shoulders.[50] Each hind leg is tied to a foreleg. All four legs are tied together and the head of the carrier comes between. To carry a deer or antelope into camp in this fashion is called *pühüno*. When the carcass is brought to camp the skinning is completed and the carcass is butchered. If the hunter had time he skinned and butchered the carcass on the spot [i.e., where the animal was killed].

If two hunters were out and one killed a deer, the one who killed the deer took the skin. The other got the front half of the carcass. Each carries his own share home. The one who killed the deer would usually divide with the other in the way described. He would give a just share to the other. He expected no present in return.

DM-PL: When a man killed a deer by himself he skinned the lower parts of the legs and tied the legs together with this skin and carried the deer home on his back. When the deer is butchered care must be taken not to cut the tendons or sinews in the back. If these are cut the man who cuts them and members of that hunting party would have bad luck in hunting. Also chopping off the head of the deer would bring the hunters bad luck. When the head has been cooked the skull is fastened to a tree [see Disposal of Parts of Large Game, below]. They did not want a skull left around because it would attract coyotes. The only bone saved in the head is a small bone in the jaw. This is called *mokano*. It is used to chip obsidian for knives and arrow points. It is also used as an awl in sewing [see Bone Tools in chap. 3].

GK-WR: The large animal were cut up just like beef. They cut all the joints off. They cut the head off at the neck. The neck was cut anywhere. Any little meat on the head is cut off and the skull is thrown away.[51]

---

[50] Riddell (1960:29) and Steward (1933:252) describe substantially the same method of carrying game.

[51] On another occasion this same consultant told Park that at least the horns were hung in a tree (see below).

Disposal of Parts of Large Game

RP-WR: When a deer was killed the eyes were taken out. If the eyes were left in the head while it was roasted the hunter would not be lucky again in hunting. The eyes are packed in sagebrush and put on a rock. Then more rocks are piled over the sagebrush and eyes. Deer can see people do this and they like the people who do it and will come to them. If they see eyes roasted along with the meat they do not like it. They say they have been treated mean. While the hunter is disposing of the eyes he talks to the deer. He says, "I am treating you good. Whenever I am out hunting you must come to me."

When the deer is killed it is opened and the intestines and the bladder are buried in the ground. The deer hooves are hung in a tree to bring good luck. The leg bones are put away the same way as the eyes are. The liver and the heart are eaten.

There is a little whirlwind that travels all over during the time that deer is hunted. The whirlwind watches to see that none of the intestines is wasted, or any other parts. If the whirlwind sees any of the parts wasted it goes back to the herd and tells them that they are not being treated right.

When an antelope is killed the eyes, bones, intestines, etc. were disposed of in the same way as when the deer was killed [see Antelope Hunting, above]. This was not done for mountain sheep. Nothing was done to bring good luck the next time when mountain sheep were killed.

JG-PL: When the hunter kills a deer and the deerskin is taken off, he spreads the skin over the carcass and talks. He says, "I am going to kill you the same way. Do not be afraid. When I am tracking, do not go away. Lie down like this deer here." While the hunter is talking he spreads the skin over the deer and picks it up again. He throws the skin over the deer as many times as he wants to while he is talking, perhaps four or five times.

A small sac near the liver — it is dark blue — is cut out. If this breaks on the meat it will taste bad. This is put away. If the hunter is in the mountain he puts it in the crotch of two limbs so it will not fall out. The hunter talks when he takes this out. He says, "I am going to find you easily." If this organ is thrown away the hunter will not be able to see deer the next time he tracks one. This is done for the mountain sheep and antelope also. Also the rabbit and cottontail [see Small Mammal Trappings, below]. The organ that is cut out and put away is called *pui'wi* [see also Rabbits, below].

In the old days the deer bones were put away.[52] Noth-

---

[52] Stewart (1941:373) received minimal data on the disposal of deer bones and other game parts.

ing was thrown away. Sometimes they cracked the bones and with a stick got the marrow out and ate it. I have never seen hunters hang the deer's eyes on trees, but I have seen eyes hanging in tule houses. I do not know why they hung the eyes in the houses.

ND-HL: The eyes are hung on a tree when a man has killed a deer. The eyes of mountain sheep and antelope are also hung up on a tree. It is not known what would happen if this were not done. Sometimes the lower jawbone was hung on a tree. This was not always done. Sometimes this bone was just thrown away. The antlers of the deer and antelope were put in a crotch of a tree or some place high off the ground.

Some organ near the liver (spleen?)[53] called *abui'wi*, was "put away" — disposed of carefully. The bladder (*sinu.pa*) was also put away. The spleen was hidden under a rock or hidden in some other place. If this is not done the deer will not like the hunter and he cannot kill any more deer. This is also true of all the four-legged animals, even such small animals as the rabbits [see Rabbits, below].

To regain his luck after being careless with the spleen the hunter must bathe and when he kills an animal such as a deer he must keep the eyes and spleen and tie them on a willow or hide them under a rock or in a crevice. The idea is to keep these organs away from other animals such as coyote, mice, birds and insects.

ND's parents told him to do these things. They did not say why they were done. It was just the custom to do these things. When asked if this was to bring good luck, ND said, "They just do that". ND thinks that when any of these things is done the hunter does not say anything to or about the animal.[54]

GK-WR: Deer, antelope and mountain sheep horns were hung in trees. Only the old timers did that. GK thinks this is done to bring good luck in hunting.

Cooking and Eating Large Game

JG-PL: Deer meat was boiled by cutting off the head of the deer and using the carcass for water and hot stones.[55] The flesh on the back of the neck [after the head was removed] was pressed together tightly and a sharp stick was used to skewer the meat together. The thorax was filled with water and hot rocks were put in to boil the meat. Meat was not boiled in baskets.

Deer and antelope heads were roasted in pits with a fire on top. The tongue was not cut out. It was roasted with the head. At the antelope drive [see Antelope Hunting, above] the heads were not roasted together. Each family had its own fire and roasted the head that it got.

The hooves of deer and antelope were roasted in a pit. When they were cooked the hoof part was peeled off. It came off easily. The hoof was put away to be sold to shamans or for beads. The flesh on the leg was eaten. The bone was cracked and the marrow taken out and eaten. Then the pieces of bone were thrown away.

Deer meat was dried on racks. Two poles were put in the ground and one pole tied across these. The meat was hung on the cross pole. The frame was erected in the shade. The meat was cut in thin strips for drying. This meat usually took four or five days to dry. It was never smoked.[56] When the meat was dry it was put in sacks and put away.

Dried deer, antelope or mountain sheep meat was pounded on the metate with tallow or a big piece of fat that starts about the middle of the animal's back and runs to the tail. This is called *tühu*. The mixture is called *tühunadamayün*. This was put away in a bag sewn out of deerskin. This was coarser than sausage.

This fat or tallow was also dried in the shade and put away. It was eaten raw with raw dried meat. A bit of meat was taken with a bite of tallow. Fat was not pounded and made into rolls. Meat, fat and bones were not pounded together and dried and made into rolls. Meat was not pounded with roots and dried. Dried meat was pounded on rocks and put on the coals to roast before eating.

Testicles and penis of game were eaten by older people of either sex.[57] The younger people were not allowed to eat the penis and testicles. JG does not know the reason for this.

Heart, liver, and kidney were tabu to boys. When a boy eats heart and trails a deer, his heart beats so hard that the herd hears it and gets away before the boy sees it. If a boy eats liver, his children will have a bluish-black spot in the small of their backs [see Birth in vol. 2]. Kidney causes the hands of a boy to sweat and when he pulls his bowstring when hunting, his fingers will slip and he will miss. A boy is forbidden to eat these organs until after he has passed through his first game ceremony [see boys Puberty Ceremony in vol. 2]. Then he is free to eat any part of the animal.

---

[53] This organ is more likely the gall bladder.

[54] Others of Park's consultants, including those quoted here, felt that prayers were appropriate at this time.

[55] Stewart (1941:377) lists this technique as common in the Northern Paiute region.

[56] Stewart (1941:376) received universal denial of the smoking of meat by the Northern Paiute. The trait is also absent in Owens Valley (Steward 1933:255).

[57] JH-PL told Park that the penis and testicles of animals were normally thrown away. Bear and badger penis bones were kept and used as beads and needles. See also DM-PL below.

Foetuses or deer, antelope, and mountain sheep were eaten. The Indians ate everything inside the game. They did not throw anything away.[58]

DM-PL: None of the deer was wasted. It would bring bad luck if the meat or any parts were thrown away carelessly. The eyes were not hung in trees. The bladder and certain organs that were not used were hung up in trees.

The heads were roasted in pits. The thorax is cooked by closing the neck with the peritoneum. Water is put in the cavity. Hot rocks are put in the water to boil the meat. The tripe of animals was kept and eaten. The penis and testicles were thrown away. The lining of the stomach was kept for keeping the blood in. The blood clots were mixed with fat and tripe and this was put in a basket of water and made into a soup.

ND-HL: All the intestines were saved and cleaned for food. Blood was put in them and they were boiled. The hearts of all animals were eaten. The lungs (*soŋo*) were eaten. The ribs were kept for scrapers. The rest of the meat was dried.

GK-WR: All of the deer was eaten except the brains, which were saved for tanning. The bones were not used. GK does not know about the preparation of bear meat. He thinks it was eaten, but he has never heard the old people talk about it.

Miscellaneous Beliefs about Hunting

TM-WR: Sweat baths were not taken by men before they set out to hunt deer.[59] Hunters bathed in the river before they started out. They bathed before they hunted any kind of game. After the bath the hunter painted himself with white paint. Bands were painted around the arms, four or five around the forearm and the same around the lower arm. The tip of the fingers of both hands were dipped in the wet paint and drawn down the front of the body from the shoulders down the torso and down the legs. It was worn until it came off.

ND-HL: When a man went hunting, he prayed in the morning before the sun came up. He asked for good luck in hunting and for good health. Sometimes when a man was out hunting he would stop and take a bath to

bring himself better luck. He also did this to regain his luck once it was lost. He prayed when he bathed. In the prayer he said *ibiamaka*. This probably means "give me". Each one would pray a little differently. Each would say different things. But always *ibiamaka* was used in the prayer. *HS-D* could not translate it into English.

When a menstruating woman handled anything that her husband used for hunting or any of the meat that he brought home he would have bad luck in hunting. Some men never went hunting when their wives were menstruating so they would not have anything happen to bring them bad luck. It also brings bad luck for a man to have intercourse with his wife the night before he goes hunting,[60] especially if it is just before she menstruates.

The death of a child or other relative does not affect a man's luck in hunting. A man can go hunting after the burial. That is the only way he can get anything to eat.

RP-WR: The sun was not addressed for good luck in hunting or gambling.[61] The charms that were carried or the spirits of the animals were addressed in asking for good luck [see Charms in vol. 2].

If a menstruating woman eats meat the man who killed the meat will have bad luck. There is no way for him to get his luck back. He had to be that way all the time. If a menstruating woman danced and touched the hand of a man in the circle it made him sick. The blood goes into the man's arms and he had pains in his arms. He cannot raise his bow.

If the guts of an animal killed in the hunt are not buried properly or if the dogs eat them the hunter will have bad luck [see Disposal of Parts of Large Game, above].

The deer always know when a man goes out to hunt. When a lazy man goes out without a gun the deer talk and they decide to go in a bunch single file and cross his path in front of him. The lazy man can only raise his arm as if shooting. The deer would laugh at him.

Four deer, one doe with a young buck and a female with an old buck (father) crossed the path of a lazy man. They played a trick on him because he was lazy and had no gun all the time. Two young bucks played far from the herd and were lookouts. When someone comes they run to the band and pass them. The band knows what that means and follows them. When they

---

[58] JH-PL gave the following account to Park: "One time a man killed a pregnant deer. He brought both the deer and foetus home. He ate the foetus himself" JH does not know why he did not want anyone else to eat it. She thinks foetuses were not generally eaten.

[59] Kelly (1932:81) states that sweating and offering prayers to the sun before the hunt were formerly the custom in Surprise Valley. Stewart (1941:373) also reports that roughly half of the individuals interviewed stated that sweating was done before a hunt. Bathing before hunting was equally common.

[60] Stewart (1941:373) received several negative replies to this from consultants. Steward (1933:252) also states that it was not required in Owens Valley. Kelly (1932:81) got affirmative responses in Surprise Valley except from one consultant.

[61] See ND-HL above. Kelly (1932:82) also reports that prayers were offered to the sun the morning of the hunt.

get to a safe place they ask each other if all are safe. The leader was told that the young buck's (*anabui'i*) mother fell back and she said she was not feeling well and she stayed behind (she was killed by the hunter.)[62]

Nowadays boys have to follow the old ways of not wasting any part of the deer. Otherwise they cannot kill any deer. When a boy brings his first meat home anybody but the boy and his family may eat it. To do so would cause the boy ill health [see Boys Puberty Ceremony in vol. 2].

JG-PL: In the old days if a man had intercourse the night before he went hunting he would have bad luck. If he had intercourse, the next morning he would not feel very well and he would be lazy. He would not go very far. He claimed it would give him bad luck.

SMALL AND MEDIUM-SIZED MAMMALS

[Several species of small and medium-sized mammals were taken for food and/or for fur by the Northern Paiute. The principal techniques used in their taking were trapping, pouring water in their burrows, or shooting with the bow and arrow. Jackrabbits were also taken in drives with the aid of nets. For the most part, food animals of these types come from the Order *Rodentia*, the gnawing mammals. Members of the the Order *Carnivora*, the flesh-eating mammals, were sought principally for the fur, although a few were also eaten. The data that follow are synthesized from bits and pieces scattered in Park's notes. They are not exhaustive of the species taken. Biotaxonomic identifications are based on additional field studies by the editor.]

Small Mammal Trapping

GK-WR: Traps were used for catching bushy-tailed squirrels, birds and mice. Traps (*wabü*) were made with two flat rocks.[63] One formed a floor and the other was propped up with a stick pointed at both ends and set on a small round rock and with a string attached at one end to the stick holding up the rock and at the other end to the bait [fig. 8a]. Pinenuts were used for bait. Ten to 20 traps were set each night. I lived up in the pinenut hills some winters and trapped all winter. I also trapped during the rest of the year. Sometimes young women made traps and caught birds and squirrels. Boys and men always trapped.

JG-PL: Grey squirrels (*kupə*) were trapped with a flat rock which is propped up with a stick and has a string for a trigger [fig. 8b]. Brush is put around the side so the squirrels can get into only one side. No bait is used. Forty or fifty traps may be set at one time. In the old days, ground for traps was owned by one man in the hills [see Property in chap. 9]. Trapping is done in the spring.[64] The squirrels are fat at that time. When the man goes out to trap on his land he takes his eldest son with him. He shows the boy how to trap. When he dies, the boy takes his brother with him and teaches him how to trap. Some women trap. These women learn from their husbands.

TM-WR, Y: Mice and rats were trapped with deadfalls made with two flat rocks. One flat rock was put on the ground. The other was propped up over this with a stick about 4 in. long and pointed at the top [fig. 8c]. The pointed end of the stick was put through some pinenuts which were the bait. When a mouse or a rat nibbled at the bait the pressure on the stick caused it to slip out and release the rock which fell on the animal.

The trapper went out to set his traps. When he had set them he carried a log or some wood home. At night he would not sleep stretched out as the other people did. He had to sleep with his legs doubled up.[65] Early the next morning before sunrise the trapper got up and went out to tend his traps. He carried his catch in a bag made from the skin of a deer two or three months old.

The traps were called *wa.bo*. The sack that the catch was carried in was called *iwəa mago*.

The rocks for the traps were not carried far by the trapper. He picks out rocks where he sets the traps. While the traps were being tended the bag was carried in the hand. When all the traps had been looked at the bag was carried home on the back with a rope around the shoulders.

[The nine species listed below were ordinarily trapped by these methods.]
1. *kubə*, prairie dog, gopher, or squirrel [Townsend's ground squirrel, *Spermophilus townsendii*; also Belding's ground squirrel, *C. beldingi*].

---

[62] This small tale, although somewhat confusing, seems to indicate that occasionally the lazy hunter also fools the overconfident deer.

[63] Although all three varieties of flat rock traps described here are said to be made with two stones, a single-stone variety for each is also known from the area. Both Steward (1933:354) and Loud and Harrington (1929:155) illustrated the "figure 4" type of trap.

[64] The season of the year when ground squirrels are reported to be most abundant is from early spring to midsummer. They remain underground during most of the rest of the year (Janetski 1979:315).

[65] No reason is given for sleeping in this position, nor is it described by other Northern Paiute ethnographers. Perhaps the position most resembles the configuration of the set trap and is maintained in an effort to keep the traps from being sprung without a quarry.

Figure 8. Traps. a (top left). String trigger type. b (bottom left). Figure 4 trap. c (top right). Pointed stick type. d (bottom right). Coyote trap. All reconstructed from descriptions given to Willard Z. Park. Drawings by Susan Lohse.

JO-PL: The prairie dog (*kubə*) was the object of most of the trapping. The usual kind of trap was made for them. They were roasted in the sand, just like a ground hog [see below].

RP-WR: The gopher (*kuba*) was trapped with a rock trap, but it was also gotten by carrying water in jugs and pouring the water into its hole.[66] When the gopher is forced to come out, it is caught with the hands by the back of the neck and killed. Some dogs are trained to stand by the hole while the water is carried and poured in. When the gopher comes out, the dog catches it and kills it.

The prairie dog (*kubə*) is taken by Thunder. When it thunders and rain comes for the first time in the season, people say that Thunder Brothers [see Mythology in vol. 2] take the prairie dogs with them. That is why there were no prairie dogs this year and last [1933, 1932].

2. *taba*, ground squirrel [whitetail antelope ground squirrel, *Ammospermophilus leucurus*].

JG-PL: The squirrel (*taba*) is nearly pink in color and with white stripes. It lives in the hills around Pyramid Lake. Sometimes it is caught in the trap set for the grey or ground squirrel.[67] It is shot by boys with small bow and arrow. Sometimes it is shot by men. These are good eating, but the grey squirrels are better. Both kinds were singed and roasted in the pit.

3. *wogotaba*, tree squirrel [western gray squirrel, *Sciurus griseus*].

JO-PL: The tree squirrel is called *wogotaba* (*wogo*, forest, *taba*, thick one). It has a bushy tail. It is eaten, but is not usually trapped or bothered. It is roasted in the sand.

4. *kawa*, woodrat [desert wood rat, *Neotoma lepida*] and *tukawa*, mountain packrat [bushy-tailed wood rat, *Neotoma cinerea*].

JG-PL: Woodrats (*tukawa*, the largest, and *kawə*, smaller) were trapped.[68] The hair was singed off in the coals and then they were roasted.

JO-PL: The woodrat, *kawa*, was found around camp mostly. It was shot and eaten. the packrat (*tukawa*) was trapped and eaten.

[Other rodents mentioned briefly in the notes as being trapped, roasted in the coals, and eaten are the following:]

5. *wooda'a*, chipmunk [golden-mantled ground squirrel, *Spermophilus lateralis*].

6. *tubagoda'a*, chipmunk [Townsend's chipmunk, *Eutamias townsendii* and *Eutamias* spp.] (RP-WR).

7. *tubagogwa*, kangaroo rat; *pa'yu*, kangaroo rat [desert kangaroo rat, *Dipodomys deserti*; Ord kangaroo rat, *D. ordi*; and *Dipodomys* spp.] (RP-WR, JG-PL).

8. *pongadsi*, field mouse [deer mouse, *Peromyscus maniculatus*, or western harvest mouse, *Reithrodontomys megalotis*] (JO-PL).

---

[66] This method is ascribed by Stewart (1941:370) to most Northern Paiute groups. Species are not identified.

[67] JO-PL told Park that traps were also purposefully set for this species.

[68] Both varieties were also reported for Surprise Valley by Kelly (1932:88), but noted as hunted only occasionally. JG-PL: packrat called *kosi*.

9. *tuba pongadsi*, mountain mouse [pinyon mouse, *Peromyscus truei*] (RP-WR, JG-PL).

The "house mouse" (also called *pongadsi*) [*Mus musculus*] was not eaten (JO-PL, GK-WR).

Hunting Medium-Sized Mammals

1. *kidü*, groundhog [yellow-bellied marmot, *Marmota flaviventris*].

JO-PL: The groundhog (*kudü*) was caught in its hole. They shove a sharpened stick in the hole and twist it until the fur is wrapped around it and then it was pulled out. The dogs were used quite often in hunting the groundhog.[69]

BB-PL: Overheard what JO said about using dogs for hunting. He claims it is not true. BB's daughter overheard that and tried to correct him but JO scolded her. BB says dogs were never used in hunting and were never used to kill groundhogs.

To hunt groundhogs, take sagebrush bark and burn it at the hole. Fan the fire with a bunch of feathers. Listen to hear the choking noise of the ground hog. When that noise dies out, the hunter puts out the fire and takes a long stick and feels around in the hole until he finds the animal. He twists the stick until he has caught the fur of the groundhog and then gently pulls it out.

The groundhog was also trapped with the usual type of lean-to trap [see Small Mammal Trapping, above]. No bait was used. The animal would come under the rock for shade and he would touch the stick and the rock would fall on him.

HS-D: *kedü* is the groundhog. To kill the groundhog, the hunter waits near the groundhog's hole. When the animal comes out he shoots it with the bow and arrow. It was cooked by gutting it and then stitching it up again. It was roasted in the skin under coals just like pinenuts.

2. *huna*, badger [*Taxidea taxus*].

HS-D: Some people eat badger (*huna*). It is smoked out of its hole and shot. It is then roasted whole in the coals.

JG-PL: Badger (*huna*) is good to eat. If they are found out away from their holes, people run after them and kill them with rocks or the badger is hit on the nose with a stick. They are easy to kill that way. If the badger gets into its hole it is impossible to get out.

The badger skin is used for an arrow quiver (*hugu'na*). Sometimes they made a cap out of badger skin. The cap was like the one made of skunk skin. It was called *huna sotüa*.

RP-WR: Badger (*huna*) was eaten in the old days, but nowadays very few people eat it. The badger is skinned and put under hot coals to roast. A hot fire is made in a pit dug in the sand. When the sand is hot the ashes are scraped out and the badger is put in. It is covered with hot sand and then covered with hot coals.

3. *poŋi'a*, skunk [striped skunk, *Mephitis mephitis*].

JG-PL: Skunk (*poŋi'a*) was never eaten.[70] It was killed with a stick when it was found. It was hit on the head with a long stick. The skunk was skinned, soaked and tanned by the damp earth process. The skin was used for a cap (*poŋi'a sotüa*) [see Headwear in chap. 5]. A long time ago everybody was hungry and they ate skunk. It was split and roasted on the coals or in a pit.

4. *muhu, sagwəda*, porcupine [*Erethizon dorsatum*].

JO-PL: The porcupine (*sagwəda*) was hit on the head with a stick and killed. They are not fast and cannot get away. The quills are singed off and the porcupine is roasted under the ashes. The quills were used for decoration and a brush was made of its tail [see Clothing and Adornment, chap. 5].

5. *kohi'i*, beaver [*Castor canadensis*].

JO-PL: The beaver (*kohi'i*) was eaten. They were gotten around Lovelock as they do not live here. They would trap them and shoot them with a bow and arrow.

6. *patsugu*, otter [river otter, *Lutra canadensis*].

HS-D: SP thinks that the otter (*patsugu*) was not eaten. It was clubbed in the water and the fur was used for wrapping the hair braids [see Hairdress in chap. 5].

JG-PL: The otter (*pasugə*) was pretty hard to kill because they live in the water. Sometimes an otter was killed. The otter was eaten a long time ago. The otter was cooked by roasting on the coals and in a pit. The skin was cut up in strips ½ to 2 in. wide for some shamans to use or it was used to wrap around the braided hair of the men. When a man got an otter skin, men came to him to buy the strips. They used to use beads to buy the strips [see Trade in chap. 9].

The otter was followed to the hole. A fire was built at the mouth of the hole and with brush the smoke was fanned into the hole. This was done for a while and then a long stick was pushed into the hole to see if the otter was dead. When the otter was dead, the end of the stick was dampened and pushed into the hole until it touched the otter. Then it was turned until it had the fur of the otter twisted about the end of the stick. Then the otter could be pulled out.

7. *pabisa*, weasel [longtailed weasel, *Mustela frenata*].

JG-PL: The weasel (*pabisa*) was eaten. A long time ago, the people ate everything. When they killed anything they did not throw it away. In the summer, if the weasel was found out of its hole it was killed and gotten out the same way as the otter [see above].

---

[69] Kelly (1932:87) also confirms the use of dogs in marmot hunting in Surprise Valley.

[70] HS-D told Park that the skunk (*poniçə*) was never killed, even for its skin.

In the summer the weasel's fur is brown with a yellow belly. The fur is not very good in summer. In the winter it turns all white. It is the best then. The weasel is hunted the same way in winter as in summer. The weasel skin was used for a tobacco pouch [see fig. 9]. The shamans sometimes used the weasel skin. Some doctors were told to get a weasel skin of a certain color. The doctor's spirit told him to get that kind and it is hard to find. He keeps the skin. When he doctors he puts the skin under the patient's back. He leaves it there all night [see Shamanism and Birth in vol. 2].

HS-D: The weasel was eaten by some Indians. It was caught by stepping on the animal as it dug its hole, just beneath the surface of the ground. The skin was used for a kind of purse, for a pouch for arrow points, flints and tobacco. The softened skin was used to wrap braids of the hair. The shaman used the skin for kits to carry their tobacco, beads, pipe, feathers, etc. Weasel skin was preserved as a keepsake by the sick. It was also used in childbirth.

8. *payona*, mink [*Mustela vison*].

HS-D: The mink (*payona*) was not eaten. The skin was used for rugs for beds. HS does not know how the mink was killed.

JO-PL: I have heard that they used to eat mink (*payona*). It was roasted in the sand.

9. *patakai*, raccoon [*Procyon lotor*].

HS-D: The raccoon (*patakai'i*) was killed with bow and arrow. It was roasted in the coals.

JG-PL: The raccoon (*patakai'*) did not live here. They lived in the timber country.

10. *pamus*, muskrat [*Ondatra zibethicus*].

JO-PL: The muskrat (*pamus*) was eaten. It was roasted in the sand.

11. *tuhu'*, wildcat [bobcat, *Lynx rufus*].

JG-PL: Wildcat (*tuhu'*) was eaten. It was killed with a bow and arrow. This skin is used for an arrow quiver. It is roasted in a pit or on the coals.

12. *iza'a*, coyote [*Canis latrans*].

JO-PL: Coyote was trapped for his skin. It was used for a quiver. He was never eaten. Coyote was also hunted [with bow and arrow]. Traps were made by piling rocks on top of each other with a stick to hold it up [fig. 8d].[71] Coyote goes into the little cave thus formed to get the bait at the back end. There is a flat rock on top held up by a stick on a round rock. The bait (rabbits) is fastened to the stick. The coyote pulls out the stick which caused the flat rock on top to fall and all the other rocks on the side to collapse. There are rocks piled on top of the flat rocks. The bait is tied on the stick just above the

round rock upon which the stick rests. This trap seems to be used only for coyotes.

13. *isha*, wolf [gray wolf, *Canis lupus*].

RP-WR: In the old days wolves were killed. The wolves used to rob the graves. Even when rocks were put on the graves the wolves would get at the corpse. The wolves carried corpses on their backs holding the corpses with their tails.[72] When a wolf killed a deer he carried it the same way. The wolves ate the corpses that they got from the graves. Wolves and coyotes were not eaten in the old days. When they were killed the skins were used to make quivers.

GK-WR: The Pauites around Walker Lake did not eat wolves and coyotes. The meat did not taste good. I heard some old men around Fallon say that they used to get hungry and kill a wolf or a coyote and cook it and eat it. The Indians around Fallon used to get pretty hungry. Wolves and coyotes were killed for their skins. The skin was made into a blanket. The hair was not scraped off.

JO-PL: Wolf (*isha*, liar) was not eaten. They were afraid of it. They did not usually kill it because it was out at night in packs.

14. *wanic*, fox [gray fox, *Urocyon cinereoargenteus*].

HS-D: Fox (*wanic*) was killed with a bow and arrow. The skin was used to make a quiver. It was not eaten.

Rabbits

[Jackrabbits and cottontails were taken in a variety of ways, including by shooting with bow and arrow, snaring with a noose, pitfall trappings, and extracting them from burrows with a stick. Jackrabbits were also taken in large drives with the aid of nets. The fur of rabbits, which was used to make rabbitskin blankets, was often considered as much of a prize as the meat. The data that follow are extracted from the accounts of seven men and one woman.

1. *kamu*, jackrabbit [blacktailed jackrabbit, *Lepus californicus*].

Drives

ND-HL, HS-D: Rabbit drives (*kamu tanoa; kamu*, jack rabbit; *tanoa*, drive) were usually held in the fall. That was when the fur was nice. The word was passed around that there was going to be a drive (*kamu nada noakwɔ*, "there is going to be a rabbit drive"). The big drives were held twice a year; once a year at Walker River and once at Pyramid Lake. People came from Walker River and Pyramid Lake to the drives.

---

[71] Loud and Harrington (1929:155) figure a lean-to trap constructed of poles and rocks for taking coyotes and bobcats. RP-WR told Park that coyotes were also taken with noose snares set at the mouth of the den.

[72] Very little is reported as to Paiute concepts of familiars for witches. These types of activities (wolves carrying corpses) are reported elsewhere in North America (see Kluckhohn 1967).

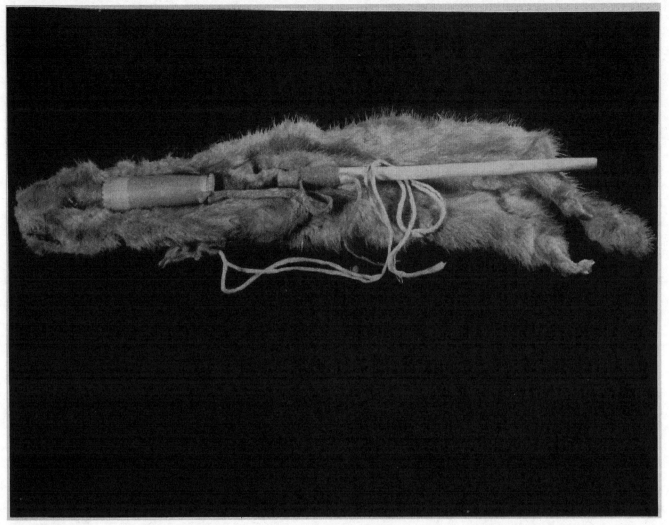

Figure 9. Skin tobacco pouch (probably mink, *Mustela vison*), with straight pipe and stem. MPM 21842a,b. Collected by S. A. Barrett, western Nevada, 1916.

The people gather together to decide on a drive. At that time they selected a leader. The leader of the drive might hold the position for several years. One of the old men who owned the nets was not necessarily appointed leader. The nets (*wana*) were as much as ¾ mi long. They were made of *wiha*. The nets used in the drive were owned by the old fellows who had the patience to make them. One man might own 50 yds or more. The nets were about 4 ft high with about a 3 in. mesh [fig. 10a].

The leader talks to the people and tells them where to place the net, like across a ravine. The leader goes out in front and builds a fire a couple of miles away from the net. The people who are to drive go to the fire to get instruction.[73] This fire tells how the rabbits are going to run. If the fire blazes up the rabbits will run slowly; if not, they will run fast. The word for this fire is *wünüpida*. When the people came to the fire the captain of the drive tells them how to spread out on each side of the ravine. Men carried bows and arrows (blunted) [see Arrows in chap. 3] which are used at close quarters when rabbits try to run away from the net.

Poles were placed 40 or 50 yds apart.[74] Men stood behind the net between the poles. The nets used in one drive may stretch out for a quarter of a mile. The men between the poles were holding the stakes.

Each man behind the net gets the rabbits that come into the space he is watching. The men who own the

[73] Lowie (1924:198) was also told by Fallon consultants that fires were built and instructions given to the hunters each day by the leader of the drive. He does not record that the config-

uration of the fire was used to predict how the rabbits would run.

[74] These distances seem too great to totally support the nets. There were undoubtedly other poles or sticks between these. The reference to "poles" probably is to the main supports — tall and perhaps thus easily seen from a distance.

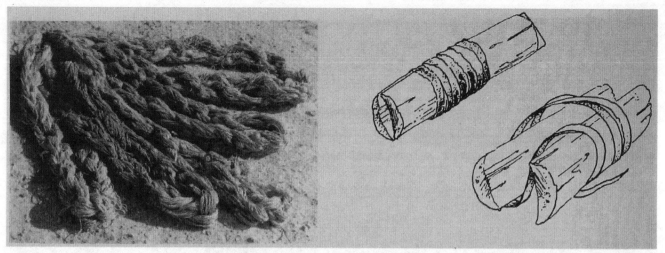

Figure 10. Rabbit hunting. a (left). Rabbit net, chained for storage. Photograph by M. M. Wheat, 1958–62. University of Nevada, Reno, Library, Special Collections Department. b (right). Rabbit call of two pieces of sage with skin of rabbit's ear between and wrapped around. Air was inhaled. PM 34-114-10/4389. Collected by W. Z. Park, Pyramid Lake, 1934. Drawing by Susan Lohse.

nets get only the rabbits they kill.[75] If one person in the drive does not get any, others would give him a few but they would keep the skins. If two men shot at the same rabbit, one would get the skin, and the other would get the rest. The first one to pick up the rabbit gets his choice. Usually the skin is preferred.

GK-WR: Jackrabbits (*kamə*) were hunted with a bow and arrows. In the rabbit drive nets were used. The nets were owned by two or three men. They were made of *wiha.*

When I was a boy they held a rabbit drive at Yerington. Many people came together and camped. The headman of the drive went out in front and made a fire. Then all the men came to the fire with their bows and arrows. The headman told everybody what to do. He told the men who had nets to put them up. One old fellow had a net about 100 yds long. Two or three men put their nets together. They were stretched on greasewood sticks. Willow was not used. The nets were about 4 ft high.

The headman of the drive told everybody at the fire what to do. Before they started the drive, the headman put some kind of medicine in the fire to give everybody good luck.[76] The headman always did that in a rabbit drive. I do not know what the medicine was. He told the men with the bows and arrows not to shoot towards the people. He talked a lot and told them everything that

they were to do. Then they spread out and drove the rabbits towards the nets.[77] The drivers shot the rabbits with their bows and arrows whenever the rabbits were close to them.

The owners of the nets got the largest share of the rabbits. They got all the rabbits that were caught in the nets. The men who were driving never took any rabbits from the nets. Those belonged to the owners of the nets. The rabbits were skinned and dried.

The headman of the drive set the date for the rabbit drive. Usually the headman of the rabbit drive was not the chief. The same man was chief of the rabbit drive year after year.

BR-L, PL: The rabbit drive is called *kamətanoa.* The nets (*kamə wanə*) for the rabbit drive were made of *wiha.* A net was about 100 ft long by about 3 or 4 ft high. The net was placed on sticks to form a "V".[78] Usually two men own the nets. At least eight or ten people, often more, took part in the rabbit drive. Nowadays 200 or 300 take part.[79]

The leader of the drive was elected by the people. He was not the owner of the nets. He would be boss of the drive as long as he was good at it. He might be boss for the rest of his life. The boss was called *kaməna.*

---

[75] Principles for dividing the catch apparently differed from area to area. Kelly (1932:88) was told that one rabbit went to each participant and the remainder to the headman; or all rabbits were divided evenly. Lowie (1924:198) was told that each person takes his own kill. This was also the pattern in Owens Valley (Steward 1933:253).

[76] This feature is not mentioned in the other ethnographic literature on the Northern Paiute.

[77] Lowie (1924:198) recounts a rabbit drive at Fallon in which the nets were set in a rectangle, with the hunters inside. They were so set six times a day in different places. The hunt lasted one month.

[78] This configuration was not reported to other Northern Paiute ethnographers. One Surprise Valley consultant told Kelly (1932:88) that the nets were set in a semicircle. They were set in an "arc" in Owens Valley (Steward 1933:253). Lowie (1924:198) reports a rectangular set for the Fallon area.

[79] According to information from Surprise Valley, formerly four to five camps or roughly 10 men participated in a hunt. In historic times, more participated (Kelly 1932:88).

The rabbits that were caught in the nets were killed with sticks. They were taken home to be skinned.[80]

Pitfalls

GK-WR: The rabbit pitfalls were called *kamu podiaru*. A series of holes 4 or 5 ft deep were dug on rabbit trails.[81] Pointed greasewood sticks were used to loosen the dirt. It was then scooped out with small willow baskets. A frame of light twigs was made to cover the hole. It was then covered with grass. Rabbits fell into the holes and were not able to get out. The pitfalls were fixed in the evening and in the morning the hunter made the rounds taking out the rabbits that had been caught during the night. This was the easiest way to catch rabbits. Many were gotten in this fashion.

Lures and Calls

GK-WR: Hunters sat in the brush in the spring and summer when rabbits had young ones. The hunter made a noise like young rabbits crying. The old rabbits heard it and came toward the brush and the hunter shot them. The noise was made by puckering the lips in some way, but GK does not know exactly how it was done.

TM-WR, Y: In the spring and summer when there are young rabbits, the call of the young rabbit was made by the hunter with his mouth and forefinger. The finger was placed across the mouth between the lips. The lips were puckered and the breath was drawn in. The old rabbits would run toward the hunter.

JG-PL: A whistle was made by putting the skin on the inside of the rabbit's ear between two sticks [fig. 10b]. This was used to imitate the cry of young rabbits in the spring. It would bring the old rabbits so they could be shot easily.

Snares

DM-PL: A rabbit trap was made of a loop of twine tied to brush along the rabbit path.[82] The loop was a little larger than the head of the rabbit. Several of these loops were set along the rabbit trail. The man set them at night and came in the morning to check his traps.

2. *tabu'u*, cottontail [mountain cottontail, *Sylvilagus nuttallii*].

GK-WR: Snares of a loop with a slip knot were hung at the mouth of rabbit holes and also along the rabbit's trail. This was used especially for *tabu'u*, the cottontail.

HS:D: Rabbits (*tabu'u*) were gotten by twisting a sharpened stick in a hole when the hunter can feel the rabbit. When the fur is twisted around the stick, it is pulled out.[83]

JG-PL: The cottontail is *tabu'u*. Cottontail and jackrabbit are about alike for eating. Both are killed with a bow and arrow. They are skinned and roasted.

Cooking Rabbits

HS-D: As soon as the rabbits were killed, they were skinned. The skin was stripped off and where it stuck around the mouth and feet the skin was cut [see also Cordage, Nets, and Weaving in chap. 3]. The meat was dried in the shade. The rabbits were hung up with the liver and kidneys. The meat keeps about two weeks. The intestines were cleaned and cooked, either boiled or roasted in the coals. The heads as well as the kidneys were given to the children. The brains were roasted.

JG-PL: Rabbits were split and hung in the shade to dry. Dried rabbits were roasted on the coals. Cottontails were fixed the same way.

When rabbits were roasted, women broke up the whole rabbit when it was cooked. Each hind leg was broken off, and the front legs were broken off. The neck was taken off and the body broken just in back of the ribs. The heart was taken out. These were all put on the sagebrush. When the rabbit was taken out of the coals it was brushed off with a sprig of sagebrush. The pieces of meat were put on the brush in front of the family and each person helped himself. There was no prayer said before starting to eat. No bits of food were thrown away before eating.[84]

The intestines of rabbits were washed, nothing was thrown away. Bones were broken and cracked on a metate and the marrow sucked out. The head and neck were mashed up to get the marrow.

RP-WR: Rabbits are pounded up, bones and all, in the mortar after they are roasted. When it was well pounded, the meat was ready to eat. Meat crushed this way was called *yuhu-sɔhɔ* (*yuhu*, fat; *sɔhɔ*, chopping).

FISHING

[Fishes endemic to the Lahontan System, of which the Pyramid Lake, Walker Lake, and Humboldt basins are a part, included the following: (1) the Lahontan cut-

---

[80] Only Steward (1933:254) refers to a celebration at the end of the drive in which the male hunters formally exchanged rabbits for seed gathered by the women.

[81] Stewart (1941:368) notes the scattered distribution of this rabbit hunting technique among the Northern Paiute.

[82] Noose snares for rabbits were also reported from Owens Valley (Steward 1933:254) and Surprise Valley (1932:88). Stewart (1941:368) lists them as common for most Northern Paiute groups.

[83] Twisting animals from their burrows with the aid of a stick was specifically denied in Owens Valley (Steward 1933:255).

[84] ND-HL reported to Park that casting bits of food to the mountains was a "Pit River" (Achomawi) feature.

throat trout (*Salmo clarki hensawi*); (2) the Tahoe sucker (*Catostomus tahoensis*); (3) the cui-ui lakesucker (*Chasmistes cujus*); (4) the Lahontan tui chub (*Gila bicolor obesus*); (5) the Lahontan redside (*Richardsonius egregius*); and (6) the Lahontan speckled dace (*Rhinichthys osculus robustus*). Of these, the most important and sizeable food fishes were cutthroat, the cui-ui, and the Tahoe sucker. The cui-ui was found only in the Pyramid Lake basin (including now dry Winnemucca Lake). These three fish species ascended the rivers during the winter and spring in large runs and were the focus of intensive fishing activities involving items of gear such as weirs and platforms, dip or lifting nets, and spears and harpoons. During other times of the year the large fish were taken in the lakes with hooks and lines and gill nets. The remaining fish species, generally referred to as "minnows," were also important although sought less intensively. They were taken with gill and bag nets and in traps of various types.

Fishing was an important subsistence activity, particularly in the Pyramid Lake and Walker Lake basins, where large fish runs were typical. It was also important in the Humboldt and Carson basins, although Park's data from these two areas are insufficient to quantify the generalization. The data that follow are prefaced by a few brief notes on fishes, their importance, and the timing of the runs. The remaining sections are divided according to the equipment types and techniques used in fishing. Additional interpretive data on Northern Paiute fishing are given by Speth (1969) and Fowler and Bath (1981). Additional technological features of net construction are given under Fish Nets in Cordage, Nets, and Weaving in chap. 3. See also Ceremonies in vol. 2 for data on celebrations held in conjunction with fish runs.]

Fish and Fish Runs

GK-WR: Fish were more important in the economy than meat. Fishing was especially important when the wild seeds failed due to lack of rainfall. Even when the women were away from the river gathering seeds or pinenuts, the men came back to fish [see Seasonal and Daily Rounds in chap. 2]. They fished almost every day in the winter and spring and quite a bit in the summer and fall.

JO-PL: Fishing was done all the time here during the winter and spring. In the winter when there was a lot of water the trout (*agai*) came. In the spring they would get *kuyui* [lakesuckers] and *awago* [Tahoe suckers]. In the summer they fished in the lake for trout, suckers and *tuipakwi* [tui chub]. A lot of fresh fish was stored away, especially *kuyui*. When all other food fails they fall back on fish.

HS-D: The first fish to come in the river at Pyramid Lake are the *tomo agai*, winter trout [Lahontan cutthroat]. They come about late November or December. Then come the *tama agai*, the spring trout [also Lahontan cutthroat].[85] The *kuyui* [lakesucker] come about late April. The *awago* [Tahoe sucker] come about that same time. The minnows are in the lake and in the river all the time. Men always went fishing.

BR-L, PL: The trout and *kuyui* start to run up the river in March and April.[86] They ran at the same time. They only went up the river during the high water. They go a long way up the river. The Washos used to come down the river about half way between here (Pyramid Lake) and Reno to catch fish. People came from Humboldt River in the spring for the run of fish [see also Trade in chap. 9].

Weirs and Platforms

[Fish weirs and fishing platforms are reported in Park's notes for the Truckee River and the Walker River. They were usually constructed together, although by two accounts not always so. Each could be used independently in conjuction with harpooning and spearing, dip and bag netting, and setting fish traps. Weirs and platforms were apparently considered to be private property, with rights to their use, as well as the use of selected places on the rivers for their construction, being inherited bilaterally. Most of the construction was in association with trout, sucker, and, for Pyramid Lake, cui-ui runs. The data that follow bring out some of the differences in construction and use of both devices, but for additional data see Speth (1969) and Fowler and Bath (1982)].

JC-WR: Fish weirs (*wəmə*) are built when the trout go up the river to spawn in high water. A meeting of the men who own the weir is held to decide upon when it is to be built.[87] There may be eight to ten platforms on each weir. The platforms are each owned by a family and are passed on from generation to generation. A man has rights not only to a platform on a weir but to one particular platform only; e.g., if he has the platform on the right bank he is the sole owner and he can use no

---

[85] See Snyder (1917) for a description of both of these runs. The first is of older mature individuals and the second of younger trout. LaRivers (1962) gives additional information on spawning periods for all of the species noted here. Stewart (1941:425) also refers to seasonal names for trout.

[86] This is a late starting date for *all* trout, but is good for the spring runs.

[87] Speth (1969) discusses the nature and composition of the remembered men's fishing cliques at Walker River. She also outlines the construction and use of weirs and fishing platforms.

Figure 11. Weir and platform fishing. a (top left). Section of a willow fish weir rolled up on the bank of an abandoned stream channel. b (bottom left). Abandoned fishing platform. c (right). Man holding large dip or lifting net. Photographs by S. A. Barrett, Walker River (a, b) and Pyramid Lake (c), 1916. Milwaukee Public Museum photographs.

other on that weir. To fish on another man's platform would cause a fight. Trouble over rights to platforms was frequent among the Indians in the old days.

JC saw weirs built on Walker River when he was young. He also saw weirs on the Truckee River near Pyramid Lake.[88] There were two favorite places on the Walker River where weirs were built. One was near his house and the other was where the highway bridge crosses the river now.

The fish weir was built across the river where the bottom was level so all the fishermen on the weir would have an equal chance. To build the weir willow poles about 2 in. in diameter were cut and sharpened at one end. These poles were also called *wamɔ*. The poles were worked into the sand of the river bed in a straight line across the river. Other poles were tied across these posts in the sand. Then sections about 6 ft long made of interwoven willow branches close enough together to prevent the fish getting through are tied to the poles in the river [fig. 11a]. These sections are called *paiaqwᵃ*. The fisher-

men build platforms on the downstream side of the weir.[89] There is one platform built out from each bank.[90] Out from the bank the platform is made by three crossed sticks with a seat of twigs and grass in the crotch [fit. 11b]. It is tied together and to the posts of the weir with string or willow.

The fishermen use dip nets to catch the fish that come up the weir [see also Fish Nets, below]. The mouth of the net is held open by two crossed willow sticks. A string runs across the fork of the sticks and another string is attached to it opposite the apex of the crossed sticks. The net is held by the apex of the crossed sticks. The string from the opposite side is held between the fingers of the hand holding the sticks. When a fish touches the string in going into the net the fisherman feels the string pull and knows that he has caught a fish. Another way to know when fish enter the net is to use this string

---

[88] All but one of the groups reported by Stewart (1941:370) verified that fish weirs were used. Kelly (1932:96) also describes weirs for the region north of Surprise Valley.

[89] Stewart (1941:370) received positive responses to the use of fishing platforms only from his Honey Lake and Pyramid Lake consultants.

[90] Speth (1969) suggests that platforms were built in the middle of the river. All of Park's accounts speak of platforms attached to the river banks only.

across the mouth of the net to attach a float of four or five mudhen feathers.

When the fisherman sees the float move or the string between his fingers jerk he slowly raises the net keeping its mouth against the side of the weir. He removes the trout and puts it in a sack hanging from his platform. Fishing goes on night and day during high water.

GK-WR: The fish weir described by JC-WR was confirmed by GK. He has fished in this fashion, catching both suckers and trout. They use different nets for each kind of fish [see Fish Nets, below]. Each platform might be owned by more than one man—sometimes as many as four. They would take turns fishing on the platform. Two might work there at the same time. The men who owned the weir held a meeting when the water was high to decide about putting it up. When the fish stopped running they took out the weir and put it away until the next time. The sections of the weir were made of willows that were ¾-1 in. in diameter. These willows were a couple of inches apart and woven together.

JG-PL: The fish weir was called *wamə*. Willows were braided about 4 ft high to make it. It was put in at an angle across the river.[91] One platform (*pa.soni*) was built about 4 ft wide near the bank. It was built over a whirlpool — one that moves slowly. Three or 4 men build the weir and each takes a night for fishing on the platform. The rights to this platform are inherited by a man's relatives. People may have a weir below a place where others spear fish. Quarrels arise and killing results from these disputes.

A dip net is used in fishing from the platform. It is used at night or during the day when the water is muddy. Then the fish cannot see the net.

BR-L, PL: Fish weirs were built on the river at high water. The weir, made of latticed willows, was put in at an angle across the river. Two sticks were worked into the bottom near the bank. Another stick was tied across these and sticks were put out from the bank to form a platform. The fisherman sat on this platform with a dip net with a large mesh. It was the same shape of net but larger as was used in winter fishing [see Fish Nets, below]. There was a string that ran from the center of the net to the fisherman's hand. When he felt something strike this string he drew the net up. One man owns this platform but he may let his friends fish there part of the time.[92]

[Several styles of fish nets were used for taking different species of fish. Large dip or lifting nets were used in conjuction with platform fishing, or occasionally were set as seines in still water. The quarry was usually trout, suckers, or cui-ui. Bag nets designed to be used to scoop fish from the water or to trap them as they swam upstream were made in different sizes depending on the species. Gill nets designed to be set in the lake, or, occasionally, in the river, were also made in different mesh sizes. Additional technological details on net construction are given under Fish Nets in Cordage, Nets, and Weaving in chap. 3].

Dip or Lifting Nets

BR-L, PL: Dip nets were 4 or 5 ft deep and 4 or 5 ft in diameter at the opening. The have a rounded bottom [fig. 11c]. They were smaller at the bottom but not conical in shape.[93] Four or five fish were caught at a time in these nets. Two sticks about 2 in. in diameter were tied to the sides of the net. The sticks were 6 to 8 ft long and crossed near one end. The sticks were not tied together where they crossed. The sticks were held by the fisherman at the point where they came together. A string was put across the mouth of the net 4 or 5 in from the top. The end of the string ran to the point where the sticks crossed. It was held in the fisherman's hand so he could feel a fish touch it as it entered the net. They had to have something like this to know when there were fish in the net for in the spring when this net was used the water was so muddy the people could not see the fish. This net was called *agaiwanə* (*agai*, trout; *wanə*, net).[94] There were different sizes of dip nets for different kinds of fish. This net was used only when the water was high and muddy. The fish would see the net in clear water and not come near it. In clear water the harpoon was used [see Harpoons and Spears, below].

On the Humboldt River the ice would freeze on the ponds. A hole large enough to put the dip net through was cut in the ice. Men with sticks scattered all the way around the edge of the pond and beat on the ice with the sticks. This drove the fish to the middle of the pond and when the man with the net felt the minnows strike the string across the mouth of the net he drew it up. Only minnows were caught in this way. The net had a small mesh but was the same size as the nets for trout and *kuyui*. The Truckee River flowed too rapidly to freeze

---

[91] Descriptions from both Pyramid Lake and the Humboldt River area speak of weirs angled across the river.

[92] This account probably refers to platforms used on the Truckee River rather than on the Humboldt River.

[93] Stewart (1941:425) noted that one consultant identified this net as similar to one shown for the Yurok by Kroeber (1925: plate 7).

[94] An additional term for these nets is *yani*, according to Barrett (1916), Speth (1969), and RP-WR.

so fish were not caught that way there. These nets could also be placed on poles worked into the sand in large still ponds at high water.[95]

ND-HL: Large nets were used to catch trout and *kuyui*. These nets were used to fish at night or during the day when the river was muddy. A platform was built over an eddy and the fisherman squatted on this with his net. The platform was about 18 in. above the water [see Weirs and Platforms, above]. The nets used for fishing from platforms had two poles crossed to hold them. The nets were tied to the poles. The poles were not tied where they crossed. The poles were about 10 ft long and were straight. When the net was open, it was about 4 ft across at the end of the mouth.

Two strings were tied across the mouth of the net. The crossed poles and the two strings were held in the left hand with the thumb on top. When a fish was felt to touch the strings and got into the net the pole closest to the body of the fisherman was lifted on the right thigh. The fisherman then reached across and lifted the further pole with the right hand. As the net was lifted, the ends of the poles were rested on the ground or the platform for leverage. As the net was lifted, the two poles were brought together to close the mouth. The fish was then taken from the net and killed with a club about 15 in long and several in. in diameter.[96] This was just an ordinary stick of about these dimensions. It was not fixed up in any way.

Bag Nets

GK-WR: GK has heard of cutting a hole in the ice on the river and catching fish with a sack-shaped net. He has not seen this done. The hole in the ice was made by breaking the ice with a pole — lifting the pole and dropping it on the ice.[97] Any kind of pole that a man could find was used. The net used in fishing through the ice was sack-shaped. It was 2 or 3 ft across the mouth and about as deep. It was attached on both sides to poles about 5 ft long. These poles were not crossed as in fishing from a platform.

The net was dipped into the water with the mouth upstream. The poles were held at an angle [fig. 12a]. No sinkers of any kind were used to weight down the bottom of the net. The other ends of these strings were fastened to a feather which was on the surface of the water when the net was in the water. The feather acted as a float. The fish entering the net touched one or more strings, which disturbed the feather float. Then the fisherman drew up his net.

HS-D: Nets were used to catch suckers (*awagu*) during the spawning season in the spring. These nets looked like a butterfly net — about an arm's length in depth. They were used along the shore.

JG-PL: A bag-type of fish net made of *wiha* was used for fishing. It was used in a shallow place in the stream. This was used a great deal. It worked on the principle of the dip net but was a little different [fig. 12a]. There is a long stick that is bent to hold the mouth of the net open. Another stick is attached to the side of the net. The ends of the sticks are held on the bottom of the river. Both sticks are held in the man's hand. One side of the net is on the bottom of the river. When the man feels a fish in the bag he pulls it up. This net is called *ze apuigwa wana*.

Gill Nets

GK-WR: Nets were used more than anything else to catch fish in the lake. The nets were about 24 yds long and about 4–5 ft high. A net was owned by one man.

Sticks were put in the bottom of the lake in shallow water near the shore. The net was placed on these stakes. It was left all night. The fish were taken out of the nets each morning and evening.

RP-WR: Nets were placed on sticks about 6 ft high all the way across the river.[98] Willow sticks about 1½ in. in diameter were placed 15 to 20 ft apart to support the net. Men walked in the water shoulder deep to place the nets in the lake. They camp on the shore. About 20 men, one from each family, camp near where the net is placed. Trout is taken from the net every morning and taken back to the homes. They are carried home in conical burden baskets.

JB-PL: They have nets in four sizes for different fish: (1) *agai*, trout; [fig. 12b] (2) *kuyui*, mullet; (3) *awago*, suckers; and (4) *pakwi*, little fish. Measure the mesh from the end of the middle finger to the big knuckle.[99] These nets were about 4 ft high and 50 to 100 yds. long.[100] Willow sticks were put down to hold the net. At every fifth stick a rock weight was suspended from the bottom of the net to keep the net straight up and down. The net was tied to sticks. The net was placed close to shore. At the ends of the net they have a long string

---

[95] This in effect turns the dip or lifting net into a gill net.

[96] JG-PL also told Park of killing fish by striking them on the head with a stick.

[97] Loud (1929) notes that "ice picks" were found in Lovelock Cave. His consultant from the Lovelock area thought shaped rocks such as these were tied to sticks and used to break the ice for fishing.

[98] This account speaks of placing nets in both the river and the lake, and thus is confusing. It may be that the nets were placed at the mouth of the river for this particular technique.

[99] This comment probably refers to the gauge size for the trout net.

[100] Fish nets in Owens Valley were said by Steward (1933:257) to be in the shape of rabbit nets.

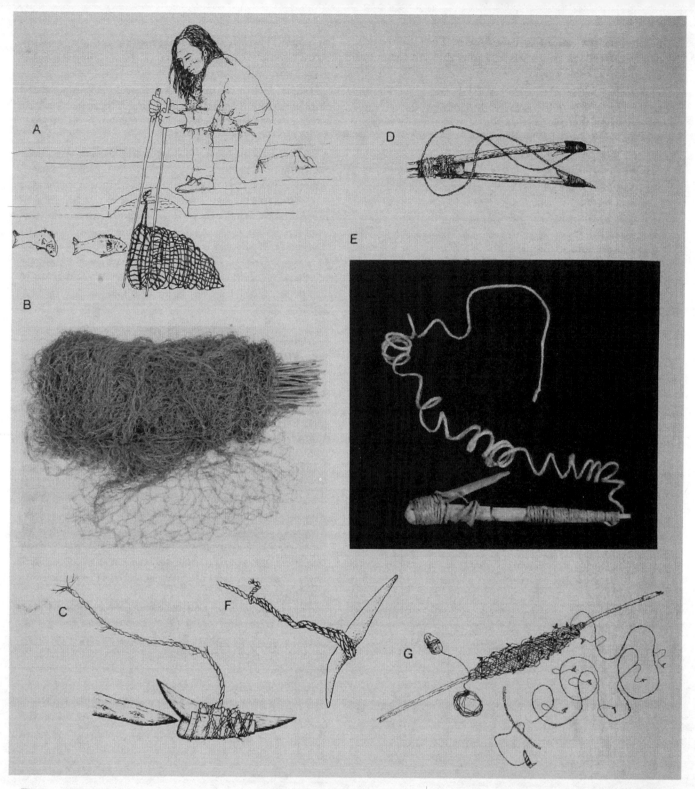

Figure 12. Fishing equipment. a. Schematic drawing of fishing through the ice with a bag net. Note float and strings to signal fisherman that quarry is in the net. b. Gill net for trout, meant to be staked across the river. MPM 21714. Milwaukee Public Museum photograph. c. Construction of harpoon head, based on PM 34-114-10/3979. d. Double-pronged fish harpoon, willow pole, greasewood shafts. AMNH 50.2/3730. e. Trout hook of greasewood, native cordage, 8.3 cm shaft. MPM 21970. f. Bone fish gorge, 3.4 cm, meant to be suspended from line with others. PM 34-114-10/3962. g. Trot line with tiny (1.3 cm) hooks of sharpened rabbit bone in folded willow splints. Meant to be thrown. NMNH-SI 19047. g collected by S. Powers, Pyramid Lake, 1876; b, e collected by S. A. Barrett, western Nevada, 1916; c, d, f collected by W. Z. Park, Pyramid Lake, 1934. Drawing of c by Patricia DeBunch; a, d, f, g by Susan Lohse.

with the end of the string tied to one end of a bunch of tule at the top. When something gets into the net, it raises one end of the tules like a flag. There is a weight at the bottom of the string at each end of the net as well as at every fifth stick. The sticks are not put in the lake bottom. They are placed to keep the net straight. The nets were placed in 20 or 30 ft of water.

Harpoons and Spears

[Both single- and double-pronged harpoons as well as bident spears were used for taking fish in the Truckee, Humbolt, and Walker Rivers and in their adjoining lakes. Harpooning and spearing fish was primarily a late spring, fall, and summer activity, as it required clear water to properly observe the fish. Some of the men interviewed on these techniques, particularly from Pyramid Lake, stated that conditions might be further improved by placing a patch of white rocks in the river bottom over which the fish had to pass. Others noted that fires near the bank of the stream would attract the fish at night, allowing fishing to continue beyond daytime. Some individuals stated that the double-pronged harpoon was often used at night, presumably improving the fisherman's chances of taking his quarry. Otherwise, the preference for styles of harpoons or for harpoons over spears seems to be a matter of personal rather than regional preference. Harpoons and spears were used from shore, from platforms, and with or without associated weirs.]

Single-Pronged Harpoons

TM-WR, Y: The fish harpoon, called *kwatino*, was made with a willow shaft.[101] At the end of the shaft there was a foreshaft of greasewood. The head of the harpoon was made of deer bone. It fitted into the greasewood foreshaft and was tied with string. The quill of an eagle tail feather was split and wrapped around the outside of the tied joint of the bone, and greasewood [fig. 12c]. Pine pitch was then smeared on to keep the quill in place and cement the joint. A hole was made in the center of the bone harpoon head. A string ran from this hole to the willow shaft just in back of where the foreshaft was attached. When the harpoon passed thru the fish's body it came loose from the shaft and turned crosswise on the other side of the fish. The harpoon was used for fishing in the river.

GK-WR: The fish harpoon had a greasewood point and willow shaft. The point fits into a hole in the willow shaft or is loosely tied to the end of the shaft with *wiha* so that when a fish is speared, the point will come away from the shaft. A small sharp piece of greasewood is

---

[101] The construction techniques described here are the same as given by Wheat (1967:64f) except that a pelican quill is used in place of the eagle quill.

tied at an angle about ½ in. from the end of the sharpened greasewood point. This acted as a barb. The barb was about ½ in. long and was tied with sinew. The string of *wiha* to hold the fish when the harpoon point came out was tied near the back of the point and close to the forepart of the shaft. GK thinks that about 10 ft of string was used. The harpoon was used to fish along the shores of the lake and along the banks of the river.

BR-L, PL: Fish spears [harpoons] are used during the spawning season. The shaft is 12 or more ft long. It is made of tule spliced together and is about 1½ in. in diameter. The point of the harpoon was made of hard bone. A string made of *wiha* was tied around the shaft and ran to a hole in the point. Where the string was fastened it was covered with a mixture of charcoal and pine pitch. Sometimes the barb of the harpoon was made of greasewood. It was long enough to go through the fish. When this point penetrated the fish it came loose from the shaft leaving the harpoon point on the other side of the fish and attached by the string to the shaft.

This harpoon was used to catch large trout. When they were spawning in the river, fishermen stood along the bank and watched the females. When the males came along they speared them. They did not spear the females for they acted as a decoy for the fishermen.

HS-D: The fish harpoon was about 12 ft. long and was called *kwatano*. The same name was used for the point. The harpoon was made of greasewood and was covered with pine pitch and then painted red with Indian paint. The harpoon was about as thick as a pencil. The greasewood was worked down to the proper size and sharpened by rubbing it on sandstone. The point was detachable and was tied to the shaft with *wiha*.

The harpoon was used on the lake and in the river. A man would sit on the rocks along the shore and wait for the fish to come along.

Double-Pronged Fish Harpoons

ND-HL: The two-pronged fish harpoon was called *kwatinyo* [fig. 12d]. The shaft was of willow and was about 15-20 ft. long. The two prongs were 8 to 10 in. long. They were made of greasewood. They were tied together on the end of the willow pole with *wiha*. The points were made of bone. Any kind of hard bone, such as deer bone, was used. The point had a barb. The point was about 1 in. long. A hole was made in the shank of the point to receive the greasewood prong. The quill of a large pelican feather was split and wrapped around the shank of the point and part of the prong. Then *wiha* was tightly wrapped around the quill and then it was covered with a mixture of ground charcoal and pine pitch. The barb projected from the quill. A hole was drilled through the thick part of the shank of the point for the string that went to the willow shaft. There was slack in this string. It was about 10 in. long.

The two-pronged harpoon was used more frequently than the one with a single point. It was used along the shores of lakes and along the river banks. To fish with the harpoon in the river the harpoon was put into the water up to 10 or 12 ft. of the shaft.[102] It was slowly advanced to where the fish were swimming around. When the point was a few in. from the fish it was harpooned with a quick hard jab. Only male trout were harpooned. The males have a red stripe along the side and during the spawning season the males are always following the females. The females are a dark silver color. Only the males are caught because the females do not taste very good. If the females are caught in the net they are used.

The men also fished with the harpoon at night. At a point where the river was shallow and flowed fast, white rocks were put on the bed of the river.[103] The rocks covered a space about 2 ft. across the river by 6 ft. in length. A short harpoon was used. The shaft was about 10 ft. long. Fish were harpooned either on a dark night or on a night when there was a moon. A fire was built on the bank so the fishermen could keep warm. A platform was built at the side of the patch of white rocks [see also Weirs and Platforms, above]. Two sticks were sunk in the river bed. Two poles ran from the bank of the river to the two upright sticks. The poles were covered to form a platform. The poles were tied to the sticks and the platform with twisted willows. ND has not heard of building a shed or roof over the patch of white rocks [see below]. They fished with white stones and spears [harpoons] all along the Truckee River. In the winter they broke the ice in these places and speared fish.

Both two-pronged and single-pronged fish harpoons were used. Both are called *kwatino*. The two-pointed harpoon was used to catch fish at night with white rocks put in the bed of the river. The white rocks covered an area of 3 or 4 ft square. A platform was built over the water where the fisherman sat to harpoon the fish as they passed over the patch of white rocks. The patch of white rocks and the platform built over the water is called *pa·habɔ*.

When fishing at night with a patch of white rocks a fire is made on the bank near the platform. The fire helps the fisherman see the fish when they pass over the white rocks. It also attracts the fish to that place.

JB-PL: Spears [harpoons] with points of coyote bone were used.[104] Coyote bone is tough. They used blackened pine pitch to cement the string to the spear [harpoon] head.

Many white rocks were put in bottom of river—6 ft square at least. When the trout cross the surface of white at night they can be speared. They would sit there and spear trout. The water was covered with a shade over the rocks, like a house.[105] With the house over the river they could fish that way in the day time. The fish would pause over the white rocks and then they would spear them.

BF-PL: BF has seen them fish by putting white rocks in bottom of river. His father used to build one on the Truckee River. He built a fence across the river with the only outlet by the patch of white rocks. He had a platform there where he sat. Two-pronged spears with barbs on the end of both prongs were used. He fished there at nights. He speared the fish when they came over the white rocks. They do not have any choice. They have to spear male and female alike. For the fence, pound poles into the river bottom. Willows woven in wickerwork are placed on the posts. The posts may be driven close together and bundles of willows put on up stream side to keep the fish from coming through. This method of fishing is called *kwatino*. The spear is also called *kwatino*.

Fish Spears

JG-PL: The true fish spear is called *tonokudz*.[106] The two points of the spear are of greasewood and are about 7 or 8 in. long. The willow pole to which they are attached is about 6 ft long.

To spear fish at night white rocks are put on the bottom of the stream for a space of about 4 ft square. A fire is made on the bank and when a fish goes over the rocks it can be seen. The fish come by the fire. The fish is speared and held down until it stops struggling and then it is lifted out. One man would spear several fish at a time. The place to spear fish is called *pahava*.

---

[102] This sounds a little deep given the length of the shaft. The water would have to be very clear to enable the fisherman to see the fish at this depth.

[103] Stewart (1941:371) lists such paving for fishing in the Pyramid Lake district and vicinity only. All of Park's Walker River consultants denied using this system.

[104] Although by description JB seems to refer to a harpoon, the historic literature gives accounts of the use at the Humboldt Sink and in the Carson Basin of a fishing spear with a fixed foreshaft of the legbone of a sandhill crane (Leonard 1839:161; Remy and Brenchley 1861:42).

[105] Steward (1933:251) also speaks of a shade over fishing stations shaped like a small house.

[106] Curtis (1926:71) speaks of a two-pronged spear for Pyramid Lake. Stewart (1941:371) received a positive response on the single-pronged variety from only two Northern Paiute consultants.

Hooks and Lines

[Hooks and lines of two sizes were used to take trout, suckers, and smaller fish such as chub, redside, and dace. The large lines for trout and suckers could have either angled hooks or gorges. The smaller lines for the "minnows" could also have either type of hook. The smaller lines were often thrown from the bank of the river or lake while the larger ones had to be carefully placed, usually by a swimmer. The accounts that follow describe both types of lines along with their hooks and the methods of placing them in the lakes and streams.]

Trout and Sucker Lines

RP-WR: A long line of fish hooks was used in fishing for trout. The long line was called *tudəmahuadə* and it had the fish hooks suspended from it. The fish hooks were made of bone and called *ohotudama* (*oho*, bone; *tudama*, hook). Both ends were sharpened. Each hook was suspended from the main line by a string tied around the middle of the hook. The line was a long grass rope. Bunches of tule were fastened to each end of it. Fishhooks were suspended from the line at 5 ft intervals. The bunches acted as floats. At each end the line was anchored with a stone. One man made this line alone. It was usually made by a man who did not have a net. The line is left in the water until fish are on most of the hooks. Then the line is taken in. Grasshoppers and worms are stuck on the hooks for bait. Both ends of the hooks were baited.

HS-D: A fishing line about 200 yds long was used in Pyramid Lake. At each end there was a bundle of tule about 2 ft in diameter. Each bundle had an anchor — a rock. Strings were suspended from the main line about a foot apart. To these were attached bones about 3 in. long and sharpened (ground on stone) at both ends. These bone gorges are wrapped with sucker meat for the big trout eat suckers. This fish line is put out in the lake. They use rafts made of three or four logs and propelled with a pole to put out the line and to take off the trout that have been caught. One man usually made the whole line.

BF-PL: Fishing was done with *wiha* ropes a couple of hundred ft. long to which about 30 bone hooks were attached. The hooks were made of bone and had a barb [fig. 12e].[107] They would tie on a small minnow on each hook for bait. The fisherman then removes his clothes. He has a large tule float in a circle around his neck. It is tied to his neck. He holds one end of a rope in his mouth. The other end is on the shore held by a man who keeps it from tangling. He swims out as far as he can and when he is at the end of the line the man on shore shouts that it is the end. He takes the float off his neck and ties the *wiha* rope to it as well as a stone sinker. This is left there until the next morning and then he pulls it in and takes off the fish. He may catch 10 or 15 fish that way. The hooks are spaced on the long rope. They hang down a couple of feet. A fish caught on one hook would move back and forth causing the other hooks to move and making it appear that the minnows used as bait were alive thus attracting other fish. BF has seen his grandfather fish this way many times.

Minnow Lines

JG-PL: Minnows were caught with a line 6 or 7 ft long. Ten or 12 rabbit bone gorges were put on the line with strings 5 or 6 in. long [fig. 12f]. These are spaced on the line. At one end of the line a rock for an anchor is tied. The other end of the line is tied to a willow stick and the anchor holds down the one end of the line. A number of minnows 1 to 2 in. long are caught at a time. Then the line is pulled up and the fish are taken off. If fishing is done in deeper waters the line is longer.

Another type of hook can be used with these lines. It is made from rabbit bones. A small piece of bone is sharpened and tied at right angles to a piece of willow about ¾ in. long. A piece of willow, 1–1½ in. long is used. The end of the piece of rabbit bone (½–¾ in. long) is put in the bight of the willow, which is then bent over double and string is tied tightly around it to hold the bone [fig. 12g].[108] A piece of string 5 or 6 in. long is tied at the angle of the fishhook and runs to the main line from which a number of such hooks are suspended. The fishhook is called *oho tutamə*. The entire gear of long line and hooks is designated by the same word.

This fishing outfit is used to catch minnows (*pakwi*). White grubs found under greasewood roots were used for bait. The head was pulled off the smallest of these grubs, and the body was stuck on the unsharpened piece of willow forming part of the hook. The fish swallow the grub and hook, and when the fish pulls, the sharp bone sticks into the side of the fish's mouth.

TM-WR, Y: Fish hooks were made of rabbit bones. A piece of straight bone about 1 in. long and sharpened at both ends was put into the bight of a wilow stick that was bent double. String forming this line (*wihabə*) was wound tightly around the willow, tying the bone to the stick. Another hook was made by putting the bone at right angles to the stick with the line wrapped around the stick and tying the stick and the bone together.

---

[107] Stewart (1941:371) gives distributional data on both the gorge and the angled type of hooks.

[108] Hooks of this same type are illustrated by Loud and Harrington (1929:41). They were obtained in Lovelock Cave.

The worm that is found on the greasewood was used as bait. This is a red worm. A white worm found on willows was also used for bait. The hooks were stuck through the length of the worms.

About 10 hooks were fastened to one fishline. The fishline was made of string made from *wiha*. The hooks were about 3 ft apart. Each hook was suspended from the main line by a string about 18 in. long. This line was used to fish either on the lake or in the river. A stick was put in the ground on each side of the river. The fish line was suspended between these two sticks in such a way as to just float the main line. The line was used all day long. The fish line was called *nanumow*. The fish hooks were called *tudɔmɔ*.

When this line was used for fishing in the lake a sinker was put near the first hook which was at the end of the line. Not far from the other end was a tule float. The end with the sinker was thrown out into the lake. The float was near the shore and the end of the line was held by the fisherman. When he felt the fish on the line he pulled it in.

Fish Traps

[Four styles of fish traps are described in the notes that follow. Two large trough-type baskets and an invaginated cone-shaped basket trap were made to be used with fish dams or weirs. A bi-pointed type with a side entrance was made to be set in the river independently. The descriptions of the designs and uses of 3 of these were obtained directly from consultants. The description of the bipointed trap comes from Park's museum specimens catalog and thus is identified as to area of origin only.]

ND-HL: A fish trap (*pazakı*) was made of willows. It was a trough-like basket closed at both ends. It was 7 or 8 ft long by a couple of ft across the top, and about 2 ft deep. A weir (*pawhuɔp*) was built across the river. Willow poles were driven into the river bed 2 or 3 ft apart. Poles were put across — close together on the upstream side of the posts. They were put close together so that the water would flow over the top of the weir in a little falls.

The trap is tied securely to the downstream side of the weir so the water flowing over the weir drops into the basket. Trout coming up the river try to jump over the weir and fall back in the trap and are killed or cannot get out.[109]

Every morning a man took the catch out of the trap. He had to wade out into the river to get the fish. A man could construct the weir and trap by himself. It was an individual undertaking. Any live trout in the trap were killed with a stick. If there were many fish running there would be four or five fish in the trap each morning. "My uncle built one of these traps when they had a dam here. There were many fish running, and he caught about 20 in one night."

JH-PL: JH knew a man who used the following kind of fish trap. It was a willow basket, tubular in shape, and loosely woven. The tube was 50 ft in length and 2 ft in diameter and was closed at both ends. In the center of the tube on one side, a round hole was made, this was 1 ft. in diameter. This basket trap was used in low water, that is in the summer or in the fall. The stream was dammed by a wall on either side so that the water must flow through the trap. This was done by building two rock "fences" about 2 ft. high for a distance of 25 yds to force the direction of the stream.[110] The water flowed through the trap but the fish having entered could not get out.

The trap was set in the water and left there overnight. Only men made this type of trap in which for the most part minnows were caught. Two or three men would make and own one of these together. At the end of the season the trap was thrown away and a new one made the following year. There was no reason for throwing away the trap. Before the trap was put in the water a prayer was said by one of the men. He would ask, "that thing under the water that makes fish to give him fish because he was hungry." No prayer was said while the trap was being made.

DM-PL: DM has never heard of the kind of fish trap described by JH [see above]. But he has heard of and seen another type. It was sometimes used above a fish dam. This trap was a willow basket pointed at one end and with a large open mouth [fig. 13a]. It had a smaller cone inside that was not closed at the bottom.[111] The fish entered this opening and could not retreat. This basket trap was called *angaque*. It was used for trout in the stream in the spring and in the fall. These willow baskets were used around Pyramid Lake. Both the men and women made them. The willows were not peeled for these baskets.

GK-WR: GK thinks that a basket trap was used sometimes for fishing.[112] This trap was about 4 or 5 ft long

---

[109] Kelly (1932:96) describes a type of trough fish trap for Surprise Valley made by crossing the vertical poles of the weir along the upper edge to form a "V." The fish try to jump the weir and are trapped at its top.

[110] Stewart (1941:370) got very little response to questions on the use of rock dams for fishing. Only two of the northernmost groups responded positively.

[111] This type of trap is also described for Surprise Valley by Kelly (1932:95-96). Steward (1933:251) reports that such a basket was used for taking fish below a willow dam in Owens Valley.

[112] Park's note: GK is rather unsure of this trap and he had to be helped in his description. However, the word for the trap was given without hesitation. He says he has seen very few of

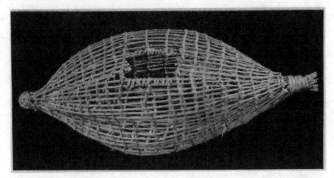

Figure 13. Fish traps. a (left). Model of fish trap, meant to be staked in the shallows with two sticks. PM 35-120-10/5186. b (right). Model of bipointed willow fish trap. PM 35-120-10/5166. Collected by W. Z. Park, Pyramid Lake (a) and Walker River (b), 1935. Peabody Museum, Harvard University. Photographs by Hillel Burger.

and about 2 ft in diameter. From his description, it would seem that the main part of the trap is a conical willow basket with the entrance for the fish between two smaller conical willow baskets fastened in the mouth of the larger basket.[113] Stakes were put in the river bottom as far apart as the length of the trap. The trap was tied at each end to one of these stakes with string made from *wiha*. One side of the trap rested on the river bottom. The trap was set near the bank in fairly shallow water. The opening of the trap was upstream. This trap was called *angaqwi*.

Men made these fish traps. They were very coarsely woven. "I guess men who had no nets made that kind and have good luck and catch fish in there."

Park — PL, WR: A bipointed fish trap with a side entrance was made either of peeled or unpeeled willow [fig. 13b]. The trap was fastened at each end to sticks that were driven into the bottom of the river. The trap was placed a few in. above the river bottom in shallow water. It was used mainly for taking "minnows" [redside, chub, dace].[114]

Fish Poison

[Only one of Park's consultants suggested that fish were stupefied or poisoned. Four others questioned on the matter either denied it or stated that they had no knowledge of such a practice. Stewart (1941:371) lists the practice for four of his most northerly groups surveyed.]

ND-HL: Fish were poisoned not in the rivers but in slues where there were minnows and chubs. ND has

seen Indians poison fish at Litchfield where there are tules and water standing. ND has only seen this done in Honey Lake Valley and in a slue several miles from Reno. The roots of the *tɔdza* [*Lomatium dissectum*] were gathered and ground on rocks.[115] About a gunnysack full was gotten. The powdered roots were scattered over the still water of the slue. Then the people took off their clothes and went into the water and splashed around to stir it. In 10 or 15 minutes the fish would be affected. The dead fish were scooped out of the water with a burden basket.

GK-WR: GK has never seen or heard of the use of fish poison. "I never hear the old people talking about poisoning fish. The only poisons they had in the old days was wild parsnip" [see Medicines, chap. 8].

Fish Arrows

[Only one out of five individuals questioned on the use of the bow and arrow in fishing had heard of the practice. He suggests that it was not a serious technique.]

GK-WR: GK has heard of young fellows shooting fish with bow and arrow, but they couldn't get fish easily that way. "I guess they were just playing. They were having fun doing it that way."[116]

Cooking and Preserving Fish

JH-PL: Fish was not eaten raw. It was cooked in the earth and not cooked all the way through because if it was not cooked all the way through it had more juice. A special soup of guts was made for menstruating girls and women. A soup of guts was made with salt and

---

them, but he has "seen that kind." This was not nearly so common a method for fishing as fishing with nets.

[113] It seems unlikely that two conical baskets are placed inside unless one is larger than the other. GK may mean that the trap is made of two baskets: one large cone and one smaller open-ended cone placed inside of it.

[114] Stewart (1941:434) also pictures this type of minnow trap.

---

[115] Of the four groups who responded positively to Stewart (1941:371) on this feature, all suggested the use of this same plant.

[116] Stewart (1941:371) received positive response on this feature from four of the twelve groups surveyed. All were north of Pyramid Lake.

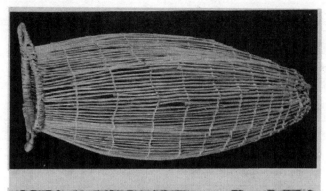

Figure 14. Fish processing. a (top). Fish basket, meant to be suspended from platform to receive fish to be transported to camp. PM 35-120-10/5187. Collected by W. Z. Park, Pyramid Lake, 1935. Peabody Museum, Harvard University. Photograph by Hillel Burger. b (middle). Fillets of cui-ui drying on a rack. Photograph by L. Creel, *ca.* 1915, Pyramid Lake. University of Nevada, Reno, Library, Special Collections Department. c (bottom). Obsidian fish knife (12.5 cm, tip broken). PM 35-120-10/5185. Collected by W. Z. Park, Walker River, 1935. Peabody Museum, Harvard University. Photograph by Hillel Burger.

water. Fish eyes were also eaten. A special basket was used for keeping the fish alive before they were ready to kill and eat [fig. 14a].[117]

---

[117] Park did not collect an example of this basket, but he did collect a special basket made for transporting fish from the fishing station to the camp (fig. 13c).

HS-D: Fresh fish was roasted in the ashes just like pine nuts. Fish were also roasted in the hot sand. First a fire is built in the sand. Then the ashes are removed. The fish is covered with hot sand and a fire is built on top.

Kuyui was dried on a rack [fig. 14b] and stored in a pit lined with sagebrush bark. It keeps a long time. Trout did not keep very long. Fish as well as meat was never smoked. When the dried fish was used it was either dampened and roasted or pounded up on the metate and boiled.

JG-PL: In the spring *kuyui* were dried on a rack. After they were dried they were stacked one on top of the other with each successive fish having its head placed in the opposite direction. Young willow branches about ½ in. in diameter were twisted and tied around each end of the stack of fish. Two or three branches were cut to the proper length for the tump line. These were twisted and tied to the willow at both ends of the bundle of fish. These willows went around the shoulders of men or around the head of women, depending on who was carrying the bundle. Fish were so carried to where they would be stored or if moving camp, to where the new camp would be.

GK-WR: Fish were dried on a rack made of two upright poles and a cross piece. The rack was built in the shade. The dried fish kept a long time.[118] Fish was never smoked.

RP-WR: Fish are taken home and cleaned. They are split down the center and the back bones are taken out. The fish are dried in the shade. No grass or plants are used to prevent spoiling or to give a better flavor. Dried fish are put under the ashes for a little while to soften the fish before cooking it. It is taken out and put in cold water. Then it is ready to eat. Fish eggs were dried and pounded into a flour on the metate and boiled to make a soup. Large trout were roasted on the coals and served on wooden platters.

JB-PL: Dried fish was used as a reserve supply. When all other food fails they fall back on dried fish. Many bury it in a pit lined with dried sagebrush branches.

Fishing Luck

[Several individuals gave Park notes on means of insuring luck in fishing. They also spoke of measures to be taken to correct a run of bad luck. Some of these were general prescriptions; others concern specific items of fishing equipment or tell of proper disposal of parts of the fish after they were caught. Some prescriptions and

---

[118] One cannot tell whether GK is referring to trout or to suckers in this passage. Cui-ui are not found in the Walker Lake basin.

practices, such as prohibitions on menstruating women associating with fishing equipment or fish preparation, are standard across the region and also apply to other subsistence pursuits (see Hunting Large Game Animals, above). Others may be individual family or local practices.]

JH-PL: Fish hooks get unlucky. If a fish is hot when it is being eaten and the eater blows on it to cool it off, the hook which caught the fish becomes unlucky. This would also apply to the net the fish were caught in.

Vomiting fish makes the net or hook that caught it unlucky. Nursing babies were not supposed to eat fish because of their tendency to vomit. This did not hurt the baby but made the hooks and nets unlucky. Fish should not be fed to dogs because they always vomited and this made the nets and hooks unlucky.

If a menstruating woman touched a net or hook it would become unlucky. It would have to be thrown away. If a menstruating woman ate fish it would make the hook, trap or net unlucky. If fish guts got on a net or hook that would make it unlucky.

A man using a fish net could pray before he used it. This was not always done. The same type of prayer was said as was said when the trap was laid in the water.

RP-WR: When cleaning the fish the woman must be careful. If she is careless she might break something inside the fish. That would bring bad luck to the fisherman. The lungs of the fish are buried. They say while they are burying them, "I want all the trout to come my way and get in my nets. Do not try to come to the others. Most of you come to my nets." A man knows when his wife has been careless in cleaning the fish because he cannot catch anything. He must try to get his luck back. The man spreads out his nets. With a burning or glowing stick from the fire he burns a single straight line the length of the net and then he repairs the net. Another way for him to get back his luck is to catch one trout. He makes a fire and scorches the fish in the flames. He turns the fish in every direction while he is scorching it. He talks while he turns the fish in the flames. He says, "I want all the trout to come my way and get in my nets. Do not try to come to the others. Most of you come to my nets. If my wife made some mistake I will start all over again."

To bring luck in fishing *kusabi* [an insect found on the water and eaten by the people at Mono Lake] are caught. These are dried and carried on the person while fishing. This charm only works for fishing. Sometimes some of the dried insects are put on the nets before starting to fish. They are chewed and spat on the fish nets or lines. At the same time the man says, "This is your own meat. You better come to it and smell it." It is thought that these insects come from fish. They are also found around Fallon.

ND-HL: If menstruating women handled the nets or the fish the husband would have bad luck in fishing. On these occasions the nets would be rubbed with fish intestines and the fluids taken from the fish. Old nets were also treated in this way to bring luck for the nets. At the same time a prayer was said. Good luck in fishing was asked for.

JG-PL: There is a small bluish organ on the liver of fish called *pui'wi*. If this is broken when cleaning the fish it spoils the nets. The nets will not catch many fish after this is broken. This is also true of rabbits caught in nets. The rabbit nets will be unlucky [see Rabbits, above]. JG does not know of anything that can be done to the nets to make them lucky again. He also does not think that there was any way to make a new net lucky.

DM-PL: If a man broke his fishing platform and fell into the water that would spoil his pool and he would have to change his fishing place.

BR-L, PL: In the old days there were two shamans who claimed that they could make more fish run when there were not many. They dreamed about the fish coming. They did this at night. I do not know if these shamans sang to make the fish come.

TM-WR, Y: TM has not heard of shamans singing or doctoring to cause the fish to run upriver. He said, "When the fish did not come the people had to go hungry. There was nothing for them to do."

VEGETABLE FOODS

[Plants used as food by the people at Pyramid Lake and Walker River and in adjacent areas included several species that produced edible bulbs, roots, seeds, berries, leaves, stalks, and nuts. Park received brief physical and ecological descriptions of many of the more common of these along with some indication of preparation techniques. He apparently also collected a few specimens for identification.[119] However, with the exception of those notes, the binomial identifications as well as some of the general information provided below are based on additional field studies by the editor (Fowler 1964–1982; Fowler and Leland 1967). Usage for common and scientific names follows that established by Holmgren and Reveal (1966). The table below is provided as a key to plant species utilized by area as given in Park's notes. None of these lists approaches being exhaustive.]

---

[119] A letter to Park dated October 31, 1934, from Dr. P. A. Lehenbauer, Professor of Botany, University of Nevada, Reno, identifies some 30 plants collected by Park. Some are given by genus name only. A few are identified only as to family. The remainder are given at the species level. Some of the binomials are now in synonymy. These names have been changed to reflect modern usage.

Plants Utilized, by Area (Park 1933–40)

	Pyramid Lake	Lovelock	Honey Lake	Walker River	Fallon	Reno	Dayton
Roots							
1. yapa	+	+		+	+		+
2. hunibui	+				+		
3. kidapᵘ	+						
4. piquid	+						
5. hüngü	+						
6. kanita	+			+		+	
7. kogi	+	+					
8. padüs	+				+		+
9. üds	+						+
10. si	+			+			+
11. moa	+						+
12. awakoni							
13. tagü	+				+		+
14. shabui				+	+		
15. tubuzi				+	+		+
16. huba	+						+
17. natsa							+
Seeds							
1. kuha	+			+			
2. wy	+			+			+
3. akü	+						+
4. pakə	+			+			+
5. atsa	+		+	+	+		
6. sunu	+		+				+
7. sopi	+						
8. wa.da	+		+		+		
9. pawia	+				+		
10. apəsᵃ	+			+	+		
11. üapa	+			+			
12. abi	+				+		
13. toib	+			+	+		
14. mudubui	+			+	+		+
Leaves and Stems							
1. kamusigi	+			+			
2. saib	+			+			+
3. tuhu				+	+		+
4. hu'unaqwi	+			+			+
5. səpiwahabᵘ		+					
6. pamasib			+				
7. obə				+			
8. toi	+			+	+		+
9. nabu				+			
Berries							
1. chokecherry	+			+			
2. elderberry	+			+			
3. wiapui		+		+	+		
4. hupui				+			+
5. pogopisha				+		+	
6. wápui		+		+			
Pinenuts	+	+	+	+	+	+	+
Acorns	+		+	?			+

[Plants from which edible roots and bulbs were taken include principally members of the parsley, lily, and purslane botanical families. Roots and bulbs were dug primarily in the spring months, or roughly from April through June. The common collecting implement was a hardwood digging stick.]

JG-PL: The *podo* (digging stick) is usually about 3 ft long and is made of greasewood. One end is sharpened with a deer bone scraper and finally sharpened with an obsidian knife. There is no kind of digging stick weight used [fig. 15].[120]

[According to accounts from Pyramid Lake, a common method of preparing several types of roots for eating was to roast them in the sand: "These roots are buried whole in the sand. . . . Build a fire on the sand, rake the ashes away and put the roots in and cover them with sand and build a fire on top" (JG-PL). Roots thus roasted could then be boiled whole or ground into flour and made into soup or mush. Some roots were also eaten raw when freshly dug. Others were merely dried and stored. "The skin of roots and tubers was scraped off on a basket tray" (BR-L,PL).[121] Although there may have been set procedures for each species, the conflicting descriptions that follow would make them difficult to affirm. The rather large number and variety of root foods listed for Pyramid Lake seems reflective of the northern Great Basin and Plateau focus on these resources as important dietary items. The processing procedures are also similar to those suggested for the Surprise Valley and Warm Springs Northern Paiute areas (Kelly 1932:100; Mahar 1953:93). The considerably smaller list of root foods for the Dayton and Walker River areas may relect a different focus. However, it may also be in response to Park's line of inquiry in these areas. There are no data in Park's notes on root gathering for the Honey Lake area, although Riddell (1960:34) indicates at least some focus on these resources in that area.]

1. *yapa* [yampa or Indian potato, *Perideridia gairdneri; P. bolanderi*]

JG-PL: *yapa* is gotten about 8 mi from Nixon, near Wadsworth.[122] The women would take water and stay overnight on trips they made to get *yapa*. This was done in the spring. A digging stick of greasewood, about 3 ft long was used. The stick was sharpened with a flint knife. Women brought *yapa* home. It was peeled and

---

[120] The weighted and handled digging stick is a feature of the Plateau (Driver and Massey 1957:213).

[121] This tray was coarsely woven in diagonal or plain twine. Kelly (1932:101, plate 25a) also describes and illustrates a "grating" tray from Surprise Valley.

[122] The site for gathering these materials is probably near Ollinghouse, Nevada.

Figure 15. End of fire-hardened hardwood digging stick. MPM 21972. Collected by S. A. Barrett, western Nevada, 1916.

eaten fresh. It was not cooked and it was not kept for winter. It was eaten right away.

BR-L,PL: *yapa* is like a sweet potato, about as thick as the forefinger. It is found in yellow clay and adobe in the canyons. It is either eaten raw, boiled or roasted. When it is roasted, it is covered with hot ashes.

JO, JB-PL: *yapa* is dried and pounded and ground on the metate and they make a soup or mush of it by boiling. It may be eaten raw when it is fresh. The skin is peeled off the potato. It is roasted in the hot sand.

HS-D: *yapah* is a white root that grows mainly around Likely, Calif., south of Alturas and Surprise Valley. They have a dark skin like a potato and grow in the ground. They are eaten raw. They are gathered in summer. They taste sweet when fresh, "taste like soaked peanuts." You can grind them into flour.

2. *hunibui* [bigseed lomatium, *Lomatium macrocarpum*].

JO-PL: It is something like sweet potatoes and the same size. It grows in the mountains and is roasted in the sand.

3. *kidap*[u] [Cusick's sunflower, *Helianthus cusickii*].

JO-PL: It has leaves like beets, and is something like a big carrot, as big as a fist. The root has dark skin. We just eat the part next to the skin. The rest of it has no taste. It is pithy.

JB-PL: Gathered in June. Eaten raw. Take outer bark off the root and eat the part between inner core and bark.

4. *piquid* [Hooker's balsamroot, *Balsamorhiza hookeri*.]

JO-PL: It grows along the foothills. Its root is dark skinned and long like a white radish. It has white meat and is about 6 in. long.

5. *hüngü* [spring beauty, *Claytonia umbellata*].

JO-PL: It grows on rocks or gravel slide on the mountain slopes and is round, gray and about the size of a radish. It is roasted in the sand.

6. *kangita* [bitterroot, *Lewisia rediviva*].

JO-PL: Grows in big clusters and the whole plant is pulled. The meat of the root is a reddish color.

JG-PL: Grows on ridges. The roots are about the length of the first finger. The tops of the plant look like a potato [?]. The skin is peeled off and the root is boiled and eaten this way without grinding.

RP-WR: *kongida* grows on the mountains. It grows spreading out on the ground. It has several pink flowers to each plant. A stick is pushed under the large root which is close to the surface. It is then pried up. The roots are roasted. They are yellow when they are cooked.

AD-R: kaŋǝtǝ grows along the foothills in sandy soil. You eat the tops just like spinach. This is an early plant; dries up in late June. Boil it like spinach or roast the roots in bunches by covering with coals.

7. *kogi* [sego lily, *Calochortus nuttallii; C. leichtlinii*].

BR-L,PL: It is peeled and roasted, or eaten raw. This tuber was found on the hillsides. A single stalk grows in a clump of sagebrush. It is gathered in May and June. A digging stick made of a sharpened piece of juniper is used to get the roots and tubers.

JO-PL: kogi and *moa* are about alike dried and then they are about like chewing tobacco. They can be eaten that way or ground and cooked in soup.

8. *padüs* [onion, *Allium biseptrum*].

JG-PL: padüs is a grass about 5 in. tall. This grows in the canyons under willows. It is gathered early in the spring. It tastes like wild onion. It is eaten raw and is not preserved. It is better when eaten fresh.

9. *üds* [onion, *Allium nevadense*].

JG-PL: üds grows under greasewood. The stalks which are 2 or 3 in. high are as large as alfalfa. There is but one stalk to each plant. In June the stalks are pulled up by the roots. A woman would gather a handful or two and take them home. The roots, stems and all are eaten raw. It tastes like an onion.

10. *si* [onion, *Allium anceps*].

JO-PL: si is a wild onion; round, white, small and something like garlic — the same size and color. It is roasted in the sand.

RP-WR: si is a plant that grows 8 to 10 in. high on the mountains. It has a bulb like a small onion. It tastes sweet. The bulbs are dug up and cooked on hot rocks. They are then soft and are squeezed into cakes which are taken home.

11. *moa* [probably onion, *Allium parvum*].

JG-PL: moa looks like garlic, is strong and has leaves like blades of grass. It is like *kogi* — dried, and then they are about like chewing tobacco and can be eaten that way. It can be ground and cooked in soup.

12. *awakoni* [onion, *Allium* sp.].

HS-D: awakoni is small, very stong, like garlic. It is one of four kinds of onions: *padus, si, uids* and *awakoni*. All of these are eaten raw. They are never cooked. Gathered in the spring; rolled up into a ball [stems] and eaten.

13. *tagü* [*Lomatium nevadense*].

JO-PL: tagü has a long, slender, dark-skinned root and leaves like a carrot. It is eaten raw or cooked in the sand.

14. *shabui* [probably wapato, *Sagittaria cuneata*].

RP-WR: A wild potato. It grows in the water. It is found when the leaves dry up. It has a yellow flesh.

15. *tubuzi* [nut grass, *Cyperus esculentus*].

RP-WR: This food is considered one of the staples at Walker Lake. It is ground on the metate and frequently mixed with other foods. It is small coconut-shaped tubers like peanuts attached to the fine hair-like roots of the plant. They taste like coconuts. The plant grows like grass in bunches. It has no flower. The entire plant is dug up and put in a coarsely woven basket. It is worked against the side of the basket until only the roots are left. The cleaned roots are stored by the meadow mouse and these are also gathered. The caches of roots are found by looking for small mounds of dirt with grass growing on top.

When a woman gathers these roots, the meadow mouse helps her. When she takes the roots from the cache, he pushes more out to her. If a woman chases a meadow mouse or makes remarks about the mouse she will not be lucky. She will not find the mouse's caches of roots or *wy* seed. A good woman says good things to the meadow mice. She asks them to be good to her and to help her find the roots and seeds. When a woman hears the chuckling sound made by the meadow mouse she knows he wants her to find his cache of roots or seeds. She knows he wants to help her.

The roots gotten from a meadow mouse's cache are not eaten by a pregnant woman or her husband. If either were to eat these roots the meadow mouse would eat the foetus just as he eats the roots.

GK-WR: tubuz is wild coconuts. This plant grows along the rivers. Wild coconuts are eaten raw when fresh. They are dried and ground and mixed with *wy* and other kinds of seeds to make it sweet. It is gathered by the meadow mice.

16. *huba* [unidentified; possibly *Balsamorhiza hirsuta*].

JO-PL: huba is similar to *piquid*. It is found on the mountain slopes.

17. *natsa* [unidentified].

HS-D: natsa is a small bush with yellow flowers that grows on the hills. The roots are gathered in May and eaten raw.

Seeds

[Seed collection was a major subsistence activity of Northern Paiutes of western Nevada as it was in much of the Great Basin. Members of several botanical families produce edible achenes, fruits, or seeds, although the plants most commonly sought were those from the sunflower, grass, goosefoot, and mustard families. Most seeds were gathered in the summer months using a stick and/or seed beater and a conical burden basket as collecting implements. The stick ("any kind of stick") or seed beater (fig. 16a) was used to knock the seeds or seed heads into either a finely twined collecting basket (see fig. 16b) or

Figure 16. Plant processing. a (top left). Alice Steve, Stillwater, using a stick to beat seeds into a basketry tray. Photograph by M. M. Wheat, 1956. b (bottom left). Close diagonal twined seed collecting basket (32.5 cm long). MPM 22086. Collected by S. A. Barrett, western Nevada, 1916. c (top right). Coiled boiling basket, probably traded from Mono Lake Paiute (35.5 cm rim diameter). MAI 13/4423. Collected by M. R. Harrington, Walker River, 1924. d (bottom right). Wuzzie George, Stillwater, demonstrating use of looped stirring stick in twined cooking basket. Photograph by L. Mills, 1953.

one of coarser weave lined with buckskin or cloth.[123] Most seeds were then "roasted in a fan-shaped basket (fig. 16d) with charcoal and then ground on the *mata* (metate). When grinding there was a skin (or finely woven

basketry tray) in front of the *mata* on which the ground flour fell. The main grinding motion was away from the body" (BF-PL). Unprocessed seeds "are stored in the ground. Sagebrush bark is put on the pile of seeds and then it is covered with dirt" (JB-PL). Seed flour mushes were cooked in coiled or twined cooking baskets (fig. 16c, d). The meal is put in water. It is stirred with a *patu* (stirrer) made of a pine branch heated so it can be

---

[123] Such lining in the historic period may have led to the gradual demise of the close-twined burden basket.

bent (fig. 16d). Then hot rocks were put in. Ten or 12 stones were used to cook with" (JB-PL).

A question by Park as to wild seed and root horticulture brought the following response:][124]

JG-PL: has never heard of burning in order to get a better wild crop of seeds or roots. "Those seeds and roots grow by the storm. When there is lots of snow in the winter and rain in the spring, there will be plenty of seeds. The Indians never burned the seeds to get a better crop" [but see RP-WR's account of *əpə*, below].

1. *kuhu* [whitestem blazing star, *Mentzelia albicaulis*].

JO-PL: *kuha* grows on the hillsides. It grows just like a tumbleweed and the leaves are greyish. It grows by Winnemucca Lake. To get it, pull the plant by the roots and dry the plant and seeds.

LA-PL: *kuha* is grey colored, 5–6 in. high. It is gathered in July. It is gathered in piles and dried for 2–3 days. They laid a skin on the ground and put the grass on it and beat it with a stick. They winnowed it in a tray basket and stored it for winter. It was roasted in charcoal in a tray basket. They ground it on a metate and made a mush out of the flour. Nowadays some of the old people mix it with flour and eat it.

JG-PL: *kuha* grows around the lake. It is smaller than alfalfa seed. It has orange or yellow colored seed [?]. The grass is about 8 or 10 in. high. The bloom is yellow. It is gathered late in July or August. A small finely woven cone-shaped basket is used to harvest the seeds. The seeds are knocked into the baskets with a seed beater shaped like a spoon. It has a short handle and is twined. It is called *sigu*.[125] The seeds are dried and piled on the metate to be rolled under the palm of the hand to free them from the husks. Then the seeds are winnowed with a tray-shaped basket. Next they are roasted in a parching tray with hot coals. They are thrown up in the air to keep them from burning. When the seeds are cooked they are cleaned and put away in a bag. When they are used they are ground on the metate and boiled.

GK-WR: *kuha* is a plant found in the desert, especially in Smith Valley. The plant looks like grass. It is small and grows on the flats or in the hills. It is not found every year. It has very small grey seeds that are oily when ground. The grass is pulled by hand and thrown in the burden basket. It is carried to a large pile which is left to dry for about a week. Then the pile of grass is pounded up and separated from the chaff and dirt by winnowing. The seeds are put on a finely woven parching tray with hot coals. The seeds and coals are tossed in the air just enough to prevent the basket from

burning. From time to time the seeds are tested between the fingers to see if they are cooked. When the seeds are cooked the large coals are raked off with the fingers. The other coals are removed by winnowing in a breeze. If there is no breeze the operator blows on the seeds as she tosses them in the air. Then the seeds are ground and they are ready to be mixed with hot water to make mush.

2. *wy* [Indian ricegrass, *Oryzopsis hymenoides*].

GK-WR: *wy* grows in the desert. The tops of the plant are cut off with a stone knife and piled in large heaps. A fire is started close to the pile. This dries the plants and the seeds fall off. They are gathered up and cleaned in a winnowing tray (*yada*). Men and women work together in gathering the seeds. The women do the winnowing. It is done in a gentle breeze. When the seeds have been separated from the dirt and coals they are put on a metate and the black husks are cracked. Then the seeds are winnowed again to separate them from the husks. Then the seeds are ground into flour on the metate. The flour is made into soup or mush. This was an extremely important plant in providing seeds. The flour from *wy* seeds was often mixed with pinenuts. *Wy* are still used a great deal. Some years due to drought the seeds of *wy* are very scarce. That is also true of pinenuts. *Wy* is gathered in July. The plants were dry and the seeds were good and ripe then. *Wy* is a good food to eat when someone has a bellyache, colic or aching bones. When a person is suffering from any of these *wy* seeds should be the only food eaten. The seeds of the *wy* are stored for winter use. The seeds would keep two years without spoiling. The seeds were stored in pits. The pits were lined with willows and sagebrush bark. After the whites came the pits were lined with gunny sacks.

RP-WR: Men help in cutting *wy* grass which grows on the desert. It is a staple food. It is supposed to be the women's job to gather it but the men help. The tops of *wy* are cut off. The seeds are dry when the plants are ready to cut. A fire is made and small bunches of the cut grass are held over it. A bunch is not held over the fire very long or it would burn. When the grass starts to burn green plants are mixed in. The seeds are dropped in a pile near the fires. These piles of seeds are cleaned in the evening.

When the people go into the desert to gather *wy* they take poles and a few sticks to make a shade. These are carried by the men. The poles are put up in the ground and covered with sagebrush. The men carry water in basket water jugs. The people here used to go to a mountain called *asaka* ("red tipped") for *wy*. When they were at *asaka* they got water about 15 miles away at Double Springs (*osaba*, "alkali") [see Place Names in chap. 1].

Wy does not stay on the plants long. The winds blow the seeds off when they are ripe. When the people are through stacking up piles of *wy* they look for mounds of

---

[124] Stewart (1941:376) got positive responses on this feature from consultants for six of the 12 groups visited.

[125] RP-WR claimed that the seed beater was used only with *kuha*. Most other seeds were gathered by beating the plants with a stick or cutting heads from stems with a knife.

dirt where the meadow mouse stores the seeds that have fallen on the ground. The women dig these up and get the seeds. It is cleaned and stored in baskets. Large quantities of seeds are gotten this way.

People go into the desert for *wy* in July and they stay there until fall. The first week they cut the grass. The rest of the time is spent looking for the caches of seed made by the meadow mouse. During the seed gathering the men come back to the river and to the lake to fish with nets. They carry the fish that they catch to the camp in the desert.

JO-PL: *wy* knocked off with a seed beater. Also the whole plant is cut and dried in the sun and then the seed knocked into a basket with a seed beater.

3. *akü* [wooly mules ears, *Wyethia mollis*].

JO-PL: For *akü*, use a seed beater woven in a spoon shape like a basket (*tsikü*). Knock it into a conical burden basket. Clean it and leave nothing but the seed. It is sacked for winter use. It is parched and winnowed and then ground for mush.

LA-PL: *aku*, something like a wild sunflower. It is gathered in July. Sunflowers are rolled between the hands to break them and any other seeds that you want to grind up fast. Roast them before you grind the seeds. Sometimes it is mixed with other seeds.

HS-D: *oap*[i][126] is a sunflower found in great abundance on sunflower mountains (Peavine) back of Reno. The mortar is used to grind sunflower seeds. Ground into flour and made into a mush.

4. *pakə* [sunflower, *Helianthus annuus*].

JO-PL: *pak*[hu] is a sunflower, with seeds that grow along the river.

LA-PL: *pakə* gathered in September after the flowers are dead.

RP-WR: *pahü* is a sunflower. The seeds are gathered and ground into meal.

5. *atsa* [tansy mustard, *Descurainia richardsonii, D. pinnata*, but also *D. sophia*].[127]

JB-PL: *atsa* is an extremely small seed. A heap of *atsa* seeds were put in the winnowing basket and roasted with charcoal. They were roasted until they smelled good. The charcoal was thrown out and the seeds allowed to cool and then they were ground on the metate. Then it was mixed with cold water, using a spoon (*soko'o*). The fan-shaped winnowing basket, closely woven, used to clean *atsa* seeds is called *samu'na*.

---

[126]This may be a misrecording for *aki*. When HS was interviewed by the editor in the 1960s, he used the term *aki* for *Wyethia mollis* and called Peavine Mountain *akigaiba*, "sunflower mountain."

[127]Although this is an introduced species, it was widely used in historic times. Because it is weedy and produces abundant seed, its use may have eclipsed that of the indigenous species.

RP-WR: *asa* ripens in July and is gathered at that time. It is stored for the winter. *asa* has yellow blossoms and grows in the river valleys. Now it grows in with alfalfa. Pull the whole plant and stack it up in piles to dry in the sun. When the seeds are loose, they are crushed between the hands to get out the seeds (red in color and very bitter). You take the husks off this way. Put the seeds in a cooking basket with hot stones and keep it moving. When they cook they pop. Then they know that it is cooked and the stones were taken out. The cooked seeds are put out to dry in the sun. They are gound on the metate into a meal. The bitterness is taken out by putting the meal in a cooking basket and mixing it with water. It is kneaded like bread. Add some more water and yellow scum comes to the top. This is removed and the operation is repeated until all the bitterness is out of it. Then more water is added to make a fine batter. This is drunk for it is too watery to be eaten with the fingers.

6. *sunu* [saltbush, *Atriplex argenta*].

JG-PL: *suno* grows along lakes and in the valley. It is a greyish plant, and grows like a big tumbleweed, in a cluster. [Fixed in the same way: parched, ground into flour and made into mush.] It is the hardest one to clean because the seeds are very small. The seeds are grey.

JO-PL: *suno* grows near the small lake and is like tumbleweeds, but has no stickers. The entire weed is gathered into a basket. It is taken home and dried. The plant is put on the metate and ground gently. The leaves are blown away and the fine fan-shaped winnowing basket (*samund*) is used. The seeds are ground on the metate. They are boiled into a mush. The *sunu* are gathered in August.

ND-HL: *sunu* seeds are gathered in September. They are knocked into a burden basket with a seed beater. The seeds are ground on a metate.

7. *sopi* [possibly mannagrass, *Glyceria* sp., or Nevada bluegrass, *Poa* sp.].[128]

JO-PL: *sopi* grows in the valley and hillside, any soft place. Grows like wild hay (probably wild rye). The seed is greenish. It is cut and dried and the seeds beaten out.

8. *wa.da* [seepweed, *Suaeda depressa*].

JO-PL: *wa.da* grows in the valley. It has a black stem, a single black stem to each plant but it grows in a cluster. The seeds are dark blackish.

ND-HL: *wadə* is a plant that grows in alkali soil. It is green in the summer but turns black when the seeds are ripe. The plant grows about the same height as alfalfa and it looks a great deal like that plant. The seed is very

---

[128]These identifications are based on Kelly (1932:99), as Park's specimen could be keyed only to the family level (grass family). Kelly records *sopibü* as *Poa nevadensis* and *P. gracellima*. Her *sopi* is identified as *Glyceria borealis*.

small. The seeds are gathered the latter part of September. A seed beater and a basket held in one hand are used to gather *wada* seeds.

9. *pawia* [curly dock, *Rumex crispus*].[129]

JO-PL: *pawia* is found in marshy places. It is knocked into a burden basket. They pound them down in the burden basket until there is nothing but seed left. This is done several times with a stick. The seeds are soaked in water for quite a while. You have to change the water every few minutes for about an hour. The red color comes off with soaking. When they take them out of the water they grind them at once on *mata*. It comes out just like a doughy flour. Shape it any way and bake it in the sand. That is the hardest seed to fix. The roots are also used. In winter when food is scarce. They take the whole root, put it in the fire and cover it with frozen ground. They only do that when they are very poor and cannot get anything else [see also Medicines, chap. 8].

10. *ápəsᵃ* [possibly Fremont goosefoot, *Chenopodium fremontii*].

JO-PL: *ápəsᵃ* has a single stem but grows in a cluster, grey, and about 18 in. tall. Grows in the valley. When it rains hard this plant grows everywhere that the water has been standing.

RP-WR: *abudza* is a plant that grows about 2 ft high. It is found in the valley along the river. It has small round silver leaves. The seeds grow on long stems. The seeds are gathered to be ground into meal.

11. *üapa* [pigweed, *Chenopodium nevadense*].[130]

JO-PL: *üapa* is grey, grows very tall, about a man's height at times. It has a brown stalk, leaves keep on spreading out, does not blossom. Seeds are in a cluster and it has very salty taste. Stalks are broken off and dried, beaten into a basket.

RP-WR: *əpə* grows as tall as a man. The stem spreads out about half way up. The leaves are at the bottom of the main stem. They are small elliptical shaped. The seeds grow on the stems. This plant grows on burnt places. People go up into the mountains and burn the brush. The next spring they go back and harvest the seeds from the plants that have grown in burnt places.

12. *abi* [Alkali bulrush, *Scirpus maritimus*].

JO-PL: *ábi* grows in the water. They wade into the water with a basket on their back and cut stalks with a knife and throw them into a basket. Then dried and the seed is beaten out. Leaves shaped like . It has

a single stem, and roots in the water. Seed same size and color as alfalfa seed.

RP-WR: *abi* grows in Fallon along the river. The plant is about 2 ft high. It has black seeds which are yellow inside. The leaves are flat like grass. It has no flower. The seeds grow on the stem very thickly. It looks very similar to *tuponi* which grows along Walker Lake.

13. *toib* [cattail, *Typha latifolia*, *T. domingensis*].

JO-PL: *toib* is a round tule cattail. Take the long stem and spread the fuzz and set it on fire. Keep on working it with a stick until the fuzz is burnt and leaves only the seed. They cook it that way. This is the same thing as *toi tsma*; the cattail is *tsma*. Instead of burning *toib*, it could be cleansed in a parching tray with hot coals shaken back and forth. The seeds drop through just as if it were a sieve leaving the fuzz in the tray. Cooking of the seeds is also accomplished by this process.

HS-D: *toi*, the yellow powder of the cattails (pollen) is called *toitsma*.[131] It is gathered into a dough which is kneaded. The dough is made into flat cakes and roasted under hot coals. When it is roasted the cake is taken out and the ashes are knocked off with a stick. This bread is called *kosino'hop*.

JG-PL: *toi* is cattail. The top part is *sima*. The small part above the cattail is broken off when it is green in color. It is then ripe. It is eaten fresh and uncooked. The seed of the cattail which is found under the fur of the cattail is gathered and spread on a cloth. In the sun it opens up and fur is peeled off. Then the cattail is burned in a fire which leaves only the seeds. The seeds are cleaned by winnowing and ground on the metate into fine flour. The flour is boiled and made into a round cake which is dried in the sun. The long root of the cattail is also eaten. It is pulled up and the skin is peeled. It is chewed and the juice swallowed. The pulp which is stringy is spat out [see also Leaves and Stems, below].

RP-WR: Cattail (*toi*) was used for food. The top part is gathered by breaking it off. The cotton-like stuff is burned off carefully so the seed drops off but is not burned. The seeds are ground after cooking with hot stones in a basket. They are ground in a mortar. Mush is not made of the seeds nor was it cooked. It was eaten in a powder form and water drunk with it.

GK-WR: The seeds of the cattail are ground into meal and made into soup. The bush part of the cattail stalk is cut or pulled from the plant. It is then thoroughly dried. A fire is built on hard ground and the cattails are put in the fire. They are stirred with two sticks. When all the fuzz is burnt off the seeds are left in the ashes. They are separated by winnowing. These seeds are gotten in the summer.

---

[129] *Rumex crispus* is a native of Eurasia according to Munz and Keck (1963:358). Thus the term *pawia* may once have been applied to another *Rumex*, perhaps *R. hymenosepalus*.

[130] Specimens gathered by Park were identified by Lehenbauer as *Chenopodium atrovirens* and *C. album*. The latter is a naturalized species from Eurasia, but was commonly used in the Great Basin in historic times (Steward 1938; Munz and Keck 1963).

---

[131] See Harrington (1933) for a short article describing the processing of cattail pollen by the Stillwater (Fallon) Northern Paiute.

14. *mudubui* [common threesquare, *Scirpus pungens*].

JG-PL: mudubui grows in ponds and sloughs. It has a triangular stem and grows like alfalfa. It is ripe in July. The women wade into the water and gather a handful of stalks into a bunch and cut them off with a knife. They take them home and spread them out on the ground to dry. The tops are put on the metate and the muller is used to work the seeds out of the stalks. The stalks are thrown away and the seeds are ground lightly in order to break the husks. The flour is boiled to make a mush.

Leaves and Stems

[Park's notes document the use of the leaves and stalks or stems of several plants as "greens." Onion stems and cattail spikes (see above) were used as well. Most of these were gathered in the spring, and for most constituted the first fresh vegetable food of the season.]

1. *kamusigi* [carved seed, *Glyptopleura marginata*].

JG-PL: kamusigi grows flat on the ground in the sandy desert. The leaves are gray. It is gathered in the spring. The plant is pulled and the leaves are eaten raw.

HS-D: kamusigi is a small green plant that grows around Virginia City. The leaves are eaten raw in the summer, about July.

RP-WR: kamɔsigi is a plant that grows close to the ground. It spreads out flat on the ground. It grows in the sand. It has a single root. It has white blossoms. The leaves and stems, but not the flowers are eaten raw. Young girls are not allowed to eat this food. The plant is said to have blood in it. If the girls eat it they will menstruate oftener. This plant is never cooked.

2. *saib* [tule, *Scirpus acutus*].

JG-PL: saib, tule. The roots of the tule are pulled by reaching into the water and grasping the tule near the roots. The root is broken off and the part under the water above the root is peeled and eaten raw.

JO-PL: The root of the *saib* is used for food. It is eaten raw. The tule is used for houses. Both kinds are used for houses [cattail and tule].

BR-L,PL: Tule roots are skinned and boiled or roasted.

RP-WR: The outer skin of the stalk of tule (*saib*) is removed and the inside is eaten raw. Tule used to grow in great quantities along the river. Now it is eaten in Fallon where there is a great deal of it. It is gathered in August. It is not kept for winter. It is eaten only when it is fresh.

3. *tuhu* [Broomrape, *Orobanche fasciculata*].

HS-D: tuhu is similar to asparagus. It grows along the river. The *tuhu* is gathered in the summer and either eaten raw or boiled.

RP-WR: Wild asparagus (*tuhu*) looks just like the cultivated asparagus. It grows in the valley. It is white. Another variety grows in the mountains. It is pink in

color and sweet in taste. It is called *pihatuhu* (*piha*, sweet) [*Orobanche crymbosa*].

4. *hu'unaqwi* [unidentified].

JG-PL: hu'unaqwi, grows on the desert. The plant grows in bunches of thick stems about an inch tall. In the spring it is pulled and the stems eaten raw as fast as they are gathered. The roots are thrown away.

5. *sɔpiwahabü* [unidentified; but see *sɔpi*, above].

BR-L,PL: sɔpiwahabü was the first grass found in the spring. The grass and seeds were eaten raw. People were hungry in the spring. They would eat anything. While men were hunting in the spring they ate the grass because they had to have something in their throats. The seeds were not gathered.

6. *pamasib* [possibly *Eleocharis palustris*].

ND-HL: pamasib is like a flat tule. It has no leaves. Grows 2 or 3 ft high. The roots are under water. This plant is a bit sweet. People broke it off and licked the sap. The sap is sweet.

7. *obɔ* [possibly miner's lettuce, *Montia perfoliata*].

RP-WR: obɔ is a plant with flat round leaves about 2 in. in diameter. It grows on flat clear spaces in the sand. It is the first plant to appear in the spring. The leaves are eaten raw.

8. *toi* [cattail, *Typha latifolia*, *T. domingensis*].

RP-WR: The roots of all the *toi* (cattail) are taken from the water. The skin is taken off and the inside chewed when fresh. They taste sweet. The roots may be dried. They are broken and split into strips. The strips were dried by putting them on greasewood. This keeps the juice in the roots. The brush was burned and the strips moved so they would not burn. Then they are put into baskets to finish drying. Dried pieces were ground into flour and made into mush. This mush also tasted sweet.

9. *nabu* [prickly pear, *Opuntia polyacantha*].

RP-WR: Cactus (*nabu*) was gathered. The needles were burnt off. It was roasted in the coals. The flat variety of cactus was used. When it was roasted, the skin was taken off and the inside eaten. Cactus was also eaten uncooked when it was fresh.

Berries

[Only six berry-producing foods were mentioned by those interviewed by Park: chokecherry, silver buffalo berry (known locally as "buck berry"), elderberry, wolfberry, currant, and juniper berries. Others such as serviceberry, other types of currants, gooseberry, etc., are known to occur and to have been used in the area although they were not mentioned to Park. Juniper berries were considered by most to be "starvation food".]

1. *toshɔbui* [chokecherry, *Prunus demissa*].

JG-PL: toshɔbui, chokecherries, were gathered in September when they are ripe. They may be mashed and made into round cakes 3 or 4 in. round and ¼ in. thick. They are eaten when dry. They are not preserved for the winter.

JO-PL: Chokecherries are gathered and mashed into pulp. They are fashioned into little cakes and put in the sun and dried. Cakes carried by people and used like chewing tobacco.

RP-WR: Chokecherries (*toishapui*) were picked by hand by bending the limbs. They were crushed with the fingers and the pulp goes through into a basket underneath. Only the seeds are left in the upper basket. They grow along the mountains. Chokecherries were dried like the berries and cooked in the same way [see *hupui*, below].

GK-WR: Chokecherries were eaten when ripe. They were also dried and stored. When the dried chokecherries were used, they were ground and boiled into a mush.

2. *hubu* [elderberry, *Sambucus racemosa*, spp. *pubens*].

JB-PL: *hubu* is picked in the fall, like grapes. It is spread to dry in the sun in a large fan-shaped winnowing basket (*samuna*). They used a sack the size of a 25 lb flour sack, woven of sagebrush, *watsi mago'* (sagebrush sack) to put them in. They were boiled (not ground) into a sort of soup. Berries and all were eaten.

3. *wiapui* [buckberry, silver buffaloberry, *Shepherdia argentea*].

HS-D: *wiəpui*, buckberry, is gathered in the summer and dried. It may be mashed in a flat basket and eaten like a mush.

BR-L,PL: *wiəpui* were pitted by lightly crushing them and passing them through a fan-shaped basket that was like a parching tray used for roasting pinenuts only it was more coarsely woven. They were mixed with meal and boiled.

RP-WR: *wiapui* grows on trees with needles [thorns] and leaves that are bluish grey in color. The trees grow along the river. The wiapui is gathered in July. Break off the limbs of the tree or use sticks to knock the berries from the limbs into the basket. Next the berries are washed by placing the basket in the river to wash the leaves away. When eaten, the flesh is crushed in a flat, fairly finely woven basket so the seeds will go out between the cracks and only the berries will be left in the tray. These berries have less seeds than *hupui*. They are also dried and cooked in the same way as *hupui* [see below].

GK-WR: *wiəpui* is wild buckberry. The berries are dried and stored for winter.

4. *hupui* [Anderson wolfberry, *Lycium andersonii*].

RP-WR: Red berries that are almost like currants and grow on the desert are called *hupui*. They ripen in July. They are gathered in baskets, dried when plentiful and placed in a hard place on the ground and dried in the sun. When eaten fresh the berries are crushed. They are put into water and crushed between the fingers. In

this way they get rid of most of the seeds. When dried the berries are softened in hot water or put in cold water and placed in the sun to soften. Then they are crushed in the same way to take out the seeds.

GK-WR: *hupui* are berries that grow along the foothills. The bush looks something like greasewood. These berries are gathered in the latter part of July and early in August. They are dried in the sand for winter use. The dried berries are usually kept in blankets in the house but they are sometimes stored in pits. The berries are not ground up but are boiled. The cooked berries are put in a basket that is like a sieve. This basket is held over a water-tight basket and the berries are mashed with the fingers. Finally only the seeds are left in the sieve. These are thrown away and the mush that has filtered through to the lower basket is eaten.

5. *pogopisha* [golden currants, *Ribes aureum*].

AD-R: The berries of *pogopisha* were dried, ground on the metate and mixed with seed flour for mush.

RP-WR: Wild currants (*huvui*) grow along the mountains. People break bunches off by hand. They are eaten fresh or dried.

6. *wápui* [juniper berries, *Juniperus occidentalis*].

ND-HL: *wapui* is juniper berries (*wápi*, juniper). When there was a good growth of juniper, when the berries are big, they are gathered and eaten. The berries are roasted in a parching tray. They are put in warm water and the berries are crushed and the seeds squeezed out with the fingers.

Pinenuts and Acorns

[Dense stands of pinyon trees are found only south of the Truckee and Humboldt Rivers and east of the Sierra Nevada (Lanner 1981). Thus, some of the Northern Paiute groups visited by Park had to travel outside their immediate ranges to gather pinenuts, or they obtained them through trade. These groups, such as the Pyramid Lake and Honey Lake people, thus may have depended on this food to a lesser degree than those people within the primary distribution of pinyon, e.g., Walker River, Fallon, etc. Park received very brief accounts of the pinenut complex from Pyramid Lake and Honey Lake people. His data from Walker River people are much more detailed.

The distribution of acorns in western Nevada is confined to the Sierra Nevada and thus excludes much of the Northern Paiute area. There is brief mention by Pyramid Lake people of gathering acorns near Doyle, California, near the southern end of Honey Lake. Others speak of occasionally obtaining acorns in trade from their neighbors, the Washo [see Trade in chap. 9]. Because of this, it is doubtful that acorns constituted much of a dietary item in the region. Their use is attested as pre-contact, however (Stewart 1941:427). They were

Figure 17. Pinenut processing. a (top left). Removing pinyon cones from trees with hooked harvesting pole. b (top right). Nuts being removed from cones at harvest site near Lovelock, 1912. Nevada Historical Society photograph. c (bottom left). Annie Bill winnowing pinenuts to remove meatless shells. d (bottom right). Wuzzie George, Stillwater, demonstrating method of parching shelled nut meats. Photograph by L. Mills, 1953. a, c by M. M. Wheat, 1958. University of Nevada, Reno, Library, Special Collections Department.

a staple crop for the Honey Lake people, often assuring against famine for two to three years (Riddell 1960:33).]
1. *tuba* (pinenuts, singleleaf pinyon, *Pinus monophylla*].
GK-WR: They go for pinenuts in August. The pine cones are full at that time. The men use a long stick to knock the cones from the trees (*tubəpi*) [fig. 17a]. While the men knock the cones down the women pile them in large heaps. These are left for about a month. The burrs open during that time and the nuts can be easily shaken out. If the cones at the bottom of the pile are not open when the nuts are shaken out, they are scattered and left a week longer. Then they are sure to open.

If the burrs are about open when picked they are put in a burden basket and beaten with a stick. The nuts are then jarred from the burrs [fig. 17b]. The pinenuts

are then dried for about a week and stored in the ground. When the pinenuts are removed from the cones, they are carefully dried before they are buried in the storage pits. If they were not dried, they would spoil.

Pine cones could also be gathered and about ten sacks placed in a trench 3 or 4 ft wide and 6 in. deep and 5 ft long.[132] The trench was covered with pine boughs or sagebrush. Fire was set to the covering. When the brush had burnt down to ashes, hot dirt and pinenuts—now separated from the burrs—were mixed together with a

[132] The method of pinenut preparation described here is for processing the "green burrs" gathered early in the season. It gives a faster return than waiting for the cones to open by natural processes.

stick and covered with dirt. This was left overnight. In the morning the pinenuts were winnowed in a coarsely woven tray [fig. 17c]. The dirt falls between the sticks and the coals are winnowed out. The pinenuts are now ready to eat or store.

Preparing Pinenuts[133]

RP-WR: Three kinds of baskets are used for this. One is a tray basket (*yadu*), coarsely woven. Another is a closely woven basket that is also tray shaped (*sayatuma*). And then another tray basket heavier and more closely woven (*tuma'a*) is also used. The first basket (*yadu*) is filled with nuts and hot coals are put on top of the pinenuts. This is shaken in a circular and up and down motion. This is continued until the nuts are cooked. A nut is tested now and then to see if they are done. Then the ashes are cleaned out by tossing the ashes and nuts up in the tray and blowing on it. The *yadu* is then covered with the *tuma'a* and the steam softens the nuts. They are ground on a metate slightly to break the shells, but the nuts are not crushed. They are rubbed lightly. Now the nuts are put in *sayatuma* and winnowed to take the shells off. If there is a wind blowing, the woman does not blow to winnow.

Now she puts the meats of the nuts back in the *yadu* and hot coals are put on and stirred [fig. 17d]. This is to dry the nuts. When they are brittle the charcoal is cleaned away in the same fashion [by winnowing]. This gives a darker color to the nuts. A small amount is now put on the metate and ground and sprinkled with water and put [rubbed] on the dark nuts. This takes off the dark color. This is winnowed again, which leaves the nuts clean and white. She then grinds the nuts on the metate, a handful at a time.

The meal is put in a cooking basket (*opu*) and water added a little at a time. At first it looks like a very stiff flour dough. Water is added until it is about the consistency of batter. She tests it by lifting it up with the forefinger. It is now ready to eat. It is cold. This is called their best food. They ate deer or rabbit with it.

This entire process is carried out in the same day. If she starts in the morning she would be finished about noon.

In the winter time when this was prepared and some was left over, it was put in serving baskets and put outside. In the morning it is frozen and considered a great delicacy—"like ice cream." It was melted a little (*awhen*, frozen too hard) on stones around the fire and eaten. During the day in winter they used to mix snow into the soup as it was made to make it almost frozen. This is

---

[133] See also Wheat (1967) for details on the processing of pinenuts.

considered a great delicacy, even today among young and old alike.

JG-PL: There was only one kind of pinenuts. There was only one kind of tree. Pinenuts are called *tu.ba*, the tree *tubap*[i]. When I was a boy we went from Pyramid Lake with my mother's father to a big mountain near Stillwater to get pinenuts. I think most of the pinenuts were around there. Every year we went there and stayed for a month or a month and a half.

BR-L, PL: Pinenuts are gotten in the mountain southeast of Austin. Another place where pinenuts grow is northeast of Fallon. They are also found east of Gardnerville and also south of Yerington. Pinenuts are stored by making a pile of burrs on the ground. The pile is covered with dried pine needles, then brush is put over the pine and finally a thin layer of dirt is put on.

HS-D: Pinenuts were most abundant around Virginia City, east of Gardnerville, and south and east of Reno except spotted places southwest of Pyramid Lake. Pinenut burrs were knocked down with a pole (*tsano*). The pinenuts are piled up in large heaps in the fall for winter use. The nuts are knocked out of the burrs with a stick and roasted. The nuts were next shelled by pounding them lightly on a metate. Then the shells are winnowed out and the nuts roasted with hot charcoal in a flat basket about 2 ft in diameter and 10 in. deep, oval shaped. Next they are ground up to a fine flour. The flour is placed in a conical basket with water and hot stones are put in. It is stirred constantly with a looped willow stick. It is like a thick gravy when it is cooked. Cooking rocks are about the size of an egg and called *tubi*.

Children used to put pinenut soup in a small basket and leave it outdoors on a cold night. The next morning it would be frozen. They would eat it that way. This was considered a great delicacy among the children.

2. *wia* [acorn, California black oak, *Quercus kellogii*].

JB-PL: *wia*, acorn, is gotten around Doyle — eastern slope of the hills around Doyle. Acorns were crushed in the mortar with the pestle. They were pulverized very fine. Wild grass was put on a place, the acorn flour was put on this mat and lukewarm water was poured over it to leach out the bitterness. This process was kept up until all the bitterness was gone. Then it was put in a basket and cooked with rocks. The acorns were ground with mortar and pestle because they are much harder.

ND-HL: Acorns (*wia*) were found around Doyle. They were gathered in the latter part of September. The acorns were knocked down from the trees with a long pole. The shells were cracked with a rock. When the shells were removed the acorns were ground. Then the acorns were ground into flour with a mortar and pestle. A concave bed of clean sand 2 or 3 ft in diameter is made. The flour is spread on the sand and covered with small cedar branches. Warm water is slowly poured on until the flour turns from pale green to white in color. The flour that is clean of sand is put in a basket. The flour that is mixed with sand is put in a basket of water. The flour rises to the top and is drained off with the water.

Other Plant Products

[The following short list adds the names and identifications of seven plants from which beverages, gum, and sugar were obtained. For plants used in manufacture or for medicinal purposes see Material Culture, chap. 3, and Medicines, chap. 8.]

1. *sudupi* [green ephedra, *Ephedra viridis*].

HS-D: *sudupi*. This is like a small bamboo. The stalks are boiled in water to make a tea.

2. *pamahabɔ* [wirerush, *Juncus balticus*, or *Eleocharis palustris*?].

RP-WR: A fermented drink was made from a plant (*pamahabɔ*) that looks like reeds. It grows about 1 ft. high. The stems are cut and soaked in water. The sap of this plant is sweet. When the stems have soaked for several hours, the liquid is put in water jugs. It is now ready to be drunk. It was intoxicating. Sometimes food was boiled in this liquid because it was a little sweet.

Both men and women drank this liquor. It left no hangover. Big crowds went out to cut the plants and make the drink. They got the plant in the morning and by noon they had filled the jugs and then they came home. They drank on the way home. The liquor was so intoxicating that some of them staggered. Even the children were allowed to drink. The effects only lasted a little while.

Some people say that *pamahabɔ* still grows along the river but it is no longer intoxicating. RP has never had any liquor made from it but her mother, AD, remembers when she drank it. Since the lake has been drying up they have not been able to make the liquor. They never made it for dances or big times. It was consumed almost as soon as it was made.

ND-HL: *pamahabɔ* is a light hollow reed, like a small bamboo [*Equisetum hyemale*]. It looks like a jointed tule. It is a water grass that grows in the river. This plant is not used. Never heard of making a drink with it.[134]

3. *sigupi* [rubber rabbitbrush, *Chrysothamnus nauseosus*].

RP-WR: Gum is gotten from *sigupi* in the summer. Dig out the roots and peel off the bark. If it is greenish in color (you have to look and see) it has gum. Peel off the outer skin and chew this part — it is greenish. Fill up the mouth and chew it into fine pieces. The bark is then spit out and the gum remains in rubberlike balls.

This they chew and it makes a delightful noise when chewed that is greatly appreciated by both sexes.

The gum from *sigupi* is chewed for a long time, day after day. It is the best kind of gum because it lasts a long time and produces a very entertaining noise. It is hard work to get the gum from the roots and people who do so usually have sore jaws the next day. Gum from *sigupi* is *sigusanaka'a*.

JB-PL: Chew the bark of the root of *sigupi* for gum. That growing near the river at Nixon is better. They do not have to chew it so long to get the rubber out.

4. *sawabi* [sagebrush, *Artemesia tridentata*].

RP-WR: Sagebrush (*sawabi*) also has a gum. It is gotten easily. It is found in the summer in little balls on the bush. It is gathered and roasted just a little in the ashes. The gum on sagebrush is called *sawapon-na'a*. It is chewed until it no longer sticks together. Then it is thrown away and a new supply is gotten.[135]

5. *tubapi* [pinyon pine, *Pinus monophylla*].

RP-WR: Gum is also gotten from pine trees. It is dried pitch made into little balls (*sanapobi*). It is taken as is and chewed. It is bitter at first, but you spit out the bitterness until it is pleasant to chew. The color is a "pretty pink"

6. *wɔkɔbihabi* (*wokokob*, common reed) [*Phragmites communis*].

ND-HL: *wokobihabi*, sugar, is gotten from cane. The sap collects on the leaves in the fall and crystallizes. The gnats collect on this by the thousands. My mother used to cut cane. When it dried a kind of sugar formed on the leaves. She knocked the sugar off with a stick and put it in bags made from sagebrush bark. The sugar formed into one lump in the bag and got brittle. Then we broke it up and ate it. It was like candy. The sugar was not mixed with other foods. We did not cook it.[136]

RP-WR: This candy was gotten late in the fall. The rain washes it off so it cannot be gathered on rainy days. It is still gotten at Lovelock. It has a brown color and tastes very much like hard candy. It melts in the mouth. Both men and women would gather it.

7. *wagapi* [Jeffrey Pine, *Pinus jeffreyi*].

RP-WR: Candy was gotten from fir trees. They have big cones but no nuts in them.[137] It is found on the leaves in a sort of sugar form. It is sweet like sugar. They knocked it off with sticks and gathered it in a bag.

---

[134] ND is undoubtedly identifying *pamahabɔ* with *Equisetum* rather than with *Juncus*. He seems not to have heard of a fermented drink in any form, however.

[135] These "sagebrush balls" are galls, probably produced by gallflies.

[136] See also Heizer (1945) for a summary of data on the extraction of honeydew or "bug sugar" from cane.

[137] This description could also refer to the sugar pine (*Pinus lambertiana*). However, the name *wogopi* ordinarily refers to Jeffrey pine in this region.

They separated it from the leaves in a closely woven basket. Just the fine leaves were left. This was taken home. It kept all winter. When it is kept a long time, it hardens into candy. Some people go after this and sell it to others. Candy from this tree is called *wagapihabi*.

WATERFOWL

[Waterfowl, including various ducks, geese, swans, herons, gulls, etc., were hunted on the several lakes, marshes, and rivers in western Nevada. The principal means for taking them were by shooting with a bow and special arrows (often with the aid of decoys), snaring, and netting. The American coot, known locally as the "mudhen," was also taken in drives. Snaring and netting seem to have been reserved for times when ducks were numerous, such as in the migratory seasons.

Much of western Nevada is within the Pacific Flyway, and thus migratory waterfowl were present in locally heavy concentrations in the fall and spring seasons. A number of species also nest in the area, thus making themselves, their eggs, and their young available through midsummer. In addition, there were some year-round residents available for exploitation.

Most waterfowl were prepared for eating by pit roasting or by cooking them on top of a bed of coals. Occasionally they were also cooked, dried, and stored for later use. The accounts that follow review the common species taken as well as the techniques used in their taking. The species identifications are based on additional field studies by the editor.]

Ducks

JG-PL: The ducks are gotten in the fall. They start to come early in September. Ducks were roasted in pits. They were split and roasted on the coals. Roasting on top of the coals is called *agwazukə*. The ducks were cleaned, the feathers plucked, and the heads cut off. The feathers were taken off the neck and head and these were roasted separately from the body in a pit. The flesh on the neck, the eyes, the tongues and brains were eaten. Pit roasting is called *aduno*. Sometimes the whole skin with the feathers was taken off the ducks and mudhens. These were used as a pillow for the baby in the cradle.

GK-WR: Ducks (*puhu*) were hunted on lakes and rivers. They were killed with bow and arrows. Ducks were either boiled or roasted. To roast, the feathers were taken off. A little hole was dug in the ground in which as many as five ducks would be placed. Then they were covered with ashes and a fire was built on top. Pit roasting is called *adinoho*.

[The following ducks were listed as killed and eaten in this manner.]

1. *sogopühü* [Cinnamon Teal, *Anas cyanoptera*].
2. *atsakutagayu* [Redhead, *Aythya americana*].
   JO-PL: *atsakutagayu* is a redheaded duck with a black bill and grey back.
3. *tohasikwad* [Canvasback, *Aythya valisineria*].
   JO-PL: *tuhatsiquad* has a grey breast and a large head. It is a large duck. This was the prize to get [see Decoy Hunting, below]. It was much like a mallard but larger.
   JG-PL: *tohasikwad*, canvas back, is also called *pizəsutu*.
4. *kuda* [Mallard, *Anas platyrhynchos*].
5. *izükoda* [Gadwall, *Anas strepera*].
   JG-PL: *izükoda* is black spotted on the breast and nearly as large as a mallard. It is grey in color.
6. *wi.gwaz* [Northern Pintail *Anas acuta*].
   JG-PL: *wi.qwaz* has a white breast, grey wings, a long neck and is almost as large as a mallard.
7. *imuduyu* [American Widgeon, *Anas americana*].
   JG-PL: *imuduyu* has a grey head with stripes of white on the head. The rest of the duck is grey. It is almost as small as the teal.
8. *agomobi* [Northern Shoveler, *Anas clypeata*].
9. *saya* [Mudhen, American Coot, *Fulica americana*].

Decoy Hunting

ND-HL: To make duck decoys (*paido'*), ducks are skinned and stuffed with sagebrush bark or tule, or anything that was light.[138] It was sewn when it was filled. The skin was still wet when it was stuffed. The legs and head were left on the skin. String was attached to the legs of the decoys. When the hunter saw some ducks coming he pulled the string to make the decoys move and he imitated the duck cry. A man would have four or five duck decoys.

When a man hunted with decoys he hunted alone. He had no one to help him. He used a special arrow with a knob just behind the point. It was called *pühü poŋos* [see Arrows in chap. 3]. The hunter was hidden in the tules. He made a blind which was made by gathering together bunches of standing tule. He wore a hat made of tules. It was made by tying ends of tules erect in a sort of a headdress. It was like an eagle feather headdress. The place where the man hides is called *obugwazubaidən*. The place where the decoys are is called *tüa*.

JG-PL: A stuffed duckskin was used for a decoy. Ten or 15 were used at a time. This was only done for can-

---

[138] See Wheat (1967:47f) for details on how decoys were made at Stillwater, Nev. For these, skins were placed over a preconstructed tule body. ND may be thinking of this method, although his and other descriptions imply that whole duckskins were merely stuffed with suitable material. Decoys are also reported for the Surprise Valley Paiute (Kelly 1932:90) but apparently did not occur in Owens Valley (Steward 1933:255).

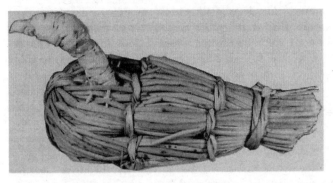

Figure 18. Duck decoys. a (top left). Decoy covered with skin of Canvasback female. MAI 13/4415. Collected by M. R. Harrington, Walker River, 1924. b (bottom left). Decoy of tules (body) and cattails (head), probably made by Wuzzie George, Stillwater. LMA 2-45482. Collected in 1971. c (right). Jimmy George, noted Northern Paiute decoy maker, with two skin-covered examples, one showing underside. Photograph by O. C. Stewart, 1936. One specimen in LMA, 1-41966.

vas back ducks.[139] [fig. 18a,c]. For shooting ducks a very small arrowhead was used. It was aimed to hit just in front of the duck. The arrow strikes the water and glances up and hits the duck. A duck hunter concealed himself behind the tules. No poison was used on duck arrows.

RP-WR: Ducks were hunted with decoys (*tüa, puhutua*). The decoys were made by skinning the ducks as soon as they were killed. The skins were stuffed with tule or feathers. Each decoy had a small rock at the end of the string for an anchor. A hunter had about 10 decoys. The decoys were put out in front of a blind where the hunter was hidden. The blind is made of tule and grass growing along the lake. The blind was a rude shelter made by standing up the tule and grass. There was no roof over it. Duck calls were not used.[140]

Snaring Ducks

ND-HL: Ducks were trapped in snares.[141] Sticks were driven into the bottom of a shallow pond about 25 or 30 yds apart. The tops had a notch like an arrow. The string was 8 or 10 in. above the water. It was stretched across the tops of the sticks. These poles were stretched out for about 200 yds. The ends of the string were attached to stakes firmly driven into the ground. About every yard a string dangled with a slip loop at the end. The loop was only about 1 in. above the water. When the duck stuck his head through the loop and went ahead it tightened up and he was caught. The loop was 3 or 4 in. across and was fixed so it was spread. These had to be watched all day until sundown. It had to be done on a day when there was no wind. ND saw two old men hunting ducks this way on Honey Lake when he was a young man, about 50 or 60 years ago [1870s, 1880s]. The name of this is *pühü hu'a* (*pühü*, duck and *hu'a*, trapping). It was too deep in Pyramid Lake to hunt ducks in this fashion. This method of hunting was used in the fall when the ducks were fat.

---

[139] Of the 11 historic Northern Paiute decoys examined in museum collections thus far, all are canvasbacks (males and females) but one, a bufflehead. A cache of painted and feathered decoys recovered from the prehistoric site of Lovelock Cave Nev., are also canvasbacks (Loud and Harrington 1929).

[140] RP-WR is probably referring here to the lack of mechanical calls rather than to voice calls. TM-WR,Y also denied the use of mechanical calls to Park.

---

[141] Substantially the same account was given by RP-WR. She called this snare *nawizo.du.na*. She added that the loops were a few in. above the water so that the ducks would be snared as they were swimming and feeding.

Netting Ducks

BR-L, PL: Ducks might be caught in a net. The net is put up in a place near the edge of the pond where the ducks come to eat. Posts are put in the water near the shore. The net is 30 or 40 ft long and about 4 ft high. It is stretched between these posts in a slight curve.[142] These nets were made out of smaller string than the rabbit and fish nets. The mesh was about 1 or 1½ in. The bottom of the net was 2 or 3 ft above the water. It was put up in the late afternoon so the ducks would get used to seeing it there and would not be frightened away. When the net is hung up the hunter goes away. He approaches it about 10 or 11 o'clock in the evening. With a stick he hits the water and all the ducks fly up. Some of the ducks hit the net and it comes loose from the posts and falls on top of the ducks so that they cannot get away. The hunter then pulls his net to the shore and kills the ducks. The net is used for ducks on a dark night. If it were moonlight the ducks could see the net and would not fly into it. The mesh of this net is not large enough for the ducks to get their heads through it. If they got their heads through the net the string would be broken. I saw a man use one of these nets to catch ducks near Lovelock.[143] The ducks had to be very numerous. There were not enough of them here at Pyramid Lake to use a net.

JG-PL: When there was a tule pond a net was used to catch ducks. A stick was put on each side of the pond. The net which was about 5 ft high was stretched across the pond. The sticks supporting the net were not put in deep. They were just strong enough to hold up the net. When a flock of ducks swooped down on the pond they hit the net and the sticks fell dropping the net on the ducks. The man who owned the net was there to watch the net and when the ducks were caught in the net he pulled it in and killed the ducks and put up the net again. He did this as long as the ducks were flying. The net was not put up in the daytime. It was put up only in the evening when the ducks were coming to the ponds to feed and stay all night.

Mudhen Drives

HS-D: Mudhen drives were usually held in the fall because at that time the mudhens were so fat they could not fly.[144] The best place for this drive used to be in a small shallow lake which was on the other side of a little ridge south from Pyramid Lake [see Place Names in chap. 1]. It was called *saiya tukəd*. It is all dried up now. It was a breeding place for mudhens. Another place was in the swamps north of Wabusca (Mason Valley).

At *saiya tukəd* men went out on this shallow lake on tule rafts. They pushed the boats with poles. The mudhens were driven to shore where they were caught by hand. The legs of the mudhens were broken and they were thrown into piles. Sometimes at Wabusca men took off all their clothes but a breechclout and waded into the water. With long poles they drove the mudhens to shore where others waited to catch the birds and kill them.

Mudhens were cleaned but the feathers were not taken off. They were hung in the shade until they were roasted under the ashes.[145]

BR-L, PL: The mudhen drive is held in October or November.[146] The boss of the drive[147] tells the people to make tule boats. He sets a day for the drive. All the men gather to make the boats [see Transportation, chap. 6].

Early the next morning right after daybreak the drive starts. After sunrise they cannot get as many mudhens. The men go out in boats. Sometimes there are two to a boat but usually only one man to a boat. Men, women and children hide behind the brush at the shore until the men in the boats drive the mudhens to shore. Then they pounce on them and break their legs.[148] Later when they have caught all they can they kill the crippled fowl. The mudhens are killed by pressing on the head with the thumb or hitting them on the head with a stick.

---

[142] The description does not indicate that the net was set at an angle to the water. Present-day consultants have said that it was usually so set.

[143] Park asked ND-HL about this technique and received a negative reply — he had not heard of it. TM-WR,Y had heard of catching ducks with nets but was not certain that nets were used by Walker River people. JO-PL had seen this done at Fallon, but thought that it did not take place at Pyramid Lake. He noted that the ducks, when frightened, flew close to the water and thus became entangled in the net.

[144] Mudhens were taken in drives in nearly all Northern Paiute areas (Stewart 1941:369). They were taken when "too fat to fly," a time likely also coinciding with their period of moulting.

[145] JG-PL told Park that mudhens were roasted in a preheated pit upon which an additional fire was built. They were split and roasted on top of the coals [see Ducks, above].

[146] BR-L,PL could be speaking of drives either at Pyramid Lake's duck lake (see above) or in the Humboldt Sink, as he was familiar with both.

[147] None of Park's other respondents noted that a leader was necessary for these drives. However, subsequent checking shows that they were common in some areas. Stewart (1941:369) also notes that it is common to have a director for communal drives for waterfowl.

[148] GK-WR noted that an additional reason for breaking the mudhens' legs beyond increasing the catch was that they scratched badly.

The men in the boats kill mudhens with bows and arrows. They have a special arrow for this purpose. The point is bulbous like a boy's spinning top [see Arrows in chap. 3]. The point is made this way so it will not go into the water when it hits the surface but will skip over the surface and hit the mudhen. This point is made of greasewood. It is tied to the arrow shaft with *wiha*. When the string gets wet it shrinks and the point will not come off. Mudhens are also killed with the bow and arrow at times other than when there is a mudhen drive.

RP-WR: Mudhens are hunted from a blind made of rocks and grass piled up in front. It has no roof. Two people hunt mudhens. One hunter is concealed in the blind while the other drives the mudhens in the direction of the blind.

Other Waterfowl

1. *naguta* [Canada Goose, *Branta canadensis*].

JG-PL: *naguta* is the honking goose. The smaller geese are called *sainaguta* [Aleutian Canada Goose, B. c. leucopareia]. They were shot with a bow and arrow in the fall. They were gotten in the fall. They were not dried because not that many were killed. They were cleaned and plucked and roasted.

2. *sigosa* [Greater White-fronted Goose, *Anser albifrons*].

JO-PL: The brown goose (*sigosa*) was shot with the bow and arrow and eaten. Its eggs and those of *naguta* were gathered and eaten. They were boiled and roasted.

3. *wahitə* [Tundra Swan, *Cygnus columbianus*].

JG-PL: Swans (*wahitə*) were killed with a bow and arrow on the lake in the winter. The swan was rather tough but it was eaten. They were prepared like geese. Sometimes the skins with the feathers were pulled off but I don't know what was done with the skin and feathers. I do not think that swans and geese were here a long time ago.[149]

JO-PL: Swans (*wahitə*) were eaten. They were shot with the bow and arrow. Swans do not lay their eggs so they did not have swan eggs.[150]

4. *panosə* [American White Pelican, *Pelecanus erythrorhynchos*].

JG-PL: Pelicans (*panosə*) were eaten. They were killed with a bow and arrow. They were prepared like the geese [plucked, roasted]. The old people ate them but now they are not eaten.

5. *wasa* [Great Blue Heron, *Ardea herodias*].

JG-PL: Crane (*wasa*). This is a blue crane, I think. They were always around the water. I think there was only one kind around here. The crane was good to eat. The big cranes were killed with bow and arrow. The young ones were caught in the nests. Men climbed up on the rocks where the cranes nested and got the young. They were cleaned and the feathers plucked. The legs and head were cut off. Cranes were put into a pit and covered with a little dirt. A fire was built on the top. It does not take long to cook them, only about 20 min. The pit was heated by making a fire in it. This was raked out before putting in the cranes. The young were killed in the early summer and the big ones were killed in the winter also.

JO-PL: Blue crane (*wasa*) was eaten. It was killed with the bow and arrow. The eggs were gathered at the little pyramid on the lake and they gathered many eggs there.

6. *kunaitu* [California Gull, *Larus californica* and/or Ring-billed Gull, *L. delawarensis*].

JO-PL: *kunaitu*, the gull, was eaten and the eggs gathered at Castle Rock [Anaho Island] where most of them live.

JG-PL: Gulls (*kunaita*) are the grey or black kind [immature California and/or Ring-billed]. The white gull is called *toha'ada* [adult of each or perhaps only *L. delawarensis*]. Both kinds were eaten. I think the gull came late. Maybe they were not here in the old days.[151] Gulls were roasted in a pit like the crane.

Eggs

HS-D: Duck and mudhen eggs were gathered all through the year except in winter. The eggs were sucked raw. Duck eggs are called *pühü naha* (*pühü*, duck; *naha*, egg). Eggs of the pelican (*panosu*), which is found only at Pyramid Lake, are also gathered. Men and women gather eggs together.

JG-PL: Eggs (*noho*) were eaten. Duck, geese and other bird eggs were eaten. They were roasted in pits. The fire on top was not too hot so the eggs would not be broken. Eggs were also boiled in a basket.

OTHER BIRDS

[Following is a list of other bird species taken for food or feathers along with some general and special techniques for their taking. Identifications are by the editor.]

---

[149] This seems unlikely, as these birds have probably not shifted their range significantly in many years. Bones from both species have also been recovered archaeologically at Pyramid Lake (Donald K. Grayson, personal communication, 1982).

[150] Tundra Swans breed in Alaska and Canada and winter in Great Basin (Ryser 1985:122). Thus JO is correct on the lack of swan eggs in the area.

---

[151] Gulls may have increased in population, but they should have been present in the region in early times.

1. *hudsi* sagehen [Sage Grouse, *Centrocercus urophasianus*].

JG-PL: Sagehens were caught where they gathered and "danced around."[152] They mated here in the spring. A hole was dug and screened with brush. The hunter got in the hole early in the morning before daylight and when the sagehen appeared he shot them with bow and arrow.[153] Sagehens were not trapped.[154]

BB-PL: Sagehens (*hudsi*) were stalked in a deerskin.[155] The sagehens are not afraid of deer so the hunter could get close to them. He shot one without throwing off his disguise and waited until the sagehens flew back. Then he shot another.

2. *kahu'u* grouse [Blue Grouse, *Dendragapus obscurus*].

JG-PL: Grouse (*kahu'u*) do not live around Pyramid Lake. They are found in the timber country.

3. *sikigi* quail [Mountain Quail, *Oreatryx pictus*].

RP-WR: Old nets were used to catch quails.[156] Seed was scattered on the snow and the net was put over this feeding ground on short sticks. The net reaches to the ground on all sides but one side was open. The quail entered on the open side and in feeding knocked down the stick which was loosely set up to hold the net. The quail became entangled and could not get away.

4. *pakodəp* blackbirds [Brewer's Blackbird, *Euphagus cyanocephalus*].

JG-PL: Blackbirds (*pakodəp*) were killed with the bow and arrow. They were cleaned and the feathers plucked and then they were roasted on top of the coals. They were not dried. Not many blackbirds were killed.

5. *atsapakodoba*, redwing blackbird [Red-winged Blackbird, *Agelaius phoeniceus*].

JO-PL: Redwing blackbirds (*atsapakodoba*) were eaten. They were mostly killed by bow and arrow by boys.

6. *pabasugu*, [American Robin, *Turdus migratorius*].

JG-PL: Robins (*pabasugu*) were killed with bow and arrow. They were prepared like the blackbird [plucked, roasted on coals].

7. *pazitono*, meadowlark [Western Meadowlark, *Sturnella neglecta*].

JG-PL: The meadowlark (*pazitono*) was eaten. These were killed with the bow and arrow. They were roasted on the coals. Sometimes they were roasted in a pit.

8. *si.duna*, snowbird [probably Horned Lark, *Eremophila alpestris*].

JG-PL: The snowbird (*si.duna*) was killed with bow and arrow. In the winter many of these can be killed. They are found in the valleys and low places in the winter. They were roasted on the coals.

9. *angə*, [Pinyon Jay, *Gymnorhinus cyanocephala*].

JO-PL: *angə* is the bluish pine nut bird. It does not have a long tail but is about the size of a magpie. It was shot with the bow and arrow. They fix a place at the water holes or spring and shoot them from there [see below].

10. *toga* [Clark's Nutcracker, *Nucifraga columbiana*].

JO-PL: *toga* has white wings and breast and is about the size of *angə*. Like *angə*, this bird was shot with the bow and arrow from a blind near a water hole.

11. *kwidagai*, magpie [Black-billed magpie, *Pica pica*].

JG-PL: Magpies are not eaten. They are caught for the tail feathers which are used by the shamans [see Shamanism in vol. 2]. They are caught in a trap (*kwidagainahu: kwidagai*, magpie; *nahu* trap).[157] To make the trap, a hole 4 or 5 in. in diameter and about 4 in. deep is dug. Two sticks are put in on each side of the hole and also in the hole. These come to about 1 in. below the surface. A stick is placed across the two sticks. Bait is tied on one side of the cross piece. A string is tied to the cross piece. A willow stick about 4 ft long is put in the ground slanting so it is several feet above the hole. The string has a slip knot and a loop goes around the hole outside the sticks [fig. 19]. Just above the slip knot the string goes around the cross piece with a double half hitch. The cross piece is jammed between the two sticks in the hole and the willow stick is bent down and the other end of the string tied to it. The bait, any kind of meat, is tied to the cross piece. When the magpie pecks at the meat the cross piece is dislodged and the willow stick jerks up and the head of the magpie is caught in the loop of the string and held fast. The magpies were alive when taken in this snare. When the tail feathers had been pulled out the magpie was set free.

12. *kwi'na* eagle [Golden Eagle, *Aquila chrysaetos*].

JG-PL: Eagles (*kwi'na*) were not eaten. They were sometimes shot with a bow and arrow. The young eagles were captured in the nest and kept in cages. One man owns a nest.[158] He always went to the same nest to capture eagles. He claimed that nest. On his death, a man in his family such as a brother or a son claimed the nest and used it.

---

[152] This is indoubtedly the nuptial display of the sagehen, known locally as "strutting."

[153] Kelly (1932:89) notes that at the "dancing" time, sagehens were clubbed rather than shot in Surprise Valley.

[154] Kelly (1932:89) reports snaring of sagehens with a noose trap for Surprise Valley.

[155] Kelly (1932:89) also reports this method, but with an antelope skin disguise. Stewart (1941:368) confirms antelope disguise hunting of sagehens for the northern Northern Paiute groups.

[156] Kelly (1932:89) notes the use of this method for sagehens. Stewart (1941:368) lists it for sagehens and doves.

---

[157] This trap form is not described by Kelly (1932), Steward (1933), or Stewart (1941).

[158] Eagle nests were considered personal property among all Northern Paiute groups according to Stewart (1941:370). The young were also gathered from these nests for their feathers by all groups.

When the young eagles were captured, each one was tied in a small basket very similar to the first cradle [see Cradles in vol. 2]. This was the way young eagles were carried home. They were kept in cages until the feathers grew.[159] Then the tail feathers were plucked out and the eagle might be kept until more feathers grew or it might be released. The tail feathers — two main ones — were plucked with the down under the tail feathers. The eagles were never killed [but see above]. The Indians did not want to kill the eagles. They did not want to destroy the eagles because they wanted to save them so there would be more eagles. There seems to be no fear of bad luck or harm resulting from killing the eagles.

Eagle cages, called *kwi'na sunobi* (*su*, willow), were of willow. They were nearly square in shape and about 5 ft high by 4 or 5 ft long and wide. They were large enough so the tail feathers of the eagle would not wear out on the sides of the cage as the eagles moved around. The cage was made in wicker work. The eagles were fed on rabbits, squirrels, mice, rats and other small animals.

Sometimes when a man goes to his eagle nest, he goes just about the time the young eagles are ready to fly. The main tail feather is plucked out and the little eagle is left in the nest.

RP-WR: They tried to train eagles. Cages and roosts were made for them. Eagles were kept chiefly to supply shamans with the tail feathers and the down [see Shamanism in vol. 2]. They were caught in the nests while young. If the young eagles were caught in the fall they had nice feathers. The feathers are plucked from the imprisoned eagles and the bird is kept until more feathers grow. When the eagle was no longer wanted, it was turned loose. When eagles are freed, they are carried out into the mountains and left. The captured eagles were never killed.

Several men might go out together to catch eagles. They owned the captured bird together. After the eagle feathers were plucked, the bird was not kept in a cage. They would not escape if fed every day. A roost was made for the eagle. When the feathers came out again on the eagle it was put back in the cage.

Five or six men sometimes owned shares in a single eagle nest. The eagle has two young each year. Both were taken. Disputes arose over the shares in the captured eagles and over the rights to the nests. The feathers are used by the shamans for wearing in headbands. They may be bought by a shaman from men who own an eagle.

Eagles are captured on a mountain west of Walker River Reservation called *tunu'u kwina'a* (*tunu'u*, top;

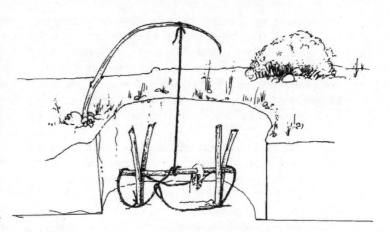

Figure 19. Magpie trap, reconstructed from description given to Park by JG-PL. Drawing by Susan Lohse.

kwina'a, eagle). Another mountain where eagles are caught is *tumə'ə kwina'a* (*tumə'ə*, rivals) east of Walker Lake. They are also captured on *tonobiduhaka* (*tonobi*, brush; *duhaka*, canyon) a mountain south of Walker Lake [see Place Names, in chap. 1].

Eagles are named after these mountains. A captured eagle is always named after the place where it was captured.

[Two birds were also named but listed as not eaten: *ada*, crow (American Crow, *Corvus brachyrhynchos*) (JO, JG-PL); and *saniki*, a little bird with yellow breast (unidentified; JG-PL)].

Shooting Birds from a Blind

TM-WR, Y: Boys and men hunted birds with bows and arrows. In the spring, a shelter like a house was built near a spring.[160] A small stick was put out over the water like a roost. When any kind of bird flew down and lighted on the stick the hunter concealed in the little house shot it with a bow and arrow. The stick was put a few inches above the water to attract the birds when they come to drink. The roost was made so it was convenient for the birds to drink from it. Birds were not trapped with deadfalls.

REPTILES AND APMPHIBIANS

[The following meager data on the use of reptiles and amphibians as food are sythesized from three accounts.]

HS-D: Animals not eaten include: toad (*pamogo*), long-legged green frog (*whagatsa*), horned toad (*pamagadsa* or *magadsa*), large black lizard (*tubotsa*), gila monster

---

[159] Caging of eagles was fairly common among the Northern Paiute (Stewart 1941:370). It also occurred in Owens Valley according to Steward (1933:257) where eagles were "raised in small wickiups."

---

[160] Blinds near springs are also described by Kelly (1932:89), Stewart (1941:369), and Steward (1933:255).

(pasiwanüna), small lizard (kwidamogus) and snake (togoko [rattlesnake]). The rattlesnake was killed for its skin which was used in making a head band. ND, present at a discussion of foods, said they used to eat snakes. He saw his grandfather eat a rattlesnake at Austin. They only ate rattlesnakes. HS-D, his wife and brother all emphatically denied this statement and ridiculed ND who stuck to his story.

JG-PL: No lizards were eaten.[161] A small lizard is called *tabasiba* and a lizard that has small black dots from its head down its back is called *kagwidə*.

GK-WR: The Paiutes did not eat snakes or lizards. The Shoshoni eat snakes. We have nick-named them "snake eaters." Shoshoni who used to come to Walker River to catch fish caught snakes and ate them. The Paiutes told them that snakes were no good for food. I think the Shoshoni ate snakes quite a bit.[162]

INSECT FOODS

[The use of several varieties of insects as food is well documented for the Northern Paiute as well as for other Great Basin people (Stewart 1941:373; Steward 1938:34). The most important insects include specific species of locusts, crickets, caterpillars, wasps, ants, and *Ephydra* fly larvae. Park's repondents described in detail only the former four food types, referring to the latter two plus grasshoppers in passing. The use of ants, or at least ant larvae, is attributed by Stewart (1941:373) to all Northern Paiute groups. Stewart (1941:426-27) also provides a long note on the use of the larvae of the fly *Ephydra hians*, known to occur near Pyramid Lake and at Soda Lake near Fallon. However, they were apparently little used in these localities. Most people associate intensive use with the Mono Lake Northern Paiute, referring to them as *kucabidikadi*, (*kucabi* [*Ephydra hians*], eaters).

Insects were generally prepared in the same manner as seeds: parched, and often ground into flour and made into mush. Preparation techniques differed somewhat according to the species. Following are Park's notes on insect preparation and use.]

1. *nizu* [Mormon Cricket, *Anabrus simplex*]

JG-PL: *nizu* are large grasshoppers, larger than crickets.[163] These do not come every year, but some years they are plentiful. About 4 years ago [1936] there were

very many. When a large bunch is seen, people go out to gather them. They are gathered early in the spring when they are nice and fresh. People go out early in the morning before sunrise to get them. Then the grasshoppers are cold and cannot travel very fast. They are picked up and put in a burden basket. Men and women do this work together. Early in the spring the grasshoppers are young and have no tail [ovipositor]. When the tail grows they are no good. In the summer they are no good. *Nizu* are killed by putting them in the fire, in hot ashes but not flames. They can also be killed by covering up the burden basket so they die in there. Sometimes the head is mashed between the fingers as the *nizu* is picked up. After roasting, the grasshoppers are put away in a bag until they are to be used. They will keep for a long time. When they are used they are ground on the metate. The flour is eaten without further cooking.

ND-HL: *ni.zu*, crickets, are gotten on the mountains. Early in the morning when the crickets are under logs and in the crevices of rocks they are gathered. A large jug-shaped basket about 3 ft high was used to hold the crickets. The colder the morning the better it is to get crickets for they move slowly when cold and will not bite. A pit was made several days before. This pit has flat rocks on the bottom. Fire is built on the rocks until the rocks are hot. Then the crickets are dumped in and more flat hot rocks are put over the top and covered with hot dirt. This is then left to roast for 2 or 3 hours. The rocks are taken off, the dirt is sifted for the crickets. Then the crickets are dried and pounded up into flour and stored in buckskin bags. The bags of flour were kept for winter. This flour was not mixed with other foods. When the crickets are pulverized they are eaten dry with the fingers and from a bowl. The crickets were gathered in the middle of June. Mush was not made from the flour gotten from the crickets and locusts and grasshoppers.

2. *kua* [cicada, *Okanogoides* spp.]

JG-PL: *kuə* is like a bumble bee.[164] Sometimes there are many of them. They are on the brush. They can be heard buzzing. They are smaller than *nizu*. They are gathered in the spring and early in the morning. When they are on the brush they will not fly away. They are gathered and taken home and roasted in the ashes. They are not ground up. They may be kept for winter if many are gathered. They will not spoil.

ND-HL: *kuə*, is a locust gotten in the late spring. It is roasted on hot coals. When the young locusts are about ready to fly they climb the brush. They are gathered in the evening or in the morning just before sunrise. The locusts are gathered in a basket. A small pit is dug in

---

[161] Stewart (1941:372, 426) notes apparent and widespread feeling that lizards were not suitable food.

[162] Stewart (1941:277) also notes widespread use of lizards and snakes as food among the Western Shoshone. Rattlesnakes appear to have been eaten occasionally, especially in historic times.

[163] Stewart (1941:373) lists crickets (*niju*, *miju*) as eaten by all groups of Northern Paiute surveyed.

[164] They are probably compared to bees because they make a buzzing sound. Stewart (1941:373) notes that they were eaten by roughly half of the Northern groups surveyed.

the ground and the locusts are put in and covered with hot ashes. It takes about a half hour to cook. Before the locusts are put in the pit a fire is burnt in it to get the ground very hot. When they are cooked the locusts are separated from the dirt by sifting out the dirt with a coarsely woven tray. The dried locusts may be ground up with seeds.

There are two kinds of locusts. One has a belly that is dark brown. It is called *atsakua*. This is the only locust that is usually eaten. The other kind, *izikua*, is not usually eaten. This is small and harder to get but it is eaten sometimes.

HS-D: *gua*, locusts, are roasted in ashes — thrown in alive. Get them in the summer time. Women and children would gather locusts. They taste like cooked [fried?] oysters.

RP-WR: Locusts (*küa*) are gotten on the brush. You do not go straight to the locust when you hear it. You go slowly and put your hands by your ears and make motions with the hands. If you do that the locusts will stay right there. Locusts are roasted in the coals as soon as they are caught. They are not preserved for winter.

3. *piəg*, caterpillar [larvae of white-lined sphinx moth, *Hyles lineata*]

ND-HL: *piəg*,[165] is a worm or caterpillar that climbs cottonwood trees and weeds to feed off the leaves. It is fat then and they are gathered for food. It is big, yellow striped and fat, about the length of a forefinger. When the worm is caught all that material that has been freshly eaten is squeezed out of the worm between the fingers and the worms are collected in a basket. The dead worms are roasted in a pit like crickets, using flat stones. (ND knows of the *piəg* that is gathered from the pine trees at Mono Lake [i.e., *Coloradia pandora*]. He says that the kind here is different. It is not gotten from the pine trees. He has never seen the *piəg* at Mono Lake.)

HS-D: *piəg* is a caterpillar. They travel in bunches in the summer. The leader is caught and a hair is tied around its neck. It is led around in a circle and tied to a bush. Then the whole bunch will stop there. It is also gotten around pine trees [again, *Coloradia pandora*]. A trench is dug around the trees. When the insects come down the trees they fall in the trench and can't get out. This insect is dried in the sun. It is eaten dry or ground into flour for mush.

RP-WR: Worms (*piəg*) that live in tall pine trees are dark greyish in color with yellow stripes on the back.

They are 1 in. or 1½ in. long with many legs. They are gotten only in July.

Men go up and dig trenches around many pine trees. The people have their own pine trees for pinenuts. They use only these trees to get the insects. If someone has no trees others will give him some. The trench is about 2 ft deep and is dug all the way around the tree. The worms cannot get out of it. They come down the trees on one particular day in July.

When the worms are taken from the trenches a fire is made nearby. The worms are thrown into the hot coals until they are dead. Then they are taken out and dried. The dried worms are stored in sagebrush bark sacks for winter use. When the worms are used they are not pounded up. They are boiled whole. A soup is made with the worms.

4. *Ants*

HS-D: A large reddish brown ant is eaten. It is called *kusabi*.[166]

RP-WR: Large black ants, vinegar ants (*a'nina*), are found in the hills. A fire is made on top of the ant hill and when the ants are driven out the eggs are gotten. Only the eggs are eaten.[167]

5. *hoatata* [grasshopper, *Melanoplus* spp.]

ND-HL: *hoatata*, grasshoppers, are not eaten by the Paiutes but the Washo eat them.[168] Where there are many grasshoppers on the weeds early in the morning before they started to move the grass would be burnt and the dead grasshoppers swept in a pile and sifted in the same way as the locusts. Then the grasshoppers were ground on a metate.

HS-D: *Whatata*, grasshopper, long horned. Some may eat them.

6. *noda* [yellowjacket, *Vespula* sp.]

RP-WR: Nests of wasps and hornets (*noda*) were gathered along the river.[169] A fire was made on top of the nest. The eggs and young are eaten. These insects are gotten early in the morning. The nests in the ground are found early in the morning when the hornets and wasps leave. The fire is built on the ground over the nest. It is left there until the next day when the eggs and young were taken out. By this time they were cooked. They were carried home in a basket.

---

[165] The term *piagi* is applied to several types of caterpillars, the most common being the larvae of *Hyles lineata* and *Coloradia pandora*. The latter, however, are confined to the Jeffrey pine forests of Mono Lake and north of Owens Valley. They are well known from this locality throughout the region, however. See Steward (1933:256), Davis (1965), and Fowler and Walter (1985) for descriptions of their preparation and use.

[166] The term *kucabi* is most often applied to the larvae of *Ephydra hians*. The application of the term "ant" here is probably a folk error. See Heizer (1950), Davis (1965), and Essig (1934) for data on the use of these insects.

[167] Ant eggs were reported as eaten by all Northern Paiute groups surveyed (Stewart 1941:373).

[168] Stewart (1941:373) also received negative responses from all Northern Paiute individuals interviewed *re* this food. Responses were positive from the Washo, however.

[169] The eggs of *nota* were reported as eaten by all but two groups surveyed by Stewart (1941:373).

7. *kusabi* flay larva [brine fly, *Ephydra hians*]

RP-WR: Mono Lake has lots of *kusabi*. They are like flies and are found on the shore. We go down and get them sometimes. Or the people down there bring them to us. We call those people *kusatikɔdu* after that kind.

SALT

[Park received only three accounts on the making or gathering of salt. All three come from the southern district (Walker River, Yerington). All three also speak of obtaining salt in Antelope Valley, primarily within Washoe territory, but obviously also jointly used. The salt described has been collected and analyzed by the Chemistry Department, University of Nevada, Reno, and been shown to contain high concentrations of the mineral halite, or sodium chloride. It also contains small amounts of sodium bicarbonate. The salt crystallizes along the edge of a dry lake in Antelope Valley, and also occurs around the edges of small spring mounds in the center of the dry lake. As stated below, it also accumulates on the surface of other soils.]

TM-WR, Y: Salt (*oŋabi*) was gotten around Topaz. It was found under the greasewood. It is found around the roots. Someone suggested that it was alkali. It is grey in color. This is gathered and covered with softened sagebrush bark. Hot coals are put on top of the bark. This melts the salt and it forms one large piece. The piece of salt is roasted in hot ashes. It is left under the ashes overnight. When it is used, two pieces are rubbed together to get the amount desired. When roasted, salt is grey in color. Salt was used to flavor all sorts of food.

GK-WR: Salt (*tubi owabi*) is from some kind of dirt— "maybe in a dry lake." It was put in a basket with a little water. This was stirred into a thick paste and formed into a cake 12 to 14 in. long and 4 in. wide. This was baked in the hot ashes. When the cake comes out it is black and hard. It was taken home and used in cooking.

This salt was gotten in Antelope Valley near Topaz. This was in Washo country, but some of the Paiutes would go up there to get salt. "Some of my old folks went up there and brought home some salt. I did not see them get it, but I saw the black cakes that they brought home." Nowadays salt is called *owabi*.

3

Material Culture

[This section incorporates the bulk of Park's data on material culture, including hunting equipment (bows, arrows, and arrow poisons), additional weapons, such as spears and shields, stone technology (knapping, manos and metates, etc.), bone tools, fire making, hide processing, basketry, and cordage, nets, and weaving. Each subsection is preceded by a brief introduction, describing the data available in Park's notes on each topic and summarizing points of agreement. Data in this section are rich in detail, and when combined with Park's (and others') collections of material items for museums, they add a great deal to our knowledge of these aspects of Northern Paiute life.]

BOWS

[Park received accounts of bow making from six men. The two most complete statements are printed here in full. Supplementary comments by other individuals are appended. Although the two principal statements agree on a number of points of construction procedure, they differ sufficiently to require printing both. The principal differences concern methods of bow reinforcement and grip treatment—both perhaps of distributional/historical significance. Stewart (1941:84) notes that the self bow was an alternative to the sinew-backed bow for some eastern and northern Northern Paiute groups. Grip constriction is described by Kelly (1932:142) for the Surprise Valley Paiute, but was apparently denied by Steward's (1933:259) Owens Valley respondents. Park (1934:I:152) provided the following note on the matter as discussed at Pyramid Lake:

> Although there are conflicting opinions on the shape of the bow, several old men insist that the bow had a constricted grip. When BB-PL brought out a small model of a bow he wanted to sell, several old men standing by pointed out the difference in the shape of the bows in the old days. They said that in the old days the bows tapered from the middle towards the ends and at the middle the bow was smaller for about the width of a hand. This they said was to enable a man to grasp the bow better. They carefully showed how the bow was constricted at the middle for a grip.

None of Park's respondents south of Pyramid Lake (four individuals) described bows with constricted grips.

All south of that area also spoke of the sinew-backed bow only as a child's toy.]

JG-PL: The bow is made of cedar [i.e., juniper (*Juniperus occidentalis* or *J. osteosperma*)]. A good strong limb of about 4 ft long is split with a rock. The end is laid on a rock and pounded with another rock until the end is split. Then with the fingers the stick is pulled apart. The bow is fashioned so the ends are smaller than the middle. There is no constricted grip. The back was strengthened with a mixture of *kuyui* eggs and bladder. This mixture is roasted before using. It is smeared all over the back of the bow and allowed to dry. This makes the bow very strong. No sinew is used.[1]

A groove is cut across the two edges[2] at each end of the bow for string which is made of *wiha* [*Apocynum cannabinum*]. A hunter carried an extra bow string wrapped around his head. When the bow was not in use the bow string was slipped off one end and the string was wrapped around the bow.

Some men painted the inside of the bow with red paint. The entire inside of the bow might be painted. The blue coloring, from a rock in which there was copper,[3] was sometimes used to paint several series of stripes across the bow. There might be two or three stripes in each group. These stripes were put on the top of the

---

[1] As noted in the introductory paragraph, respondents were of different opinions on the use of self *vs.* sinew-backed bows. Kelly (1932:143) states that in Surprise Valley only boys used the self bow. Steward (1953:259) states that large game bows were sinew-backed and small game bows were self bows in Owens Valley. Riddell (1960:48) assumes by the absence of any description of sinew backing that the bows of the Honey Lake Paiute were self bows. Stewart (1941: 384, 432) refers of a "self bow" (*soroado*) of limited distribution, but excluding the Pyramid Lake Paiute. The term *soroado* (*sogoadi*) is literally 'old time bow.' Whether it refers specifically to an earlier style of self bow or was merely being used to refer to "bow" as opposed to "gun" (now also *adi*) is a matter for speculation.

[2] Steward (1933:259) states that the Owens Valley self bow was grooved at both ends.

[3] See also Lowie (1924:245) for a description of painting with pulverized "copper rock, *puirupi.i*" (*puitipi*, literally 'green rock').

solid red. They made their bows look good that way. The backs of the bows were never painted.

A man always made his own bow.[4] If he had a boy 16 or 18 he made a bow for the boy. He did not make such a strong one. He made a plain one without fish glue on the back.[5]

ND-HL: Tops of young junipers were taken and split. They are about 2 in. in diameter and about 4 ft long. When it was split it was trimmed down. A bow made from juniper is called *wa'adu*. Bow made from oak is called *wiɜadu*.[6]

The bow was dried for a week or more.[7] It was put in the sun to dry. The back is covered with sinew. At the ends of the bow the sinew is left hanging 4 or 5 in. To these are tied the bow string. When not in use the bow string is untied and the bow put in the bag [quiver].

The largest part of the bow is at the grip. It tapers to both ends. There is a consricted grip on the bow. The bow tapered from both sides of the grip to the ends. The inside of the bow was flat. The back side was rounded.

The bladder of the *kuyui* was used for glue. Bladders were rolled in sunflower leaves[8] when they are green and put in ashes to cook. Then it is mashed up and shaped into a loaf and dried. It was rubbed on when moistened like belt dressing. A flat rough rock used to scrape off the cake. The rock is already moist. Then it is put on the bow with the hand. Glue is called *sa'go*.

The sinew has been dried. When it is used it is soaked. The entire back of the bow is covered with sinew.[9] The sinew is evenly laid. There is no special strengthening at the grip. The sinew that sticks out past the end of the bow is allowed to dry. It gets very hard. It is hard like iron. The bow string is tied to this projecting sinew at both ends of the bow. There is a loop already at both ends of the bow string. When it is placed over or taken off, the bow is bent and the loop is hooked or unhooked. (Now ND says one end is tied and the other end has a loop.)

The bow string is made of sinew or *wiha*. It was of two strands. The bow string is called *pagakwi*. The arrow is held between the thumb and the first finger and the third finger is also pulling the bow string.[10]

The Paiutes never used mountain sheep horn or antlers to strengthen the bows. Indians in Idaho use horn this way, it is said.[11]

HS-D: Bows made from juniper were usually 4 to 5 ft long. For smaller game a bow about 3 ft in length was used. Juniper which was often used in making bows was never heated.[12]

The sinews taken from the backs and legs of deer, antelope, or mountain sheep were used in making bows because they were longer. The sinews in the backing form a loop at each end. The bow string is attached to these loops.

Red and yellow lines were painted on the back of the bow.[13]

The Paiutes hold bows at a slight angle to shoot [fig. 20]. Pit Rivers and Washos hold it in horizontal posi-

---

[4] See also Lowie (1924:245) and Kelly (1932:142) for lack of a bowyers' craft. Steward (1933:259) states that bows were made by professionals in Owens Valley, although one consultant denied this was true.

[5] See note 1 above for discussion of the self bow. Steward (1933:259) and Kelly (1932:143) also attribute self bows to young boys. JG's age estimate of "16 or 18" seems higher than that implied by either.

[6] ND came from Honey Lake, which is within the distribution of oak (*Quercus kelloggii*). Surprise Valley Paiute attribute oak bows to the Achomawi (Kelly 1932:142). Lowie (1924:245) lists "Paviotso" bows of *tsisaBi* [perhaps either *ciabui*, wild rose (*Rosa woodsii*) or *tiabi*, serviceberry (*Amelanchier alnifolia*)] *poɤonoBi* [perhaps currant (*Ribes aureum*, *R. cereum*)], or *ugwogowᵃ*, "the last-named being used for arrows as well." The latter is likely *wokokobi* (or *wokʷokobi*), common reed (*Phragmites australis*), with the confusion resulting from the application by many people of the term *adi* to bows and arrows together. Stewart (1941:384) lists self bows of willow (probably narrowleaf cottonwood (*Populus angustifolia*) and juniper for the Paiute of Carson Sink and sinew-backed bows of juniper and serviceberry for Pyramid Lake. Steward (1933:259) notes in addition to juniper, water birch (*Betula fontanalis*; now *B. occidentalis*) for Owens Valley. It is clear from all accounts, however, that juniper was favored.

[7] HW-Y: the wood was tied firmly to a straight stick for drying. GK-WR: the young cedar was bent slightly and dried. It was round on the back with a flat surface inside.

[8] Probably either wooly Wyethia (*Wyethia mollis*) or arrowleaf balsam (*Balsamhoriza sagitatta*). HW-Y speaks of glue (*tsago*) made of fish intestines.

[9] JB-PL stated that it formed a single layer. HW-Y suggests two layers as does Stewart (1941:384). Steward (1933:259) notes that several were used in Owens Valley. HW-Y says sinew backing was called *ahodəm*.

[10] Primary arrow release also noted by Steward (1933:263), Kelly (1932:144), and Riddell (1960:49). Kelly (1932:144) says the arrow was held to the left of the bow. This description by ND is of a secondary release. All others described primary release.

[11] This is probably correct for the area, although Curtis (1926:71) states that the "powerful recurved bow of mountain-sheep horn was not uncommon" among the Paviotso. See Lowie (1909:192) for description of Northern Shoshoni horn bows.

[12] Kelly (1932:142) states that the "limb was warmed and scraped" in Surprise Valley. Steward (1933:259) states that in Owens Valley, "treating with fire and ashes in some way straightened and supposedly gave elasticity."

[13] See JG's account of painting, above. Steward (1933:260) describes specimens from Owens Valley with crossbands painted on the inside (red and blue).

Figure 20. Billy Biscuit, Pyramid Lake, demonstrating use of bow and arrow release method. Note skin quiver across his back. Photograph by W. Z. Park, Pyramid Lake, 1934.

tion.[14] No guard was worn on the hand while shooting with the bow.[15]

The Paiutes had very strong bows. An old fellow from Susanville went to the Bannocks on a visit. They were about to hunt buffalo so the Paiute went with them. The buffalo stampeded. The old Paiute told one of the Bannocks to take him on a horse up to the herd. They found the leader of the buffalo herd and the old fellow shot at him. At close range he shot all the way through the buffalo.[16]

BR-L, PL: Bows were made from young juniper. They were about 3 ft long. The wood was smoothed with a flintknife. The wood was dried for about a month before it was smoothed. The greener the wood the better, they say. If the wood is old it might break. Deer sinew is rolled on the leg to make the bow string.[17] It is about 3/16 in. in diameter. When the bow was not in use the string was taken off the bow and put away. If this is not done the bow does not work so well and it does not last as long.

ARROWS

[Accounts of arrow making were given by five men. Four are represented here. Principal differences in the accounts concern the material used in arrow manufacture as well as some of the specific features of tip design and fletching. Since individuals come from different areas, preference of materials may be influenced by availability. For example, marshes in the general vicinity of Pyramid Lake were good sources of common reed (*Phragmites australis*). However, materials preferences might also be influenced by an arrow's purpose, as some of the following statements seem to indicate.]

ND-HL: Arrows were made of chokecherry, *təshab* (*Prunus virginiana* var. *demissa*). The ones made by ND are about the length of arrows in the old days.[18] The stick for an arrow was straightened by heating it in a fire and then holding it between the teeth.[19] Then it is sighted. It is tested for straightness by putting the shaft on the forefinger of the left hand about one third of the way from the end and twisting the other end with the right hand. If it is true, it makes a little humming noise when it spins.

The flat rocks with a single groove in each are used. The rocks are 4 in. by 2 in. The rocks were put together on the arrow and the arrow was pulled back and forth and turned around to smooth the shaft.[20] The rocks were called *pa'ab'* [fig. 21a].

---

[14] Kelly's (1932:144) Surprise Valley Paiutes also associated the horizontal shooting position with the Washoe and Achomawi. Steward (1953:263), says bows were held "diagonally in front of body" in Owens Valley. Riddell (1960:49) says that a bow held at a 45° angle with the top to the left is Pit River; Northern Paiute position is vertical.

[15] Kelly (1932:142) speaks of buckskin wristguards in Surprise Valley and Stewart (1941:384) lists them for groups adjacent to Pyramid Lake. Steward (1933:263) notes that they were absent in Owens Valley.

[16] Kelly (1932:144): bows could "shoot hard—50'; a well shot arrow penetrated a deer 3 or 4 inches."

[17] Stewart (1941:384) suggests both two-ply and three-ply bow strings for Pyramid Lake. The twisting process is the same as for manufacturing cordage of hemp (see Wheat 1967:58 and Cordage, Nets, and Weaving, below).

[18] Park collected three arrows from ND. They ranged from 80 to 83 cm (AMNH 50.2/3643-5). Stewart's (1941:384) consultants from Pyramid Lake and vicinity did not give length figures. Those from areas farther east and north suggested 2-3 ft. Kelly (1932:143) gives the following dimensions for Surprise Valley arrows: for bear and elk, 3-4 ft; deer and antelope, 3 ft; birds, *ca.* 15 in.

[19] Riddell (1960:48) also suggests this method, as does Kelly (1932:143). Stewart (1941:385) lists its presence for all Northern Paiute bands surveyed. Steward (1933:260) suggests that willow was heated and bent by hand.

[20] Steward (1933:260) describes several grooved stone "straighteners," some of which may be smoothers. Kelly

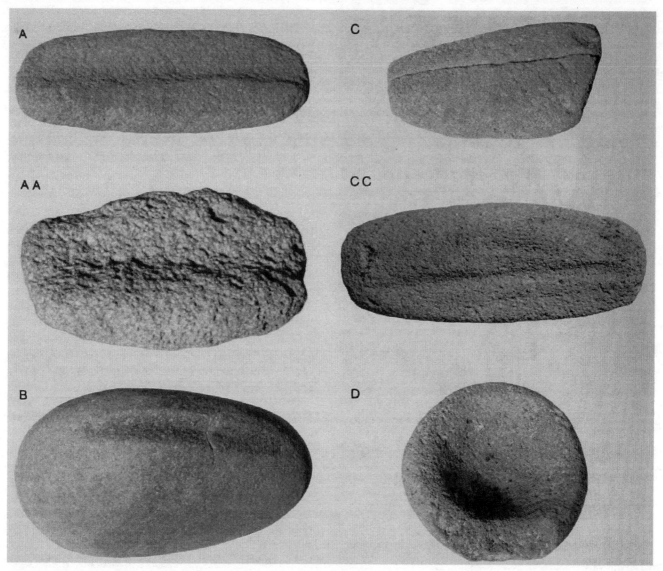

Figure 21. Bow and arrow making. a, aa. Scoria shaft rasp in two parts, both grooved (a, 10.5 cm, and aa, 7.3 cm long). MAI 13/3891. b. Shaft straightener for cane arrows, groove darkened and smooth (12.5 cm long). MAI 13/3888. c, cc. Tufa wood rasps for bow making and other wood work (c, 15 cm, and cc, 14.5 cm long). MAI 13/4409. d. Scoria mortar, used in mixing paint to pitch arrows (8.5 cm diameter at rim). MAI 13/3893. a, b, d collected by M. R. Harrington, Pyramid Lake, 1924; c at Walker River.

The end was hollowed out to take a greasewood point. The point is larger than the arrowshaft. These were used for small game. For deer and other large game arrow points of obsidian were used. Large cone-shaped greasewood points were used for hunting ducks. It would glance along the top of the water when shot at ducks, just as a flat rock will skim along over the surface when thrown.[21] The cone-shaped arrow point was about ¾ in. in diameter. These are called *pühü poŋos* [fig. 22]. Rabbit arrows are called *kaməpoŋos*. These are blunt but smaller than duck arrows. Arrows with obsidian points are called *pagapʾ*. Arrow points of obsidian are called *taka*. *Kwasipagap* is a complete arrow. The arrows with no points used by boys are called *poŋos*.[22] The bow and arrow together are called *adü*.

(1932:143) describes smoothers as two flattened and grooved stones. See fig. 21 for shapes of both from museum collections. Stewart (1941:385) lists two-piece "staighteners" (*paavi*) as present at Pyramid Lake, but absent from Honey Lake. They may have been principally for hardwood shafts.

[21] Steward (1933:260-61) describes and illustrates duck arrows with foreshafts "wrapped with sinew to form a bulge making the arrow skip on the water." See also fig. 22.

[22] The difference between the terms *pagapi* and *poŋosa* seems to involve point attachment: i. e., *pagapi* is obsidian-tipped while *poŋosa* has only a greasewood foreshaft. Kelly (1932:143)

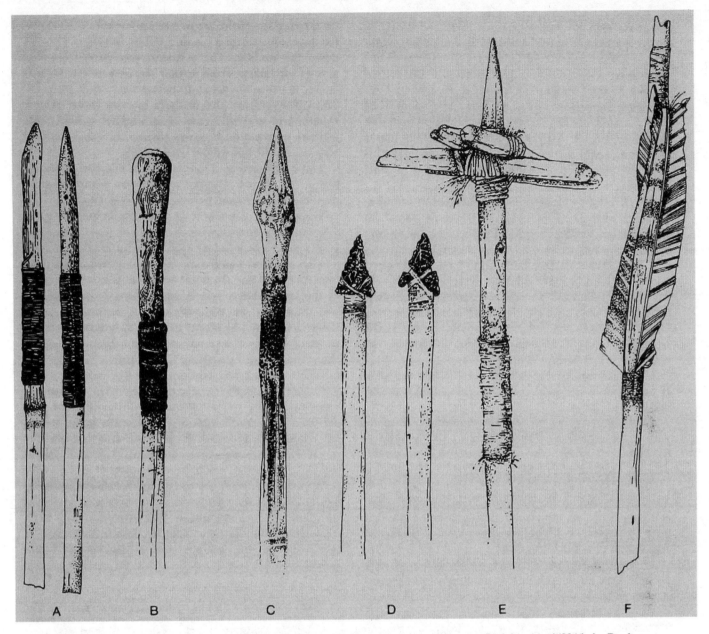

Figure 22. Arrow types. a. Composite, greasewood foreshaft, cane shaft, for small game. PM 34-114-10/3915. b. Duck arrow, greasewood bunt, cane shaft. PM 34-114-10/3959. c. Rabbit arrow, greasewood plug, serviceberry shaft. PM 34-114-10/3958. d. Game or war arrow (model), obsidian point, rosewood shaft. AMNH 50.2/3777. e. Bird arrow alternative, crossed greasewood pins. MPM 21980. f. Spiral fletching. a, b, c, d collected by W. Z. Park, Pyramid Lake, 1934; e collected by S. A. Barrett, western Nevada, 1916. Drawings by Susan Lohse.

The feathers on the arrows were split by pulling them apart. It was started about ½ in. from the end. Then the edge was smoothed by scraping with an obsidian knife. The feathers were trimmed with glowing coals.[23]

A little of the feather [shaft] is left on the end on the stripped side in order to tie it. The end nearest the nock (picigu) is tied first. Tugasawa are the feathers on the arrows. They are fixed in a spiral in order to make the arrow go straight.[24] Owl, sagehen, eagle, and wood-

notes that hunting and game arrows are called baqubᵘ in Surprise Valley.

[23] See HS's account, below. Kelly (1932:144) gives the length of Surprise Valley Paiute arrow feathers as 5-6 in. If they were longer, they were cut. She says nothing about trimming.

[24] Riddell (1960:48) assumes that feathers were radially attached. Steward (1933:260) states that "occasional feather spiraling seems accidental" in Owens Valley. Stewart (1941:385) lists spiraling for all Northern Paiute bands.

pecker feathers are used on arrows.[25] The top wrapping on the feathers is *nutamɔ*; *piwɔtamɔ* is the bottom wrapping. Feathers are lashed on with sinew (*tamo*). Then the lashing is covered with pine pitch.[26] Paint is used around the shaft under the feathers for decoration. They are never painted on any other part of the shaft. The shaft is called *tupadɔpⁱ*. Arrows were made any time that they were needed. Arrows had no distinguishing marks but a man could tell his own arrows.[27] A boy made his own bow and arrows when he was old enough to start hunting.

HS-D: Willows for arrows were gathered in summer. Bamboo cane [*Phragmites australis*] that is found in Winnemucca Valley, Lovelock, Fallon, along the Carson River and in other places is also used in making arrows. The cane for arrows is gathered in the fall. Cane is better than willow for making arrows. It is lighter and very strong. The weight throughout the length of the cane is more even than in a willow. Cane arrows shoot straighter. Cane growing in the mountains around springs is the best for arrows. It is strong and less brittle than the cane that grows along the rivers.

Chokecherry (*tɔshabuⁱ*) is often used to make arrows. It was about as good as cane. Wild rose (*siabɪ*) was also used.[28]

Compound arrows for war and hunting were made with a mainshaft of cane, a foreshaft of greasewood (*tonobɪ*) and a point either of greasewood or obsidian. The shank of the foreshaft was inserted in the hollow cane and tied with a sinew.[29] The point is put into a V-shaped socket in the foreshaft. If it fits snugly, the arrow is ready for use; if not, string is tied around it once. The point is fastened in the socket of the arrow with warm pine pitch [fig. 22d].

Hunting arrows are feathered. Those used in war are not feathered for the people have no time to put feathers on them. Also, if the arrow has no feathers it is harder for the enemy to see it coming.[30] The feathers were split down the middle. The feathers were fastened to the arrows with sinew. Each feather was fastened in a radial curve, to cause the arrow to twist when it was shot [fig. 22f]. *Who'siabɪ* are the feathers on the arrow. When chokecherry and wild rose were used for arrows three feathers were put on.[31] Arrows from these woods always stayed straight but willow would warp.

Hot coals were used to even up the edges of the feathers on the arrows. The red woodpecker feathers[32] were used most of the time because they were easy to get.

Greasewood points were usually used in hunting while the obsidian points were used in warfare. The greasewood points were a little larger than the shaft of the arrow.[33] The greasewood was ground into a point with a grooved piece of sandstone, the point being rubbed in the groove in the stone. There was a special arrow for mudhens and ducks and for the rabbit drive. Instead of being sharp the point was blunt. A piece of greasewood 2-3 in. long was fitted into one end of the shaft. An arrow was straightened by wetting it with saliva. Then it was heated in a small fire, and immediately put between the teeth and bent in the proper direction. When the arrow was straightened to the satisfaction of the operator who squinted down the length of it after each bend, it was run through the groove in the piece of sandstone in order to polish it. Arrows were painted with red and yellow marks so each man would know his own.[34]

Arrows were never carried in the hand when in pursuit of game or the enemy—only the bow was carried in the hand. The arrow quiver was carried on the back diagonally from the right shoulder. Points of the arrows would be in the bottom—the largest part of the quiver.[35]

---

[25] Kelly (1932:144) lists arrow feathers as from the wing feathers of sagehen, goose, swan, duck or crow. Riddell (1960:48) lists duck wing and sagehen tail as preferred at Honey Lake. Steward (1933:260) lists hawk and eagle feathers from birds raised in captivity in Owens Valley.

[26] Kelly (1932:144) does not discuss lashing but states that feathers were secured with fish glue or juniper or pine pitch. Stewart (1941:385) lists both alternatives for all bands. Steward (1933:Fig. 3e) illustrates feather attachment: quill attached at bottom, quill folded back and attached at top.

[27] But see HS-D below.

[28] Alternative materials for other Northern Paiute groups include (GK-WR) rosewood; Owens Valley (Steward 1933), cane or willow; Kelly (1932:143), Surprise Valley: "rose (*tsiabɪ*), currant (*pohonobɪ*), service (*wükwükobü* and *tüabɪ*) and possible young cattail (*toibü*)." Serviceberry arrows were made for boys only, although she notes that she saw duck arrows of that material at Beatty, Oregon. Riddell (1960) lists serviceberry and arrow cane for Honey Lake Northern Paiute.

[29] See JB's account, below.

[30] An unfeathered fishing arrow was used rarely in Surprise Valley, according to Kelly (1932). Steward (1933:260) also lists unfeathered fishing arrows for the Owens Valley Paiute.

[31] The number of feathers listed is usually three for Owens Valley (Steward 1933:260); invariably three for Surprise Valley (Kelly 1932:144). Riddell (1960:48) says always three unless they didn't have enough, then two. Lowie (1924:245) suggests either two or three; Stewart (1941:385) lists two or three.

[32] Identification is probably Northern Flicker (*Colaptes auratus*).

[33] This statement probably refers to width rather than length.

[34] There seems to be some controversy over the matter of arrow painting. Kelly's (1932) consultants say arrows were not painted. Stewart (1941:385) says that this was frequently done. Steward (1933) shows painting over sinew.

[35] But compare the following by JG-PL: "When a man was carrying nothing on his back the arrow quiver was slung on his back. The string made of *wiha* was over the left shoulder. When a man was on the trail all the arrows were in the quiver until he came on the track of a deer, when he took an

JB-PL: Arrows were made of *wakokob*ª, a kind of bamboo [*Phragmites australis*]. A hot rock with a groove the size of an arrow is used. The arrow is worked in the groove to straighten it. This is done while the rock is hot [fig. 21b].[36]

The arrow was wrapped all the way along to prevent its splitting.[37] The bamboo was cut about half way between the joint and greasewood inserted up into the joint. It was wrapped with sinew to keep it in. The greasewood projects from ½ to 2 in. The arrow head is put on the end where the greasewood is.

Eagle feathers were used on arrows, usually three feathers about 2 or 3 in. along the arrow with wet sinew.

BR-PL: There are four kinds of arrows:[38] 1) a blunt point used for rabbits; 2) a sharpened wooden point with foreshaft of cane and point of greasewood used for prairie dogs;[39] 3) poisoned arrow with a flint head used for big game; 4) and a bird arrow. About 1½ in. from the end of the bird arrow, a string was tied around the shaft a couple of times and two cross pieces about 2–3 inches long were put on each side. Those are tied on with two more cross pieces running in the opposite direction. The end of the arrow is blunt. It was used for small birds for close shooting. [fig. 22e].

Figure 23. Quiver of coyote skin. PM 34-114-10/3926. Collected by W. Z. Park, Pyramid Lake, 1934. Drawing by Susan Lohse.

Arrow Quivers

HS-D: The arrow quiver (*hugu'na*) was made of buckskin. It was made of a single piece of skin. It was not made on a frame. The quiver was large enough to hold as many as a hundred arrows. Sometimes it was made from an entire coyote skin. [fig. 23].

HW-Y: the quiver (*hugutna*) is made of coyote skin or of the skin of some other very fast animal. A wild cat skin is good for an arrow quiver. It holds many arrows.

---

arrow in his hand to be ready to shoot. When an arrow was needed it was pulled from the quiver with the right hand. The arrows were in the quiver with the points projecting. The feathered ends were in the bottom of the quiver. If the points were in the bottom of the sack it would be too hard to pull them out."

[36] Straighteners for cane arrows in Owens Valley are rounded rocks with grooves across the convex surface: "bun-shaped" according to Steward (1933; see also Liljeblad and Fowler, 1986: fig. 3a). Fig. 21b illustrates a cane shaft straightener collected by M. R. Harrington at Walker River in 1924. S. A. Barrett collected examples of this same style at Pyramid Lake in 1916.

[37] Only one of the five men interviewed mentioned this continuous wrapping.

[38] Steward (1933) lists special arrow designs for game and war, rabbits, ducks, birds, and fish for the Owens Valley Paiute.

[39] Probably ground squirrels (*Spermophilus beldingi*, *S. townsendii*).

Arrow Poison

[Three types of arrow poison were described by the nine men and one woman Park interviewed on the subject: (1) rotted deer meat, liver, or blood poison; (2) rattlesnake poison; and (3) red ant poison. Three individuals described the use of the first, five the second, and two the third. Rattlesnake poison was most popular at Pyramid Lake, and red ant poison at Walker River. Three accounts are reproduced below, with supplementary notes added where pertinent.]

HS-D: Arrow points were dipped in rotten venison.[40] After the venison had dried and rotted in the sun, it was rubbed on a stone until it was in the form of powder. The powder was dampened and with the finger it was smeared on the point of the arrow. The arrow head was

---

[40] JB-PL suggests specifically rotten deer liver, and RP-WR says deer blood mixed with the air sac of trout. Lowie (1924:245) notes poison of "mixed livers of different animals." Stewart (1941:385) lists poison of decayed deer meat as used by all Northern Paiute bands with liver present at Pyramid Lake and Lovelock and decayed deer heart blood also at Pyramid Lake. Steward (1933:263) lists three types of poison for the Owens Valley Paiute: (1) a yellow mineral (*moata*); (2) decayed substance from a "sack"/gall bladder on the left side of deer, mountain sheep stomach, dried; and (3) a concoction of several substances, including dried deer heart blood. Kelly (1932:145) lists poison from deer's *akwatsi* which she suggests is probably the spleen. It is more likely the gall bladder.

fixed on the shaft so that it easily came away and left the arrow point in the wound.[41] They used poisoned arrows to hunt deer, antelope and mountain sheep.[42] The poison was carried in deer or badger skin pouches. Sometimes the poison was carried in the quiver with the arrows.

AM-PL: For arrow poison, you cut off the head of a rattlesnake and take the poison sack.[43] Dip the arrow heads in the poison. Poison is called *tutaigəpə.* AM's father would take him out hunting when he was a boy. His father would sneak very close to the deer. When he shot the deer only a scratch or a light wound was necessary with the poison. The arrow shaft usually drops out but the head with the poison stays in the wound. He tracked the wounded deer and if it gets dark he goes home and starts out early the next day to track it again. When he finds the deer he butchers it and brings it back. He leaves any he cannot carry. The poison never harms the meat.[44] AM thinks poison made from rotten deer meat would be too weak,[45] and would only last a short time —two or three days at the most—then it would lose its strength. Rattlesnake arrow poison was used in warfare.[46] If a person were shot with an arrow poisoned in this way the wound would begin to swell. If there were no Indian doctor around who understood this kind of wound[47] the person would die. The doctor takes out a piece of flint and then sucks the blood—black stuff. The poison does not harm the doctor.

GK-WR: To make arrow poison, red ants were killed and mashed up with the blood of deer, or mountain sheep. This mixture was dried. When it was used, it was dampened and smeared on the arrow points.[48] GK has not heard of rattlesnake poison used on arrows.

ADDITIONAL WEAPONS

[The following are notes on miscellaneous weapons either described briefly or denied by Park's respondents.]

---

[41] See illustration of hunting arrow, fig. 22d.

[42] Confirmed by Kelly (1932:145), Steward (1933:263), Lowie (1924:245).

[43] Whole head of the rattlesnake, according to BB-PL; rattlesnake "grease" according to BR-L, PL.

[44] Confirmed for various types of poisons by Steward (1933:263) and Kelly (1932:145).

[45] Neither JG-PL nor BB-PL had heard of deer meat poison. On the other hand, JB-PL told Park that "a very few used rattlesnake poison, but most did not believe in it."

[46] This use also confirmed by Steward (1933:263), Kelly (1932:145) and Lowie (1924:245).

[47] That is, if a man did not have rattlesnake power? See Shamanism, in vol. 2.

[48] GK-WR: This poison would kill a man very quickly.

Sling

JG-PL: The sling[49] was called *tukwiboin.* The string for a sling was made of *wiha (Apocynum cannabinum).* Tanned skin from just above the deer's ankle was used. This skin was tougher.[50] Holes were made in both ends of the skin for the strings. One string was about 2 in. shorter than the other. The strings were about 2½–3 ft long. The longer string was wrapped around the middle finger several times near the base of the finger, with the end of it between the first and second fingers. The end of the shorter string was held between the thumb and first finger.[51] This string was released when the sling was whirling. A stone, a quarter the size of an ordinary fist or smaller was used. Stones that were somewhat rounded were selected. Flat stones were not used. The stones were called *tupi,* the word for any kind of rocks or stones. Clay balls or pellets were not used with the sling.

Slings were used for small game such as rabbits, sagehen, etc. They were used when a man could not get close enough to shoot with a bow and arrow. Slings were not used for large game or in warfare.[52]

Spears

JG-PL thinks that spears were not used.[53] [But see Warfare in chap 9.]

Rabbit Clubs

JG-PL stated that rabbit clubs were not known. *HS-D* stated that clubs were used to kill rabbits.[54]

---

[49] One of Riddell's (1960:49) Honey Lake Paiute consultants described the sling, called *pagas' tutabin°.* Stewart (1933:259) states that "slings, made of leather in recent days, were of minor importance" in Owens Valley. Stewart (1941:386) lists slings used as childeren's toys for all Northern Paiute bands.

[50] Riddell (1960:49) states that the Honey Lake Paiute slings described were entirely of leather with a diamond-shaped patch in the center.

[51] Riddell (1960:49) states of the Honey Lake Paiute sling: "One thong had a loop to go around the middle finger. The end of the other thong was held between the thumb and forefinger."

[52] ND-HL told Stewart (1941:386) that slings were used for war and hunting in addition to being used as toys.

[53] Kelly (1932:145) notes that in Surprise Valley, spears were also apparently unknown. Only one consultant thought otherwise. Steward (1933:259) states that in Owens Valley "spears were used little if at all, except in fishing." One Pyramid Lake consultant also mentioned the thrusting spear as a war weapon to Stewart (1941:385).

[54] Presence reported by Steward (1933:386) for Owens Valley and by Stewart (1941:367) for all but the Surprise Valley Paiute (see also Kelly 1932:88). These clubs were apparently not thrown (Stewart 1941:367), thus perhaps differing from

Shields

JG-PL: A few warriors had round shields which were about 4 ft in diameter. They were made of deer skin and put around a frame of chokecherry wood (a hard wood) and hard willows [fig. 24]. Only a few had these shields.[55]

HW-Y: Shields (*topu*) were made of deerskin (from the back of the neck and hardened) and were about 24 in. in diameter and circular. They were put on a wooden hoop, and tied in back like a drum. There were two small holes in the shield so that a man could put it before his face and look through. These were captured in a fight if possible.

Armor

HS-D: Dried buffalo and horsehide were used for armor.[56]

STONE TECHNOLOGY

[Stone technology was probably but remnant knowledge by the time Park worked in the area. It is obvious from the manuscripts and notebooks that he inquired into the subject, but the information he received from five individuals was minimal and sketchy. Some other implements are described in sections on Hide Processing, below, and Hunting, in chap. 2.]

Obsidian Sources

JG-PL: Obsidian, *pizu'mp* was obtained from a hill near Eaglesville [*sic*, Eagleville] in California. *Takakuda'wa'* ["arrowpoint hill"] is the name of the hill.[57] Arrowpoints of this are called *taka*. People went from Pyramid Lake to this hill for the obsidian. This hill was in the territory

Figure 24. Shield, rawhide over chokecherry hoop; crossed lines in white clay. PM 35-120-10/5191. Collected by W. Z. Park, Pyramid Lake, 1935. Drawing by Susan Lohse.

belonging to *kidutuka*, ["marmot eaters" or Surprise Valley Paiute]. This is around Surprise Valley, around Cedarville. Sometimes five or six men went for the obsidian. They brought back enough to make knives and arrow points. These were made when they brought the obsidian home.[58] If they had enough they gave their friends some. Some of the obsidian was sold, usually for arrows or beads measured on the back of the thumb from the end of the second knuckle.[59]

RP-WR: Obsidian for knives, arrow heads, etc., was gotten in the mountains south of Walker Lake, near Hawthorne. The place where obsidian was gotten was called *takatubi?i*.[60]

Knapping

JG-PL: Knives and arrowpoints were flaked. First the flint [obsidian] was cooked, softened, under hot ashes.[61]

---

the Southwest variety of curved rabbit sticks (see Underhill 1953:112-13).

[55] Shields of rawhide with wooden rims and decorated with feathers were described by Stewart's (1941:385-86) Winnemucca Valley and Pyramid Lake consultants.

[56] Armor denied by all of Stewart's (1941:386) consultants. HS-D may be referring to shields as described in note 55. That the comment may refer to the Bannock or Northern Shoshoni is also possible (see Steward (1943:315)).

[57] HS-D: "Obsidian was obtained from northern Washoe County." ND- HL: "Obsidian (*piza^{mu}*) was obtained from the mountains around Surprise Valley." Riddell (1960:50) notes Honey Lake Paiute reference to a "Flint Mountain," *dakakudak^w*, a hill near Gerlack, Nev. Kelly (1932:131) notes a large deposit at the south end of Cow Head Lake in Surprise Valley. The latter deposit is approximately 40 mi north of JG's source near Eagleville. Nodules of obsidian are scattered in various places from roughly Leadville, Nev., north and west. The exact location of this particular *takakudak^w a* is unknown.

---

[58] JB-PL: "They chipped off whatever they wanted and carried it home in a buckskin bag where it was used to make knives (*wi.hi*) and arrow points (*taka*)."

[59] See Miscellaneous Beliefs and Customs in vol. 2 for methods of measuring, and Trade, chap. 9.

[60] The exact location of *takatubi?i* is unknown. However, good obsidian quarries are said to be located at Mt. Hicks and Aurora Crater southwest of Walker Lake (Lonnie Pippin, personal communication, 1982). GK-WR confirms the name and general location.

[61] See also Stewart (1941:383) for mention of heat-treating "flint" at Pyramid Lake and Lovelock. Kelly (1932:141) also

The obsidian was heated and then allowed to cool until it could be held in the hand. Buckskin was wrapped around the thumb[62] and the obsidian was flaked with a piece of horn about 4 in. long. The name of the bone flaker is *mo'kano*. It was flaked with a stroke toward the operator's body.[63] The end of the deer horn was used or it was broken off so there would be a jagged edge to catch the obsidian.[64]

Knives

JG-PL: The regular knife, called *wi.hi*, was about 7 or 8 in. long. It had a point and in the middle was about 2 in. wide. Only the point was sharp. The handle was not sharp so when it was held in the hand it would not cut the hand.[65] Sticks were not attached to the obsidian knives for handles [fig. 25a]. Steel knives are now called *wi.hi*.

RP-WR: Knives were used for skinning and cutting meat. An outline of a knife owned by RP is included here [fig. 25b]. This is about the usual size and shape of knives that were used for cutting hair, thread, skin for moccasins, skinning, butchering, etc. Longer and more slender knives were used for fine work [fig. 25c]. These were called *wihi* or *taka wihi*. The long slender piece of obsidian was held in the hand and worked with a sawing motion. Both edges of the knife were sharp the entire length of the blade. It was grasped around the end of the blade without any protection for the hand. A stick was never fastened to the knife blade for a handle. Any sort of handle was unknown.

ND-HL: Stone knives (*wihi*) were not fastened to sticks for handles nor were knives wrapped. When cutting, the operator draws the knife toward himself as in using a spokeshave. The motion is the same in chipping flint by pressure. [But also from ND on another occasion:] When ND saw the spears, etc. in Plate 45 of Loud and Harrington (1929), he said (b) was nearly like a Paiute

knife with a handle. Earlier in the summer [see above] he said obsidian knives were never provided with handles.[66] The handle was 4 to 5 in. long. It was willow. One end of the handle was grooved for the obsidian blade. The blade was held in place with pine pitch and then firmly held in place with a string [fig. 25c]. To cut with one of these knives a line was made with a quick scratching movement toward the operator. Then a deeper cut was made.

Drills

ND-HL: Drills, *wadoduin*[a], were made of flint or obsidian. The drill is shaped much like an arrowpoint except that it is longer and more slender. It is fastened to a willow shaft just as an arrowpoint is fastened to the arrow shaft.[67] The drill is revolved between the hands like a fire drill.

Mortar and Pestle

JG-PL: The mortar, *paha*, and the pestle, *pahagun*[o], were made by women.[68] It takes a long time to make a mortar. The bluish hard rock is gotten for the pestle.[69] The mortar is made of softer rock.[70] The pestle is from a

---

describes warming stone on coals prior to flaking. Lowie (1924:225) presents J. W. Powell's (1895:27-28) account of Ute stone working including heat treating. Steward (1933:262) notes heat treating of blanks held in cedar splints wrapped with moist buckskin for Round Valley (north end of Owens Valley).

[62] Steward (1933:262) notes that buckskin was placed on the hand when flaking in Owens Valley. Stewart (1941:383) also lists a buckskin pad for flaking for most Northern Paiute groups surveyed. Kelly (1932:141) received two Surprise Valley Paiute accounts of flaking: one with and one without the pad.

[63] See also ND-HL, below.

[64] That is to create a friction surface.

[65] Riddell (1960:50) described a Honey Lake Paiute skinning knife owned by one informant as similar in shape; i. e., pointed at one end, rounded at the other, ovoid, but in this case 3½ in. to 4 in. long and 1½ to 2 in. wide.

[66] There may be two types of knives under discussion here. Kelly (1932:141) notes that Surprise Valley Paiute knives were of two sizes with some hafted and others not. They were carried at a man's waist in a special sack that also contained his fire drill and hearth. Steward (1933:277) also describes two types for Owens Valley: (1) a "skinning knife" of obsidian, 8 in. long, one end pointed, the other concave and unhafted; and (2) a hafted knife 4½ in. long (see his figs. 3i and 3j). Stewart (1941:382) also lists both types for various Northern Paiute bands.

[67] See section on Arrows, above. Apparently ND is referring to the manner of fastening with pitch and then binding with sinew. Stewart (1941:383) also notes drills were attached with glue. Steward (1933:277) notes "T" shaped drills recovered archaeologically in Owens Valley were not reconized by consultants. Riddell (1960:50) lists "flint" drills for working buckskin for the Honey Lake Paiute. Stewart (1941:383) also lists hafted drills for Pyramid Lake and Winnemucca Valley but notes in addition that some knives were also used as drills by all Northern Paiute groups surveyed.

[68] Stewart (1941:381, 431) received conflicting reports on the indigenous manufacture of mortars. One consultant reported that they were made in the Lovelock area. Others attributed their manufacture to coyote, deer, or the *saidoka*, the previous occupants of the Humboldt Sink (see Mythology in vol. 2). Kelly (1932:139) reports some use of archaeological specimens by Surprise Valley Paiute, with one consultant remarking, "What would we use those for? We have no hard seeds." Steward (1933:240) notes that they were not used by the Owens Valley Paiute, but were by the adjacent Death Valley Shoshoni.

[69] Stone identification possibly greenstone, or a fine granite.

[70] Stone identification probably scoria or other volcanic material.

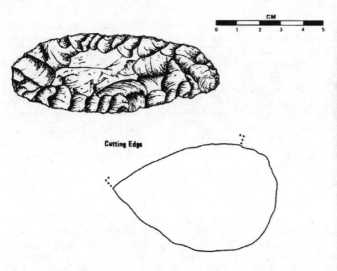

Figure 25. Stone knives. a (top left). Drawing of obsidian knife used for cutting and scraping inside of hide for tanning (9.9 cm). PM 34-114-10/3928. Collected by W. Z. Park, Pyramid Lake, 1934. b (bottom left). Outline of knife owned by RP-WR, from Park's field drawing (10 cm). c (right). Obsidian blade (13.2 cm) and hafted knife (13.6 cm) with buckskin-wrapped handle. MPM 21784 and 21955. Collected by S. A. Barrett, Walker River, 1916. Drawings by Patricia DeBunch.

foot to a foot and a half long. The pestle is shaped and rounded by pounding with a piece of rock. The pestle is made tapering to a sharp end. With the sharp end of the pestle the rock for the mortar is pounded until the bowl is formed. The pestle was not ringed.[71] The pestle is also called *tutabino* [fig. 26a].

The mortar and pestle were often used for pinenuts and acorns. With a mortar and pestle the nuts could be ground more quickly than with the metate. The mortar does not grind seeds so finely. The metate was used for fine seeds. These could not be ground in a mortar. The mortar and pestle were not carried when moving camp. They were cached to be used when the family returned to that camp site.[72] A few families still use the mortar and pestle although its use is not general. In the old days the mortar was probably not used as commonly as the metate.

Bedrock mortars were made in the pinenut hills.[73] JG has seen them in the Pine Grove Range west of Wellington. These mortars were made at a place where

people camped every year. The pestle was left at the mortar. These bedrock mortars belonged to certain families, but anyone could use them. Shades were not built over bedrock mortars.[74]

HW-Y: The mortar (*paha*) has a large depression with a smaller round hole in the center. The seeds are ground in the hole and the flour banks up and is held in the depression in the stone. Women made the mortar and pestle (*pagun*).

Metate and Mano

JG-PL: The metate is called *mata*. The muller is called *tusu* [fig. 26c]. The smaller seeds, about the size of alfalfa seeds, were ground on the metate. Pinenuts were ground with the mortar. The metate was usually buried near the camp along the river where the family stayed in the winter and spring.[75] It was not carried to the pinenut hills in the fall for the mortar and pestle were kept there for grinding the pinenuts. The metate is used today in almost every family. It is used to grind pinenuts, seeds and wheat or other grains. It was possible to grind seeds faster with the mortar than with the metate.

HW-Y: Only one side of the metate (*mata*) was used for a grinding surface.[76] The metate is used for grinding

[71] Ringed pestles are common in California (Jennings 1974). Ringed "ice picks" were also reported from Lovelock Cave (Loud and Harrington 1929:plate 54) and might have been shown to consultants by Park. The pestle in Figure 26a is at least grooved.

[72] Kelly (1932:139) also notes that mortars were cached.

[73] JG-PL is probably speaking specifically of the Pine Grove Range west of Wellington, Nev., rather than everywhere in pinenut country. Bedrock mortars were used by the Mono Lake Paiute (Davis 1965:12) for pounding dried meat and berries. Stewart (1941:381) reports their use for pinenuts, acorns, and other seeds by various Northern Paiute bands. Riddell (1960:49) also notes their use by the Honey Lake Paiute.

[74] Park is probably asking here with reference to the Washo practice of pounding acorns under a shade (Price 1962).

[75] Kelly (1932:139) notes that a small-sized metate was carried on journeys in a burden basket. See also HS-D, below.

[76] Although not noted by Park's consultant, the two surfaces of metates may have been used for different purposes. Lowie (1924:204-5) notes that one surface was used for crack-

Figure 26. Ground stone tools. a (top left). Stone mortar (34.5 cm) and pestle (33 cm) of type used to grind pinenuts and acorns. MAI 13/4405, 4406. b (bottom left). Wuzzie George, Stillwater, demonstrating use of mano and metate to grind pinenuts. Photograph by L. Mills, 1953. c (top and middle right). Metate (45 cm) and mano (18 cm) used to grind pinenuts and seeds. MAI 13/3882. d (bottom right). Wooden mortar (32.5 cm) and stone pestle (52 cm) used to grind pinenuts and acorns. MAI 13/4407. a, d collected by M. R. Harrington, Walker River, 1924; c at Pyramid Lake.

pinenuts and small seeds. It is used more than the mortar and pestle. The muller (*tusu*) is rubbed back and forth on the metate with both hands.

Every family had a metate. It was made of hard rock. The old people do not like any other kind. The muller and metate were chipped into shape with a flat rock.

HS-D: Mortar (*podanu*) and metate (*mata*) were used in grinding seeds. Mortars were usually not carried when the family moved. Metate and muller, *tusano*, were always

taken along. Parching trays might be cached with the mortar and pestle to be used when the family moved back again.

Miscellaneous Stone Tools

JG-PL: Adzes and wedges were not used. Only slender willow poles were split. This was done by pounding one end with a rock and then with the hands, the pole was split apart in the cleavage started by the pounding of the end.

Poles that were driven in the river bottom in the construction of weirs were not sharpened more than the

---

ing the shells of certain hard seeds while the other was used as the flour grinding surface. JB-PL and RP-WR also say only one side was used.

ragged point made when the pole was broken from the tree. The poles set in the ground for the frame of the house were not sharpened. Holes were dug in which the poles were placed. Stone hammers and axes were not used.[77] For a hammer, a stone was used without a handle.

BONE TOOLS

[Park received few direct statements on the manufacture and use of bone tools— awls, scrapers, and flackers being primary. But, some additional comments on these and their uses are given in the context of discussion of clothing and basketry manufacture, hide processing, and the making of stone tools. See especially the latter for the discussion of flackers.]

HS-D: A needle (*mokano*)[78] is made from a small narrow bone in the deer's foreleg. It is sharpened on stone. It has no eye, but it is used like an awl. Sinew (*tamo*) is used in sewing and on the backs of bows. It is used with this needle.

ND-HL: The small bone of the forearm of the deer is sharpened by rubbing on a stone. There is no eye in the bone. It is used in sewing as an awl. The men usually made the awl (*witu*). In sewing the awl was pushed through and the garment was turned so it could be pushed through again [from the other side].

JB-PL: The thigh bone or rib bone of deer, seasoned well and scraped to sharpness, was used as a scraper to dehair deerskin. A deer scraper was used to make the greasewood digging stick (*pǝdǝ*). It [the digging stick] was finally sharpened with an obsidian knife.

HOUSEHOLD TOOLS

Cooking Stones

HS-D: Each household had about 12 cooking stones. These we carried along in a buckskin bag each time the family moved.[79]

Hot Stone Lifters

RP-WR: The hot cooking rocks were picked up with a willow stick fastened in a triangle. It was tied at the

apex where it was held. Another straight stick was used to work the rocks onto the triangular stick. The triangular stick is called *padu*. The stick used for getting the rocks onto the loop is called *tuzikwituinyo* [fig. 27a].

Stirring Sticks

RP-WR: A willow stick looped at one end is used to stir mush. It is about 2 ft long. It is twisted back on itself and bent and the handle is tied in several places along its length. It is called *padu*.[80]

HS-D: A spoon, *sɔkɔ*, is used to stir and ladle out mush and to take rocks out of the cooking basket. It has a handle about 18 in. long. The frame and handle are of wild rose. It is woven with willow strands.[81] The handle is double. It is simply an extension of the frame of the spoon.

FIRE MAKING

[Five men described the fire making process to Park. All agreed that a drill using an arrow as a mainshaft was most typical. One account of the process is given below, with references to details contained in the others. Supplemental notes on fire tending and the slow match are also added.]

Fire Drills

HS-D: Fire was made with a drill (*wa'i*) [the hearth; fig. 27 b,c]. The hearth was a flat piece of cedar[82] about 5 in. long.[83] The drill was made from sagebrush gotten in

---

[77] Kelly (1932:138) also notes that the Surprise Valley Paiute did not have axes. Stewart (1941:383) reports the use of broken cobbles for chopping and natural cobbles for hammering among all but one Northern Paiute group.

[78] There may be some confusion in terminology here, as *mukan.u* is ordinarily reserved for the bone or antler flaker (see Stone Technology, above), and the term *witi* for an awl.

[79] The count of cooking stones at 10 to 12 was confirmed by JB-PL and RP-WR.

[80] RP-WR gave the term *padu* for both the looped stirring stick and the looped stick used to lift hot stones from a cooking basket—perhaps one and the same implement in some areas. Stewart's (1941:377, 382) data suggest the widespread use of a pair of straight sticks to lift hot stones and a looped stick (*patu*) to stir mush. He also notes the use of a "paddle" [probably wooden] among some groups.

[81] Stewart's (1941:382) data also include this implement, apparently with a woven basketry blade or scoop, but suggest its use more as a dipper or spoon.

[82] Stewart (1941:381) also notes a preference for juniper by his Winnemucca Valley and Pyramid Lake consultants. Others interviewed by Park suggested hearths of sagebrush — old sagebrush. This wood was listed by Stewart's (1941:381) Lovelock and Stillwater consultants as well as others farther east and south. See also Lowie (1924:223) and Steward (1933:276) for data on sagebrush hearths and Kelly (1932:142) for juniper hearths.

[83] HS-D does not list the number of holes in the fire drill. JB-PL told Park there were either 4 or 5 holes. BB-PL said there were 5. Stewart (1941:381) lists the number of holes as an "indefinite number" for all bands surveyed. Lowie (1924:222) notes 4 pits, probably for the Stillwater Paiute. Kelly (1932:142) notes 2–4 or more for the Surprise Valley Paiute.

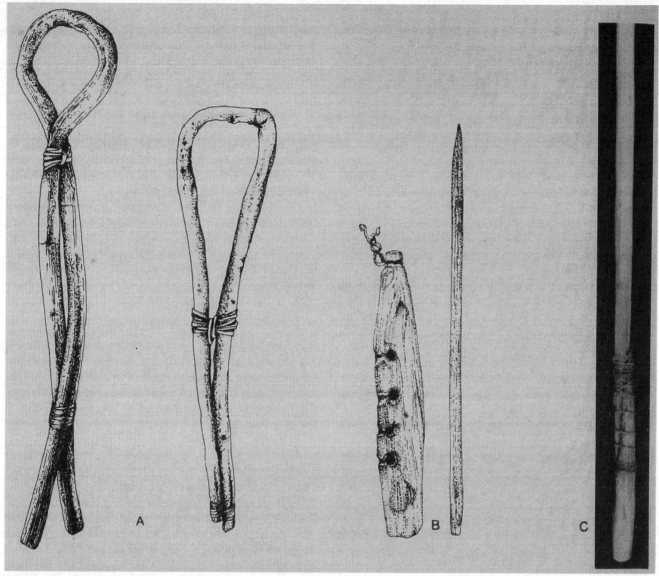

Figure 27. Household equipment. a. Cooking tools, including looped stirring stick collected by R. H. Lowie, Pyramid Lake, 1914 (AMNH 50.2/7903), and triangular stick used for stirring and lifting hot cooking stones, collected by S. Liljeblad, Fallon, 1965. Idaho State Museum of Natural History 5370. b. "Paiute" fire drill and hearth, collected by P. S. Sargent, Nevada, 1926. LMA 2-13001a,b. c. Honey Lake composite fire drill with tip of sage. Collected by W. Z. Park, 1934. AMNH 50.2/3663. Drawings by Susan Lohse.

the mountains. It was more brittle there. The drill, about 5 in. long, was fixed so that it could be fitted on a cane arrow.[84] The greasewood point was taken out of the arrow and the fire drill was fixed to the arrow shaft. It is impossible to get a long piece of straight sagebrush so an arrow must be used to lengthen the drill. When dried willow was used for a drill it was not fitted to the arrow.[85]

The hearth was held in place with one foot and the drill revolved between the hands.[86] Sagebrush bark was used for tinder.

---

[84] Compound drills using either cane arrows or hardwood (willow) for shafts and foreshafts of sage are also described by Lowie (1924:222), Steward (1933:276), and Kelly (1932:142). Stewart (1941:381) lists compound drills or hardwood preferred over cane. BB-PL noted that the foreshaft was either wild rose or chokecherry rather than sagebrush.

[85] Fitting could be either by inserting the new tip into the cane shaft or lashing it to a hardwood shaft (see also Kelly 1932:142) and Lowie (1924:222). Simple drills were denied by most of Stewart's (1941:381) consultants.

[86] JB-PL: "Hearth held in place by placing knee on each end." BB-PL: Held between the feet [while in a squatting position?].

The fire drill point is carried wrapped in a piece of buckskin. It is kept with the flat cedar hearth in the arrow quiver.[87] Fine sagebrush bark for tinder was also carried.

JG-PL: Men usually made fire with a fire drill. Women sometimes used a fire drill, but not often.[88] Men always carried fire drills when they went hunting. Men usually drilled for fire because they always had the fire drill. Quartz was not used for fire making.[89]

Fire Tending

JB-PL: A fire was started with sagebrush bark as tinder and sagebrush wood. Then greasewood was used because it did not burn so rapidly. When people were in the mountains, they used whatever wood was available, mostly cedar, and pine if it could be found. Dry limbs were found and broken up with the hands. A large limb was put on the fire before going to bed. The fire would burn all night long, particularly in the fall, winter and early spring or during cold weather. Some men in the family group would get up once in a while and put a little wood on the fire. No one was designated to do this. Any man in the group might do it.

During the warm weather, the greasewood coals were covered with dirt or sand when the people went to bed. In the morning the sand was raked off and the fire was built again. This way they had a fire in the morning quickly without using the fire drill.[90]

The Slow Match

CW-PL: A roll of bark from sagebrush[91] about 1 ½ in.

in diameter and several feet long was ignited and carried around to all camps to light their fires. They used this to carry fire on a trip. Before the match is lighted it is called *wasiba.* Fire is *kasobə* and when the match is lighted it is also called *kasobə.*

HIDE PROCESSING

[Seven accounts of skin dressing, six by men,[92] were elicited by Park. All agree substantially on the general procedures. The principal point in contention has to do with whether hide smoking has always been practiced. The most detailed description of each aspect of the process is in the accounts of the four consultants quoted below. Variants are added in the footnotes.]

Skinning

BR-L, PL: When an animal is skinned, a cut is made starting at the neck and going to the crotch. The skin is cut inside the leg and around the top of the hoof. Then the skin is pulled off.[93] This must be done very carefully when skinning a deer for the deerskin is very thin. Only a little of the fat on the inside of the deerskin is scraped off before it is soaked.

Dehairing and Fleshing

BR-L,PL: When the skin was just taken from the animal it was soaked in water for two days. Then it was put over a stake 3 or 4 ft high.[94] The bone from the foreleg of the deer was sharpened with flint.[95] With this

---

[87] According to Kelly (1932:142), the Surprise Valley Paiute carried the firemaking kit either in the quiver or in a special sack tied to the waist.

[88] Surprise Valley Paiute women kindled fires—taking turns rotating the drill (Kelly 1932:142).

[89] Stewart (1941:381, 431) also notes the absence of fire kindling with stone, except by hearsay for a group on the Snake River Plain.

[90] Stewart (1941:381) and Riddell (1960:32) also note covering coals to preserve fire as common practice. See also the former for alternative method: allowing fire to burn into the roots of sage. Lowie (1924:223) and Steward (1933:276) specifically comment on the difficulty of kindling fire with a fire drill—perhaps the key factor in attempts to preserve fire. Riddell (1960:32) states that fires were not allowed to go out if at all possible. Steward (1933:276) also notes that hearths were made by men with special powers in Owens Valley.

[91] Stewart (1941:381) lists a slow match of rolled sage as common. Lowie (1924:222) and Kelly (1932:142) note that the sagebrush was specifically braided. Kelly (1932:148) states that it was a three-strand braid and that an individual stated that it was "about the size of a woman's forearm and was braided hard."

[92] Stewart (1941:383) notes that skin dressing was done by both men and women in most Northern Paiute bands. Kelly (1932:118) found it to be principally the craft of women in Surprise Valley, although with occasional assistance by men.

[93] Kelly's (1932:118) description of skinning is nearly identical, except for supplementary information noting that the ears and horns were normally left with the head rather than the hide and that hoofs were sometimes left attached to the hide. GK-WR also noted the latter practice and added that the tail was normally slit underneath so that the skin went with the hide. Skinning was also the same for mountain sheep.

[94] HS-D referred to the skinning post as the trunk of willow, about 1 ft. in diameter and 4 ft. long, with one side shaved smooth and leaned up against the house. See also Wheat (1967:78f) for details of the process and comments on new procedures.

[95] According to JB-PL, either the bone from the deer's foreleg or a deer's rib bone, seasoned well and scraped to the sharpness with "flint," was used as a fleshing and dehairing tool. Both types, each showing evidence of sharpening, were collected by Park and one is illustrated in fig. 28. Lowie (1924:227) reports dehairing with a horse rib scraper. Kelly (1932:119) was told that only the largest of the deer's ribs could be used for dehairing.

Figure 28. Hideworking. a (top left). Dehairing and fleshing tool, made of radio-ulna of deer. MPM 53106. Collected by S. A. Barrett, Walker River, 1916. b (top right). Basalt flesher and knife, used to scrape inside of hide for tanning and for cutting (12.8 cm). PM 34-114-10/3927. Collected by W. Z. Park, Pyramid Lake, 1934. Peabody Museum, Harvard University. Photograph by Hillel Burger. c (bottom left). Johnny Dunn, Pyramid Lake, removing hair from hide with draw knife. d (bottom right). Willie Jones, Walker River, stretching drying hide to soften. c, d photographs by M. M. Wheat, *ca.* 1965. University of Nevada, Reno, Library, Special Collections Department.

the hair was scraped from the soaked skin [fig. 28]. Both ends of the skin were then tied with skin or the skin from the two legs was tied together at each end. Then one end of the skin was tied to a post by the skin of the leg. A stick about 3 ft long was twisted to wring out the water. Then the skin was left overnight [see also under Tanning, below].

Tanning

ND-HL: Any kind of brain[96] is used for tanning (*tüsoŋoyo*). These should be roasted or boiled first. When the brain is cooked it is pulverized and put into a big basket of water (in winter, lukewarm water; in summer, ordinary temperature) and worked around to make sort of a suds-like soap. The roasted brains may also be put in a clean white cloth (not pulverized for this method).[97] The skin is then put in the water[98] and it is squeezed

and pulled and worked to be sure that the skin is uniformly soaked with solution. The skin is soaked until the water comes through the pores of the skin—one or two days. Then the skin is taken out and hung from a tree and a stick is put through the other end and it is twisted for about an hour. Then the skin is spread in the sun for a few minutes. When it is seen that the skin is drying it is worked by hand to make it soft and smooth. This cannot be done on a cold day. It must be done in the sunlight when it is warm. When the skin is dry, it is rubbed with a rough rock.[99] This process softens the tanned skin. ND tans a skin each year in this way. He makes moccasins and gloves to sell from it. The skin, after tanning, is called *kwasüb.* Scraping the hair is called *püwhano.*

Skins that were to be used with the hair left on were tanned by rolling them up with damp earth, burying the roll in the damp earth, and leaving it until the skin

---

[96] According to BR-L,PL, the brain of any animal could be used—rabbit, deer, mountain sheep, and now horse and cow.

[97] *HS-D:* Brains were wrapped in a very thin piece of buckskin. Stewart (1941:383) lists the use of the pericardial sac for the purpose in two Northern Paiute bands.

[98] *HS-D:* They are placed together in a very large basket. *RP-WR:* [roasted deer brains] are chewed by the men and spat into a basket of water. The skin is soaked in this water.

[99] Riddell's (1960:47) Honey Lake consultants also referred to a "rough stone, about the size of a mano . . used to clean the inner surface." GK-WR and JG-PL also note the same. The basalt knife [fig. 28] collected by Park at Pyramid Lake was also said to be used for scraping the inside of hides. See also ND's description of the use of broken cobblestone as fleshers, below. RP-WR noted only that the hide was rubbed, pulled, and stretched with the hands until dry and soft.

was thoroughly dampened but not wet.[100] This usually took from 24 to 36 hours. When it was taken out sagebrush bark was broken up fine and was put in a basket with warm water and brains and was mixed until it was thin like gravy. This mixture was rubbed and twisted until the mixture was worked into the skin. Cobblestones were broken and the rough broken sides were rubbed over the insides of the skin. When the small crevices in the rough side were filled with particles, another piece of rock was used. The scraping was done in the sun. Deer skins and the skins of other large animals (antelope, mountain sheep, etc.) were tanned this way. It was called ɔsɔkɔɔ. The damp place where the skin was buried was called sɔkɔbɔ.

For groundhog, coyote, otter skins and skins from other small animals, the brains were soaked in water and rubbed on the smooth side and the skin rolled up and left one day and one night. The hair is not scraped off. Then the skin is stretched and worked to make it soft and dry. The skins that are tanned in this way are fresh. The fat and gristle are pulled off with the fingers before the brains are rubbed on. Small skins tanned with hair on were called iwaɔabɔ. [See Clothing and Adornment, chap. 5, for uses of these small skins.]

Smoking

ND-HL: For smoking, a small hole was made in the ground. Hot charcoal was put in the hole and covered with dry willow clear of all knots. The willow was cut in short pieces. The hot charcoal causes the willow to smoulder. The tanned skin is sewed up so only one end is open. No stick frame is made to hold the skin over the fire. It is held by hand for 10, 15 or 30 minutes until it is the desired shade of yellow. Smoking is very old among the Paiutes.[101]

GK-WR: I (GK) have never seen smoking of skins here (WR). People at Pyramid Lake did that but people here never did. They say that if they smoke a skin it will not spoil so quick when it is rained on. When a skin that has not been smoked gets wet it hardens. Smoking prevents this.

---

[100] JG-PL stated that hides were pegged to the ground. Clean earth was put over them so that they would absorb moisture. The skin was rubbed and pounded with a rough stone while the earth was still on it. See also Kelly (1932:119).

[101] Both Kelly (1932:119) and Riddell (1960:47) discuss hide smoking by the same means. Neither comments as to the antiquity of the trait. Lowie (1924:227) records a term for it, but again without discussion. Stewart (1941:383) lists smoking as a widespread but not universal feature of Northern Paiute skin dressing techniques. *RP-WR*: Both men and women smoke skins. A woman smokes the skins for her dress so she will have just the color she wants.

HS-D: The Paiutes did not smoke skins in the old days. This process was learned from the people who were north of Fort Bidwell, around Beatty [Oregon].

BASKETRY

[There are seven accounts of basketry manufacture and basketry types in Park's notes. One, a lengthy account by RP-WR, is given in full below. One other, also printed in full, is based on Park's own observations of a basket weaver at work. Other notes, including some that discuss features that may be of distributional significance, follow these. See also Child Rearing in vol. 2 for an account of the construction of basketry cradles, and Fishing in chap. 2 for data on basketry fish traps.

Park collected several baskets for the American Museum of Natural History, the Lowie Museum, and the Peabody Museum of Archaeology and Ethnology. He may have intended to study them and include a more detailed analysis of these specimens as part of his ethnography. Some of the specimens he collected illustrate this section.]

Fiber Preparation

RP-WR: Willows were gathered for baskets late in the summer.[102] When the twigs are reddish in color is the best time. Then the willows are strong. In the spring the willows break easily.

The twigs are split three ways by biting with the teeth to start the ends. One of the split ends is held between the teeth. Each of the other ends is taken between the fingers and pulled down 2 or 3 in. and then the fingers are slipped down for a new hold [fig. 29a].

The inside coarse part of the willow in each strip is peeled off by holding it between the teeth and stripping the outside away from it [fig. 29b]. If the willow strips are to be used to form the dark designs on the basket the brownish bark is stripped off at once[103] after splitting in the same way as the useless inside part of the willow is stripped away.

The white smooth strips are made by drying the split willows. When used, these strips are peeled. To do this, the dried strip is put between the first and second finger of the left hand; i.e., the fingers are held horizontally and the strip is pulled straight downwards. Willows for

---

[102] Steward (1933:270) states that in Owens Valley willows were cut only in winter. Kelly (1932:120) notes that willows were considered best in the fall by Surprise Valley Paiute. See other accounts printed below for other opinions.

[103] In effect, this process leaves some of the inner layer of the bark on the stem. This apparently absorbs the dye better than a stem totally free of bark.

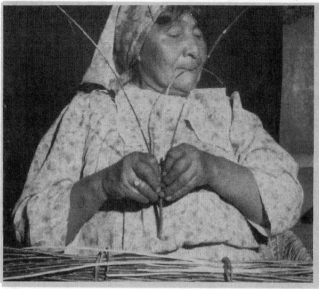

Figure 29. Processing willows. a (left). Wuzzie George, Stillwater, splitting willow for baskets. Photograph by M. M. Wheat, *ca.* 1958. University of Nevada, Reno, Library, Special Collections Department. b (right). Rosie Plummer, Walker River, removing pith from split willow. Photograph by W. Z. Park, 1934.

the rods of baskets are scraped off with a knife while they are still green.

Techniques of Manufacture

Twining
RP-WR: Twining is called *tukwicipi*. It is used to make cooking baskets, trays, bowls, spoons, seed beaters, cone baskets and water jugs. Twining for cooking baskets and bowls starts at the bottom. While working the bottom, the basket is held upside down. When the sides are reached, it is turned right side up and the side nearest the body is worked. The basket is constantly turned to keep the twining directly in front of the body. Both the bottom and the sides are worked from left to right. Trays are started at the small end and worked form right to left.[104] When the right hand edge is reached, the tray is turned over and again woven from left to right . Spoons and seed beaters are started and worked in the same way. Cone baskets and water jars are started at the bottom and worked in a circular fashion like cooking baskets and bowls. New rods [warp] are added to cone baskets to make them wider at the mouth (see Kelly 1932: fig. 5). They are added to water jars until the

middle is reached, and then they are broken out as the jar gets smaller toward the neck.[105]

Coiling
RP-WR: Coiled basketry is called *nazihidu*. Serving baskets were made in coiled ware and were very fine. These were called *nuhapi*. Three rods were used for very fine work.

When the coil is started, the first round is stitched without an awl. On the second round, an awl is used for stitching. The basket is worked upside down until the bottom is finished and the curve of the sides starts. Then the basket is turned right side up and worked. Coiled baskets are always worked from the outside, near the edge. A right handed person made the coils counterclockwise looking into the basket.[106]

The awl is put through at a slant from left to right. Care must be taken not to split the stitches. If the awl is

---

[104] *JB-PL*: Winnowing baskets are started with two rigid elements. The cross strands [weft] alternate over the rigid elements. Then after six cross strands they go over alternative strands. [The two rods spoken of here form the outside rim of the tray. His second statement apparently refers to the use of close simple twine to start the tray, later shifting to diagonal twine. Kelly (1932:126) also notes the left-to-right progression of twining, although she states that it is not exclusive.]

[105] Park is undoubtedly referring to Kelly (1932:126:fig. 5). However, this figure differs from the method of introduction observed on most of Park's baskets in collections. Kelly's figure shows the introduced rod folded in half to produce two new rods. Rods on baskets collected by Park are sharpened at one end and added next to an existing rod to form a pair to be caught by a single weft stitch.

[106] The direction of coiling described should be leftward, given an exterior work surface. JO-PL (see below) in speaking of the direction as "clockwise" also presupposes an exterior view. Kelly (1932:122) states that in Surprise Valley, coiling runs clockwise when seen from above, and work of a left-handed weaver in the area runs counterclockwise. Steward (1933:271) describes wares from Owens Valley as running clockwise as seen from the basket bottom.

put through straight, the stitch just previously made will split. Stitches of foundations are not split.

Designs

RP-WR: Design elements were very simple; narrow bands were put around the basket, or rough diamonds, or rectangular dark spots.[107] When the basket was made, the design elements were marked off with warps of willow that did not have the dark bark scraped off.[108] These were painted with *tuboŋ*, a yellowish chalk gotten in the hills near Schurz. This is put into the fire until it turns red and is soft and chalky. Then it is ground and mixed with water. It is applied to the design with a small twig. When dry, the chalk is washed off with cold water. This leaves a design that is black. The design is fairly permanent. The chalky paint will not color the willows in the basket that have been scraped smooth and white. It only colors those willows that have the rough natural bark left on.

Willow material [weft] can also be colored with this rock before baskets are woven. To do this, the willows are soaked in water with this powder. When the basket is completed, it is rubbed vigorously and the color, a dark brown, comes out clearly.

Basket Types

RP-WR: The cooking basket (*opo*) is made by twining [fig. 30e]. RP and AC say that a rim is necessary to make this basket serviceable for cooking. Although the cooking basket is porous when made, they say that when used, the small holes fill up with meal and it is water tight. The smaller, bowl-shaped basket (*süzida*) is also made by twining [fig. 31b]. It does not have a rim. These are the baskets from which mush is eaten. Cooking baskets are not pitched on the outside. "It would melt."

There are three kinds of twined trays.[109] The small fine twined tray (*tumaʔa*) is used for separating fine flour from the coarse meal [fig. 30d]. A larger and slightly coarser tray (*saʔya tumaʔa*) is used for winnowing small seeds [fig. 31a]. Parching trays (*yada*) are woven slightly coarser and larger [fig. 32b].

A cone-shaped basket (*kudusi*) about 2 ft high is used to gather pine cones [fig. 32a]. The mouth of the basket is made in open twine. Unlike other baskets, both warp and weft are unsplit willows. Smaller ones for collecting seeds are made in close twine [fig. 30f].[110] Water jugs (*süosa*) are made to carry and store water [fig. 30c]. They are twined and pitched [see below].

Spoons made by twining are called *ignyo*. The small spoon is for eating mush, and the large spoon is used to dip the soup or mush from the cooking basket into the small bowl-shaped individual baskets [fig. 31d].

Seed beaters (*sigu*) are made fan-shaped and with handles [fig. 33c]. They are used to beat seeds into the fine woven cone basket or onto a tray.

The fine coiled serving basket is called *nahapi* [fig. 31c].

Pitching

RP-WR: Water jugs are covered with pine pitch. A fire is built and rocks are heated. Pine pitch is put on hard ground where it will not soak into the ground when melted. The hot stones are put on the pitch. The pitch is melted in a shallow pit. Before the jug is dipped in the pitch, red paint is smeared over the outside of the jug. This makes the pitch adhere better. The jug is put in when the pitch is melted. The jug is turned around to get the pitch all over.

The owner of the pitch melts more than she needs for her jugs because other people would want to dip their jugs in the pitch again. When the pitch comes off a jug it is dipped again. They paid for this with beads.

Pitch is sometimes put on the inside as well as the outside of the basketry water jugs.[111] The pitch is heated before it is put inside. The jug is slowly turned until the pitch is spread over the inside of the jug. While the pitch is hot, it spreads easily. Some do not put the pitch on the inside because it flavors the water. The pitch gives the water a bitter taste. The bitter flavor of the water can be prevented by half filling the jug after the pitch had first hardened with a fine dry clay. The jug is then shaken well. The powdered clay is poured out and the jug is washed out with water. Then the water tasted all right. That takes away the bitterness.

Women who are menstruating are not allowed to be present when the jugs are pitched. If menstruating women are present, the pitch will not boil up. It would collapse when boiling and turn black—it would be spoiled. It

---

[107] Other designs are present on Northern Paiute baskets from this and other areas. See figs. 30-32 for examples.

[108] This statement is less than clear. It is possible that Park is correct in stating that it is unscraped warp rods that form the basis of the design—over which unscraped pieces of weft would also have to be placed. However, it is also possible that his statement should have read "weft" instead of "warp."

[109] Three grades of twined trays are typical in the central Northern Paiute area. JG-PL speaks only of two in his account (see below).

[110] Neither Steward (1933) nor Kelly (1932) speak of whole-rod twined burden baskets. Most specimens examined have wefts of split willow. Whole-rod wefts are more typically Washoe.

[111] Pitching jugs on the inside has a scattered distribution according to Stewart (1941:387).

Figure 30. Basketry. a (top left). Unpitched water bottle, also used for seed storage (54.7 cm length). MPM 22106. b (middle left). Close diagonal twined winnowing tray, plain twine borders (52 cm length). MPM 53115. c (bottom left). Close diagonal twined pitched water bottle, personal canteen size (33.5 cm high). MAI 13/4178. d (top right). Close diagonal twined winnowing tray with heavy plain twined borders (51 cm length). MPM 22104. e (middle right). Close diagonal twined boiling basket (22 cm high). MAI 13/4422. f (bottom right). Small close diagonal twined seed collector (35.5 cm length). AMNH 50.2/3618. a, b, d collected by S. A. Barrett, Walker River, 1916; c, e collected by M. R. Harrington, at Stillwater (c) and Walker River (e), 1924; f collected by W. Z. Park, Pyramid Lake, 1934.

Figure 31. Serving baskets. a (left). Small open diagonal twined winnowing/serving tray (32 cm length). MAI 13/4418. b (top right). Close diagonal twined mush bowl (15 cm rim diameter). MAI 13/4177. c (bottom right). Coiled mush bowl (17.5 cm rim diameter). MAI 13/3822. All collected by M. R. Harrington, Walker River (a, b), and Stillwater (c), 1924.

was then thrown away and the menstruating woman was told to leave. Then a new batch was started. This applied to a pregnant woman as well as a menstruating woman.

When boiling pitch collapsed and turned black, the other women asked each other which if one of them were menstruating. When they found the culprit, all the women reproached her and even reviled her before they sent her away.

While the pitch was cooking, the women talked so it would stick to the jugs. They talked to an animal *odzaza*, that eats manzanita leaves. It is like a rat but RP has not seen this animal. The women said, "Bring us good rich pitch and put some of your own flesh and blood in it." The women can tell when the *odzaza* is boiling pitch. The best pitch is gotten from where the porcupines gnaw on the pine trees.

Observations on a Basket in Progress

An old woman was observed making a twined burden basket at Reno. After the basket was started, a piece of cloth or canvas was put in the bottom to hold the willow rods from falling together. The basket maker sat with the bottom of the basket on her lap and wove from left to right, turning the basket after tying two or three rods so that she was always working on top. The twining elements were pulled tightly with the right hand while the rod was held properly spaced with the left hand. Then the two crossed wefts were held by the thumb and third fingers, the first two fingers holding the rods in place, while the wefts were passed around the next rod.

When a new rod was introduced (see illustration of method of introducing new rods in burden baskets in Surprise Valley) [Kelly 1932: fig. 5], the end was sharpened or beveled with the teeth or with a knife. After twining around two or three rods, water was sprinkled with the right hand upon the next few rods to be tied, and the wet fingers were drawn the length of the wefts. When a new weft was to be introduced, it was first soaked in a can of water for about a half minute. Before the preceding weft was used up, the new piece was put under the preceding one and the two were then twined around the next four or five rods. The end of the new piece and that of the preceding one stuck out and when dry, were broken off. At each round of the weft, the basket maker sat the basket on its bottom to see how it was shaping.

Other Comments on Basketry

JG-PL: In the old days coiled baskets were not made.[112]

---

[112] Kelly (1932:120) also suggests the recentness of coiling in Surprise Valley, noting that several specimens show technological innovations foreign to native techniques. Stewart (1941:433) also was told by several individuals that it was recent. Curtis (1926:70) states that "all Paviotso baskets are

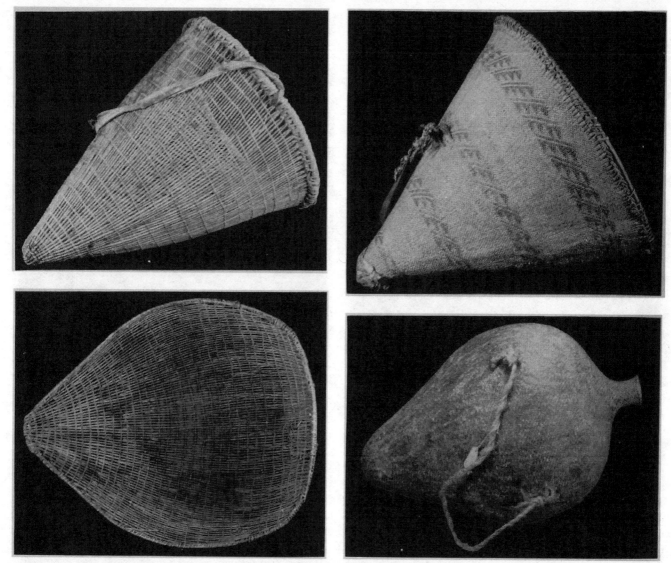

Figure 32. Twined baskets. a (top left). Open, plain twined burden basket used to collect berries and pinenuts (44 cm length). AMNH 50.1/7906. Collected by R. H. Lowie, Pyramid Lake, 1914. b (bottom left). Open, plain twined winnowing/parching tray (81 cm). MPM 21883. Collected by S. A. Barrett, Walker River, 1916. c (top right). Close diagonal twined burden basket (76 cm). MPM (no number). Collected by S. A. Barrett, western Nevada, 1916. d (bottom right). Close diagonal twined pitched water bottle of size used in camp (60 cm). Collected by M. R. Harrington, Walker River, 1924. MAI 13/3808.

Women learned to make them after they saw them in stores. Coiled basketry is called *tusihi* (sewing). All twined baskets are *tugwicɔ*. A water jug is called *su.osᵃ*.

Willows were colored for basketry by burying the coil of split willow in the ground for two or three days where horses had urinated.[113] Split willows colored in this fashion were used to make the marks on the hoods of cradles to designate the sex of the child. Nowadays yarn is used for this purpose.

Fine twined winnowing trays were called *samuʔno*. The coarse parching tray was called *ya.ta. Tudəwkidənᵘ* was

made by the twining process.   '' although he figures coiled wares in his plate (titled "Paviotso Basketry," opposite p. 74). Lowie (1924:233) does not comment on the practice, nor do Riddell (1960:43-44) or Stewart (1933:270-271). Museum collections contain few coiled pieces from Pyramid Lake, but more from Walker River.

[113] *HS-D*: "The willow material for baskets was colored by soaking it in water with the bark of redberry [?] bush for several days."

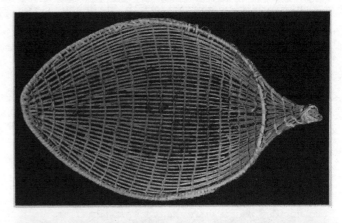

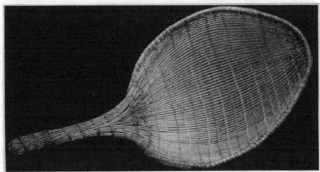

Figure 33. Bag and seed beaters. a (left). Bag of continuous length of three-strand braided sagebrush bark. Braid sewn together with native string. AMNH 50.2/3656. Collected by W. Z. Park, Pyramid Lake, 1934. b (top right). Seed beater/berry crusher (42.5 cm). LMA 1-29032. Collected by W. Z. Park, Pyramid Lake, 1934. c (bottom right). Seed beater (58 cm). Collected by C. F. Nesler, Walker River, 1921. MAI 10/5315.

the small tray used to seed chokecherries[114] [fig. 33b]. The seed beater was called *si.ku*.

All the flat baskets—parching trays, seed beaters, etc.—were started at the small end, the end away from the handle. One weft was carried from left to right[115] then the basket was turned over and the weft was worked back to the other side and again the basket was turned over. The rim is put on with the top of the tray facing the worker. The ends of the wefts are turned over when the tray is completed, and the rim lashed on. Then the ends are broken off. The rim is sewed to the first and second weft from the edge.

The small round cup or bowl used to serve individuals mush is called *su.zida*. This cup is not water tight at first. Pitch is not used on it.[116] After soup has been in the cup the little holes fill up and the cup can then be used for drinking water as well as for soup. There is no

rim or border put on this basket. These baskets come in different sizes.

There are two kinds of burden baskets. One is a coarsely woven conical basket standing 2½ to 3 ft. high. It is called *tubakəwanə*. The other is woven closely. It is the same size and shape. It is called *wanə*. It is made like a water jug (e.g., close-twined) [see figs. 30, 32 for examples].

HS-D: The spoon is called *sɔkɔ*. The handle is about 18 in. long. The frame and handle are of wild rose [*Rosa woodsii*]. The spoon is woven with willow strands. The handle is double. It is simply an extension of the frame of the spoon. This spoon is used to stir and ladle out mush and to take the rock out of the cooking basket.[117]

JO-PL: The willows are gathered in the fall. The branches that have turned red are taken. The branches are scraped with a knife for rods. The outer skin is scraped off. It is used for tying the split willows when they are still wet. Do not dry them before splitting. Split

---

[114] This statement refers to a large, open-twined sieve made on the design of a seed beater. See fig. 33b.

[115] This statement agrees with that of RP-WR above.

[116] Stewart (1941:387) reports the use of pitch on food bowls for the Honey Lake Paiute. Two specimens in the Field Museum collection from Pyramid Lake are also pitch-coated. The practice was apparently rare, however.

---

[117] For example, the handle is doubled back on itself before the twining is added. HS-D is the only individual to report a hot rock lifter with mesh added. Spoons, or dippers, are also noted by Kelly (1932:123) for Surprise Valley.

each branch in three pieces; then dry them and take out the pith.

Sometimes simple color (brown) is given to stitches with the bark still on the sticks. They got yellow dirt by the lake for dying. They buried the material in the ground with the yellow dirt. Some old people use the root of the fern gotten in the mountains.[118] This latter is just used for decoration and is very black.

For cooking baskets three rods are used.[119] Each tie [weft] is around the three rods. The base is started with a single rod. When that is used up, start in with three rods. The three rods are introduced to overlap at the ends. Coiling is always clockwise. "Maybe some of the left-handed people wove the other way."[120]

The rods are dampened when used. They are soaked for an hour as was the stitching material. When they come to the end of a stitch they run it under the previous stitch and break it off right away. Do not wait until it dries.

The round coiled basket is easier to make than the oval coiled basket (statement later contradicted). The edge of the coiled basket is not caught with any special stitch. The edge of a coiled oval basket has a border with a stitch around the top rod between each stitch catching it to the next rod. It crosses underneath the rod. Some single rod coiling. Very bad in sample seen.

They do not put pitch on the inside of water jugs, just the outside. Pitch heated and spread on outside of water jug with a stick.[121] Water jug started at bottom with four cross rods [see Kelly 1932: fig. 6]. At neck leave out rods—every other one.

OTHER CONTAINERS

[Included here are some miscellaneous notes on the manufacture and use of containers other than baskets. They are probably not complete.]

Platters

RP-WR: A wooden platter (üino)[122] or bowl was made for serving fish. A piece of wood was cut or burned off a dry stump. It was uneven on the bottom. It was then roughly shaped. It was burned and scooped out with obsidian knives. The platter was oval shaped. There were depressions in both ends where the juice collects from the roasted fish. Every family had one of these wooden bowls. Baskets were also used for platters[123] and bowls.

JG-PL, AD-R: JG-PL has not heard of any kind of wooden meat platter or wooden dish used in the old days. AD-R has not seen wooden platters or bowls. They only used basketry dishes.

Pottery

JG-PL: JG has never heard of any kind of pottery being made or used either at Pyramid Lake or at Humboldt Lake—Lovelock.[124]

RP-WR: RP has never seen or heard of the making or use of any kind of pottery. Mud dolls and other figures were made of mud and clay by children in play. They did not keep such objects. They left them there in the mud when they quit playing. "I used to do that way myself before."

Bags

[Park does not give any accounts of the manufacture and use of skin or fiber bags, although they are occasionally mentioned in connection with storage of various foodstuffs. He did collect an example of a braided bag of sagebrush bark from Pyramid Lake, however (fig. 33a).]

CORDAGE, NETS, AND WEAVING

[Park received accounts of cordage manufacture from three men, fishnet manufacture from two men and one woman, and weaving from seven men. Cordage was extremely important to the Northern Paiute life style as can be seen from the frequent mention throughout this text of wiha, Apocynum string. Nets, whether for rabbit hunting or fishing, were also important throughout the area. And nearly all Great Basin families, at the least, wrapped themselves in rabbitskin blankets. Other types of woven products, such as pelican skin blankets, shirts, etc., were also made by similar manufacturing techniques and are thus discussed here.]

---

[118] Bracken fern root [Pteridium aquilinium L.] was commonly used for basketry designs by the Washoe and other Sierran groups.

[119] The coiled cooking basket has a scattered distribution among the Northern Paiute according to Stewart (1941:387). Twined boilers were more typical.

[120] This statement appears to contradict that of RP-WR (see above), but probably does not. JO views the basket from the exterior.

[121] Kelly (1932:124) also speaks of applying pitch to the exterior of water jugs with a stick. The pitch is placed on the stick and then the stick is held over the fire to melt the pitch.

[122] Stewart (1941:387) notes that the term üano is applied to an "angular" twined basketry tray.

[123] This probably refers to the use of twined trays as platters rather than to a more specific type of basketry platter.

[124] Stewart (1941:389) also received a negative response from all individuals surveyed on pottery manufacture. The reference to pottery manufacture in the Humboldt Sink in Zenas Leonard's journal of 1833 (Wagner 1904) is undoubtedly better placed in Owens Valley (Stewart 1941:426).

Cordage

JB-PL: Wiha [*Apocynum cannabinum* L.] was gathered when dry [fall]. It was then dried more and scraped with a knife [to remove buds, small branches, etc.]. Then it was cracked lengthwise with the teeth. The dry fiber was broken away by cracking it against your leg. Breaking away the sticks [core] leaves the fibers. It was softened by rolling it between the hands. The fibers of one stalk were divided into about three parts, and straightened out. They were then rolled into two strands. First wet the fiber in the mouth. The two strands are then rolled by keeping the two parts separate and rolling away from the body on your thigh [fig. 34b]. Then roll the two strands together [to ply].[125] *Wiha* grows around JB's place longer [in fiber size] than any other place.

Fish Nets

ND-HL: Fish nets were made with a shuttle (*tudaŋaotunᵃ*, or *wanadunᵃ*) and a gauge (name not known) [fig. 34a]. The shuttle was 8 or 10 in. long and 1 to 1½ in. wide. Each end was deeply notched and pointed.[126] The gauge was about 6 in. long. The width of it depended upon the size of the mesh desired.[127] The string for the net was wrapped around the shuttle. When each knot was made (ND does not know how the knots were made),[128] it was slipped onto the gauge and worked back as each succeeding loop was slipped on.

Seine and other square and rectangular nets were started at the end. The cone-shaped dip nets were started at the point and built up spirally. Hoops and poles were added to some nets.

RP-WR: Nets were made of *wiha*. They were made by the old men. The mesh was about 2½ in. The mesh was measured with a willow stick marked at the proper place. The net was made "almost like crochet work." String was wrapped around the willow stick about 10 times to make each knot [row?] in the net.

GK-WR: Nets were made of *wiha* by men. When the nets were made the mesh was measured with the fingers—two fingers for a sucker net and three for a trout net [see also Fishing in chap. 2 for additional descriptions of net types].

Weaving

BR-L, PL: The skin of rabbits is used to make a blanket. The skin is best around November. Then the rabbits are hunted and the rabbit drive was held.[129] They wanted the skins to make the blankets. In the summer the rabbit skins are brown and the hair is hard and falls out. In the fall the skins turn white and the hair is soft and does not fall out. The Indians say the rabbits are "ripe" then.

GK-WR: Rabbits are skinned at the time they are killed. That evening the skins are cut into strips. To make the string, a knife is held in the mouth and with the hands the skin is cut into the countinuous strip by cutting it in a spiral [fig. 34c].[130] The strips of skin are then rolled into two-strand string. Each strip is doubled to give the two strands and the next strip is put through its loop.[131] The fur string for the entire blanket is thus rolled into one long piece. Women may help with rolling the twine which is done by placing a stick through one end to keep it from turning and then the string is rolled on the thigh. GK can cut and twist into string 40 or 50 skins in half a day. The twisted string is hung in the sun to dry [fig 34d].

The blanket is made on a frame. Two poles are set in the ground. A cross piece is tied across the top and another tied across the two upright poles several inches from the ground.[132] The string made from the skins is put between these cross pieces passing around each cross piece [fig. 34e]. Grass string (*wiha*) was formerly used for weft. Now flour sacks are cut in strings for that purpose. The weft is started at either the top or the bottom. Two fingers are inserted between the warp of skin strings to space the weft. The weft is put through with the fingers. Men always make the rabbit skin blankets.[133]

---

[125] See also Wheat's (1967:55f) excellent description of the process. Plying is accomplished by rolling the two completed elements together on the thigh in a motion *toward* the body.

[126] Stewart (1941:388) also lists carved shuttles for net making as present for all but his *küpa* (Lovelock) band. The alternative in most areas was a simple stick shuttle.

[127] Separate gauges of wood were suggested by some of Stewart's (1941:388) consultants and denied by others. Alternatives were finger measurements, stone gauges (?), or using the end of the shuttle.

[128] All fish nets and rabbit nets thus far examined in museum collections are made with a sheet bend knot, which is easily done with a continuous strand of cordage.

[129] Rabbit drives traditionally occurred in the fall. See Lowie (1924:288) for a description of a drive held near Fallon, Nev.

[130] See Lowie (1924:228) for a description of cutting the whole rabbitskin in a spiral to obtain a single strand. Wheat (1967:75) also illustrated the process.

[131] This is apparently not plying, but rather doubling the strand. Examples of rabbitskin blankets from the Peabody Museum and the American Museum of Natural History collections are 2-strand, S-twist. Chaining the strips is also implied.

[132] Both the two-post and the four-post weaving frames were used by the Northern Paiute (Stewart 1941:388). Two-post frames were also used with and without cross pieces. See Lowie (1924:288) for an account of the four-post frame. Kelly (1932:137) indicates that the Surprise Valley Paiute attributed the four-post frame to the "Nixon Paviotso."

[133] Stewart (1941:388) notes that women were reported nearly as frequently as men as the makers of blankets.

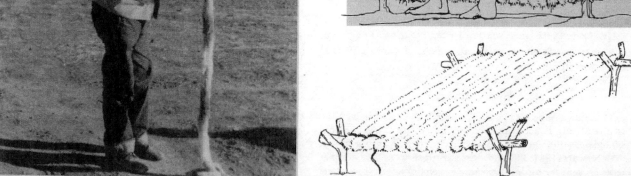

Figure 34. Nets, cordage, and weaving. a (top left). Shuttle (32 cm) and gauge (19.3 cm) for net making. PM 23-114-10/3963. Collected by W. Z. Park, Pyramid Lake, 1934. b (middle left). Johnny Dunn plying native cordage. c (bottom left). Jimmy George cutting rabbitskin into strips for making warp for blanket. d (top right). Jimmy George twisting fur warp for rabbitskin blanket. Note twisted strips drying on house in background. e (middle right). Upright loom for making rabbitskin and other woven products. Warp may be wrapped vertically or horizontally. f (bottom right). Four-post horizontal loom for making duckskin skirt. b, c, d photographs by M. M. Wheat, 1958–62. University of Nevada, Reno, Library, Special Collections Department. Drawings by Susan Lohse.

A married man has a rabbit skin blanket large enough for two people to sleep on. A single man has a blanket half that size. A man with a wife and children would have a blanket large enough for them all to sleep together. A blanket lasts for two or three years.[134]

JO-PL: Skins are wrapped together and spun together.[135] Their ends are tied together. Then roll it with a stick on one end and the other end held by a person or tied to a tree. It is rolled on the thigh, two strands together. It is dried before they make the blanket.

Blankets are made on a frame, usually built into a tree.[136] We hardly ever use a four-post frame; use only two posts.[137] JO has seen a four-post frame but considers it harder to weave that way. We usually weave with a two-post frame and weave it [the weft] up and down. It is much easier that way. Start either at the top or the bottom to weave across—have done it both ways. The cross weave is with *wiha* measured with three fingers between each cross weave. Two strands are in the cross weave: open twine. It takes about 30 skins for a blanket large enough for two people.[138] A blanket will last about 10 years. They can use cottontail and jackrabbit skins or any other fur they have for a blanket.[139] The frame for weaving has no name, but the blanket is *kamuwiga*.

ND-HL: Five skins were cut into strips about ½ in. wide and used to make one length for the blanket. About 25 strips in all were used for the blanket. The strip from one skin is doubled and rolled on the thigh. It is spliced with *wiha* before the string is rolled.[140] As it is finished on the thigh, the string is rolled into a ball.

The blanket is woven in a frame of two upright poles with one stick across the bottom and one across the top. These sticks are usually tied so they will not move.

The dry string is dampened before weaving which starts at the bottom of the frame. The weft used to be *wiha*. There are two strings for the weft, which cross between each warp [i.e., are twined]. Weaving is started at the left edge and moves towards the right. When the right edge is reached, the weaving with the next higher wefts starts again on the left.[141]

Feather Blankets and Skirts

JB-PL: Pelican skin blankets were made from young birds that were about ready to fly. They are made in the same way as a rabbit blanket.[142]

BR-L, PL: Women's skirts of mudhen skin and feathers were made just like a rabbitskin blanket except that they had the strings running around instead of up and down.[143] To make this skirt, four posts were set up with cross pieces between each pair [fig. 34f]. The cross pieces were set far enough apart to make a skirt sufficiently large. The length of the cross pieces determined the length of the skirt. The string made from mudhen skin was wound around the two cross pieces. Then the top and bottom layers were sewn in open twine with string.[144] The wefts were 1/2 to 1 in. apart. A small slit was left in the back of the top of the skirt and a string was put around the top. The women stepped into the skirt and pulled it into position and tied it with the string. The string was tied on either side, in front, or in back.

If women did not have any skin to make a dress, they made a skirt with tule. The tule was placed closely together and held together with wefts of *wiha* or string made from sagebrush bark. It was done in open twine. [see also Clothing in chap. 5.]

---

[134]Opinions differed among Park's consultants as to how long rabbitskin blankets lasted: two to ten years. See the other account below.

[135]See account of ND-HL below and note 140.

[136]This two-post frame was apparently made by leaning both posts against the branch of a tree. The branch then served as the stabilizing cross piece. Weaving may be on a horizontal warp.

[137]Again, Lowie (1924:228) describes the use of the four-post frame. See also BR-L, PL's account of its use for skirts, below.

[138]This estimate is somewhat lower than the numbers given by ND-HL and HS-D. Fifty skins for a single blanket and 100 for a double are more typical.

[139]Stewart (1941:388) also notes the use of wildcat, woodrat, muskrat, meadow mouse, squirrel, mole, and rarely, coyote fur in twisted strips for blanket making.

[140]ND is apparently referring to making a continuous loop of a single skin preparatory to chaining them together, as suggested by Kelly (1932:137) and Wheat (1965:76-77). An alternative explanation is that each skin is spliced to the next with cordage. Lowie (1924:222) states that two skins were tied together and doubled by rolling them on the thigh. Others were tied on when needed.

[141]Kelly (1932:137) notes the feeling in Surprise Valley that if rows were not started on the same side, the blanket would "wrinkle."

[142]Kelly (1932:137) notes that the Surprise Valley people were aware of mudhen skin blankets produced by the "Nevada Paviotso." Steward (1933:270) also notes their production in Owens Valley.

[143]BR's statement is not clear here. He seems to imply that the feather strips run around the woman's body, thus creating a tubular skirt. However, he could merely mean that the warping for this skirt is in the horizontal direction rather than the vertical.

[144]This statement could be interpreted in two ways, i.e., the two surfaces could be twined independently, thus creating a tubular skirt, or the two surfaces could be joined together by twining, as with a rabbitskin blanket. If the former is what is really implied, a slit would have to be made in the garment by cutting. If not, the slit would be made by leaving part of a required side seam open. Although confusing, it appears that the tubular skirt is implied.

4

Houses

[Accounts of houses and/or house building were secured from 10 individuals, including seven men and three women. The most lengthy and detailed accounts were by JG-PL and ND-HL. These are printed in near entirety below. GK-WR, RP-WR and AC and LG-F also gave good descriptions of construction details for their areas. Excerpts from their descriptions are included where details differ. Points of agreement and disagreement by other individuals are included in the footnotes.

Housing construction and house types varied somewhat across the region. Some of the variation seems attributable to materials availability; e.g., the use of grass *vs.* cattail *vs.* tule. Some also seems to be regionally influenced; e.g., the use of a vestibule and bark covering on the mountain house by groups in close proximity to Sierran California. Styles and designs were also in part dependent on the seasons. The most clearly established house types are the mat-covered winter house, the pine-bough- and often earth-covered mountain house, and the circular windbreak. Less well established types are the brush kitchen, the four-post storage platform, and the four-post shade. The former two are probably legitimate for most areas with semipermanent camps. The latter is of questionable antiquity. See also Subsistence, chap. 2, for additional data on the function of storage platforms; see Puberty in vol. 2, for menstrual structures.]

WINTER HOUSES

JG-PL: The winter house, *no.bi*, is made with a frame of willows [fig. 35a]. The poles of the frame, which were called *sainobinawat* (or *wa·ta*), were 2–3 in. diameter and 10–12 ft long. They are placed in a circle in holes from 18 in.–2 ft deep. The holes were dug with sharpened sticks. The number of holes depended upon the size of the house. Usually the house was about 12 ft high and about 8–10 ft in diameter. The size depends on the size of the family.[1] The poles are about 2 ft apart. At the door, they are 3 ft apart. A hoop is then made of

willow about 1 in. thick. The hoop (*nükɔdɔp*) is about 2½ ft in diameter. The poles (*wa'ta*) are put in the ground slightly slanting toward the center of the circle. A ladder is then made by lashing cross pieces to two poles with twisted willows. This is leaned against the poles in the inside of the frame. A man goes up on the ladder and bends over the poles and lashes them with twisted willow to the hoop. The upright poles project for about 4 to 8 in. These ends are not cut off.

Willow poles 1–1½ in. thick are then lashed horizontally around the frame of the house. These are lashed to the upright poles with willows. There are three of these running around the frame.[2] They stop at the door which is about 4 ft high. One piece of willow is tied across the top of the door. The two upright poles beside the door are a little larger than the other uprights. These are called *nükɔdɔp*. The door always faced east. I think that was on account of the weather, wind, rain and snow.[3]

In the old days the willows for the frame were dug up and the roots broken off.[4] A tall slender willow or cottonwood was selected and the roots uncovered. If the roots were green and could not be broken off a fire was built in a hole on the roots. The fire was kept burning until the roots were dry and could be broken. The men did this work. Men also build the frame. When the poles are ready, it takes about a day to fix the frame. When all the materials are gathered, it takes about 1½ days to finish the house.

---

[2] Interior frame of three rows of lashed willows was also confirmed by other consultants, although ND-HL mentioned specifically four rows. The number may depend on the size of the house as these tie together the overall framework. Exterior reinforcing rods are also added to Pyramid Lake grass-covered houses according to Wheat (1967:108) and to tule-mat-covered houses according to Kelly (1932:105).

[3] See Stewart (1941:377) for distribution as a common feature; also Steward (1933:264) for Owens Valley and Wheat (1967:108) for Pyramid Lake. Kelly (1932:105) notes orientation in Surprise Valley is away from prevailing winds.

[4] ND-HL provided the following on cutting willows: "Willows for houses were broken off and then trimmed with a flint knife. Sometimes the willow was broken off and burnt off to the proper length. Only small willows were cut down. Chipped first with a stone knife held in the hand without any kind of padding and then the willow was broken off."

---

[1] HS-D, ND-HL, and BR-L,PL also noted that the overall size of the house depended on the size of the family. This house is not built around an excavated pit. Kelly (1932:104) for Surprise Valley and Wheat (1967:104) for Fallon also note the lack of excavation.

The women make the tule mats. It requires about half a day to make the tule mats if the tule is already gathered. Tule mats are made by putting four willows on the ground about 1 ft apart. These are about 1–1½ in. in diameter and 4 ft long. They are evenly spaced to make a mat about 5 ft long. Tules[5] (*saib*) [*Scirpus acutus*] are laid thickly across these sticks and then four more willow sticks are placed on top. Thin green willows are twisted in the hands to soften. The sticks with the tule between are tied tightly together with these twisted willows. These mats are called *sigwa*. The mats are put on the frame, beginning at the bottom. Both men and women do this. The mats are lashed to each one of the upright poles. The bottom row is put on all around the house. The next row overlaps the lower one about 6 in. They are tied on with small tule.[6] These are put all over the house except over the hoop on the top which is left open for the smoke to escape [fig. 35b]. The mats are so thick that the snow and rain do not come through. There was no covering for the smoke hole.[7] It is left open all the time even if there is snow or rain. The smoke hole in the *no·bi* was called *ka·nitupa* (*kani*, house, *tupa*, mouth). A house made with mats of tule alone is called *saino·bi*. On some of the houses in the valleys no tule is used. The mats are made entirely of *waiyabə* [*Elymus cinereus*]. A house made with mats of tule and *waiyabə* is called *ka.ni*. This is the regular name of the house a long time ago.[8]

A hole was made in the center of the floor for the fire. This hole was about 6 in. deep and about 2 ft in diameter (name of the hole not known). The hole was not lined with rocks.[9] No rocks are on the outside of the hole.

The door was covered with a mat made especially to fit. It was tied to one of the door posts and opened to

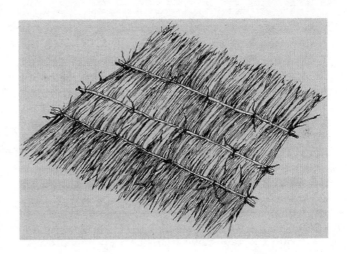

[5]Although JG and others refer to the use of tule (*Scirpus acutus*) in house construction, it should be kept in mind that cattails (*Typha latifolia*) were also used (see RP-WR below). Some of the confusion is the result of the western American tradition of designating both tules and cattails as "tules." Unless the consultants gave the native name of the plant (as JG did in this case), the designation should be viewed advisedly.

[6]Tule (*Scirpus acutus*) can be quite fragile. The reference here to "small tule" may be to *Juncus balticus*.

[7]ND-HL and GK-WR note the lack of a smoke hole covering. Kelly (1932:105) says that smoke holes in Surprise Valley were covered with a blanket in cold weather.

[8]There is considerable confusion in the literature as to the application of the terms *kani* and *nobi*. JB-PL told Park the following: "The grass or tule covered houses were called *kani*. Any kind of house was *nobi*. This includes the shades. The shades on four uprights were called *haba*. Circular windbreaks made of brush were called *saiwabi wənanobi*." *Kani* is the older Uto-Aztecan term (Miller 1967).

[9]Also confirmed by ND-HL. See also Kelly (1932:105) for the same feature.

Figure 35. Housing. a (top). House frame of willow poles. Photograph by W. Z. Park, Pyramid Lake, 1934. b (middle). Cattail mats for houses, construction detail. c (bottom). Cattail mat covered house. Photograph by S. A. Barrett, Pyramid Lake, 1916. Milwaukee Public Museum photograph. Drawing by Susan Lohse.

the side. The doorway was called *yü·hü*. Tules were spread all over the floor. They were spread so thick that one could lie on it. Sometimes the grass *waiyabɔ* was spread on the floor instead of tule. The grass or tule covering on the floor was used only when it was cold—fall, winter, and early spring. When the covering was packed down, more grass or tule was cut and spread on top. The old covering was not cleaned out.[10] The covering of tule was fairly deep so it made a bed. The beds were placed against the wall. When sleeping, people always had their feet toward the fire.

A pile of wood was by the door. Baskets were hung around the wall. Bow and quiver were stuck in back of the cross piece that ran around the house. The water jug always was by the door. Adults and children who were big enough drank out of the jug without a cup. Small children were given a drink with the bowl or cup used for serving mush.

Sometimes short poles, about 5 ft high, were placed in the ground about 5 ft in front of the door of the dome-shaped house. Poles ran from the top of these to the door posts. Cross-beams were lashed on these and the two sides and the top were covered with tule mats. In case they had this entrance, a door was placed on this entrance but not to the house proper. Only the outside entrance had a door. The porch or shade in front of the door is called *yü·hü*, the same word as for door.[11]

The best place in the house was opposite the door.[12] The man who owned the house (it was felt that the man was the "boss" and owned the house, not the woman) slept there. When it rained all the people sleeping in the house moved as near to him as possible because the wind and the rain came from the west and drove in through the smoke hole in such a way as to make part of the house near the door wet.[13]

In one house there would usually be about four adults—man and wife and her parents or even her brother—and three or four children. Sometimes there

would be a small cluster of houses, four or so. All the people in these houses were related. When a man got married he always went to live with his parents-in-law. The father-in-law owned the house and he was looked upon as the head of the family.

The houses were not always built under trees or very close together.[14] Some camps were a long ways from water and the people had to carry water in jugs. The old man in the family decided where the family would build the house. A sandy place was best for the house for the water drained off quickly and in winter the ground would not be muddy. When the family moved the house was torn down and the poles and tule mats were taken to the new site if it were nearby. If the move were very far the house was simply deserted. No other family would use a deserted house. The family might return and occupy the old house a second winter.[15]

The winter house (*no·bi*) was a good house. The wind and rain did not come through. Only a little rain came through the smoke hole. I lived in one of these houses when I was a boy and it kept out the wind better than these board houses. At night a big log 4 or 5 ft long was put in the fire and the log burned all night long and kept the house warm. The wood that was put on the fire at night was called *mu·zanɔ*. Wood burnt on the fire during the day or for cooking was called *kuna*.

There was no feast or celebration when a family moved into a new house and no ceremony to bring good luck to the house or its occupants.

AC,LG-F: A willow frame was built in a circle—8 to 14 ft in diameter. The frame was called *maiwɔmɔsubi* (*maiwɔmɔ*, to put up; *subi*, willow). The circle was about 2 ft in diameter at the top. Tule mats (*sigwatu*) were made by drying tule (*toi*) [*Typha latifolia*] and putting them across four willow sticks evenly spaced. Sticks were put on the top of the mats and these were tied together. The mats were tied on to the frame of the house. Each mat overlapped the mat below it. Houses were 8 or 10 ft high and called *toinobi*. The fire was built on the ground in the middle of the floor space. Greasewood was burned. Sagebrush bark was used as a mattress.[16] I (AC) lived in one of these houses. There was my father, mother and three brothers and me. There were six of us.

[10] According to ND-HL, "the floor of the house was covered with *waiyab* [*Elymus cinereus*] or tule. In the spring or summer when new tule or grass could be gathered the old floor covering was burned and the floor was covered with fresh grass or tule."

[11] ND-HL also suggests a vestibule entrance for tule houses: "Entrance to the house built by building out from the door two or three feet with grass or tule mats. This was roofed and the side covered." See also Steward (1933:264) for similar entrance to Mono Lake houses. Stewart (1941:377) also suggests that the trait is widespread among Northern Paiute groups.

[12] In Owens Valley, the place of honor was also opposite the door (Steward 1933:263, 264). ND-HL also confirmed this for Park.

[13] The prevailing direction of the weather at Pyramid Lake is as JG-PL describes it. See also Kelly (1932:105) for orientation of Surprise Valley houses away from the prevailing wind.

[14] Winter sites were often chosen for proximity to wood, according to ND-HL. BR-L,PL noted that houses built in the open were generally smaller, often because of the lack of sufficient building materials, and were sagebrush-covered.

[15] BR-L,PL told Park that houses usually lasted two years. People lived outside in the summer in the square or rectangular shade. On separate occasions, ND-HL confirmed and denied reoccupation of houses a second season. See Note 20.

[16] HW-YR: Cottonwood tree (*singabi*) bark was used for a bed. The bark was softened by rubbing between the hands. Rabbit skin blankets were used for covering.

RP-WR: Houses were located in the valleys. Stalks of *toi* (cattail) were used to cover houses. The stalks were tied in bunches about 6 in. thick.[17] Each bundle was tied in three places with willow bark. The bunches of tule are placed on the willow frame of the house, fastened to the poles with willow bark split in halves. The bundles are 6 or 7 ft long and 4 or 5 ft wide. The men tie the tule together, and women help them lift them up to put on the walls. The men lift them to the roof. Both men and women gather the tule. *Saib* [*Scirpus acutus*] has round stems and cannot be used so well for houses. Only *toi* [*Typha latifolia*] is used to build houses.

Mountain Houses

JG-PL: Winter houses were also built in the mountains. These are made with pine branches. The circle the size of the house is dug out to a depth of about 2 ft. The poles are set in the same way as the other house then pine branches are put on. The house is covered with dirt.[18] The house is called *ka·ni*. There is more slant to the house posts of the *ka·ni* than to the *saino·bi*. The *ka·ni* is probably more dome-shaped than the tule house.[19] After the house is finished the floor is dug out. My grandfather told me one time that was the way they built a house in the mountains near Stillwater. Near the bottom of the house the dirt banked up outside is about 6 or 8 in. deep. Near the smoke hole the dirt is not so deep, only 3 or 4 in.

ND-HL: When people wintered in the pinenut mountains they dug a space about a foot deep where the house was to be built. The frame was made of willows and was covered with *waiyab* [*Elymus cinereus*]. Willow poles were put in the ground about 1½ ft. The poles were 12–18 in. apart. At the top the poles were lashed to a willow hoop with twisted willow twigs. This hoop was about 2 ft in diameter. Three or four circles of willows ran around the framework. The poles in the frame were

called *wa.ta* (pole). The main circle was called *anabiwükədəp*. The circle at the top forming the smoke hole is called *kanituba* (*kani*, house, *tuba*, mouth). The door is called *yühü*. *Kapipad* is the space opposite the door in the house. *Kasimonad*, interior of the house; *podanº* is the fireplace.

If the house was to be occupied only during the harvesting of pinenuts, the frame was thickly covered with *waiyab* and pine branches. If the house was to be used for several winters,[20] branches of the grass would be sewn together like a broom. Flat bunches were woven through in open twine.[21] Each end of the grass was tied in this way. These bunches of grass are tied on the frame of the house. The bunches of grass were put on in rows like shingles with each row overlapping the one below it. This house had a long doorway [vestibule, see above].

In the old days houses were built for the winter along the ridge above Nixon on the west side. The river was too high in the old days to build houses down under the trees. These houses were also covered with *waiyab*. Tules were made into mats just the same way as the grass. The mats were put on the house overlapping the mats below.

If no one dies in the family the house is occupied for the entire winter. In case of a death the house is either burned or torn down. A deserted camp was not used by anyone else even for a temporary residence. ND knew of no reason for avoiding the deserted camp of another family, even one's own deserted camp. He thought that it was just their habit. There seems to have been no fear of a deserted camp.

GK-WR: Semi-subterranean houses were not built.[22] The houses in the pinenut country (called *kani*) were built like the houses in the valleys. They were circular with a frame made of pine branches instead of willows.[23] The number of the main poles that were set in holes in the ground was determined by the size of the house and the amount of material available. The poles

---

[17] RP seems to be describing a house constructed of separate cattail bundles. There is no mention of mats, although her statement below that the bundles are 4–5 ft wide might indicate otherwise.

[18] There is scattered information on earth-covered houses for the Northern Paiute. Steward (1933:64) suggests their presence in Owens Valley and the Mono Lake area, and in Fish Lake Valley. In all three locations, the houses were also built over excavated pits approximately 2 ft deep. Curtis (1926, plate 78) also suggests earth covering for Pyramid Lake houses and Riddell (1960:42) describes the Honey Lake valley earth-covered sweat houses as presumably a Maidu trait. They are also noted in ethnohistoric sources (Fowler and Liljeblad 1986).

[19] There seems to be some confusion here. Given the size of the timbers used for the earth-covered houses, they were probably more conical then dome-shaped; but perhaps with a lower over-all profile.

[20] ND-HL also told Park the previous day: "If a family returned to the same place the next winter, they did not use the house of the past winter. They built a new one near the old one. The old house was left to fall down. When they came back the timber of the old house was not used in the new. There was no reason I know of for this practice."

[21] Twined grass mats are also described by Wheat (1967:108). This type of house usually also has exterior reinforcing rods to keep the grass mats in place.

[22] This is in conflict with the above descriptions, but probably represents little more than another variant.

[23] See also Steward (1933:263) for description of the pine-branch-covered mountain house. It may, however, have had a ridge pole. BR-L,PL also noted to Park that people might stay in the pinenut country during the winter. If so, they built a house with a frame of pine tree branches and covered it with sagebrush, dead pine boughs, and pine needles.

willow branches or cedar bark. The hoop was about 2 ft in diameter. The poles forming the frame were called *wadəgwaməpə*. The frame was covered with bark from dead pine or cedar [juniper] trees. Dry pine needles were heaped (great quantities) over the bark to keep it warm. The side of the house was not banked up with dirt. The pine needles were kept from blowing away by putting dry pine boughs over them. The house was dome-shaped. The smoke hole (*kanituba*) was never closed or covered.

There was a covered entranceway about 4 or 5 ft high by 3 ft wide and about 8 ft long. It was covered with bark and pine needles just as the house was covered. The door (*natsəgwanəpə*) was made of skins. There was a door covering at the entranceway and at the doorway to the house. The ground forming the floor was not covered.

GK lived in one of these houses in the mountains above Yerington (Pine Nut Mountains). It was warm and dry. The house was built in the mountains after the pinenuts were harvested. The house was built in the pine grove owned by a certain family. They stayed there all winter.

SHADES AND PLATFORMS

JG-PL: In the summer, a shade (*ha·ba*) was built. Four or six poles, if a large shade was wanted, were put in the ground (fig. 36b).[24] Two poles were put across in the crotches of the upright posts. They were lashed in place. Poles were lashed across these 2 ft or 3 ft apart. These cross pieces projected 2 ft to 3 ft. Willow foliage or tule mats like the ones used on the winter houses were placed on top to form the roof. The fire was built a little to one side of the shade. The family slept and ate under this shade in the summer.

A small shade, called *pa·soni* was also built.[25] Four poles are put in the ground. The poles stand about 6 ft above the ground. It forms a square of about 4 ft. Poles are put across these posts. They are close together; they touch. This is a storage place for dried fish, meats, etc. Rabbit and other game and fish are hung underneath. This is built near the house, usually in the sun. The dried fish, etc. are in burden baskets or parching trays. The foliage and limbs of willows are cut and placed over the top of the food stored on this platform. The

Figure 36. Shelters. a (top). Winter camp, with cattail house and adjacent brush windbreak/kitchen. Photograph by J. Mooney, Walker River, 1892. NAA-SI. b (middle). Shade of posts roofed with cottonwood branches. Photograph by S. A. Barrett, probably at Walker River, 1916. c (bottom). Frame for sweat house. Photograph by S. A. Barrett, Pyramid Lake, 1916. b and c Milwaukee Public Museum photographs.

were set in the ground slanting toward the center of the house. The tops of the poles were bent over and tied to the house. The poles were tied to the hoop with twisted

---

[24] GK-WR did not think that the shade set on four posts such as is used today was used in the old days. He never saw the shades when he was a boy. Lowie (1924:220) also notes that they may be recent.

[25] ND-HL had never heard of this type of storage platform. The term *pa·soni* is also applied to the fishing platform (see Fishing in chap. 2). Wheat (1967) notes the use of shades as storage platforms as do Kelly (1932:106) and Riddell (1960:42).

leaves and branches of willows are cold and will preserve the dried foods on the platform. Every house had one of these storage platforms usually built about 10 ft away from the house. The food stored on the platform was well covered with leaves so rain or snow would not spoil the food.

BRUSH WINDBREAK

JG-PL: A circular pile was made of sagebrush or other brush. The walls of this were about 5 ft high. Sticks were placed in the ground 5 ft to 6 ft apart. This brush was tramped down so it would not blow away. The wall had an entrance on one side. This was called *hunino·bi* [fig. 36a]. A fire was built in the middle of the circle. This may be built near the *no·bi* and used for cooking. It is also used in the summer. Some of the family may sleep in the circle and some sleep outside.[26]

GK-WR: A semicircle of brush was built in the old days for shade. The wall of this was taller than a man. It was made by standing willow branches with foliage left on in the ground in a semicircle. The shade was open on the shady side, towards the north. This shade was called *haba.* The shade was occupied during the summer.

During the good weather, cooking was done outside the *kani* in a place that was surrounded by a circular or semicircular pile of brush.[27] This shelter was not made carefully like the *haba.* Brush was piled about 3 or 4 ft high. This was called *uninobi.* During the good weather women sat in this enclosure grinding seeds or making baskets. Old men sat there and made string from *wiha* or made nets.

CAVES

BF-PL: The caves have never been used as dwelling places but have been used as a temporary shelter in case of a storm or for people traveling.

BF knows of no story about the Lovelock Cave. Originally Pit River Indians lived around there and lived in the cave. He does not know about burying the dead in caves.[28]

---

[26] Circular windbreaks are a widespread Basin feature (see Steward [1933:265], Riddell [1960:42], Lowie [1924:220], and Stewart [1941:377]). Some of Kelly's (1932:106) information suggests that these and shades were formerly the only dwellings. HS-D called them *tuna nobi.*

[27] ND-HL: A circular brush ring (*huninobi*) made near the house was used for cooking purposes during warm weather.

[28] Stewart (1941:380) reports that four of the 11 groups surveyed noted the use of caves as temporary shelters only. Burial in caves was reported for two groups, but other members of those two also denied the feature.

SWEAT HOUSE

[Park received eight accounts of sweat house construction and sweating. The three most complete accounts are given below as well as excerpts from three others. They describe slightly different methods, uses, and values of sweating, all of which have also been reported in the literature. Sweating and sweat houses are apparently recent in the region, having entered the area from different geographic points. The Pyramid Lake–Lovelock –Honey Lake complexes are said to be of "northern" origin, with the latter perhaps from a different northern source. The Yerington complex may be southern, perhaps *via* Mono Lake and ultimately Bishop. Walker River seems to have lacked the complex until quite recently.]

JG-PL: The sweat house came from some Indians up north, in California or Oregon.[29] The Paiutes got the sweat house around 1880. The people came from around Susanville and Surprise Valley. They took sweat baths and the people at Pyramid Lake learned to take a sweat bath from them. There was a man from Fort Bidwell who came to Pyramid Lake to live when I was about 18 or 20 years old.[30] He got married and stayed here. He used to take sweat baths. The people at Pyramid Lake learned to take sweat baths from him.

The sweat house was made from a willow frame [fig. 36c]. It was small, just large enough for three or four men.[31] The frame was dome-shaped. This was covered with blankets.[32] A pit was dug in the center of the house. Five or six rocks were heated outside and rolled into the pit in the house. Then the men got in the house with a

---

[29] Four of Park's eight consultants on this subject suggested a northern origin for the sweat house. Others did not comment as to its history. Most of Stewart's (1941:430) consultants also suggested its recent acquisition from northern tribes. However, one of Kelly's (1932:203) suggested the aboriginality of the complex in Surprise Valley. de Angulo and Freeland (1929:318), who worked in that area briefly in the 1920s, noted its acquisition from Warm Springs people. Neither Lowie (1924:305) nor Riddell (1960:42) comment on this historical question for Pyramid Lake, Fallon, and Honey Lake. Riddell (1960:42) does attribute the large communal ceremonial and sweat house at one Honey Lake village to Maidu influence. The large, earth-covered communal sweat houses of Owens Valley as described by Steward (1933:265) are also of California origin.

[30] The name of this innovator is not recorded.

[31] Substantially the same structure was described by HS-D. See also Kelly's (1932:203) account for Surprise Valley, Riddell's (1960:42-3) for Honey Lake and Steward's (1933:266) for Mono Lake.

[32] HS-D suggested the use of skins as a covering. In Surprise Valley, sweat houses were covered with rye grass, sage, willow, and probably deerskin. Riddell (1960:43) presumes hides or tule mats for Honey Lake Valley. ND-HL told Stewart (1941:379) that sweat houses were also earth-covered.

cup full of water. They covered up the opening and a little water was sprinkled on the hot rocks with the finger.[33] As soon as they sprinkled the hot rocks one of the men started to talk (pray). They prayed, they talked a hell of a lot. They said, all beating their chests with their fists, "hi., hi., hi.," etc. Then they started to talk: "We are here now, inside here we are taking a bath now. We want you to take the sickness out of us.[34] This is the best medicine. These rocks here and the water and the steam coming out are good medicine. This water that we spray on the rocks makes everything grow and makes things alive. That is why we spray the water on the rocks, to make us strong so we can live a long time." This is all I can remember. There was more talk in there. They stayed in there and sweated until they got through talking. I think they were praying to those rocks and that water.

When they were through talking they went outside and stood around for four or five minutes and took a bath in cold water.[35] Clothes were not put on for a while. They did not feel very good. They felt dizzy and sort of weak. They had to lie down for a while before they put their clothes on.

Women also took sweat baths. Sometimes men and women took sweat baths together.[36]

Udutnabagin° was the name of the sweat house. The sweat bath was called *udutnabagiɔ*. The sweat bath was called *tupinabagia* (*tupi*, rock or stone; *nabagia*, bath or swim; *udut*, hot.)

BR-L,PL:[37] The sweat bath (*tupinabagia*; *tupi*, rock, *nabagia*, swim) was learned from the Bannock. The sweat house was a round dome-shaped frame of willows. It was large enough for only one person at a time. It was covered with tule and brush. Rocks were heated and

rolled inside and water was sprinkled on the hot rocks. The rocks were placed at one side of the house.[38] The bather pours cold water over himself as he comes out of the house. If the sweat house is near the river, he jumps in the river instead. The sweat house was often quite close to the river. Both men and women use the sweat bath. The sweat house is *tuzino·bi* (*tu·zi*, small, *nobi*, house).

The sweat bath was used any time during the year but not much in the summer. It was frequently used in the fall because the steam felt better then, the weather was colder. Sweat baths were not taken in preparation for hunting.[39] BR says he has heard of the practice among other Indians but the Paiutes did not use the sweat bath for that purpose. The sweat bath was learned from the Surprise Valley Paiute and from the Bannock. The people at Wadsworth had the sweat bath when I was a boy (about 65 years ago). I think they learned about the sweat bath a good many years ago. I think there were sweat baths when my father was a boy.

JB-PL: The Paiutes at Pyramid Lake learned the sweat bath from the people in Honey Lake Valley. It was not used much at Pyramid Lake. They bathe in the lake and in the river here. The people in Honey Lake Valley got the sweat bath from people west of Susanville. These people built a large round house, about 20 ft in diameter.[40] They built a hot fire in the house and men and women went in there to sweat. Men and women bathed together. The Honey Lake Valley people also have a smaller sweat house.[41]

TM-WR,Y: A circular house just large enough for two people to sit in was made with a willow frame and covered tightly with grass and tule. The sweat house was called *namosain*.[42] There was no hole in the roof, which was dome-shaped.

A shallow pit was dug at one side of the circular floor and a large flat rock was put into the pit. A fire was built on the rock and burnt until the rock was hot. When the rock was hot, the fire was raked off to one side or the fire was allowed to die down and the ashes left on the rock. Water was then sprinkled on the rock. When the

---

[33] HS-D: "Four or five rocks about 12 in. in diameter were heated outside and rolled into the pit inside the hut. Basket of water was taken in with bathers who sprinkled the rocks and blew on each other to circulate the steam."

[34] Kelly (1932:203) also notes prayers in conjunction with sweating. Prayers were specifically addressed to the sun according to Kelly (1932:203) and Lowie (1924:308). Stewart (1941:380) gives the distribution of the use of the sweat house as a curative agent.

[35] A cold bath was required by the Honey Lake and Pyramid Lake Paiute according to Stewart's data (1941:380). However, according to Lowie (1924:308), a river plunge was made at Fallon but not at Pyramid Lake. A cold water bath was optional in Surprise Valley (Kelly 1932:203).

[36] Both men and women sweated together according to JB-PL and HS-D. Lowie (1924:308) is not clear on the point. Kelly (1932:203) indicates women occasionally sweated with their husbands but also did so with other women.

[37] BR-L,PL may be speaking more of sweat houses at Pyramid Lake than at Lovelock. Locational data by him are not always clear.

[38] Rocks placed to the side in both Surprise Valley and Honey Lake according to Kelly (1932:203), Riddell (1960:Plate 3b), and JB-PL's and TM-WR,Y's accounts to Park.

[39] This was a function of sweating at both Surprise Valley and Honey Lake according to Kelly (1932:203) and Stewart (1941:380).

[40] What is perhaps this same large communal structure is described by Riddell (1960:42) for the village of *Mata*.

[41] JB-PL also gave an account of the smaller house with rocks to one side that agrees with BR-L,PL's account.

[42] This term appears to derive from *muusa*, the word used for the large communal sweat house in Owens Valley (Steward 1933); the term is ultimately of Yokuts origin.

people in the house were perspiring freely they came out of the sweat house and bathed in the nearby creek or river.

Men and women both took sweat baths. Two men would take a bath together and women took baths together. Men and women did not go into the sweat bath at the same time.

Before a person with a cold went into the sweat house he drank a drink made by boiling *todza* [*Lomatium dissectum*] in water. The sweat house was only used for sickness. It was not used for cleanliness. One person may take a sweat bath alone or two to four may take a bath together. A man may build a house just large enough for himself or he may build a larger one. The sweat bath was called *tubinabagiab* (*tubi*, rock; *nabagiab*, swim or bath). Shamans did not prescribe sweat baths for their patients.

GK-WR: I never saw the sweat bath around here (Walker Lake). It was used by the Shoshoni. When the Paiutes want a bath they go into the river where there is water.

RP-WR: Sweat bath is taken by people around Bishop. This was done by the California Paiutes. Not practiced around Walker River. "They take a bath in the river." Practiced by Bishop peoples to rid themselves of some pains. It is not practiced for bathing purposes.

HW-Y: I think that I was the only Paiute at Walker Lake to use the sweat bath. I learned it from a Ute from White Rock. He lived here with me for a long time. This was about 17 years ago.

5

Clothing and Adornment

CLOTHING

[Several types of garments for men and women were described to Park by 14 consultants from various locales. It seems clear from the accounts that dress varied to some degree, within local populations as well as across the region. Factors influencing styles included the local availability of materials, the personal skills and preferences of individuals, and the season of the year. The use of buckskin and/or hide clothing in particular seems to have been a positive reflection on the man's skill as a hunter and provider.

Several people suggested that the older and more typical garments were aprons (often called skirts) of various materials for women and breechclouts/loin cloths and shirts for men. In addition, and when materials were available, women wore knee-length skin dresses and men wore skin pants. Leggings, or, better, leg wrappings, were also described for both sexes for use in winter or when out in the brush. The one-piece buckskin moccasin and/or sagebrush or rush sandals were typical footwear. Headdresses and hair styles as well as other features of personal adornment also seem to have varied across the area.

The accounts that follow have been rearranged in some cases into the categories given. They are the most complete. Supplementary materials and additional points for discussion are contained in the footnotes.]

Sewing Clothing

ND-HL: Each sex sews its own clothing. Women make the clothing for their children. All the garments are sewn with sinew. The small bone in the forearm of the deer is sharpened by rubbing it on stone.[1] There was no eye in the bone. It was used as an awl (*witü*). In sewing, the awl was pushed through and then the garment turned so it could be pushed through again.

GK-WR: Both sexes made the clothing. They helped each other. Sewing was done with a true needle made from some kind of hardwood [fig. 37] or bone. The

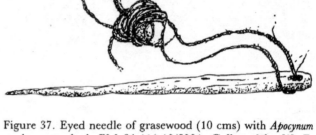

Figure 37. Eyed needle of grasewood (10 cms) with *Apocynum* cordage attached. PM 34-114-10/3921. Collected by W. Z. Park, Pyramid Lake, 1934. Drawing by Susan Lohse.

needle had an eye.[2] The thread was of *wiha* or milkweed. It was softened and beaten up with sticks and the fibers taken out [see Cordage in chap. 3]. Deer sinew was also used for sewing. It is stronger than *wiha* and was used for sewing moccasins and dresses and shirts of buckskin.

HS-D: Women generally do the sewing for clothing. They help one another when they are sewing. Men also sew. They use a needle from the narrow bone of a deer's foreleg. Deer and antelope sinew (*tamo*) was used in sewing.

Women's Clothing

Aprons and Skirts

RP-WR: The wives of lazy men or men who were not good hunters had to make skirts of twisted grass.[3] The grass skirts were woven [i.e., twined] close like a basket only finer. They reached the knees. They used a grass which was much like *saib* [*Scirpus acutus*] but it did not grow as tall. It was only about a foot high and was

---

[1] The identification of this bone is likely part of the radio-ulna.

[2] Eyed needles are viewed as a recent innovation by most. They are probably copied from White models. Unless they were exceedingly fine, it is doubtful that they were much used on clothing.

[3] Skirts of sagebrush bark, rushes, or other fiber were also noted for most of the area by Stewart (1941:394). Kelly's (1932:106) Surprise Valley consultant attributed fiber skirts to widows and the poor.

Figure 38. Women's clothing. a (top left). Wuzzie George, Stillwater, twining sagebrush clothing. Photograph by M. M. Wheat, *ca*. 1958. b (bottom left). Twined sagebrush skirt (based on descriptions). c (top right). Wuzzie George in twined tule dress. Photograph by M. M. Wheat, 1953. d (bottom right). Woman's buckskin dress. MPM 22004. Collected by S. A. Barrett, western Nevada, 1916. a and c, University of Nevada, Reno, Library, Special Collections Department. d, Milwaukee Public Museum photograph. Drawing by Susan Lohse.

called *pamahab* [spike rush, *Eleocharis palustris*]. The grass skirt was called *pamahanagwi* (*pamaha*, grass; *nagwi*, skirt or dress). Skirts were also made from the bark taken from the trunk of large willow trees.[4] This skirt was made like a rabbit skin blanket [i.e., twined]. The bark and grass skirts came about halfway to the knees. Skirts covered only the front of a woman [fig. 38b].

If a woman's husband provided her with a skin, she cut a hole near the head for the neck. The skin was draped over the back and came below her knees. It was gathered at the waist with a belt. The grass apron was worn with the skin. The breasts were not covered, the skin coming just a few inches below the neck. The apron was called *nagwi*. The skin draped over the shoulders and falling down the back was called *kwasünagwi*.

A long time ago some of the women had no skirts at all. At a dance these women would borrow skirts from women who had them. When a woman loaned her skirt she sat at one side all curled up and waited until the woman brought her skirt back. The women would not dance without a skirt.

BR-L,PL: If women did not have any skin to make a dress they made a skirt with tule.[5] The tule was placed closely together and held together with wefts of *wiha* or string made from sagebrush bark. It was done in open twine. These tule skirts came below the knees. *Pamahanakw[i]* was a tule or grass skirt made from *pamahab[i]* [spike rush, *Eleocharis palustris*].

Women also wore skirts made from a small piece of rabbitskin blanket or mudhen skin and feathers. It was made just like a rabbit skin blanket. The skirt made of mudhen skin had the string made from the skin running around while the rabbit skin blanket had the strings running up and down [see Weaving in chap. 3 for construction details]. A small slit was left in the back of the top of the skirt and a string was put around the top. The women stepped into the skirt and pulled it up into position and tied it with the string.[6] The string was tied on either side, in front, or in back. Women also made skirts of two mountain sheep skins sewn together at the sides.

My grandmother told me that when she was a girl the women wore skirts but nothing above the skirts. In the winter a cape which was a small piece of rabbit skin blanket was worn over the shoulders.[7]

JG-PL: Women wore a skirt that came just above the knees made of *pahahab[i]*. This was a plant that grows at the mouth of the river in running water. The stems are hard to break and are smooth. The women pulled them in the summer and spring while they are green and wove them into a skirt. After summer the stems dried and they could not be used.

Some women also wore a single apron (*nakwi*) of buckskin.[8] There was nothing worn in back. The apron came down halfway to the knees and came halfway around the hips. It was held up by a belt. This apron was also made of a coyote, badger, or two or three rabbit skins. These skins were tanned by soaking in damp ground [see Tanning in chap. 3]. Men also wore this apron [see Men's Clothing, below]. My grandfather told me about this. He told me the people were hard up for skins.

JS-R: A mudhen skin apron was worn. A string of buckskin was tied around the waist or sagebrush bark was used. The string was tied in a knot on the side or in front. The mudhen skin was hung over the belt.[9] Sometimes this was worn only in front, sometimes it was worn front and back. Some women wore nothing. They just held something in front of themselves when they walked.

The men occasionally wore the same arrangement [i.e., a loin cloth; see below]. Some women did not have dresses. Only women whose husbands were good hunters had buckskin dresses. Some women wore grass skirts.

The people at Pyramid Lake had more buckskin clothes than the people at Honey Lake. The people at Fallon, Schurz and Yerington traded red paint and beads for buckskin clothes.[10]

HW-Y: Women wore a sagebrush bark skirt (*sawabi nagwi*) that came below the knee.[11] These skirts were made of string twisted out of sagebrush bark. The string was woven into a skirt in the same way a rabbit skin blanket was made. Sagebrush bark was also used to make a sack [shirt, dress] worn by men and women. It was called *watsi tasub*.

AC,LG-F: Skirts (*wa.tsi nagwi*) were made of sagebrush bark. The bark was twisted into string and woven into a skirt. It was woven like a rabbit skin blanket [fig. 38a, b].

---

[4] JO-PL also noted that fiber skirts were made of willow bark. "They had to keep dampening the bark skirt when it got dry or they had to make a new one."

[5] Although the account is not clear, BR probably refers to a double-twined apron rather than a true skirt.

[6] In this case BR is probably describing a true skirt. It is apparently made in tubular fashion [see Weaving in chap. 3].

[7] BR's grandmother was probably from Lovelock and is thus describing the styles there. Rabbitskin capes were also worn in other areas [see Capes and Robes, below].

[8] Stewart (1941:394) also lists the front apron of skin for various Northern Paiute groups. Badger skin apron was called *yohi* (DM-PL).

[9] This account refers to a whole skin apron rather than one of twined feather cloth (see below).

[10] ND-HL: "The Indians around Pyramid Lake and Honey Lake and the Indians in northern Nevada made skirts of buckskin. The Indians around Fallon made skirts of grass and tule because they had plenty of material."

[11] Wheat (1967) describes in detail the construction of these bark garments.

Dresses

RP-WR: If a man was a good hunter, his wife made a dress of two skins [fig. 38d]. The two seams made by sewing the skins together were on the sides. The hole for the neck was not trimmed. The uneven edges of skin around the neck hole were folded inside. The front of the dress was decorated [see under Men's Clothing below]. The dress reached below the knees. The bottom of the dress as well as the arm holes were cut to have a fringe. This dress was worn the year around. It was taken off when the women went to bed. People slept naked.

When a woman borrowed a skin dress in order to dance she gave her friend the grass skirt that she wore.[12] This the woman who loaned the skin dress put on. She sat to one side and watched the dance until her skin dress was returned to her.

BR-L,PL: If two skins could be had, a woman's dress (*kwasəp*, buckskin dress) was made. The two skins were sewn together with the seams on the side. Openings were left for the arms and neck. If there was enough material, elbow-length sleeves were sewn on.[13] The dress was sewn with sinew. The head part of the skin formed the upper part of the dress. The skin from the neck of the animal was left hanging in back of the dress. In front the extra part of the skin was cut off.[14] The front of the neck of the dress was cut in a circular shape. The dress opened about half way down the chest. It was closed with one or two buckskin thongs. There were fringes around the edge of the neck and armholes. The skin was tanned and the smooth side, the side from which the hair had been scraped, was turned out on the dress. There was nothing worn under the dress. It was worn the year round.

Dresses were also made from mudhen skins (*saiyapühü*, mudhen skin). The skins were cut into string and made like rabbitskin blankets [see Weaving in chap. 3]. The dress came from the shoulders to just above the knees. The short feathers on the skin are twisted into twine. The dress has a V-shaped neck and has neither collar nor sleeve. Men usually made these dresses, but "some women knew how". This dress was worn the year around [*sic*]. Both sexes wore these.

In the hot summer weather, the women's mudhen skin dress was replaced by a deerskin skirt (*napi sapo*) that went from the waist to a few inches above the ankle. A few women wore a buckskin dress made in the same way as the dress of mudhen skin. Most of the women wore nothing in the summer or they might wear a two-piece skirt which came about half-way to the knee (*mawgoni nakwi*: *mawgoni*, woman; *nakwi*, skirt).[15]

Leggings

BR-L,PL: In the old days, the women did not wear leggings. Skin was scarce. My mother told me that the women went without anything above their moccasins. About 60 years ago the women wrapped buckskin around their legs up to their knees.[16] In the winter, sagebrush was also wrapped around the legs. The sagebrush bark was worked into string and was braided 2 in. to 4 in. wide and wrapped around the legs (*wisa wüpa'aga*: *wisa*, leg; *wupa'aga*, wrapping). Women wore these leggings sometimes. The leggings were worn only in winter and when away from camp. They were worn for warmth and to protect the legs against scratches from the brush.

Men's Clothing

Breechclouts and Loin Cloths[17]

BR-L,PL: A breechclout was worn. It was called *napiza po·bˀ*. A belt was put around the waist and a piece of skin came between the legs and over the belt with the end hanging down in front and back. This piece was 4 in. to 8 in. wide. The part used passed between the legs and was wide at the ends. Probably when there were only men around or when a man was out trailing deer, he took the breechclout off so it would not chafe the legs.

ND-HL: A breechclout was worn with pants. The breechclout (*napizapogo*), is made of a soft piece of buckskin that goes between the legs under the belt front and rear with the ends loose like short aprons in front and back. The apron-like piece hanging down in front that forms part of the breechclout is called *topada*, the same as the woman's single front apron.

---

[12] RP tells basically the same story here as in her description of the borrowing of bark skirts. A note by Park indicates that she and her daughter found this borrowing exceedingly funny and could hardly stop laughing over the telling.

[13] Kelly (1932:106) considers sleeves to be a recent innovation for Surprise Valley as does Wheat (1967) for Fallon. BR's account of mudhen skin dresses and shirts indicates that they were sleeveless. JB-PL also told Park that women's dresses were made of two skins and were sleeveless, fringed at the armholes, and belted.

[14] JO-PL adds: "The head part of the skin they tucked under until they needed it for moccasins when they would cut it off the dress or the shirt." The neck skin of the deer was considered the toughest and best for moccasins (Riddell 1960:45, Kelly 1932:110).

[15] This account seems to refer to the double apron, a common California feature. Kelly (1932:106) notes it for Surprise Valley. Stewart (1941:394) also notes a scattered distribution for it among the Northern Paiute.

[16] This account is not clear, but it seems to suggest that buckskin leg wrappings as well as bark wrappings are recent.

[17] Kelly (1932:106) suggests that the breechclout may be recent, being associated with Plains-type clothing. Stewart (1941:394) notes the use of both for several bands.

JG-PL: JG has never heard of a breechclout. His grandfather told him about the clothing that the people wore in the old days but he did not tell him about a breechclout. He said men wore an apron [loin cloth] in front.[18]

HS-D: The breechclout (*sasinub*) was worn by the men. It was actually made of buckskin but it might be rabbit-skin. It passed between the legs. Men who are not good hunters weave sagebrush bark to wear as breechclouts. The loin cloth (*pishoni*, also diaper) was also worn.

GK-WR: A breechclout (*napizəpogo yəp*) was worn by the men and women.[19] The breechclout had flaps both in front and in back. The flaps hung several inches down on the legs. The breechclout was about 8 in. wide. It was made of buckskin. Sagebrush bark was used to make aprons which were worn at the front and back when people had no buckskin. Rabbit skins were also used for aprons. Lazy people who did not hunt wore these clothes.

HW-Y: Men wore a sagebrush bark apron (breechclout) called *pinugakwasi*ᵃ.

Shirts

JB-PL: A shirt for men was made from a single skin doubled and sewn down the sides. A hole was cut for the neck. The shirt hangs below the genital organs. The buckskin was always white. A long time ago they did not smoke their skins [see Tanning in chap. 3].

ND-HL: Young boys wore a robe made of the skin of young deer about a month old; this had white spots. A round hole was cut in the middle of the skin for the neck. A slit of 3 or 4 in. was made down the front. This was tied in front with a single string. The sides were sewn up leaving arm holes. The edges were not trimmed. These jackets or white shirts came to about the hips. The bottom edge of the garment was not cut straight across. No belt was used for this jacket. This was called *iwa'abᵊ kwansugaiyu*.

Older men made jackets from two skins (*kwasü*) [fig. 39a]. These were sewed together at the top, at the shoulders. There was the same kind of neck hole. These jackets came a few inches down the thighs. Like the boys'

jackets the edges were trimmed with a fringe. The bottom was cut with fringes that were dangling pieces of buckskin about 3 in. long. These were made by cutting the bottom edge of the garment. At the arm holes there were either these fringes or a serrated edge like a saw.[20] A fringe was also sewed across the chest. Sometimes short pieces of fringe were sewn on the top of the shoulders. A belt (*nati*) was worn with this garment.[21]

Sometimes beads were put on the strings of the fringes sewed across the chest [see also Beads, below]. Often the bones from the paw of the wildcat or the small bones in the lower leg were used. One long bone alternated with a short bone on the string. On the end of the string there was a deer dewclaw or the tip of a deer hoof.[22] There were four or five beads on each string. A hole was bored in the tip of the hoof and the string put through. A knot was made in the end of the string. The tip of the hoof was up with the knot in the hollow of the hoof. A string of beads was worn across the chest. Sometimes the beads were around the bottom edge. If they had enough beads another row was sewn across the front of the dress below the belt. Men only wore the beads on the chest and at the shoulders. Women wore them on the chest, below the belt and on the bottom edge of the dress.

A fringe was made of porcupine quills [see also Quillwork, below]. The porcupine quills were boiled with yellow juniper berries.[23] The quills turned yellow. The quills are hollow. When they are dyed they are pressed flat between the fingers. A quill is wrapped spirally on the buckskin strings of the fringes. When the quill is nearly all around the buckskin string another flattened quill is put under [?over] the first one and the wrapping continued. Four or five quills were put on each string in this fashion. The last quill on each string was held in place with a half hitch. The wrapping of quills sometimes comes about half way down the string of the fringe. These fringes were worn across the chest. These fringes do not make any sound but the ones with the beads do. The fringes made with deer hooves make a very nice sound when the person wearing the dress walks.

These garments are the same for both men and women except the women's dresses are longer, they come to the

[18] Park's note: "In most cases, it was found that informants meant an apron rather than a breechclout. To them a piece of buckskin passing between the legs proved on closer questioning to mean a piece of buckskin or other material was covering the genitals and hung down several inches on the legs but was in the form of an apron. When the wearer, male or female, sat down, the apron was put between the legs." Again, Stewart (1941:394) lists both the apron and the breechclout.

[19] Stewart (1941:394) got positive response for women wearing a breechclout from only one group: the Lovelock Paiute. Kelly (1932:107) also confirms this usage for Surprise Valley. However, Park's account here may refer to the loin cloth or double apron as discussed in note 17.

[20] Shirts of this same construction are also reported by Kelly (1932:108) for Surprise Valley.

[21] Stewart (1941:391) lists buckskin belts as universal items of men's clothing in the area.

[22] Stewart (1941:391) notes decorations of bone tubes and dew claws as well as other ornaments. Kelly (1932:117) notes the use of rabbit-foot bones, dew claws, etc., sewn on garments or worn around the neck and wrists.

[23] Kelly (1932:107) states that quills were dyed yellow by boiling them with lichen (*Evernia vulpina*) found on dead juniper. Quill embroidery and fringing were also practiced in Surprise Valley but the nature of the work is not fully known.

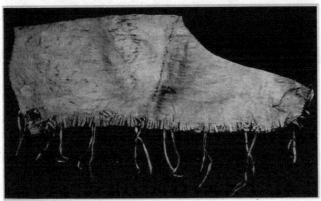

Figure 39. Men's clothing. a (top left). Shirt of type similar to that described by Park. MPM 22007. Collected by S. A. Barrett, Pyramid Lake, 1916. b (bottom left). One side of buckskin pants/leggings. MPM 22005. Collected by S. A. Barrett, Pyramid Lake, 1916. c (right). Man wearing rabbitskin blanket. Photograph by R. H. Lowie, Pyramid Lake, 1914. Neg. #118575. Courtesy Department of Library Services, American Museum of Natural History.

knees or a few inches lower. The men's garment is more of a jacket, it comes to about the hips.

Pants

ND-HL: The men wear pants (*kusa*) that are like cowboy chaps [fig. 39b]. These are held up by strings on the sides that are attached to a belt worn under the jacket. The pants cover the legs only. A breechclout is worn with the pants. The pants are of buckskin, loose like modern trousers. The two legs of the pants were not sewed together at the crotch. The two legs were separate pieces. They came to the ankles.

The buckskin pants were cut out with a flint or obsidian knife. There was no pattern. They just guessed the size. The seam was on the inside of the leg. On the inside of the legs the pants came up 2 or 3 in. below the crotch. It was cut curving upward so that the outside of the pants came almost to the hip. A fringe about 3 in.

wide was sewn down the outside of the leg. This fringe was called *si·tu·da*ʸ. This ran the full length of the pant leg. The tops of the moccasins came above the bottoms of the pants. The moccasins worn by men had tops 2 to 3 in. high.

The buckskin used in dresses, jackets, pants, breechclouts, etc. was not smoked. A long time ago the Indians did not smoke buckskin [see Tanning in chap. 3].

JG-PL: Men who were good hunters were the ones who had buckskin clothes.[24] The lazy people used mudhen skin and feathers. They would take the whole skin off the bird. They left the feathers on. It took about 10 of these skins to make pants for a man. Strings of *wiha* were used to sew the skins together. Around Fallon they use this *wiha* to sew duck skins. Here (Pyramid Lake) they use it for mudhen skins and buckskin. These pants came to just above the knees and opened on one side. The string of braided *wiha* was put all the way around the waist to hold them up. The string was tied either on the side or in front or in back. They also made a shirt the same way.

They had no leggings [see below]. Sometimes when the men came home from hunting their legs would be all bloody from sagebrush scratches.

Leggings

ND-HL: Knee-length leggings (*witsaw pa*ʔ*agan*) were worn only by the men. Each legging was a rectangular piece of antelope skin. It was wrapped around the leg once and tied with a single string at the top, just below the knee. These came over the tops of the moccasins. The leggings were worn over the pant legs for protection going through the brush.

BR-L,PL: In the winter men on the hunt wore buckskin moccasins and leggings of buckskin or sagebrush bark[25] wrapped around the legs up to the knees. These were worn to protect his legs from the brush and also for warmth. Good hunters wore badger skin leggings instead (*wisawü pa*ʔ*aga*, leggings; *wisa*, leg; *wupa*ʔ*aga*, wrapping).

HS-D: Buckskin was wrapped around the leg below the knee, and was called *witsawupuganu* or *witsasahuma*. These leggings were worn in winter or even in the summer when traveling through thorny brush. They were worn by men, women and children.

Capes and Robes

JG-PL: In the winter, a small rabbitskin blanket was worn over the shoulders by both men and women [fig. 39c]. People also had small robes made of different kinds of skins.[26] My grandfather told me he saw one old man make a small blanket of mountain rat skins. He skinned the rats and spread the skins out flat. The blanket was only large enough to cover his chest. He covered his chest with this blanket when he went to bed at night. He also wore it in the daytime in winter.

When a man had a fine large robe, he was a rich man. Skins such as cow, antelope, deer, horse and those of small animals were softened with the hair on and used for this. They were softened by burying them in damp ground [see Tanning in chap. 3].

RP-WR: Men wore the same cape as women [see RP's account of women's skirts, above]. This was one skin with a hole near the top for the head. It hung down the back. A man wore this with a sagebrush apron.

Belts

RP-WR: Belts were made of swan feathers mixed with the green and blue breast feathers of the male ducks. The swan skin was cut in strips. Thread of *wiha* was wound around the swan skin and the duck feathers which made strips of alternating white swan down and green or blue duck feathers.[27] The duck feathers were fastened to the swan skin. The belt was from one to 2 in. wide. These belts were used to gather the dress. Children held up the loin cloth with this belt. Men wore these belts or plain ones of buckskin.

Gloves and Mittens

RP-WR: The Paiutes did not make or use any kind of gloves or mittens.[28] Even in winter no covering for the hands was worn.

---

[24] Statements *re* hunting skills and the acquisition of buckskin clothing were so often repeated by Park's consultants as to become cliches.

[25] BR suggests in his account of women's leg wrapping that those of sagebrush bark were "braided" [i.e., plaited].

---

[26] Stewart (1941:393) lists robes made of furred skins of deer, mountain sheep, wildcat, badger, and coyote. BR-L,PL also noted the use of mudhen skin robes made like rabbit skin blankets.

[27] Such belts were not suggested to Stewart (1941:391), and thus may be special items manufactured by a few. The technical description is not clear but may involve plying swandown strips and duckskin strips over *wiha* cores and then plying those so that the colors will alternate. This could then be sewn on the swanskin strip.

[28] Gloves and mittens were denied by all of Stewart's (1941:393) consultants. Kelly (1932:113) notes the use of mittens of rabbit fur in Surprise Valley but questions their antiquity.

Children's Clothes

HS-D: Children wear in winter the same clothes as adults. In the summer they went naked.

Arm Bands

HS-D: Men wore armbands of skin—gopher skin, or other soft fur. Armbands were worn on the forearm.

Footwear

Skin Moccasins

BR-L,PL: In the old days there were not many people who had buckskin moccasins. Skins were too difficult to get. Only the few who were the best hunters got enough skins to have buckskin moccasins. Other people made moccasins from twisted sagebrush bark. These were called *wasimoko* [see below].

To make buckskin moccasins (*moko* or *kwasamoko*) the skin was folded and the foot placed so that the inner side of the foot is along the folded edge [fig. 40a].[29] With a knife the skin is cut around the shape of the foot except on the side of the fold. The cut edge is sewn with sinew or *wiha*. A hole is then cut for the opening to put on and take off the moccasin, and the tongue which comes above the ankle is sewn in. One or two strings were used for tying.

The sole for the moccasin[30] is usually made of badger skin because it "doesn't wrinkle when it gets wet." A worn sole is replaced if a piece sufficiently large can be found. If not, a piece of skin is sewn over the hole as a patch. The strongest moccasins are made of badger skin [fig. 40b]. The hair is not scraped off. The hair side is outside. The badger skin sole of the moccasin is not tanned.

Men made the moccasins. They made the footwear for the women, but "sometimes a few women knew how to make moccasins and they made their own." Moccasins were worn all year around. Sagebrush bark that has been softened by rubbing is put inside the moccasin before it is put on the foot. This keeps the feet dry and warm in winter.

ND-HL: No socks were worn but there was a high top moccasin. Tops came to 4 to 5 in. above the ankle.

The tops were sewn on the moccasin [i.e., they were separate]. They were worn year round. A long thong is used to tie the tops that are wrapped around the legs. Women wore the moccasins with a high top. Some of the men wore buckskin pants with which they wore the short moccasin.

AC,LG-F: Moccasins (*sogomoko*) were made of buckskin. The pair that AD-R has came from Susanville. They have a trailer about ¾ in. long and about 1 in. wide. No other moccasins that were seen—and they are frequently worn by the old women—had trailers. All the informants at Pyramid Lake and Reno denied that moccasins were made with trailers.[31]

Bark Shoes or Sandals

JG-PL: Moccasins of twisted sagebrush bark were called *wasimoko* [fig. 40c]. To make them, the outside bark from old sagebrush is pulled off in long strands. It is rolled on the thigh and then two strands are rolled together (ca. ¼ in. in diameter). These moccasins came just to the ankle. They are not as high as those made of buckskin. One strand starts at the top of the foot, runs over the toe and then the length of the bottom of the foot and over the heel and up in the back as far as the ankle. If this string is long enough, it is then doubled back and close to the other strand. These strings are put as close together as possible and then the tying weft is in open twine with the elements close together as in a fine parching tray or water jug.[32] Loose sagebrush bark was rolled to make it soft and put in the bottom of the moccasin. It was put in both in summer and winter. The bark was put just on the bottom of the moccasin. This bark lasted about three weeks. Then fresh bark was put in. These moccasins did not last as long as buckskin moccasins. When a moccasin got a hole, it was not repaired. It was thrown away and a new one made. These were worn in the snow. When wet they did not pull apart or go to pieces.

Pamihabi [*Eleocharis palustris*] was also used in making shoes like the sagebrush moccasins [fig. 40d].[33]

---

[29] This seems to match the moccasin described and figured by Kelly (1932:110f) and equated by her with Wissler's (1910:151) Number 8 pattern. BR suggests that a separate tongue was sewn in.

[30] BR seems to imply here that the one-piece moccasin had a separate sole. Perhaps it is only that it can be soled when worn out. Lowie (1924:218) reports that the badger skin moccasins were made with the hair side in. ND-HL and JB-PL both referred to the use of badger skin for soles, noting that it was not tanned. Hard-soled moccasins are a Plains feature.

[31] Kelly (1932:111) describes and illustrates this type of moccasin, complete with trailer.

[32] Although this description is not clear in details, the moccasins referred to are probably similar to the ones described by Kelly (1932:109). These are also multiple warped, the ends of the warp being folded upon the upper foot. These in turn are essentially the same except for materials as those described by Barrett (1910) for the Klamath. Fig. 41c is of a sandal collected by Kelly in Surprise Valley.

[33] Lowie (1924:218) discusses and figures sandals. Although JG's mention of these is too brief to add construction details, in all likelihood these are also the multiple warp variety. Kelly's (1932:109) consultants noted that tule was not good for sandals. Sagebrush wore longer.

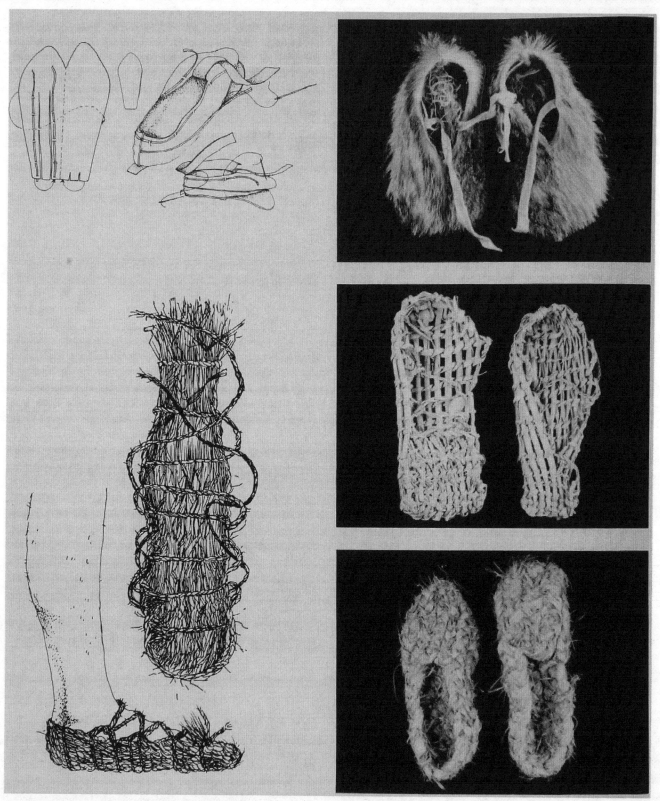

Figure 40. Moccasins and sandals. a (top left). Moccasin pattern, after AMNH 50.2/3722, collected by W. Z. Park, Pyramid Lake, 1934, and Kelly (1932, fig. 2). Woman's version has higher ankle flaps. b (top right). Child's badger-skin boots. Idaho State Museum of Natural History 5004. Collected by S. Liljeblad, Stillwater, 1970. c (bottom left). Sagebrush sandals, diagonal/plain twined. LMA 1-28208. Collected by I. T. Kelly, Surprise Valley, 1930. d (middle right). Man's tule sandal. AMNH 50.1/7965. Collected by R. H. Lowie, Fallon, 1914. e (bottom right). Winter shoes of braided sagebrush bark. AMNH 50.2/3724. Collected by W. Z. Park, Pyramid Lake, 1934. Drawings by Susan Lohse.

In the old days, people went barefoot around the house. When they went out to gather seeds or hunt they put on moccasins. Today many old people are seen around the house barefooted. This is especially true of Walker Lake where people of both sexes were seen about the house without any footwear.

RP-WR: People did not go barefoot around the house. Moccasins were put on as soon as the people arose in the morning and worn all day until retiring at night.

AD-R: Sagebrush bark was used to make sandals, like a slipper. The soles were thick. They were tied on with string.[34]

Overshoes or Snow Boots[35]

RP-WR: Sagebrush bark was softened and the fibers were combed out. These were rolled into a string and woven into a shoe with a legging which comes to the knee (*nubamaka*: *nuba*, snow; *maka*, shoe).

One pair of these would last through a big storm. The soles could be renewed with the same material. Extra pieces were made in the same shape as the sole and put inside the shoe for an inner sole. The use of a snowshoe with a rigid frame was unknown to RP [see Snowshoes in chap. 6].

HS-D: A wide sandal, "something like an overshoe" was made of tule (*toi*). I do not know how this was made and I do not know its name. Sagebrush bark was stuffed between this tule overshoe and the moccasin.

JG-PL: People made shoes of braided sagebrush bark for winter [fig. 40e]. They did not have snow shoes of any kind for walking on top of the snow.

Headwear

Basket Hats

RP-WR: Basket hats (*kütunano*) in twined work, like the cooking baskets, were worn by women. They were worn when carrying burdens or when they went out to get seeds to protect the head. The basket was made especially for wear. It was not used for other purposes such as eating or drinking [see below]. There were no rims on these baskets. They were made to fit the head tightly. Basket hats had more and larger designs than cooking baskets. The designs were bands and diamonds [fig. 41a].

AC,LG-F: A basket was made to wear on the head. Only women wore these hats. They were used for drinking water. This basket was called *susida*.

BR-L,PL: Women wore baskets on their heads. These were bowl-shaped baskets that were also used for serving mush. Women washed the basket and put it on their heads when they went out. There was no basket that was used only as a hat. All of these basket hats were used for eating mush. Not all of the women wore baskets on their heads.[36] Some women went bareheaded most of the time.

Skull Caps

ND-HL: Men and women wore a cap made out of buckskin. It was like a skull cap. It was cut to fit over the head and the hair left hanging down the shoulders. It was worn year round. The hat was called *kwasüsotiya*. The hat came over the forehead and covered the top of the head. There was no brim to the hat at all [fig. 41b].[37]

HS-D: While hunting on a hot day men wore a small piece of buckskin over the back of the head. A few men wore badger skin caps.

BR-L,PL: Men wore a sort of skull cap made out of deer skin. "It didn't have a good shape. I think that the skunk and badger skin caps were not worn in the old days.[38] A few years ago I saw men wear these caps" [fig. 41c].

Headbands

ND-HL: Headbands (*zowɔpaga*) were made out of the neck skin of mallard with the feathers on it. The skin was cut in strips an inch wide. Sagebrush bark was used for a core around which the mallard skin was wrapped. Both men and women wore this headband.

The bald eagle is called *pazia*. The black American eagle is called *kwi'na*. The breast feathers of this eagle are taken off but the down is left on and the skin is cut in strips to be used in making a headband in the same way as the mallard skin. The part of the eagle that is used is called *pihihukap* [fig. 41d].

BR-L,PL: Men wore the tail feathers of magpie.[39]

---

[34] AD's description is also too brief to characterize the construction to these, but the mention of tying the sandals on with string supports the notion that it is multiple-warp shoes being described. These were laced onto the foot [see fig. 40c].

[35] Overshoes are listed by Stewart (1941:395) for Fallon, Yerington, and Walker River people as well as for several more northerly bands. JB-PL told Park of sagebrush bark boots that came 4 to 5 in. above the ankles. Stewart (1941:436) illustrates several sagebrush bark boots from the John T. Reed collection, Lovelock, Nev.

[36] Stewart (1941:392) lists basketry hats as common but by no means universal head wear for the Northern Paiute.

[37] Skin caps with visors are reported by Kelly (1932:114) for Surprise Valley.

[38] Stewart (1941:392) lists men's caps of tanned buckskin, fawn, and antelope, mountain sheep lamb, muskrat, beaver, badger, wildcat, and coyote. Lowie (1924:217) also notes that badgerskin caps were occasionally worn as does Kelly (1932:114).

[39] JG-PL noted to Park that he thought the use of magpie feathers by other than a shaman was recent. The description of this headwear is not clear. It probably refers to an eagleskin

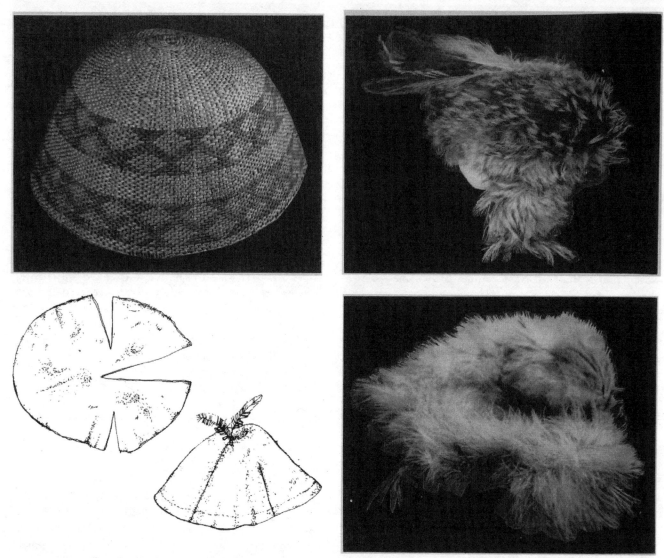

Figure 41. Headdress. a (top left). Woman's diagonal twine basket hat. MPM 22124. Collected by S. A. Barrett, western Nevada, 1916. b (bottom left). Man's buckskin cap, unconstructed and finished, with feathers and horsehair attached. PM 35-120-10/5188. Collected by W. Z. Park, Pyramid Lake, 1935. c (top right). Man's coyote-skin cap decorated with eagle feathers. MAI 13/4148. Collected by M. R. Harrington, Stillwater, 1924. d (bottom right). Eagle-down headband. MAI 13/4430. Collected by M. R. Harrington, Walker River, 1924. Drawings by Susan Lohse.

The fine feathers from underneath were used. The size of the head was measured and the dry skin of an eagle with the small feathers still on was put on. Magpie tail feathers were stuck in like a bank around the head. This man's headdress was called *pihi hukab*.

JG-PL: Some people who had buckskin would fix beads on a band of it and wear this around the head. Some bands were decorated with porcupine quills which were sewed on with sinew. Eagle feathers would be stuck into the band at the back of the head.[40] One of two feathers

were worn. Only men wore these feathers.

Head bands were made of feathers. Many women wore woodpecker feathers, the red ones (probably Northern Flicker) [*Colaptes auratus*]. The feather is stripped except for the tip. The quills were then woven together with sinew. Only one row of feathers is used.[41] Porcu-

---

headband with magpie feathers, although a cap of eagleskin is also possible.

[40] Several individuals commented to Park that feathers were not worn in the hair or in the headband all of the time. BR-

---

L,PL noted that "feathers were not worn in the hair in winter as they could get wet and be spoiled and considerable value was placed on eagle feathers. In summer, one or two eagle feathers were worn in back of the head held by a band."

[41] Park collected some examples of headbands with feathers for the Peabody Museum. Most of these are extremely simple, with feathers of gull, magpie, etc., made to stand vertically in a two-ply band. Other, more elaborate bands of flicker feathers may be in imitation of California practices.

pine quills are arranged in the same way. These feathers and porcupine quills are used for headbands and belts. A piece of sinew was left at each end of the belt or band for tying. These were made by both men and women. No bird scalps were used, nor were headdresses made from human hair.

Some people had little ponies. They would take the hair from the tail of the pony and braid it. If the hair was white, they would dye it yellow or green. This would be worn as a forehead band. Both men and women made them, wore them and dyed them.

HW-Y: Men wore a deer skin band around the head. One feather was stuck in the band. These head bands were called *watsotaya*. Some men wore squirrel skin head bands.

BR-L,PL: Women often wore head bands of twisted tule or sagebrush.

Other headwear

HS-D: The war bonnet came from the Bannock.[42] Very few Paiutes had them. HS does not know when the Paiutes first got them. They were used as a decoy in warfare. When the battle went against them the war bonnet was left on a bush to make the enemy think they were still there and then they sneaked off.

GK-WR: Hair nets were made of *wiha* and worn by both men and women.[43] "I remember my old uncle wore a net on his head." These hair nets covered only the top of the head, like a skull cap. Each person made his own hair net usually, but sometimes a man would make a hair net for his wife. "I have seen the old people make these nets." The hair net or any kind of hat was called *sotua*. Very few men wore a feather in the hair or in the hair net. The hair net was worn on any occasion. It was worn every day.

RP-WR: In the spring the bark was peeled from the long green shoots of willow. The pieces of bark were tied together and placed on top of the head. The ends fell down the back and down the side of the head. Only the women wore these wig-like things. This was used as a protection against the sun. It kept them cool.

PERSONAL ADORNMENT

[Treated under this topic are such matters as hair styles, nose and ear piercing, tattooing, depilation, and the uses and manufacture of paints. Park received short accounts on all of these topics from several individuals, and what follows is structured so as to bring out differences of opinion or suggested regional variations. Most respondents, however, seemed to agree on the general features within each topic.]

Hairdress

HS-D: The hair was worn long. The men wore their hair in two braids which fell over the front of the shoulders. The braids were wrapped with fine fur such as weasel. One or two feathers were worn hanging down. The hair is parted in the middle.

Women wore their hair braided in two braids which fell down their backs. The women did not wrap their hair in fur. At big dances the women wore their hair unbraided and brushed out down their backs.[44] Women cut their hair on the death of a relative. Men never cut theirs.

RP-WR: Hair was worn in braids mostly by the men. The women wore their hair loose down the back. The men used weasel or beaver fur for tying the braids. No paint was put on men's hair. The part in the hair was not painted.[45] The braids were not artificially lengthened.

Women wore the hair loose. Stripes of white paint ran across the hair.[46] The paint was put on in stripes horizontally. The stripes started at the top of the head and were put on 2 or 3 in. apart the full length of the hair.

Nothing was done to prevent the hair from turning gray.

JG-PL: Both men and women parted their hair in the middle. Red paint was put on the part. Both men and women painted the part. The paint was wet before it was applied. Paint was not put on any other part of the hair. JG has not heard of women using white paint on their hair [see RP-WR, above].

The women did not braid their hair much. It was parted and combed down the back. A band of string around the head held the hair in place, or the hair was tied at the back with *wiha* or sagebark string. Men wore

---

[42] JG-PL and GK-WR also concurred that the war bonnet was obtained from the Bannock, and quite recently (perhaps the middle of the last century). HS's comment on leaving war bonnets probably refers to a single incident.

[43] Stewart (1941:392) obtained a positive response on the use of a hair net from only two bands: Honey Lake and Yerington.

[44] Essentially the same account as Kelly (1932:114–15), except for wearing the hair brushed down the back. She was unable to verify this style although it had been reported for the area by de Angulo and Freeland (1929:139). Kelly also notes the use of three braids for both sexes in Surprise Valley.

[45] Stewart (1941:392) lists painting of the part for roughly half of the bands surveyed. The primary distribution of this feature is in the north, however. See also GK-WR below.

[46] Stewart (1941:392) notes that white paint was used in the hair by only three of the 12 Northern Paiute groups surveyed. JO-PL told Park that women pasted their hair down tight with white paint. It was put on when wet to get a wavy effect.

the hair in braids starting at the side of the head and falling down the chest. The braids were not artificially lengthened. Long ago they did not braid their hair. They just let it hang.

In the old days, flowers were not worn in the hair or over the ears by either sex.[47] There was no way of getting rid of lice in the hair. JG thinks there were no lice in the old days.

When the Indians got scissors, they cut the boys' hair. The hair was cut short on the sides and on top. A small tuft of hair 4 to 5 in. long was left in the middle of the top of the head.[48] The boy started to have his hair cut this way when he was about seven. When he got to be a big boy, about twelve or thirteen, they stopped cutting his hair and it was allowed to grow. I do not think they cut the boys' hair before they had scissors. The girls' hair was not cut at all.

GK-WR: Men and women wore their hair long, parted in the middle and put over the back. Sometimes it was braided, sometimes not. The hair could be done up in two braids. It was parted in the middle of the head. The braids of hair were tied with string or small pieces of beaver fur. Sometimes half of the braid was wrapped with strips of fur and sometimes the braid was only tied at the end with string or fur. Men especially wrapped their braids.

Sometimes the hair was worn in a single braid down the back.[49] Other times the two braids were worn falling over the chest. Both sexes wore the hair either style. The hair might not be braided but simply fall down the back or over the shoulders and on the chest. The part in the middle was not painted. HR has seen Bannock Indians with paint on the forehead and in the part of their hair. The Paiutes did not put paint on their hair.

"When I was a boy, I saw the old people—and I did it too—take deer fat or tallow and the marrow from the bones and put it in small baskets to keep. They kept some all the time. They would rub the tallow or marrow on the hair and then comb it in. I guess they got rid of lice that way." Mud plaster against lice was not known.[50]

Figure 42. Hairbrushes. a (left). Porcupine-tail hairbrush. MPM 22059. Collected by S. A. Barrett, western Nevada, 1916. b (right). Hairbrush of wild rye roots, buckskin-wrapped. NMNH 19065. Collected by S. Powers, Pyramid Lake, 1876. Drawings by Susan Lohse.

GK has never heard of flowers being worn in the hair or over the ear either in daily life or at dances by either sex.

RP-WR: Children's hair was cut with a flint knife. Boys' hair was cut until about seven years of age, the same with girls. Children would cry when their hair was cut as it pulled. "Could hear children crying from both sides of the river when their hair was cut."

Hairbrushes and Combs

ND-HL: Both men and women used a comb (*wunədsu*). The comb was made from a porcupine tail [fig. 42a].[51] The bottom of the tail had very hard quills. On the top side the quills are taken out. The tail is skinned and stuffed with sagebrush bark. It is sewed and stuffed when it is still fresh. When it dries it becomes hard. It has the regular shape of the tail when it is stuffed and sewn. The quills continue to grow (come out) in the comb. The quills are trimmed from time to time to keep them even.

---

[47] Sarah Winnemucca Hopkins (1883:47) reports that girls wore crowns of flowers in their hair at annual spring festivals. Park's question is probably in response to this.

[48] Hair cutting with stone knives is reported by Stewart (1941:392) but no details are given. The tufted style described here may be in imitation of Plateau or Plains hairdress.

[49] This was also reported to Park by JS-R as a favored style for women.

[50] Stewart (1941:392) got positive responses on this feature from consultants from five out of the 12 bands surveyed. JG-PL also told Park that he had not heard of this use.

[51] Kelly (1932:115) also describes this comb. Stewart (1941:392) gives its distribution.

RP-WR: A hair brush was made from *waiyaba*, wild rye [*Elymus cinereus*] which grows in bunches in the valleys.[52] The seeds are used for food. The roots are dug up and a handful of the grass 12 to 14 in. long is tied together in the center. Then the bunch is doubled over and again tied in the center [fig. 42b]. The ends are evened off in the fire. This also hardens the ends. It makes a good brush that is good and strong. It is called *wunadzo*.

AD-R: Another type of brush is made from rabbitbrush (*sigupi*) [*Chrysothamnus nauseosus*].[53] In the fall when the branches are dry, a handful is gathered and tied together at one end. This brush has long straight twigs. It is tied in a bundle by wrapping string at one end of the bunch of twigs. The brush is 6 to 8 in. long. It is called *wǝnadso*, the same as the porcupine tail brush.

Tattooing

HW-Y: Both men and women were tattooed. To tattoo, a grass was chewed and mixed with ashes from pinewood.[54] It is very black. A porcupine quill is used to prick the skin and apply the coloring. Children were tattooed when they were about 10 years old. The operation was performed on both boys and girls by the mother or grandmother.[55] Boys were often tattooed with a horizontal line on the cheek that reaches to the corner of the mouth. Women may have straight lines on the chin or lines running obliquely downward from the corner of the mouth. They also have a straight line on the bridge of the nose. Both sexes were also tattooed on the hands and wrists.

HS-D: Tattooing (*nabawits*) was for both sexes, but girls were tattooed more than boys. A porcupine quill, a rabbit bone or some other small bone was sharpened. Charcoal was dissolved in water and used for coloring. A sister, aunt or mother performed the operation. Men never did the tattooing. Boys and girls were tattooed around 14 or 15 years of age. Straight lines were tattooed on the cheeks, nose, chin, back of the hand. Both sexes used the same marks. Tattooing was not very elab-

orate. One individual had only several lines on the face or hands.

JG-PL: Greasewood or cedar [juniper] was burned to charcoal. This was mixed with water until the mixture was very thin. A needle was made by breaking off a rabbit bone. It was broken off so that it was very sharp. With a stick dipped in the dissolved charcoal, the design was painted on the hand, arm, face, etc. Then with the sharp needle, pricks were made in the skin along the designs. The women had legs and toes tattooed.[56] Bands were tattooed around the leg above the ankle. Straight lines were on the thigh and on the toes. Straight lines were made on the arms and hands.[57] A person tattooed his own arms and legs and nowadays with a mirror a person tattoos his or her own face. In the old days the face was probably tattooed by another person. Tattooing on the face included lines on the cheeks, bridge of the nose, chin, at the corners of the mouth, sometimes a dot on the upper lip if there was no mustache.

The tattoo marks have no meaning. Tattooing was done just to make people look good. It was not done for luck.[58] While a person was being tattooed or was tattooing himself, he did not talk or pray.

Nose and Ear Piercing

ND-HL: The septum of the nose was drilled and a small piece of bone—usually the bone from the forearm of the porcupine—was worn in the hole. It looked pretty good. Any sharpened bone was used for a drill. Or a porcupine quill could be used. The quill was just stuck there and not forced through. The quill worked its own way through. When it came through on the other side it was pulled through and a stick was used to make the hole larger. Only a few people did this, men especially.[59] A boy might have his septum drilled when he was between 10 and 15 years old. The bone was worn in the septum permanently. It was sometimes taken out to clean and then it was put back. The bones that ND has seen in

---

[52] Grass hairbrush construction is described by Wheat (1967:88f), as well as by Kelly (1932:115). Stewart (1941:392) lists its distribution.

[53] This type of brush was also described to Park by ND-HL and HS-D.

[54] GK-WR noted the use of *sudupi* [*Ephedra viridis*] mashed with rocks and put on the end of a sharp bone as material for face and body tattooing.

[55] Kelly (1932:115) states that in Surprise Valley children were not tattooed and that it apparently had no connection with puberty. Stewart (1941:390) found scattered reference to tattooing children or young adults but found that most groups felt that it could be done at any time.

[56] Stewart (1941:390) notes tattooing on arms, legs, and other parts of the body for most Northern Paiute groups surveyed.

[57] JG-PL stated on another occasion specifically "wrists and fingers."

[58] Park's note: JG has never heard that the Indians believed that the souls of untattooed people enter rat holes or are trodden underfoot. He insists that it is done only for show.

[59] Stewart (1941:390) lists nose piercing as rare for females, more widespread for males. Kelly (1932:117) notes that it was apparently rare in Surprise Valley. Riddell (1960:46) notes that Honey Lake people considered it a "sporty affectation." GK-WR was of the opinion that only "chiefs" wore a bone in the nose.

the septum were just plain white. They were not painted.[60]

RP-WR: The ear lobes were pierced. The lobe was squeezed tightly between the fingers until it was numb. Then it was pierced with a sharpened sagebrush stick that had been burnt a little in the fire. This prevented the lobe from getting sore. The sagebrush stick was left in the hole until the wound healed. When it was taken out, a string of *wiha* or buckskin was put through the hole so it would not close up. The string was left in until the wound was thoroughly healed. Then green stones about 1 in. long are suspended from the ears with deer sinew. Pendants were also made of abalone shell gotten from California. Only women wore the pendants in their ears. The hole was drilled in the shell with a deer bone. A deer bone was used to shape and cut the shell for a pendant.

The green and blue stone used for ear pendants was gotten east of Hawthorne. That is the only place this kind of stone was found. DL, the interpreter, thinks it was turquoise.[61] It was sometimes used to make a pipe. The place where this stone is gotten is not known today. Many people have looked for it.

BB-PL: The ear lobes were commonly pierced.[62] Beads were worn as ear pendants for special occasions. For every day wear a stick was put in the hole in order to keep it from closing.[63] Both sexes wore ear pendants. Beads were suspended by a string. The purpose was ornamentation.

A boy's ear lobes were usually pierced by his mother. It is done while the child is still in the cradle.[64] A dried badger's penis that has been sharpened is used to pierce the ear lobes.[65] The bone in the penis is about .8 in. in diameter when it is dry. It is also used as a needle.

---

[60] One of Kelly's (1932:117) informants reported seeing one old man with a bone and "feathers" in his nose. This is more commonly a Plateau feature.

[61] The green stone described here is probably serpentine rather than turquoise, based on the suggestion that it was used in pipe manufacture.

[62] Stewart (1941:390) lists ear piercing for only some women and some men in most groups surveyed. JG-PL: "I saw a lot of people that way not very long ago."

[63] JG-PL noted the common use of a stick of greasewood as an ornament. GK-WR noted that bone tubes were used for everyday wear.

[64] No specific reason was stated for this practice, and the age at which it was done apparently varied. Kelly (1932:117) notes that some pierced the ears of infants to secure health and longevity — and also to prevent crying. Stewart (1941:390) notes that for most groups it was commonly done when they were children. GK-WR stated that fathers pierced the ears of their sons when they were one to two years of age.

[65] This same instrument was also described to Park by ND-HL.

Depilation

JG-PL: In the old days the Indians had no hair on their faces. Hair did not grow on their faces.[66] The eyebrows were not touched in the old days. A few years before I was born the men started to pull out their eyebrows. They had tweezers then. These were made out of iron. They pulled out the eyebrows leaving a narrow straight line of the eyebrows.[67] When they painted their faces, they painted a line above and below this line of eyebrows. The women did not do anything to their eyebrows. Only the men did this. My father plucked his eyebrows this way.

ND-HL: In the old days young men pulled out their eyebrows leaving only a narrow straight line. Each hair was caught between the fingernails and jerked out. The beard was also pulled out with the fingers.[68] The women did nothing to their eyebrows.

Paint

HS-D: Black paint (*tunupi*) was made by burning pine pitch under a basket.[69] The soot was collected from the basket and mixed with deer fat. This was used on the face and body.

Red paint (*pizəpi*) was also sometimes mixed with grease. White paint (*ibi*) was always used with water or saliva. It was never mixed with fat. Red paint and yellow paint (*oapi*) were always carried in a small buckskin bag [fig. 43a]. Women also have a supply of paint.

Yellow paint is gotten around the southwestern corner of Pyramid Lake. They get it and soak it in water. The part that settles to the bottom is used for paint. This yellow paint is used to keep the buckskin bright on the cradle. It is also used to paint the body. To have the body painted is *nabizasi*. The command the doctor gives the spectators to put on white paint is *ubishas* [see Shamanism in vol. 2]. The mark put on the body or face while doctoring is *naboni*. White paint is gotten near Virginia City and also at a place south of Dayton called White Chalk Mountain. Right after birth the baby is powdered with red paint.

GK-WR: Yellow paint (*oapi*) was gotten in the mountains southeast of Walker Lake. It was used to color deerskin clothes, moccasins, cradles, and for personal

---

[66] Stewart (1941:392) got positive response on depilation of beard from nearly all informants questioned.

[67] Kelly (1932:115) also states that it was a practice of youths and girls in Surprise Valley.

[68] Stewart (1941:392) notes the use of a stone flake for this purpose as well as one's fingernails.

[69] BF-PL told Park that black paint was obtained by burning greasewood under a blanket or skin. The soot was then mixed with water to apply.

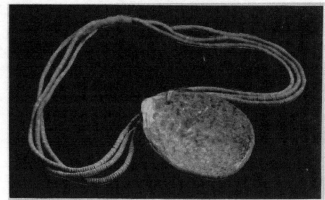

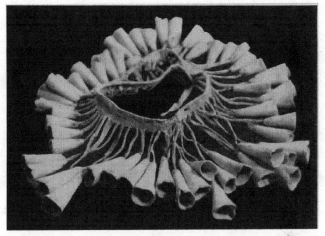

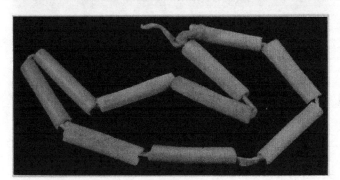

Figure 43. Personal adornment. a (top left). Buckskin bag for personal supply of red/yellow ochre. NMNH 19061. b (middle left). "Bricks" of processed red ochre paint. MPM 21825. c (bottom left). Woman's necklace of wing bones of swan. Park private collection. d (top right). Necklace of duck-bone beads said to have been used as money. Abalone shell pendant may be museum addition. NMNH 19062. e (bottom right). Necklace/belt of mountain-sheep phalanges. NMNH 19057. a, d, e collected by S. Powers, Pyramid Lake, 1876. b collected by S. A. Barrett, Pyramid Lake, 1916. c collected by W. Z. Park, Pyramid Lake, 1934.

adornment.[70] It was found in small pieces. It was not dissolved as white paint but was used just as it was found.

White paint (*ibi*) was gotten in the mountains. All the rocks were taken out. It was dissolved in water. The fine white paint goes to the bottom. The sediment is moulded in any desired shape and dried and kept for later use [fig. 43b]. It is dampened again when it is used. The Indian doctors use this paint most of the time [see Shamanism in vol. 2]. Red paint is gotten and fixed in the same way as white paint.[71]

Everybody paints his face at the big dances. Paint was put on the arms and legs. Red paint was put on first and then designs were made with white and yellow paint. White paint was used on the face after the red paint was put on as a trimming to make stripes. Paint was put on every day at the dance after they washed in the morning.

[70] GK-WR noted to Park that buckskin shirts and dresses were painted with yellow paint along the seams. He had not seen paint put on any other part of the clothing.

[71] Wheat (1967:27) discusses the use of red pigment. Stewart (1941:391) lists the colors of paint, their uses and distributions for the region.

JG-PL: A good complexion is gotten by mixing red paint with water and this is applied to the skin and left until it peels off. "It peels the skin off and even removes the hair." It leaves the skin soft and lighter in color than before. For this beauty treatment, the red paint is mixed with water. It cakes harder on the skin. Men and women both would practice this.

Red paint was put on babies after washing them immediately after birth [see Birth in vol. 2]. It was mixed with water and put on the baby all over to peel the skin off. When the red paint has peeled off, more paint is mixed with marrow of deer or duck bones and applied to the baby. Men and women use this mixture of paint and marrow for decoration.

BR-L,PL: At dances, the women sprinkled their hair with white paint. They put on as much as they could. The face and all exposed parts of the body were painted red, white and black. They painted themselves with stripes or dots or anything they wanted to fix themselves [see also Hairdress, above].

GK-WR: When a man went hunting when there was snow on the ground, he would sometimes put red paint under his eyes and on the lids—"he put red paint all the way around his eyes." This was to prevent snow blindness. Eye shades were not known.

I have never heard of coating the body with mud for warmth.

ORNAMENTS

[Park's notes contain scattered references to the manufacture and use of beads and quillwork. For the latter, especially, details are sorely lacking. Additional data on the use of beads are found in the section dealing with trade in chap. 9.]

Beads

RP-WR: All kinds of beads were called *nama hibi*, "personal belongings." *Namaku* is the word for any kind of beads used in the old days.[72] *Somibi* are the beads used today in decorating baskets [i.e., glass seed beads].

The wing bones of swans[73] were cut in lengths of 2 or 3 in. [fig. 43c]. These were strung on buckskin and worn around the waist and around the neck. The thin breast bones of ducks were tied on the string with the swan bones [fig. 44b]. Holes were made in the duck bones and they were strung on the string. A duck bone was strung between every two swan bones. These beads made a pleasant sound when the women danced. These beads were worn every day.

Another bead was made from a snail-like shell [i.e., *Olivella bipleata*]. "These were the main kind of beads" [fig. 44c]. These were gotten from the ocean. The shells were hard like bone. The largest were about 5 in. in diameter and about 1 in. long. No one has these beads nowadays. These shells were called *potu*. Small holes were drilled by thinning the end by rubbing the shell on a rough rock. Then the hole was drilled with a sharp bone. When the shell was rubbed on the rock, it was often rubbed down enough to rub off the end, and in that fashion the hole was made. The shells were strung alternating with the univalve shells or several of these were strung together and then a piece of abalone shell. The abalone shell was cut in one particular design [fig. 44a]. This was done with the rough rock used on the other shells. This rock was called *pa'abi*.[74] This might have been a sandstone. Small pieces of the stone were chipped off and used like a file.

The abalone shell was gotten the same place as the univalves. RP does not know where these shells were gotten, but she thinks that the Indians went through Sacramento to get to the ocean. The old people who made the trip used to say that the Spaniards were already there when they went to get shells[75] [see Trade in chap. 9].

Another bead was made of juniper berries (*Juniperus monosperma*).[76] The juniper berries were picked while green. The skin was removed by boiling and then the berries were dried. A hole was then bored through the middle of each berry. They were strung on *wiha* and worn around the neck or used to decorate the belts. The straight or slightly curved bones from swan's wings, cut in pieces about 1 in. long, were sometimes alternated with juniper berries on a string. They make a sound the people like. These beads were never used for money.

HW-Y: Beads [*namaqwi*] were used for money. Shell beads were gotten in California, near San Francisco. Beads were made from a tiny spiral shell (*pota*). These were especially valuable. They were used by shamans. These beads were picked up on the sea shore. The people did not buy them. Both men and women made the

---

[72] The term *namaku* is probably *namaka* 'to exchange,' referring to the use of beads in trade.

[73] Also noted by Kelly (1932:117). The swan is the Tundra Swan, *Cygnus columbianus*.

[74] This is the same term as applied to the arrow shaft straightener/smoother.

[75] GK-WR was of the opinion that people went to California only after they got horses. BR-L,PL had heard that they went "before whites came." Shell beads, including *Olivella* and *Haliotis*, are well represented in prehistoric sites in western Nevada (Hughes and Bennyhoff 1986).

[76] ND-HL noted that these berry beads came out "white as bleached bone" when dried. They could also be dyed black with unidentified roots. See also Kelly (1932:117) for use of juniper berry beads by the Surprise Valley Paiute.

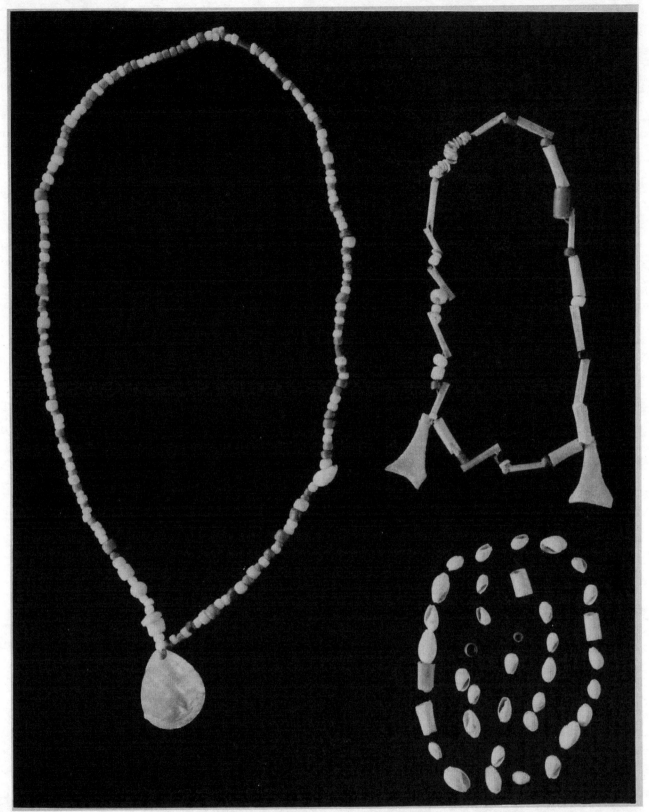

Figure 44. Necklaces and beads. a (left). Necklace of shell and glass trade beads, abalone pendant. Note single olivella bead. PM 35-120-10/5194. b (top right). Necklace of miscellaneous bead types, including duck sternum pendants, quills, wing bones, clamshell, and glass trade beads. PM 35-120-10/5182. c (bottom right). String of olivella and cut bone beads. PM 35-120-10/5183. Collected by W. Z. Park at Pyramid Lake (a) and Walker River (b, c), 1935. Peabody Museum, Harvard University. Photograph by Hillel Burger.

trip to get beads. Bone beads were also gotten in California. They were also used in gambling.

Beads were owned by both men and women. The beads were measured on the finger joints and by the hand when they were exchanged [see Methods of Measuring in vol. 2].

BR-L,PL: Beads were made of bird bones and from the bones of small game (*ohosomibi*). The bones are cut in various lengths and they are then strung on *wiha* fiber. BR's father went to California in '49 and around Santa Cruz he got some shell beads. They were the shape of a peach pit, were red, brown and white in color.[77] A hole was drilled in the shells and they were put on a string and worn around the neck and waist. All the different kinds of beads were used for money. Not everybody had beads. Only those had them who were industrious and knew how to make them.

GK-WR: Beads (*somibi*) were made of shell gotten in California—see string of beads purchased from GK's wife [fig. 44a]. Nowadays, people get these beads by searching around an old Indian campsite. They are quite rare today. (Probably some of the beads on the string are old trade beads, but they are all thought to have been picked up on the beach in California.) The univalve on this string is called *pota*. The round piece of shell near the large piece of abalone shell on the string is called *suigi*. The abalone shell is *puidwa*. The white bone-like beads are called *tuhagwədada*; the red beads with black centers *atsagwədada* and the black beads *tuhugwədada*.[78] Beads were strung on sinew or *wiha*.

JB-PL: Bones from the forepart of a deer's foot were strung on *wiha* for beads. Dew claws were alternated with these on the string. The forefeet of deer make a string about 18 in. to 2 ft long [fig. 43e].

ND-HL: Beads were made of the claws of bears and eagles. They were strung and worn as necklaces. Paiutes did not make beads or pendants from flint or obsidian.

Quillwork[79]

DM-PL: Porcupines were killed and then the quills were pulled out of the body. The points of the quills were cut off with a flint knife. The dye was prepared and the quills put into it. The quills were dyed only yellow and green.

The yellow dye is made of the yellow stuff that is found on the bark of the juniper tree.[80] Long ago there were some certain rocks which were found at Sutcliffe which were used for a green dye.[81] The dye rocks were put in a basket of water, and then the boiling rocks were put in. The rocks are stirred around with a stick so the basket would not burn. When the right color was reached the boiling rocks and the dye rocks were taken out of the basket and the quills put in. The quills are left in the dye until they were the desired color. The dye was used for other things besides quills. Feathers were also dyed in this.

Porcupine quills were woven together with sinew and then the woven piece was sewed to a piece of buckskin with sinew.[82] This piece would be very stiff. Porcupine quills were used for headbands and belts.

HS-D: Porcupine quills were used to decorate the front of shirts and the front of women's dresses [see Men's Clothing, above]. The quills were colored by rubbing them with red paint. They were not dyed by soaking in the juice of redberry (?) bark as with a material for baskets. Both sexes did the work of decorating clothing with porcupine quills.

AD-WR: Porcupine quills were strung on a dress. Holes were put in the center of the quills and they were put on a string like beads. They were not stuck through the dress.

[77] The identity of these beads is not given; brown may be digger pinenuts.

[78] These are merely color terms in this case applied to beads. The red beads are Cornaline d'Aleppo, or "Hudson's Bay beads" (Orchard 1975:100). The type called *suigi* are white clamshell.

[79] Quillwork may be late in the region, and specifically associated with buckskin clothing.

[80] See Kelly (1932:107) for identification of juniper lichen as *Evernia vulpina*. She also provides some notes on quillwork for Surprise Valley.

[81] These "green rocks" may have contained copper sulfate or some other copper compound.

[82] No details are given on the methods for quillwork. In Surprise Valley the techniques had also been forgotten (Kelly 1932:107). See ND-HL's description of fringe wrapping with quills under Men's Clothing, above.

6

Transportation

[Included in this section are miscellaneous notes on tule balsa construction, snowshoes, burden carrying, and horse gear. Tule balsa boats were the principal watercraft used on the lakes and marshes of western Nevada. Park received construction details from four individuals: three men and one woman. Four men and one woman also described the manufacture and use of snowshoes. Additional data on these matters will also be found in other sections, such as those on Hunting and Fishing, in chapter 3, and Trade, in chapter 9.]

THE TULE BALSA

JG-PL: The tule balsa was about 6 ft long.[1] Seven bunches of tule, each about 6 in. in diameter were used.[2] Each bundle was tied with tule.[3] The bundle was tied the full length of the tule—a wrapping about every foot. The balsa was built with a wide center and pointed at both ends.[4] It was built up with five bundles of tule: one at the bottom, two above and outside this bundle and two inside[5] of these bundles. Finally two bundles were lashed on top and on the outside of these giving a boat-shaped depression inside. The seven bundles were lashed together at the ends. Then lashings were made to hold the bundles together the full length of the boat. The lashings were about a foot apart [fig. 45a].

The balsa was poled [punted] by a man sitting in the bottom.[6] The pole, called *wata* (any kind of pole), was pushed against the lake bottom. This balsa carried only one person.[7] It was used only on shallow water, not on the river.

JG has never seen this balsa used at Pyramid Lake. It was used at Humboldt Lake, Stillwater—a lake beyond Carson Sink; water flows from the Sink into this lake—Carson Sink and probably at Honey Lake.[8] These balsas were not used on lakes where the water was deep

---

[1] Stewart (1941:380) lists 8–12 ft as the more common length. However, his consultants may have been speaking of a two-person balsa. Those pictured in Wheat (1967:46) and Lowie (1924:263), both single-person crafts, appear to be roughly 7–8 ft long.

[2] Most published accounts refer to balsas made of large bundles of tules; see, for example, Kelly (1932:150), Wheat (1967:40f), and Lowie (1924:249). Steward (1933:258) briefly describes a balsa made from a single tule bundle. Stewart (1941:380) lists three bundles as common, with one of his Pyramid Lake consultants noting the use of four or more bundles. GK-WR noted the use of three primary bundles: one shorter for the bottom center and two longer ones at each side that would be drawn together for the prow and the stern.

[3] Lashings of cattail (*Typha latifolia*) were preferred by Fallon area people because of their increased strength (Lowie 1924: 249; Wheat 1967:41). Kelly (1932:150) reports the use of bark twine lashing in Surprise Valley. HS-D also told Park that balsas, presumably in the Mason Valley area, were lashed with *wiha* (*Apocynum cannabinum*).

[4] Fallon balsas have an upturned prow and a rounded stern (Wheat 1967:43; Lowie 1924:249). Surprise Valley balsas were pointed both fore and aft to move in either direction (Kelly 1932:150). Those in Owens Valley were either double-pointed or "rather shapeless" (Steward 1933:258).

[5] Park's use of "inside" here would apparently yield a boat with the following cross-section:

Although JG-PL does not speak of gunwales, the last two bundles applied might serve this purpose. Fallon two-bundle balsas have small bundles of cattails attached fore and aft and joined on each side for this purpose (Wheat 1967:44).

[6] Poling, or, better, punting, is reported in most other Northern Paiute areas as well (see for example Kelly 1932:150; Riddell 1960:51; Lowie 1924:250; Wheat 1967:46; Stewart 1941:382). Kelly (1932:150) also reports paddling with a pole and propulsion with the hands and feet for the Surprise Valley area, although the latter means was said to be used by those "unable to swim."

[7] One-person balsas are also most typical in other Northern Paiute areas, although those for two or more persons are occasionally reported (*cf.* Kelly 1932:150; Stewart 1941:380). HS-D also told Park of two-person crafts wherein one man stood in back and punted while the other sat in the center, facing forward.

[8] Honey Lake balsas were used principally for netting fish (Riddell 1960:51). Kelly (1932:150) lists their use in Surprise Valley as for duck and goose hunting. Lowie (1924:249) also notes their use for duck and mudhen hunting at Fallon. HS-D reported to Park that they were used only for mudhen hunting and driving (probably in Mason Valley). It seems clear from all accounts that they are principally shallow water craft.

Figure 45. Tule balsa boat. a (left). Jimmy and Wuzzie George, Stillwater, with tule balsa boat. b (right). Jimmy George poling tule balsa boat in Stillwater marshes. Photographs by M. M. Wheat, *ca.* 1958. University of Nevada, Reno, Library, Special Collections Department.

such as at Walker and Pyramid Lakes. The balsa was called either *toisak*[i] or *saisak*[i] depending on whether it was made of cattail (*toi*) or tule (*sai*).

RP-WR: *Saib* (tule) was used for boats (*saki*). First make two bundles of tule, each about 2 ft in diameter and tapered at the ends. These are tied at both ends and in the center in three places. Two bundles are tied together for the bottom, and two more are used for the sides (one on each side) so that it is shaped in canoe fashion. The balsa is 7 or 8 ft long. One man, or sometimes two, go in each boat. Each man makes his boat in one day. The boat is discarded after one day's use.[9] A new one is made next time. A pole is used to propel the boat. The boatman pushes with the pole on both sides of the balsa. Poling is done by the man in a kneeling position. Boats are tested by getting in and standing up. They row around in this position to see how buoyant it is and how fast it will go. Women never go out in a

boat. These boats are used only in driving the mudhens. No fishing was done with boats.

BURDENS

JG-PL: If a woman had something to carry, she put it in a conical burden basket on her back [fig. 46a]. For carrying the burden basket, a tumpline was made of sagebrush bark rolled on the thigh. This line was a half inch in diameter and was called *wasidəgəp*.[10] Twisted willow branches were used for a tumpline in carrying wood, as was the line of sagebrush bark. The tumpline of willow was called *subinamabüsugin*, (*subi*, willow; *namabüsugin*, twisting).

---

[9] After use in the Fallon area, the balsas were beached and allowed to dry for later reuse (Wheat 1967:47). Balsas became waterlogged in use.

[10] Stewart (1941:389) lists pack straps of both skin and fiber as used universally among the Northern Paiute. Fiber tumplines of either two- or three-ply, or three-strand, braids apparently have a scattered and overlapping distribution over the region. RP-WR described a tumpline (*anakapuin*) as "braided" of *wiha* (*Apocynum cannabinum*). She also noted the use of strips of deerskin as alternative tumplines.

Figure 46. Transportation. a (top left). Wuzzie George, Mabel Wright, and Minnie Houton trekking with burden baskets and poles. Photograph by M. M. Wheat, *ca.* 1958. University of Nevada, Reno, Library, Special Collections Department. b (bottom left). Woman with burden basket, using forehead tumpline. Photograph by R. H. Lowie, probably at Fallon, 1916. Neg. #118586. Courtesy Department of Library Services, American Museum of Natural History. c (top right). Snowshoe, willow hoop, and rawhide lacing. PM 35-120-10-5190. Collected by W. Z. Park, Pyramid Lake, 1935. d (middle right). Pad saddle with hand-made stirrups and horsehair cinch. MPM 21958. Collected by S. A. Barrett, Pyramid Lake, 1916. Milwaukee Public Museum photograph. Drawings by Susan Lohse.

When taking up a burden, burden basket, bunch of wood, etc., a woman kneeled on the ground and put the tumpline over her head.[11] Bending forward, the weight of the load was taken on the back. Then the woman put both her hands on the ground and lifted herself to her feet.

Usually a man used a net for carrying and women used the conical burden basket. Sometimes a dip net was used for carrying purposes. A carrying net was not made.[12] A fish net was used if it was at hand. The top of the net was tied together and the burden carried with the top across the man's shoulders just as when he carried a burden with a strap. Men got their burdens on their backs in the same way [as women] except they put the tumpline over the shoulders.[13] The tumpline came around the shoulders and chest 2 or 3 in. down from the top of the shoulders.

When camp was moved, the household effects were put in the burden basket. After the woman gets up with the burden basket the father lifts a child that cannot walk and puts it on the top.[14] The child's legs hang over the woman's shoulders. The man carried the water jug with the line around the shoulders. He carried his bow and arrow in his hands.[15] When he has the water jug on his back he carries the quiver in his hand. When he was carrying nothing on his back, the arrow quiver was slung on the back with the string over the left shoulder. When an arrow was needed it was pulled out of the quiver with the right hand. The arrows were in the bottom of the quiver. If the points were in the bottom of the sack it would be too hard to pull them out [see Arrows in chap. 3].

When a man is out hunting, he carries a rope made of sagebrush bark. He wears the rope wound around his waist. When he kills a deer, he skins it and butchers it. If he cannot carry all of it he takes the hind quarters with the heart and other viscera and hangs up the front quarters until he can return for it. The hind quarters are carried in the skin. When the deer is skinned the legs are cut off at the knee joints. The skin is peeled down about half way on the lower joint. The left hind leg is tied with the right front leg. The bone projecting prevents the "granny knot" from slipping out. Half the deer is inside the skin. If the skin of the legs was long enough it formed a tumpline with the forelegs and hoofs in front of the carrier [see Butchering Large Game in chap. 2]. I saw my uncle carry a deer this way. He told me that his father showed him how to carry deer that way. The rope carried around the hunter's waist was used to hang the half left behind in a tree where animals such as coyote could not reach it.

SNOWSHOES

[Park's notes contain four descriptions of snowshoe manufacture. Of the four, that by ND-HL is the most detailed and is printed in full below. Notes from the accounts of others are also presented, as the snowshoes described differ. No attempt has been made to illustrate the differences described. One type of snowshoe collected by Park from ND is also shown in fig. 46c. See also Clothing in chap. 5 for a description of other winter footwear.]

ND-HL: Snowshoes (*su·kü*) were made from a frame of green willow about ½ or ¾ in. in diameter. This is bent into a hoop [fig. 46c]. When the willow is dry, the mesh of the snowshoe is woven into the frame with rawhide. Two main strings, heavier than the others, run in each direction.[16] Then two strings of each pair are about 4 in. apart. The two pairs cross in the middle of the hoop. These strings are about ½ in. wide. There are usually about four other smaller strings woven in and out in each direction, running parallel to the two pairs of main strings.[17]

The foot is placed on the crossed four main strings, and a single strap is tied across the instep to the straps of the mesh of the snowshoe. The snowshoe is not tied on at the heel of the foot.[18] This is done so that at each step the back of the snowshoe drops down and the snow on the mesh falls off. This snowshoe is used for walking on soft snow. When frozen snow is reached, the snowshoes are taken off and carried.

---

[11] Kelly (1932:148) notes the use of a sagebrush-bark head pad under the tumpline. Stewart (1941:389) notes the same for one other Northern Paiute group. Consultants from two of his areas mentioned the use of a basket hat under the tumpline.

[12] Neither Kelly (1932:148) nor Stewart (1941:389) specifically differentiates the type of container carried by either sex. Stewart (1941:389) notes the use of carrying nets of pieces of rabbit netting as well as a "hammock-shaped" carrying net.

[13] Kelly (1932:148) attributes the difference between head *vs.* shoulder suspension more to the weight of the burden than to sex.

[14] Kelly (1932:148) also notes this feature.

[15] See also section on Arrows in chap. 3.

[16] According to HS-D, the first two strands were "grass" rope placed about 2 in. apart. Stewart (1941:395) also lists "vegetable cord" as a common alternative for lacing.

[17] Riddell (1960:51) received a similar description from a man from Honey Lake.

[18] Park probably means here that the heel was free to be elevated. The specimens he collected from ND-HL have 40 cm. cords attached to the mesh close to the toe grip, presumably to further secure the feet (see fig. 46c). Riddell's (1960:51) informants spoke of Honey Lake snowshoes being tied tightly to the feet with a "sort of moccasin" as the footgear. Kelly's (1932:149–50) informants also suggested two methods of fastening snowshoes, both leaving the heel free.

When walking with snowshoes, a stick is carried in the right hand to use as a cane.[19] This stick is called *nuba nadzitənə*. Indians did not like to walk with snowshoes. The size of the frame made it necessary for them to throw the foot out to the side at the same time putting it forward.[20] This was so different from the customary way of walking in which the foot was put directly in front of the other — the way in which ND walks today — that men found it uncomfortable. Men walking on snowshoes often caught the snowshoes on something or tripped themselves and fell on their faces. The stick carried in the hand was to help prevent these falls as well as being useful in climbing.

Snowshoes were hung up in any convenient place, either outside or inside the house when not in use. When the snow melted, the strings were taken from the frame of the snowshoes and saved for future use. The frames were thrown away.

Women did not use snowshoes.[21] They did not travel much in winter. There was no belief about keeping the snowshoes away from the women.[22]

BB-PL: Snowshoes (*sukü*) were made in a circle about 12 in. in diameter with a frame of *tüabi* [serviceberry, *Amelanchier alnifolia*]. This wood is strong. Also snowshoes were made of juniper. Seven or eight sticks crossed the frame.[23] Skin was then woven back and forth across the wooden cross pieces. Snowshoes were used in winter to hunt deer. When they move camp in winter, two go abreast with snowshoes and pack the snow down. The others follow. Only the men wear snowshoes.

HW-Y: Snowshoes with a round frame are used around Sweetwater. The frame was made of cedar and formed a circle about 14 in. in diameter. Two sticks were tied across the middle of the hoop. The sticks were tied to the frame with buckskin. The foot was placed across the sticks in the center of the snowshoe. The snowshoe was tied to the foot with buckskin (see the snowshoes figured in Dixon's Northern Maidu [Dixon 1905]).

HS-D: Snowshoes (*səkü*) were used. They were round, about 22 in. [?] in diameter. The frame was of willow about ¾ in. in diameter. Two pieces of grass rope were tied across the frame in the middle. These were placed

about 2 in. apart. Buckskin thongs also paralleled the grass rope. These thongs were interlaced leaving ¾ in. mesh. Buckskin thongs were used to tie the snowshoe to the feet. Only men wore snowshoes. They made them.

HORSES AND TACK

ND-HL: The people had horses (*pugə*) before the whites came to this country. Before the coming of the whites, horses were gotten from the Bannock of Idaho.[24] Only a few Paiutes had horses in the early days. They were brought home and the horses increased. The Paiutes learned to make the saddle and other riding gear from the Bannock. This was a long time ago.[25]

The saddle (*kwasünadudnə*) was made of deerskin. The hair of the deerskin to be used was not scraped off. It was made of two pads about 2 ft long by 6 or 8 in. wide and 3 or 4 in. thick [see fig. 46d].[26] These were held in place by buckskin strings at both ends of the pads. The strings are long enough to hold the pads high up on each side of the horse's back. The pads were stuffed with hair scraped from deerskin. At the back of the pads there was a harness called *nagwasisaniga* that went under the horse's tail. The seat of the saddle was formed by a pad made of a large piece of buckskin which was about 3 ft long and about fourteen inches wide in the middle. It was roughly elliptical in shape. This piece of buckskin had the hair scraped off and was not stuffed. Only the pads running length-wise on the horses were stuffed with hair.

The stirrups (*nadakadu*) were made by cutting a flat piece of juniper and bending it in the shape of a horseshoe[27] [fig. 46d]. Buckskin was tied across the ends. These were tied with buckskin to the buckskin running across the two pads.

There was a cinch with a flat belly band about 3 to 4 in. wide made by weaving horse hair. The belly band of the cinch was called *nagoihisamap"*

The bridle was called *tubəsəniga*. The rope had two half hitches that were put in the horse's mouth and over the chin with a running end on each side of the horse's

[19] Use of a support stick was also noted for Honey Lake (Riddell 1960:51).

[20] The same interference with walking was noted to Riddell (1960:51). HS-D told Park that it "makes a man tired to walk with them."

[21] Kelly's (1932:150) and Riddell's (1960:51) informants also agreed that women did not use snowshoes.

[22] Kelly (1932:150) reports a belief on the part of one Surprise Valley person that "cooking" — boiling or frying — snowshoes would bring snow.

[23] Two of Kelly's (1932:149–50) informants described "slatted" snowshoes, although of different configurations.

[24] Riddell's (1960:52) respondents also identified the "Cow Eaters," probably the Bannock, as the source for Honey Lake horses.

[25] Park provides the following note: "ND's father knew how to make this riding gear when he was young so it must have been taken over from the Bannock more than 60 years ago at least" (1870s).

[26] Kelly (1932:148) described the Surprise Valley saddle as "an affair of soft deer or antelope hide stuffed with deer hair. It had no wooden horn frame."

[27] According to Kelly (1932:148), Surprise Valley stirrups were also of juniper, but "round."

face.[28] A hair rope (*wətigəp*) was used to lead and tie the horse.

A whip (*nagwiba*) with a handle made from straight deer horn about 10 in. long was used. A hole was drilled at both ends of the handle. At one end there was a buckskin thong that went around the wrist. At the other end there were two lashes made of braided buckskin 18 in. to 2 ft in length.

[28] This type of "war bridle" is also described by Lowie (1909) for the Bannock and Northern Shoshoni.

7

Dogs and Horses

[Dogs, and occasionally eagles, were the primary pets of the Northern Paiute. Horses were also considered pets or "tame animals" once they were obtained *ca.* 1820 (Layton 1978; Rusco 1976). There are some differences of opinion among Park's respondents as to whether dogs were used in hunting. Stewart (1941:422) also received mixed statements on the subject in his Culture Element Survey. The data that follow are meager on both topics (dogs and horses)].

RP-WR: Dogs and horses were the only tame animals that the Paiute had.[1] The dog was called *wisipugu* (*wisi*, fur-bearing; *pugu*, horse).[2] The Paiute dog was small. It had pointed ears. Dogs were used in hunting. They could trail deer.[3] The dog was also used in the antelope drive to keep them running. Dogs were not eaten.[4]

Horses (*pugu*) were small. The Paiutes found the horses already here.[5] These horses were already tame. They only had to be caught. They could be ridden as soon as they were caught. They did not buck. The males were not castrated. This kind of horse is no longer found here. When a man died his horses were killed [see Death and Burial in vol. 2]. That is why that type of horse died out. Wild horses were also eaten. They were called *kaib' tuhida* (*kaib'*, mountain; *tuhida*, horse).

JG-PL: The old word for dog was *iza' poku* (*iza'*, coyote; *poku*, pet). Dog and coyote are brothers. The dog had pointed ears like the coyote. The dog was not usually used for hunting, but sometimes it was. The children played with dogs just as they do now. Dogs were not given names.[6] When dogs came into the house people said, "*isha*, go away, get out." This was only said to dogs — never to people. Dogs were not used for carrying burdens.[7] They were not good for watch dogs. They were never eaten.

Horses were called *poku*. A long time ago they were called *tuhut*.[8]

JB-PL: The dog was used in hunting.[9] Dogs would get the game in close so they could get a good shot at it. Dogs were fed by putting some mush on the toe of a moccasin. They would always leave dogs in camp when they went on an antelope drive.

The Paiutes got horses from people on the Snake River [Northern Shoshone/Bannock]. They would go up there and buy horses. The trip would last a month or two [see Trade in chap. 9].

JO-PL: Dogs were called *sogoduish* (*sogo*, on foot; *duish*, pet). They were bought from each other and eaten when people were starving. They looked more like a coyote. They were used in hunting. The dog would tree animals, would drive deer (*tühita*) up on a rock and keep it there. Dogs were also used in the rabbit drive and the antelope drive.[10]

HS-D: Dogs were called *sogo pugu* (*sogonuma*, man walking on foot). Dogs were not used for hunting. They

---

[1] Eagles were kept in cages by some and became "tame" (see Other Birds in chap. 2).

[2] The term *puggu* is better translated as 'owned animal.' It, along with the term for mule deer (*tihidda*), was applied to the horse as well.

[3] Both Steward (1933:252) and Kelly (1932:148) affirm the use of dogs for deer hunting. Stewart (1941:422) notes that dogs were not very plentiful aboriginally, and that roughly half of the individuals he interviewed thought that they could be used for hunting deer, mountain sheep, and antelope.

[4] Stewart (1941:419) found that the eating of dogs was denied by all consultants.

[5] This may be a vague reference to a tale motif accounting for the origin of horses.

[6] Kelly (1932:148) also found no references to the naming of dogs by the Surprise Valley Paiute.

[7] De Angulo and Freeland (1929:322) refer to the use of dogs for packing burdens by the Northern Paiute. Kelly (1932:147) found little verification for this. Only when pressed did consultants suggest that one might so use a very strong dog.

[8] *tuhut* (*tihita, tihi?ya*) is the term for mule deer in the Pyramid Lake dialect.

[9] Stewart (1941:366–7) received some substantiation for the use of dogs to drive deer, antelope, and mountain sheep.

[10] Park's note: BB-PL overheard what JO-PL said about using dogs in hunting. He said that it is not true. BB's daughter overheard that and tried to correct him but JO scolded her. BB says dogs were never used in hunting and were never used to kill ground hogs [see Small and Medium-sized Mammal Hunting in chap. 2].

were fed by putting acorn mush on the dog's paw or while the master was eating he would put mush on the toe of his moccasin and the dog would lick it off.

Horses were called *pugu*, the same word as for dog. The horses were formerly small and their hooves were covered with hair.[11]

---

[11]The reference to hair on the hooves of horses may be to a thick growth of hair on the fetlocks, overlapping to some degree the hooves.

8

Medicines

[Park's field notebooks contain a number of miscellaneous accounts of the use of plant and animal medicinal remedies. Most of those described were within the pharmacopoeiae of various individuals, rather than within the province of the shaman. Uses varied throughout the area, often for the same plant, as individuals discovered new properties or began to favor one medicine over another. Additional data on most plants will be found in the WPA project report by Train, Hendrichs, and Archer (1933) on Nevada Indian medicinal plants. Additional data on theories of disease and other means of treatment are contained in the section on Shamanism in vol. 2. The identifications, unless otherwise indicated, are by the editor.]

PLANT MEDICINES

1. atsagwasobə [Artemisia douglasiana][1]

RP-WR: For fever or for colds a bed is made of warm ashes and a thick layer of atsagwasobə is put over the ashes. The patient sleeps on this bed for the night. The warm ashes cause the brush to steam. Sagebrush [big sagebrush, Artemisia tridentata] is also used for this treatment. The sagebrush might be mixed with other brush.

2. atsanazakodid [possibly Asclepias cryptoceras][2]

JG-PL: This is a plant that is spread over the ground. The leaves are big and round. The flower is small and pink. The root is dug up and dried and ground into a fine powder. The powder is put on a sore and it dries the sore and heals it very quickly. It is a good medicine.

3. hi·wabi [Hermidium alipes]

JG-PL: The plant called hiwabi[3] grows on the ground. It is a creeping plant with large leaves. The flower is

pink and round. The roots which are nearly white are used. The roots were dried and ground into a powder. The dry powder was put on a sore. When I was a boy I fell and cut my knee and we used to have that medicine. They fixed it for me and I put it on and covered it with a rag. That was so the sore would not get rotten. To clean the sore some of the powder was boiled. The old powder was washed off and the fresh dry powder was put on. This powder dried and healed the cut very quickly.

4. iza' pijə [unidentified, but probably a fungus sp.]

JG-PL: This medicine was called iza' pijə. It is an old dry root found growing among the sagebrush. It has a very fine dark brown powder inside. This was used on sores. It caused the sore to dry and heal. It was put on the sore dry. It was especially good for sores on babies. The sore was first washed with cold water and then powder was put on.

5. kangə [Shadscale, Atriplex confertifolia]

JG-PL: Sage, like the kind that is ground up for sale, is called kangə. For a cold the leaves are mashed up and put on the chest and held in place with a bandage. The leaves are boiled and the liquid is drunk while the person has the leaves on his chest.

DM-PL: The leaves of kangəpə are gathered and boiled. It is used for a liniment for sore muscles and aches. It is also drunk for colds.

6. kangənatusiwabi [possibly purple sage, Salvia dorii][4]

JG-PL: This plant is good for a dose [gonorrhea]. Nearly all the Indians on this reservation have the dose. They get it in town in Lovelock, Wadsworth and Stillwater and spread it all over. The leaves are stripped off the plant. The leaves are boiled and the liquid drunk. The patient drinks a great deal of this and he urinates frequently and this cleans him out. This is called kangənatusiwabi. This medicine smelled like sagebrush. It is found in the canyons. It has small leaves, a little larger than sagebrush.

---

[1] A specimen gathered by Park was identified by P. A. Lehenbauer of the University of Nevada, Reno, Department of Biology, as Artemesia vulgaris — now A. douglasiana.

[2] By description this may also be Hermidium alipes or hiwabi as described in Number 3, below. The accounts of the two plants are by the same consultant but in different years. Asclepias cryptoceras also fits the description.

[3] This plant is described by Train, Hendrichs, and Archer (1933:86) as well as by Stewart (1941:429). It is still well known today.

---

[4] See also Number 29, tubisiginup, below.

7. *kawa siin* [lichen, sp. unknown]

AD-R: Moss from rocks on the mountains—the black variety—is called *kawa siin* ("packrat urine"). This moss is scraped off the rocks. It is boiled and the liquor is drunk for venereal disease.

8. *kjbu natuswabi* [possibly *Angelica linearloba*][5]

RP-WR: This medicine (*kjbu natuswabi*) is a plant not a bush. It has not been seen by RP. They only bring back the roots. It is used for pneumonia or for someone spitting blood. They use the root (it has thick roots) that are soft even when dried. They scrape the dry root into boiling water. It makes a bitter drink. This is drunk at intervals of an hour. Soon the person stops the spitting of blood. At the same time the pain stops. It is a most efficacious remedy. This plant grows way up in the mountains where the climate is cool. It is gathered over around California. It is found in the mountains—up on top—on the other side of Smith Valley.

9. *hunabi* [antelope bitterbrush, *Purshia tridentata*]

AD-WR: There is a tall plant (4 or 5 ft high), a kind of brush growing in the mountains called *hunabi*.[6] The leaves are picked and dried in the sun. They are boiled and drunk for stomach ache or for constipation. It makes them vomit and moves the bowels. It is gathered when the leaves are green at the end of June. It is also used for worms in the intestine. If is found near Hawthorne.

10. *kudagwavə* [unidentified]

RP-WR: When people go up into the mountains for pinenuts or any other place where there are lots of rattlesnakes they tie a plant to their ankles. This plant [*kudagwavə*] grows in the water in the mountains. It is tied to the moccasins or to the ankle. It makes a noise something like the warning of a rattlesnake that is heard when water is flowing. The snakes can hear this. They do not like it and it drives them away.

11. *kwibanobu* [slim stinging nettle, *Urtica dioica*]

JG-PL: Nettles (*kwibanup*)[7] are used for hives and itches. The root is boiled and the juice is drunk. The roots were broken up and boiled until the water was almost black. JG drank it all day long while it was hot. "I drank it for about 6 days and the itch was all gone. I did not scratch any more and I lay down and slept at nights. I drank it for about 10 days and I was all right. It killed that." Nettle leaves were also used to whip aching arms and legs for rheumatism. They whipped all over. "My father used that kind. It hurt so he could not stand it but he got better."

RP-WR: The nettle plant (*quibanobu*) grows 3 or 4 ft high along the river. It has big leaves. The stalk and leaves are gathered and used to hit wherever they feel pain—in legs or arms. This is for rheumatism or pains in the limbs. It causes the limb to swell up and become inflamed. When the swelling goes down the pain goes away with it.

12. *kwidətunabə* [heliotrope, *Heliotropium curassavicum*]

RP-WR: Eating *kwidətunabə*, a plant found along the lake, caused baldness. Baldness was called *kai zopuhugayu* (*kai*, no; *zopuhugayu*, hair). There was no treatment for baldness. There was no treatment to prevent baldness. Nowadays people rub bald spots with bacon rind. That is supposed to make the hair grow.

13. *mugutuhupi* [Nevada dalea, *Psorothamnus polydenius*.]

AD-R: A tea was made from *mugutuhup*, and was used for light colds and also for a physic. The bark is used. This is a brush 2 to 4 ft high. It doesn't have leaves but many branches. It is greyish greenish white. It grows in sandy soil. The branches are broken off and the bark is removed.

DM-PL: The brush called *mogatuhup* was broken up and boiled. It was drunk for flu during the epidemics of 1917 or 1918. This medicine was also used in the old days for sore throats, colds and pneumonia [see also Bear Hunting in chap. 2].

14. *muipə* [sacred datura, *Datura meteloides*]

JG-PL: The Indians around Bishop used the root of a plant called *muipə*[8] to discover things or see things that they could not see with ordinary powers. The first man to discover this dreamed about it. He had to find it on the mountain. He found four plants but they did not have enough limbs.[9] The last or fifth had enough limbs, so he pulled the plant and took it home. It is not eaten

---

[5] Train, Hendrichs, and Archer (1933:36) identify "*kiba natisuah*" as *Angelica* sp. They said that a root by this name was examined at Yerington and was obviously an umbelliferous plant. It was said to grow in the Sweetwater Mountains, which seems to agree with RP's location. *A. linearloba* is found in the Sweetwater Mountains.

[6] Train, Hendrichs, and Archer (1933:126) also list various uses for this plant.

[7] See Train, Hendrichs, and Archer (1933:146) for various uses for this plant.

[8] Stewart (1933:318), citing an MS by Chalfont, suggests that the narcotic "*mu-e-pa*" may not be jimsonweed or datura. Essene (1935) identifies his "*man-oph-weep*" as datura. Park asked AD-R about "*muip*" and she replied that she had not heard of it. A man from Bishop who was at her camp at the time also did not recognize the name *muip*. He stated that the Indians at Bishop could occasionally eat a very small amount of wild parsnip (probably poison hemlock, *Conium maculatum*) in order to numb themselves—a kind of drink. Several people interviewed by Stewart (1941:415, 444) also recognized "*muipō*" as the name of a very powerful medicine from Bishop.

[9] Stewart (1941:444) was told by a man from Pyramid Lake that the plant could only be found at night and that its roots grew in five directions.

right away. When he eats it he prays to the plant and it tells him how both the Indian and the plant are put on this earth and that they are friends. He states in his prayer that he is going to eat a piece of the root. He asks the plant not to harm him and show him things he could not see ordinarily. A small piece of the root is then chewed and swallowed. It makes the man who eats it feel as if he drank a little whiskey. He is elated and happy. Then very soon the eater can see things that other people cannot see. He can see things that people have lost. This is a dangerous medicine if it is not used this way. It will kill anyone who does not use it the right way; i.e., talk to the plant and pray.

When the person who ate the root has found what he was looking for, he must go to running water to bathe and pray while bathing to the water and the plant. If this is done, there will be no harmful effects from eating the root.

This root does not grow around Pyramid and Walker Lakes. The Indians at these places do not eat this root. Only the Indians at Bishop use it. JG learned about how the Bishop Indians use it from his uncle and cousin, Dan Vorhees, at Schurz.

This one is a bad one. If you don't use it right that medicine will make you crazy or kill you. One time, down at Bishop, a young fellow ate that medicine and didn't use it right. It led him way out where there was no water or food and he died. The people found his tracks and found him there dead. That medicine killed him.

You can't keep that medicine in the house or close to you. It would kill all your family and you too. Bury the root in the ground some distance from the house. If you don't talk to that medicine right when you pray to it, it will lead you out on the mountain someplace. Or if you carry it around with you three or four days, it will make you sick.[10] The people don't touch it nowadays. It was pretty strong medicine.

It was not very long ago. I have an uncle down at Schurz and Yerington. One time I went over to Yerington and the people were telling stories. Then he, my uncle, told a story: a woman lost $30.00. It was stolen. Nobody could tell her where it was. My uncle said that he would give some of that medicine to a little boy playing around there. He took out his medicine and talked to it and the boy swallowed it. Then he went on playing. After a while he went over to a haystack and dug out some dirt and picked up a little bag. He put it on the pile of dirt he made in playing. Then my uncle called the boy over and had him take a bath while my uncle talked to the medicine and told it to leave him. The boy had picked

up beads, pins, needles and other things in addition to finding the money. That medicine would make him see those things.

My uncle had that medicine down at Yerington, but it doesn't grow there. It grows in the country east of Bishop.

15. *namagəd* [unidentified]

AD-R: The plant called *namagəd*[11] grows along the Carson River. It grows about 4 ft high and has yellow flowers. It has leaves like the wild parsnip. To use it, pulverize the root and sprinkle the powder on open or fresh sores. A piece of the root was also sucked for a sore throat. The root is dug in July. It is dried and used at any time.

16. *pagabibə* [false hellebore, *Veratrum californicum*]

JO-PL: The plant called *pagagibə*[12] grows like corn. The root is like a potato. It is mashed up and smeared over swollen parts on arms and legs. It is used mostly for rattlesnake bites as it draws out the poison. The root is the only part of the plant that is used.

JG-PL: The plant called *pagagiv* grows with flat long leaves about 5 in. long. The root is used. A flat rock the size of the palm is used to grind it with water and then it is applied to swellings. This plant grows in the canyons around the springs. It has no flower.

DM-PL: The roots of the *pagagib* were tied on the ankle or calf to drive away rattlesnakes. The snakes do not like this plant and they will stay away from anyone who has it.

When anyone was bitten by a rattlesnake a band of red paint was put around the limb above the bite. Horse hair from the tail or string was tied above the band of paint to stop the circulation. The *pagagib* that has been ground on a rock was put on the bite. In the old days a man always carried some of the ground *pagagib* root when he was away from camp.

HS-D: This plant (*pagagiv*[a]) grows up in the mountains near springs and beside creeks in cool places. It is used for medicine for cuts, sores and snakebite. It grows about 18 in. high. It is gotten in the fall when the plant is dry. The root is grated and chewed. The juice is swallowed for colds. The grated root is applied as a poultice to sores and snakebite.

ND-HL: When an ankle was sprained the skin all around was scratched to let out the blood and then the wound was plastered with mashed *pagagib*. It was also used when a bone was broken. It was not necessary to have a shaman treat fractured bones. Anybody might

---

[10] Stewart (1941:444) was also told that the medicine would kill its possessor if kept too long.

[11] Kelly (1932:196) identifies "*na.mogu.d*" as *Penstemon deustus* in Surprise Valley. The plant described here does not seem to be the same, however.

[12] See also Train, Hendrichs, and Archer (1933:147) for additional uses of this plant.

set a fracture and put a splint on. They would first drain the blood off and then use the *pagagib* to heal the wound.

17. *pawagabish* [sweet anise, *Osmorhiza occidentalis*]

JB-PL: Dry the roots of *pawagabish*[13] and chew the inside of the root for colds and pains in the chest. After the whites came with utensils they boiled it and made a tea which was used for sore eyes and for sores.

AD-R: This plant (*pawabapic*[a]) is used as a liniment. The root is the part used. The root is twisted. It grows in the mountains near streams.

18. *pawia* [curly dock, *Rumex crispis*]

AD-R: The roots of *pawia*[14] are ground into powder and put on a sore to dry it. It is also used for cuts. It is a very good medicine.

19. *sawabi* [big sagebrush, *Artemesia tridentata*]

RP-WR: Sagebrush (*sawabi*)[15] leaves are ground on the metate when the leaves are dried or green. The ground leaves are mixed in cold water. This makes a paste which is put over the body for a fever. The leaves of the sagebrush are boiled and the water drunk for a cold.

Sagebrush leaves are also ground and mixed with tobacco. This is wet so it makes a paste. This is applied to children for fever or put on swellings on adults or children.

Small pieces of sagebrush are also stuffed into the nostrils for colds and headaches. Sagebrush blossoms are dipped into water and then the hair is combed with the branch of blossoms when a person has fainting spells. At the same time the person talks and tells the spirits that cause the fainting spells to stay far away. "This makes the person think straight."

AD-R: Sagebrush (*saiwabi*) leaves are boiled and the liquor drunk for diarrhea and a strong solution was used as an emetic. When the stomach ached badly an emetic was taken. Sometimes it was also taken for a headache.

20. *saiyagab*[u] [erisastrum, *Eriastrum sparsiflorum*][16]

JG-PL: The plant called *saiyagab*[u] grows about 4 ft high. The flower is sky blue. It has many branches. The plant is pulled and the stalks are used. They are boiled and the water is drunk for stomach trouble. Enough is drunk so that in a few minutes nausea is produced and the entire insides are cleaned through the mouth. If the person does not vomit the medicine will kill him. When a person drinks this he can feel his stomach move. He lies down where it is warm even if he is sweating and covers himself with a blanket.

21. *sigoabə* [death camas, *Zigadenus venenosus, Z. paniculatus*]

AD-R: The plant called sigoabə[17] is like a wild onion and grows about 2 ft tall. It grows on the mountains on bare spaces. The small bulbs growing on the ends of long roots are roasted by covering them with hot coals. They are then mashed and put on swollen parts or used for rheumatism. They are put on like a poultice. The plant is gathered after July.

AD-WR: There is a sort of onion, or a plant that looks like an onion, called *sikawabu*. The white root is what is gathered. This is ground on a metate and spread over swollen parts. It feels very cold and reduces the swelling.

22. *su.bi pi.tukwə* [coyote willow, *Salix exigua*]

AD-R: The dried roots of willow (*su.bi pi.tukwə*) are gathered and boiled. This is taken for venereal disease— probably gonorrhea.

23. *sudəpi* [Ephedra, *Ephedra viridis*]

JB-PL: The stems of *sudəpi* are dried and pulverized in a mortar. The powder is used on sores. When they had utensils for boiling they used it as a tea. It is also used as a beverage now but it was not in the old days.[18]

24. *tosi tonig* [possibly yarrow, *Achillea millefolium*][19]

AD-R: The plant called *tosi tonig* is used for flu or a cold in the chest. The root is boiled and the liquid drunk. The patient keeps covered in a warm room. No cold water is drunk. For a sore throat a small piece is chewed and the saliva is allowed to flow down the throat. For cuts and sores, pulverize the root and smear it on the cut or sore. For kidney trouble, boil one cup of root in one gallon of water. Drink the liquor. For a cough in the early stages, soak the leaves for a few hours before using. Also in taking the sweat bath, sprinkle the hot rocks with the soaked leaves.

---

[13] See also Train, Hendrichs, and Archer (1933:109) for additional uses of this plant.

[14] See also Train, Hendrichs, and Archer (1933:131) for additional uses of this plant.

[15] See also Train, Hendrichs, and Archer (1933:44) for additional uses of this plant.

[16] Stewart (1941:429) identifies "*saiagava*" as *Psathrotes annua*. However, this rather flat plant seems not to fit the description given here by JG-PL. Stewart was also told that if one did not vomit after ingesting the plant, one would die.

[17] JG-PL also called the plant *kogiatanop*. This name and *sigoab* are both applied to the two species of death camas (*Zigadenus venenosus* and *Z. paniculatus*), apparently without discrimination.

[18] JB-PL is quite correct in stating that the beverage is generally used—also by the non-Indian population. Its medicinal uses probably have historical precedence.

[19] Train, Hendrichs, and Archer (1933:48) also identify "*tods-e-tonega*" as *Aster frondosa*. Kelly (1932:196) identifies "*dotsi toniga*" from Surprise Valley as *Heracleum lanatum*, cow parsnip. The latter might fit the description given by AD-R here, except that cow parsnip also grows in the valleys. My own work in the 1960s failed to precisely identify this plant although there was much discussion of it by collaborators.

The plant has leaves like carrots. It grows 2 to 4 ft in height. It is found near mountain streams. It is gathered in early summer and dried and preserved.

JO-PL: The plant called *tositonigad^u* has leaves like carrots and grows 1 to 2 ft high. It grows on the mountains. There is a great deal of this on Peavine at Reno. Dry the root and then chew it raw. It is good for colds.

25. *tonobi* [greasewood, *Sarcobatus vermiculatus*]

AD-WR: For decayed teeth, a piece of greasewood brush or root is heated in the fire until it burns or is blackened. When it cools sufficiently to put it inside the mouth they put it on the aching tooth and hold it there.

JG-PL: Bleeding was induced to cure a bad headache.[20] A sharp stick of hardwood, perhaps greasewood, was used to prick or scrape inside both nostrils until bleeding started. This was done by the sufferer himself.

26. *toza* [*Lomatium dissectum*]

JO-PL: The plant called *toza*[21] is boiled and drunk for colds. It is also smoked for a cold. They use the root. Cut it up not too fine or you cannot draw it. It may also be smoked for pleasure. A red-tipped cigarette is made from *toza* now.

HS-D: The plant called *tosə* is gotten any time of the year. The root is cut into chips which were thrown on a fire made in the house. The fumes were inhaled for a cold. The shredded root of this plant was smoked in pipes in place of tobacco. The root was also cut in thin slices and boiled. It was used for colds. It has a strong bitter taste.

AD-WR: The plant called *tawza'a* is gotten in the mountains. It grows like a potato or the shape of a parsnip. The root is used for a cold. It is smoked and inhaled for a cold, pains in the head and dizziness. It is also boiled and drunk or the head washed in it. It is eaten for a sore throat. To do this, chew some of it and swallow the juice. Spit out the residue. It can also be mixed sometimes with tobacco for smoking purposes. It is smoked only this way for a cold or pain in the head (headache).

DM-PL: The plant called *todza* is the most common medicine. Every family has some of it in the house. It is used for all the common ailments and injuries.

JG-PL: The plant called *todza* is also used for the dose. The root is split and boiled and the decoction is drunk. It tastes bitter and greasy. It is also used for a cold and as a poultice for sores. For this purpose it is first roasted in the ashes.

AD-R: The plant called *todza* is boiled and drunk when the patient can't pass water because of venereal disease. It is also used to stupefy fish [see Fishing in chap. 2].

BR-L, PL: The plant called *tawza* is gotten the year around. It is boiled and the broth is oily. Rub this on joints for rheumatism. It is also good for pimples, sores and aches.

27. *tozituna'abə* [peppermint, *Mentha canadensis*]

RP-WR: Wild peppermint (*tozituna'abə*) is good for colds. The leaves are picked fresh and put in the nostrils. It clears the head. A bunch of the peppermint is spread out on the ground and a person with a fever or a cold lies on it.

28. *tubi* [mountain mahogany, *Cercocarpus ledifolius*]

AD-WR: A small bushy tree (*tubi*) grows in the mountains. Take the bark and dry it. The bark is good for tuberculosis or anyone who spits blood. The dried bark was boiled in water. Any amount was made and stored in water jugs. The red tea made from this was drunk.

29. *tubisiginob^u* [purple sage, *Salvia dorii*]

AD-WR: In late June when the leaves of *tubisiginob^u* are green this plant is gathered. The leaves are dried in the sun. The plant grows in the mountains and is about 1 ft high. It has small leaves, round and green. Strip off the leaves and dry them and preserve them. When needed the leaves are boiled and the head is washed with it or it is drunk for a headache. It is also used for a cold as a drink. When the head is washed for pain, the plant takes the fever from the head and keeps the head cool.

30. *tupi* [unidentified]

HS-D: There is a red berry called *tupi*. The bark of the vine was boiled and the liquor drunk as a physic.

31. *tu.pəziBu* [possibly *Penstemon deustus*][22]

BR-L, PL: There is a small plant called *tu.pəziBu* that is gathered in the spring in the hills. It is a small plant growing 4 or 5 in. high. The green leaves and stalks are gathered and dried. When dry it is put away but first it is ground between two flat stones. It is used for chapped and cracked skin. The cracked sores are washed and the powdered leaves are sprinkled on.

---

[20] Kelly (1932:196) also notes the association of headache with blood being "too thick" according to Surprise Valley informants. The cure there was to slash the forehead between the eyes and let the blood flow. This cure is also recognized by other Nevada Northern Paiute.

[21] See also Train, Hendrichs, and Archer (1933:97) for numerous accounts of this widely used plant. Stewart (1941:429) and Kelly (1932:197) also provide data on uses.

---

[22] Train, Hendrichs, and Archer (1933:112) identify "*too-buzz-see-bee*" as *Penstemon deustus* as well as pennyroyal (*Monardella odoratisima*). The description by BR-L, although very general, could fit either plant. Train, Hendrichs, and Archer (1933:113) list one of the uses of *Penstemon deustus* as for treating sores of various types.

32. *wahapəbi* [juniper berries, *Juniperus osteosperma*][23]

RP-WR: Juniper berries (*wahapəbi*) are selected for the ones with red coloring on the ends. These are put under hot ashes. A person suffering from pains or rheumatism squatted over the ashes so the steam from the cooking berries comes up around him. The patient may squat over the cooking berries all night. Only the juniper berries with red coloring are good for medicine.

JO-PL: The leaves of juniper are made into a tea and used for medicine. They are also burnt like an incense and breathed. This drives the cold out. When a person is sick they put some on the stove and let it smoke.

33. *za'abupijə* [puffball, *Ballarrea phullordea*]

JG-PL: Another medicine for sores is called *za'abupijə* (ghost paint). It is gotten from mushrooms that grow under the trees along the river. The mushroom used is the shape of a ball. The powder inside of the ball-like top is used. It is put on a sore dry. The sore is first washed. Sores on the limbs are bandaged after the powder is put on. If the powder is dry then the bandage is taken off and the sore is healing. If it is still damp it must be treated with powder again.

34. burrs [probably cockleburr, *Zanthium strumarium*][24]

AD-WR: Burrs growing along the water are used as medicine. When the burrs are strong (when the plant is dry) they put a burr on the sore gum and rub it. "That takes the pain, poison and blood out."

35. wild parsnip [probably cow-parsnip, *Heracleum lanatum*]

JG-PL: Wild parsnip is roasted on the coals and split in two. The pieces are tied on both sides of an aching joint. It is also good for rheumatism.

36. *tsinibab* [unidentified]

RP-WR: This is a small tuber chewed and the juice swallowed for a sore throat. The tuber was cut in pieces, and holes cut in them, which were then strung and dried. Gotten on Mt. Grant.

ANIMAL MEDICINES

1. badger [*Taxidea taxus*]

RP-WR: For goiter, mumps and swellings, the bladder of a freshly killed badger is put in the mouth and the juice is swallowed. Two little glands, oblong in shape, greyish in color and about 1 in. or a little less long are found close together near the bladder of the badger and are called *ada.'*. These are dried and then ground up fine. When used the powder is moistened and made into a paste. This is applied externally for boils, swellings and a sore throat. The intestines are dried by hanging up the entire intestine. When it is used a piece is boiled and when soft it is eaten for diarrhea. The fat between the skin and flesh is chewed raw for consumption.[25]

AD-R: The juice from the badger's bladder or *ata'* was used as a medicine for swellings and mumps. The juice in the bladder is also used to rub on the swollen penis resulting from venereal disease. It is also warmed and used to rub on swollen parts and on boils. AD claims that goiter was unknown in the old days.

2. deer [*Odocoileus hemionus*] and antelope [*Antilocapra americana*]

Br-L,PL: The marrow from the large bones of the deer and antelope was rubbed on sunburnt lips, chapped hands, scratched hands, arms, legs, etc. When people had been travelling through the brush all day or when men had been out hunting and had gotten scratched, sunburnt or chapped they used this. The marrow was used when a supply was on hand. It did not keep very long. It was not always used because people did not always have marrow.

3. porcupine [*Erethizon dorsatum*]

HS-D: The quills of porcupine were used to treat toothache. The gums around the aching tooth were pierced with the quill to let out the bad blood.[26]

4. *magasa'a* [horned toad, *Phrynosoma* sp.]

RP-WR: When someone has a pain in the arm he catches a horned toad (*magasa'a*). He puts the toad on the afflicted limb. At first the toad is small but when it has been there a few minutes it is very big. It is about ready to burst. Then the person takes the toad off and lets it go. He places the toad under a bush and thanks him. The toad carries away with him all the bad blood (poison). Some old women still do this.

HS-D: Horned toads (*pamagadsa*, or simply *magadsa*) are not killed for if they are preserved a man can go out on the desert without danger of thirst. Sore muscles and rheumatism are treated by scratching the place where the pain is with a live horned toad.

5. *tupaz* [leopard lizard, *Crotaphytus sp.*]

JG-PL: A lizard is chewed and applied to injuries for medicine. This medicine is called *tupaznatuzwə* [*tupaz*, lizard; *natuzwə*, medicine). When the chewed piece of lizard is rubbed on the injury the person talks to the

---

[23] Train, Hendrichs, and Archer (1933:93) also list numerous other uses for this plant.

[24] This weedy species has spread throughout much of the area in recent years. It is not known whether there is an indigenous Nevada form.

[25] Kelly (1932:197) also reports the use of badger fat in Surprise Valley as a remedy for heart trouble.

[26] This use was confirmed by AD-WR.

lizard and asks it to heal the wound. That kills the pain and prevents the injury from swelling.[27]

6. *paba tupodz* [probably chuckwalla, *Sauromalus obesus*]

JG-PL: The brother of my grandfather, Captain Dave, had this medicine here one time. It is called *paba tupodz*. It is a lizard, but larger than the kind around here. When that lizard sees people going along, it whistles. This lizard comes from around Benton (east of Bishop). You can't see the lizard during the day—only hear its whistle. When you want to kill one, you go early in the morning—before sunrise—to the rocks where they live. You kill it with a gun.

That medicine is for injuries. Captain Dave had a small piece that cost him $5.00. One day his horse dragged him under the wagon and hurt him pretty bad. He made people get out of the house. Then he chewed some of the medicine, spit it on his hands and rubbed it all over the places where he was hurt. He talked to it.

I went over there in two days and he was walking around, cured. I asked him about it and he told me about that medicine. When he talked to the medicine, he asked it to cure his pains, to make the swelling go down and to help him. That is what he prayed. Captain Dave got this medicine from someone around Bishop. He went there visiting. Some of those older people at Schurz know that medicine.

7. *pipuz* [stink bug, *Eleocles* sp.]

AD-WR: There is a beetle, a black one, that stinks when it is touched and is called *pipuz*. It is gotten when under the ground. It is good only when gotten from underground. It is brought to a patient with tuberculosis. The person puts the beetle in the mouth and allows it to discharge the stink into the mouth.[28] This fluid is swallowed. The legs are taken off the body and the body is left in the mouth but not swallowed. Repeat this operation with a number of stink bugs. The bodies of the bugs are taken out and thrown away.

OTHER

1. *pa'abi* [either tufa or pumice]

RP-WR: A light greyish rock that is very light in weight and soft is gotten around Mono Lake. It is ground with a small mortar and pestle such as the one pur-

Figure 47. Small (6.5 cm rim diameter) stone mortar and pestle used to grind pumice to treat trachoma. AMNH 50.2/3648. Collected by W. Z. Park, Walker River, 1934.

chased from BG at Yerington [fig. 47]. The rock is ground into a fine powder. The dry powder is sprinkled in the eyes for bad cases of trachoma. It is left in the eyes until the tears wash it out. The powder is put in the eyes before going to bed. On awakening, the eyes are rubbed to loosen the caked powder.

AD-WR: There is a stone gotten from Mono Lake called *pa'abi*. It is rocks that have been in the water for a long time. It has a rough surface. It is gotten only there. For eyes with blindness, get these rocks from the shore of Mono Lake. Grind them up fine into a powder. Put this in the eyes in a dry form where the white spot is forming (cataract). You "have to stand it" (must be painful). Put it in just once. Sleep with it there. Then the eyes are rubbed to get it out. The tears wash it away. Another person removes with (finger) nails any that remains under the eyelids. Then they can see all right.

2. *yadubi* [specularite].

RP-WR: A powder (*yadubi*) which looks like ground copper is found under large rocks not far from Fallon. It was given by the Indian Father. It is found where he and his wife used to stay. The powder is gotten by reaching under the rock and taking any amount needed.

It is put on the face and head of the insane. When the powder is put on someone prays to the Indian Father. Anyone can apply the powder and pray. It is not necessary to have a shaman do it. This medicine is still used. It is very expensive. The people in Fallon still get it.

---

[27] This account by JG may refer to the same incident and lizard as Number 6 below. The term *paga tupodz* merely refers to a "big lizard"—probably the chuckwalla. The term for leopard lizard is often used as a cover term for other lizards.

[28] Kelly (1932:197) reports the use of "*pipus*" beetles in the same manner in Surprise Valley as a cure for heart trouble.

ND-HL: It was very rare to break bones in the old days. When ND was a young man he never saw a crippled Indian or an Indian with broken bones. The Indians years ago did not have trouble with their eyes. Even the old men had good sight. In the old days even the old people had good teeth.

HS-D: No eyeshade was worn to prevent snow blindness which was common. Nothing was rubbed on or under the eyes either to prevent the blindness or to relieve it.

JG-PL: When the hands or feet froze they were rubbed a little with snow and then the hand or foot was buried in the snow until the feeling returned.

9

Political Organization

[Park's notes on political organization include primarily data on chieftainship and the conduct of group meetings. To these have been added miscellaneous notes on inter-tribal relations, including warfare, trade, and visiting, as well as concepts of property. Additional notes on these topics are to be found in Bands, Ranges, and Intergroup Relationships in chap. 1.

Chieftainship and Meetings were discussed by six individuals, three from Walker River, two from Pyramid Lake, and one from Honey Lake. The following accounts are the most complete and representative. Accounts from Pyramid Lake and Walker River agree that "election" or community approval of a chief/headman was required. The accounts also distinguish this position from that of hunt, drive, and dance leaders (see Subsistence, chap. 2, and Music and Dance in vol. 2). A major role of the chief was apparently advisor on matters of the proper conduct of life. Whereas one account from Walker River suggests that each chief had an assistant who acted as a spokesman, such a position was specifically denied by people at Pyramid Lake—although one individual noted that such a person was called upon to narrate and interpret the journey of visitors (see Visiting, below). Group meetings were somewhat formalized, according to most, with smoking playing an important role. Positions differ as to whether women and younger men had much of a role in speaking on such occasions, although the advice of all was sought in decision making. The chief summarized consensus on issues at the end of discussions.]

CHIEFS

JG-PL: There were a number of chiefs. There was one political chief who talked for everybody. In addition there were chiefs of the rabbit drive, mudhen drive, antelope drive, deer hunting, dances, etc. These chiefs decided when these undertakings were to start. The big chief called no tribal or band meetings.[1] The big chief had nothing to do with setting the dates for the drives. When a big dance is held he gets up during the day and talks to the people. He makes his speech before the gambling starts. The big chief admonished the young people to get married and to take care of the old people and to provide food for them and to have children. He warned the married men and women not to fool with others' spouses and not to fight.

A chief was a bigger man than the Indian doctors. The chief was over the shamans. They had to do what the chief told them. I think the chief was a bigger man than the shamans. In the old days some of the chiefs were shamans. Some had the power to ward off arrows and bullets and could doctor sick people as well. The chiefs in the old days had more property, such as skins, beads, etc., than the shamans. It was felt, however, that most chiefs were also shamans.[2] The chiefs who were shamans were very powerful because they were more powerful than anyone else. Today, Abraham Mahwee is both a chief and a shaman.

Abraham Mahwee is chief at Pyramid Lake. His interpreter is Joe Green. Captain Dave was the chief before Abraham and before Captain Dave, Natches Overton, Captain Dave's uncle was chief. Both of these chiefs had interpreters.

The Indians held a meeting to elect a chief after Captain Dave died. Abraham was an old man and he knew more than the young fellows. That is why he was elected chief. In the old days there was only one chief for each band. In the old days the chief had no talker or assistant. He had to talk to the Indians himself. When the chief died a meeting was held to elect a new chief. The dead chief's son did not succeed him. They elected

---

[1] JG seems to be responding to a query regarding extra-local meetings. He later talks about the chief calling meetings of local interest (see Meetings, below).

[2] On another occasion, JG said the following with reference to chieftainship and shamanism: "[A very powerful shaman] was chief at Pyramid Lake until he gave his chieftainship to another man, Captain Dave. His name was Humboldt Natches and then he changed it to Natches Overton. Captain Dave was not a shaman. These two men were about the same age, perhaps Captain Dave was a bit older than Natches. Captain Dave was Natches's uncle (sic). Johnson Sides was not a shaman. Old Winnemucca was both a chief and a shaman. He was a powerful shaman. He had stronger power than other shamans. He could doctor people who had been shot. Young Winnemucca was also a chief and a powerful shaman."

another man who was a good talker. The chief had no one to help him talk. He was the one who talked.[3]

BR-L,PL: The chief was a man who was well known and accepted by the others as a leader. When there was a big hunt or a drive, he told the people what to do. Being a good warrior was not a qualification for chieftainship. If ten or twelve people wanted to fight, the chief could not say no. The chief did not usually take part in the fight. He stayed back.

GK-WR: A man was elected chief because he was a leader. He could talk. Usually a man who had made a lot of speeches that the people liked was chosen chief. The most essential qualification for chieftainship was to be able to make speeches. A chief must be able to make speeches that the people like. The chief always speaks last in the meeting. He sums up the opinions expressed in the other speeches. He makes his decisions on the basis of the majority opinion expressed by the old men in their speeches. The chief is called *poinabi*. The head man of the rabbit drive is called *kamupoinabi*.

RP-WR: The chief was elected by the people. He was an outstanding man. The son of a chief did not succeed his father.[4] Chiefs for war might be appointed. They were men who could not be killed. They got their power from the bear. *Iza'a dua'a* was a war chief. He told the people when to hold dances. He was not a doctor. He was invulnerable against certain kinds of wounds.[5]

MEETINGS

JG-PL: When anything was to be decided, a meeting was called. There was a chief for every communal undertaking. The chief of the rabbit drive or a hunt for any kind of game set the time for the drive or hunt. If all the people were camping close together, the chief went outside his door and shouted to all the people to come over and smoke with him. The old people always talked about having a smoke when they wanted to talk something over. All the men came to the meetings. When they decide something, they have a meeting at night. The meeting starts right after dark. This meeting is held in the house of the chief or if the meeting is to decide a drive, it is held in the house of the captain of that particular drive. Only the men attended these meetings.

The women never came to the night meetings. They would go to a meeting held in the day time.[6]

When all the men have gathered in the chief's house, they sit around in a circle. He fills his pipe and lights it and passes it to the man on his right. The pipe always goes around the circle counter-clockwise, never the other way. Each man takes two puffs and passes the pipe to the next man. When the pipe has gone all the way around the circle the chief starts to talk. He tells them where the drive is to be held and where the camp is to be held. If anyone disagrees with him, he speaks up and suggests any other plan that he might have. Then the other men join in the discussion. From the opinions expressed in the discussion, the chief decides the majority opinion and he does what most of them want. The chief has no larger house than anyone else.[7]

When the chief talks, no one answers him or repeats his words.[8] While he is talking everyone sits quietly and listens to what he says.

GK-WR: In the old days, the chief called the meetings. He acted as his own messenger, going to all the camps and telling the people that on a ceratin day there would be a meeting to talk things over. During the meeting a pipe was passed around among the old men. There was no fixed direction for the passing of the pipe. When I was a boy I saw the old men come together many times to talk things over. They sat around a fire and kept the pipe going around.

The chief made the first speech. The chief stood up and talked loudly so all the people could hear. The chief talked about a little of everything. He told the people it was time to hunt ducks, birds, deer or other game, to gather pinenuts, to hold a rabbit drive or to hold a dance. He told the men not to fight and the women not to quarrel. He told them to be good people. He told the young people to be good and not to steal and get along with their friends. He told the young girls not to run around but to stay home until they got married and to have children. He told the people not to be lazy but to gather seeds and hunt. He talked a great deal and told the people what to do. Other men were heads of rabbit-drives, of mudhen drives, antelope drives, chief of the dance, head of a big duck hunt.

Meetings of the entire band were held to decide about dances, war and other affairs that concerned the group.

---

[3] Stewart (1941:407) received positive response on the use of an announcer or "repeater" from one of two individuals at Pyramid Lake. Otherwise, all others who knew of such individuals were from more northerly Northern Paiute groups. But see also JG's discussion of the use of a repeater under Visiting, below.

[4] Stewart (1941:407) also received negative replies to the question on patrilineal succession.

[5] Powers of this type can exist outside the realm of shamanism (see Shamanism, in vol. 2).

[6] Both Stewart (1941) and Kelly (1932) are silent on the matter of women's attendance and participation; but see ND-HL's account below.

[7] ND-HL (see below) specifically states that chiefs had larger houses, partly to accommodate meetings.

[8] JG is consistent in his denial of the existence of such talkers or repeaters (see above); but see also the comments of HW-Y, below.

All the people in the band came to these meetings.[9] The old men did all the talking. When all the opinions on the matter at hand had been expressed, the chief voiced his opinion and made the decision. His decision was final. Women attended these meetings but they never made speeches before the band.[10] They would talk about the question among themselves, but they never made speeches at the meetings.

HW-WY: The chief called the meetings. He told all the people to gather together to talk things over. When the chief spoke there was a man sitting beside the chief who "talked right after him." He repeated the chief's words. He repeated the chief's words in a loud voice so all the people could hear. He talked louder than the chief. The chief was called *poinabə.* The repeater was called *nədənəgədiidə.* Anybody could act as repeater.

ND-HL: Messengers were sent out with a message of a meeting or dance to be held in a certain number of days. They carry strings with knots, one knot for each day between their departure and the day of the dance or meeting. The messenger unties a knot for each day that passes while he is traveling. The knots are made in string (*wihabi,* string made of *wiha*).

Meetings were held both during the day and in the evening. The people sat in groups in a circle. The chiefs and the important men sat near the front, nearest the middle of the circle. The sexes were mixed. A family usually sat in one group.

The meeting might be held in a tule or grass-covered house (*kani*). The chief usually had a larger house than the other people in the band. The meetings were sometimes held in his house. The people in the band help the chief build his house so he can have a larger place. In the evenings even if there is no meeting the old men go to the chief's house and sit around and smoke. The chief had the pipe which was passed around. The older men had tobacco which they took to the chief's house for smoking. At a meeting of the band the pipe is passed around before the talk starts. The pipe continues to circulate while speeches are made.

When the chief calls a meeting, he announces it before evening. If there are other camps near him he shouts, "You men come to my house tonight and smoke with me. I have something to tell you." The chief makes no announcement of what the meeting is to be held for. While the people are gathering, the old men sit around

and smoke. The women come to the meeting with the men. The children play outside the house or around the circle if the meeting is held outdoors.

When all the people have gathered the chief gets up and makes a speech telling the people the purpose of the meeting. During the speeches the pipe is continually passed around among the old men. The chief does not have an assistant.

After the chief had made his speech, members of the band spoke giving their opinion. If the women had suggestions or wished to express an opinion, they were free to speak. Sometimes young men got up to express an opinion, although it was the old men who usually decided things.

INTER-TRIBAL RELATIONSHIPS

[Several individuals from all areas contributed data toward aspects of this topic. Most numerous are data on warfare. Although opinions occasionally differed, most agreed that skirmishes and battles took place most often with the Modoc and Pit River peoples, and much less frequently with the Maidu, Washoe, and Shoshone. Opinions also differed on the proper conduct of battles, including such matters as to whether scalping was practiced aboriginally, and whether armor and shields were used. A number of people recalled fragments or whole sequences of tales of battles fought. It is likely that statements about occasional warfare with a particular group may refer to single incidents—now somewhat generalized. People also recalled times of early contact and battles involving Whites.

Data on trade were given by but a few individuals. None of the accounts is particularly full, but each adds notes on the topic that are not necessarily part of the published literature. See also Bands, Ranges, and Intergroup Relationships in chap. 1].

Warfare: Friends and Enemies

HS-D: The Paiutes were friendly with the Bannock and Shoshone. They had no trouble with the Indians to the south—those of Mono Lake and those of Yosemite Valley. The Paiutes fought more with the Modocs and Pit River Indians. These fights were usually caused by stealing women. [When the Pit River people stole Paiute women,] the women were raped and tortured, while captive children were tortured and killed. The Paiutes did not steal Pit River women often. There are just a few cases of stolen Pit River women.

The Paiutes fought with the Modocs around Alturas, Likely, Aden, Fall River and Lakeview [see Tales of War, below]. The Digger Indians (*takoni*) around Susanville and Greenville were not enemies. The Paiutes

---

[9] Just how large these gatherings were and how encompassing of other than those conveniently at hand is not stated. Probably all people at Pyramid Lake or at Walker River, for example, rarely came together.

[10] ND-HL (see below) implies that women did speak, but also suggests that decision-making was largely in the hands of men.

did not go to war against the Washo either. A small group might have a fight with some Washo.[11]

RP-WR: The Paiutes have no trouble with the Indians around Bishop or the Washo. They got along well with the Shoshone (*tubong*). They didn't marry Shoshone women.[12] A long time ago they did not know these people. When the Paiute began travelling around Elko, Nv., they met the Shoshone. A long time ago Bannocks used to come to Walker River for a big dance.

Paiutes fought with the Pit River (*sai*). Some men from Schurz used to go up and help the people at Pyramid Lake when they were fighting the Pit River people. A few of them would bring back Pit River women as wives. They captured the women in war against the Pit Rivers. RP's husband's great grandmother was captured from the Pit River Indians. There are also a few other people around Schurz who have a little Pit River blood due to this kind of marriage. Just young fellows did that. They took one wife.

CW-PL: The Paiutes fought with the Shoshone. They lived around Duck Valley, Wahee [Owyhee]. Paiutes got horses from the Shoshoni. They got them from war with the Shoshoni. Horses got away and became wild and these developed herds of wild horses in the mountains.[13]

BR-L,PL: The Paiutes never fought with the Bannocks. They are Indians.[14] They went away from here and went to Idaho. They went from here to the east, met some people and stayed with them, married the women and took their ways and called themselves Bannocks. They always stayed over there (Idaho) after that and came to be big in numbers.[15]

One time the Paiutes were going to fight the Washo. The Washo became frightened and threw away their bows and arrows and ran into the timber. The Paiutes could not catch them. After this some of the old Washoes came

to Pyramid Lake and dried fish and took them home with them. There was plenty of game in the Paiute country so they never went in to the Washoe country to hunt. The Paiutes called the Washoes *Washu.*

GK-WR: The Paiutes never fought among themselves. I never heard of any trouble with the Klamath. I was never up that way. I have heard that the Washoes around Gardnerville were mean people.[16] The Paiutes had trouble with them. The Washo lived in Washoe Valley, between Carson City and Reno, and Washoe Lake. The Paiutes [from Walker River?] never went into that country. The people around Bishop were called *pitən-nagwət.* The Paiutes never fought these Indians.

Warfare: Procedures

ND-HL: The battle is entirely in the hands of the chief. As they moved toward the enemy the chief talked to his men in the evening. He would send out scouts to the high points along the course of march. The party stopped in the evening and the chief talked to his men. He instructed them in what they are to do in the battle. He tells them about his experiences in war. He tells them that when the enemy starts shooting to watch the flight of the arrows. When they look as if they are going to fall about ten feet in front of a man he must dodge for they are the ones that will hit him. When they look as if they are coming right at a man, they will go over him.

The chief talks to his men every night when they are on the trail. He does not get up and give a speech but he talks softly so the enemy cannot hear the echo.

When a party is going to attack, the shaman has nothing to do with the party. The shaman does not predict the outcome of the battle while the warriors are on the warpath. The shaman goes along as a doctor but in the band he is just like any other warrior.[17]

Bows and arrows were the chief weapons in fighting. Warriors carry a bone spear. This is made from a brush (*tü.abi* [*Amelanchier alnifolia*]) found on the mountains.

---

[11] BB-PL: "In the old days the Paiutes were good friends with the Washo but one time two women were coming to Reno on the train. Some Washo men attacked them and they died as a result. After that there was trouble between the Paiutes and the Washo." Stewart (1941:440) reports that "the individual encounters between Washo and Paiute resulted in some deaths, no war."

[12] GK-WR: "The Paiutes fought with the people around Humboldt County [Shoshone?]. They stole women from these people and brought them to Yerington and Schurz. I (GK) do not think the Paiute stole children from these people."

[13] This account may refer to a specific event in which horses were stolen. See HS-D's account above.

[14] "They are Indians" means that they were kinsmen; i.e., Paiutes. The Bannock speak the Northern Paiute language and were originally from Oregon country.

[15] The Bannock also played an important role in Northern Paiute history through continued contacts throughout the late nineteenth century. Kinship between the Bannocks at Fort Hall and all Northern Paiute groups is still recognized.

---

[16] GK-WR: "My uncle, Captain Sam, told me that the Washo were bad people. He said they were very wild and mean. The Paiutes had nothing to do with them. We have never had a war with the Washo. The Washo always tried to kill Paiutes when Paiutes came into their territory. I do not think that the Paiutes tried to kill Washo when they came into our country. Now the Paiutes are very friendly with the Washo." BF-PL: "Heard the Paiutes fought the Washo but never saw that. His grandfather told him that Washo never liked the Paiutes."

[17] Neither Kelly (1932) nor Stewart (1941) comments on the use of shamans in war. But the Washo and the Klamath are known to have enlisted them to make the enemy vulnerable (Warren L. d'Azevedo, personal communication, 1985; Spier 1930:30).

The shaft is about 3/4 in. in diameter and about 4 ft long. A piece of sharpened bone about 6 in. long—it is like a flat knife with both edges of the blade sharp—forms the point. This spear is carried in the arrow quiver. The spear point is sticking up. In fighting men never wanted to come close to the enemy, but when their arrows gave out they pulled out the spear and rushed in to fight at close quarters with spears.

The spear is held near the end of the shaft with the right hand. The arm and hand are bent back to hold the spear upright in *back* of the arm. The bow is held in the left hand and is used as a kind of guard. This is the position for advancing. The spear is held in this position so the enemy cannot catch it with his spear or bow. When the thrust is made the bow is brought close and in front of the body. With a quick jerk of the wrist the point is brought down and pointed forward. The rest of the thrust is carried out with the entire arm. The spear is called *sigica*.

The arrows were poisoned, but the spear point was not poisoned.[18] ND thinks that this spear was not used by the Walker Lake Paviotso.[19] Only the Paiutes who fought the Pit Rivers had this spear.

The arrow quiver was worn diagonally across the back. The top of the quiver was at the right shoulder. ND demonstrated with a coyote skin the position of the quiver. No armor was worn. The Pit Rivers wore the hard thick skin from elk as armor. Clubs were not used in war, nor were shields used.[20]

The best runners were sent out ahead as scouts. Usually about four scouts were sent out. The scouts were sent out early in the morning. The rest of the war party waits until they return. If the scouts do not find the enemy's track or signs of them the party travels until night. Again, early next morning scouts are sent ahead to look for the enemy.

Bird or animal calls were not used by scouts. No signals were given by the scouts. If the enemy is seen the scouts try to sneak back to their camp without being seen (see reference to bird and animal calls used by the Northern Paiute scouts in Spier 1930)[21] When the attack on the enemy is made men shout and make as much noise as they can.

The most important element in war is to surprise the enemy. Every effort is made to cover the presence of the war party until the moment of attack. The time considered best for the attack is in the grey light when dawn begins to break. When enemies are killed the beads, clothing, etc., are not stripped from the bodies. The bows and arrows are not taken. The only loot is the baskets that may be found in the enemy's camp.[22]

If the Paiutes were victorious the chief went among the slain enemy to select the scalps with the longest hair. Four or five scalps might be taken. These were taken home. The scalps were put on a straight pole. Each scalp was put on a willow stick which was lashed to the top of the pole. The men danced around the pole every night for a month or longer.[23]

The good singers, about three, sing and beat drums. Three young men who were the best dancers dance the war dance. The step was a double little hop on one foot and then on the other. The dancers shave their faces and have their bodies painted with white and red paint. At the end of the dance the spectators clap and shout. The dancers have locks of hair from the scalps fastened to their shoulders or tied to their hair at the temples. This dance was called *tuwɔnuga*. The scalp is *tuwɔpi*. This is probably a dance that came from the Bannock.[24]

Sometimes some of the slain enemies were flayed. The skins were brought home. They are filled with sagebrush bark and grass. The skin of the feet and hands was not taken but the skin of the face and head was taken. When it was stuffed it was stood up by the pole during the dance. Only one skin was taken. When the dance was over the stuffed skin and the scalps were burned. ND's grandfather told him about this. He has

---

[18] Kelly (1932:187) speaks of poisoned war arrows. She describes the spear as 4 to 5 ft long, tipped with a 4 1/2 in. obsidian blade. It was used for close combat. Some Surprise Valley Paiute denied its use.

[19] Stewart (1941:385) got a positive response to the use of a thrusting spear only at Pyramid Lake, Winnemucca, and Owyhee (Miller Creek).

[20] Stewart (1941:386) received negative responses throughout the Northern Paiute area on the use of armor. But shields are reported for Honey Lake, Pyramid Lake, Fallon, Walker River, and Owyhee (Miller Creek). Kelly (1932) got conflicting reports as to the use of armor by Surprise Valley people. Circular or fan-shaped shields, however, were well known. BR-L,PL commented to Park that "very few had this shield."

[21] Spier (1930:32) says of the Klamath: "Scouts do not use animal cries like those of the Northern Paiute." This statement may have occasioned Park's question.

[22] Given that baskets took considerable time to make, they may have been considered desirable prizes. However, on another occasion, ND-HL told Park that "the baskets, beads and blankets of the enemy were gathered in a pile and burned."

[23] Kelly (1932:178) received an account of a scalp dance, featuring a central pole, from one Surprise Valley individual. Others denied that scalping was practiced. Riddell (1960:76) likewise received a detailed account from a Honey Lake respondent of such a dance held in their territory. According to Spier (1930:33), the scalp dance was common among the Klamath.

[24] If not specifically from the Bannock, the dance probably can at least be attributed to northern sources; e.g., the Klamath.

never seen it.[25] ND does not know how the human skin was taken from the body.

Men going to war would paint their bodies with red and white paint. Straight lines were put on the face and body, big stripes across the chest and around the legs. This was done because they were pretty angry. After one day if the fight was to be continued they washed the paint off and repainted themselves. When the fight was over the paint was not taken off. It was allowed to wear off.

JG-PL: When men went to war they smeared their faces with red paint. Perhaps one side would be white and the other side black or red. Bands of paint were put around the arms, legs and body. These bands were usually about as wide as a man's hand. This made them look pretty wild and it made their enemy think they were tough men.

I do not think the Paiutes scalped their enemies. I never heard of their doing that. The Indians over in Idaho do that. They hang the scalps up and dance around. The Paiutes never cut off the heads or any other parts of the bodies of the slain enemy. In the fight with the Pit River near Sutcliff [see Tales of War, below], the Paiutes buried a Pit River chief who was killed in the fight. They left the other Pit River dead lying there.[26]

A few warriors had rough shields which were about four feet in diameter. They were made of deer skin and put around a frame of chokecherry wood and hard willows. Only a few had these shields [fig. 24, chap. 3].

GK-WR: GK thinks that slain enemies were scalped. The scalp did not include the ears. The scalp was cut low on the forehead and below the temples and up and above the ears and around the back of the head. Then the scalp was pulled off. Only the scalp was taken, bodies were not mutilated. The scalps were kept by the chief. When a dance was held the scalp was put on top of a pole in the middle of the dance grounds. I don't know what this meant. The scalp was used for the circle dance that lasted for five nights. When the dance was over the scalp was put away until the next dance.[27]

[Park recorded the following accounts of encounters between the Paiute and hostile Modoc and Pit River peoples. Those given are the most complete, but several individuals Park interviewed knew of these and other incidents. As narratives, some may be accounts of the same battles, expanded or elaborated with other motifs.]

War with the Modocs.
ND-HL: When ND's great grandfather was a little boy, a band of Modocs came upon Paiutes who were getting suckers (*a'wago*) from Long Valley Creek (*suhu*).[28] The Paiutes were camped along the creek. The Modocs attacked the Paiutes. Some of the men took the women and children away from the fight to protect them. The fight was out in the open. They get the worst of it when they fight behind the brush. They cannot see the arrows coming. The Modocs had round shields made from stretching buckskin on a willow hoop.[29] The Paiutes never used shields. Other Modocs had round shields covered with dried skin. The men with shields crept close to the Paiutes holding the shields in front of them. The Paiutes always faced the enemy in order to dodge the arrows. The Modocs held their bows horizontally while the Paiutes held theirs vertically. When the fight started the warriors got separated and there were many individual struggles. The Modocs scalped their own dead, so the Paiute could not get the scalps.[30] The Modocs carried off their wounded. The battle lasted all day. The next day the Paiutes followed the Modocs. They found many corpses left behind around Honey Lake.

Some years later there was a camp of Paiutes on the west shore of Pyramid Lake. The women and children were around the camp. Most of the men were away. At this time ND's grandfather was between fifty and sixty.[31] It was in the spring. The Modocs surprised the camp and killed most of the people. Only a few Paiutes got away. The Modocs took everything that they could carry. They killed the Paiute women and took the chil-

---

[25] Spier (1930) makes no mention of flaying an enemy and dancing around the stuffed skin at the scalp dance. The Klamath did take body parts (hands, feet, ears, heart, lips, etc.) as war trophies, however.

[26] Others agreed with JG that scalping did not occur. BR-L,PL stated that "scalps were taken only when people were very angry at each other." He also stated that very few prisoners were taken. "They tried to kill the enemy instead of capturing him." ND-HL agreed that "the hands of killed enemies were not cut off for trophies." JG-PL and JB-PL both speak of burying the chief after a Pit River battle (see Tales of War, below).

[27] Scalping and the scalp dance are probably late arrivals in Northern Paiute territory, especially as far south as Walker River.

---

[28] Long Valley Creek terminates in Honey Lake. The specific site of this battle is not recorded, but fishing for suckers, validated by Riddell (1960:38) probably occurred in Long Valley proper (near Doyle, Calif.) rather than at the extreme headwaters of the stream.

[29] Park collected two round shields at Pyramid Lake (see Fig. 24 in chap. 3). Spier (1930:32) also attributes the round hand shield to the Klamath.

[30] According to Spier (1930), both the Modoc and Klamath scalped enemies. He does not report any special feeling about the dead having to be "whole" for cremation—a possible justification for taking their scalps. The Klamath always tried to return their dead killed in war to their own territory for cremation.

[31] If the relationship term is correct (and not an extension), this battle may have taken place in the 1840s.

dren with them. When the men arrived at their camp they found nothing but dead and ashes. The Modocs drove the Paiute children along. They made captive children eat the flesh of dead Paiutes.[32] They fed them this way morning and evening. When a child gave out from fatigue they threw it in the fire and when it was cooked they gave the flesh to the other captives. It took the Modocs about three days to get to Aden [Calif.]. They stayed around Aden.

The Modocs took all the clothes away from the captive children so they would not run away. They made the children carry wood and water and work around the camp. Some Modoc men married the captive girls. One of them married two girls. They held dances in the spring over the Paiute scalps. Two of the Paiute girls married to a Modoc wanted to get away. One day one of the girls found the place where her husband kept his tools for making fire. The two girls agreed to escape that night but one of them backed out. One girl stole the fire tools and a piece of mudhen skin blanket. The Modocs danced all night. Just before dawn when everyone was asleep the girl sneaked out and crossed the Pit River. She floated down stream and hid. The Modoc looked for her all day. That night she came out of her hiding place and started for Pyramid Lake. After several days she arrived. The girl was pregnant when she arrived among the Paiutes. The child was brought up as a Paiute.

ND's grandfather was a chief. His name was adabuga', 'Jaw.' He called the Paiutes together. He sent a messenger with an arrow with ten knots made of buckskin on it. In ten days they were going to meet. If the people whom the messenger invited were willing to join in the fight they tied an arrow to the one he carried. The messenger went to Nixon, Fallon and Schurz. Then he came through Mason Valley. The messenger was sent out after the girl who got away from the Modocs and came back to the Paiutes. She came home and told the Paiutes where the captives were kept.

Hundreds of Paiutes gathered at Pyramid Lake in response to the message. The women came too. They started to make ready for war. The men made many arrows. The women made moccasins and gathered seeds. These seeds were not to be eaten until they were on their way home from the Modoc country. The girl escaped in the spring and by fall the Paiutes were ready to start against the Modocs.

It took three days for the Paiutes to get to the Modoc country. They kept scouts out in advance all the time. The scouts were relieved often so they would always have a fresh man in advance. Some of the Paiutes were on horses. They came upon the Modocs in Round Valley near Aden, California. They waited until night to creep upon the Modoc camp. The Modocs were holding a pow-wow. At daybreak when the fires were dying down the Paiute attacked. They surrounded the Modoc camp. They killed men, women and old people. A few men captured Modoc girls. The Modocs had sent all the captive children north. The old chief would not allow the Paiutes to keep the Modoc girls so most of them were killed. One Modoc woman was reserved for the Paiute women to eat alive.[33] A few Modoc girls were brought back and married to Paiutes. Their descendants are known today among the Paiutes as having Modoc blood.

Another band of Modocs from still further north drove the Paiutes back. The Paiutes lost only two men. One was killed pursuing some Modocs. The Paiutes did not scalp on this expedition.

The Paiutes held a dance before they left Pyramid Lake. The dancers faced the northwest, towards the enemy's country. The only dance they held when they got home was when the women danced around the captive Modoc woman and ate her alive.

This fight occurred 95 to 100 years ago. ND's mother was eight or ten then. It was before the Whites came.

Pit River Battle.

AM-PL: One of the Paiutes went to capture little eagles. He was also digging for potatoes. He spent the night there at the other end of the lake. Two other Paiute men started out northward and passed his camp early in the morning. On the other side of the hill from there these two found the Pit Rivers in large numbers at what is now the Round Hole.[34]

On their way back they warned the eagle hunter of the presence of the *Sai*. He had a dog and he went to where eagles had a nest and got in there and left the dog outside. As he lay there the eagles paid no attention to him. Then the Pit Rivers came over the hill and he saw them. He saw the enemy near the two Paiute scouts. The best runner was very tired and could not go very fast. One was all in and tired. A Pit River went around and was shot in the neck by a Paiute who waited on the other side of the hill for him.

---

[32] Spier (1930) does not report this for the Klamath/Modoc. HS-D, probably referring to the same story for which he acted as interpreter, stated that they say that the Pit River people (Achomawi) used to make captives eat their own children.

[33] HS-D, again probably referring to this story, on another occasion stated that the Paiutes captured a Pit River woman and tied her to a stake, and the women danced around. "Each woman bit a piece out until she was dead." Spier (1930:34) reports that the Klamath made prisoners dance very close to the fire [as torture] and sometimes clubbed them. However, since most were sold or kept as slaves, they tended not to kill them.

[34] This place name is no longer in use, and the location of Round Hole is thus uncertain. It may be between Tule Peak and the present California border.

He made a special noise to signal the other scout to let the other know he had killed an enemy. That made the other feel better and gave him more strength. He told the freshest runner to go ahead and warn the Paiutes while he would stay and fight the Pit Rivers. He got to Willows[35] where some of the Paiutes were fishing. They decided to fall back and fight the enemy at Nixon. The chief refused to retreat.

The women were gathering *sunu* (a kind of seed). The scout told them the enemy was coming. They picked up their baskets and started for the hills away from the lake. Then the scout came to the men fishing.

The man in the eagle nest threw away his bow and arrow sack while he was watching. He captured two small eagles that could fly. He tied one to each forearm and tried to fly with them but the two were not strong enough to raise him. Then he tied them closer to his wrist and tried to fly again. This time they could lift him. He escaped down the cliff with these eagles. They flew him to the bottom of the cliff. Now the Indians are too heavy and they cannot do this. When he got down he put the two eagles in a little cage he had and he took them home (*kuina'*, 'eagle'). The enemy was ahead of him then and he followed them over to where his people were. He found where they had killed and cooked and eaten his dog. When he got close to Willows the battle had started.

The women got in a small cave so the Pit River started fires in the mouth of the cave.[36] The women smothered to death and then the Pit River dragged the bodies out. They would take out the intestines and stretch them over brush. They massacred the Paiutes that time. One of the Paiutes was strong. He was shot full of arrows and he ran to where three men were hiding. He pulled out the arrows and used them against the enemy. The Pit Rivers had a shield to cover the face. One came where these people were. They did not shoot arrows at him but grabbed him and cut his head off. Some Paiutes escaped by swimming to a cave that had to be reached under water. Two unmarried women ran toward the Indians at Nixon. A young man started to come with them but he could not keep up. They warned the people at Nixon. They got ready and went over to help but the *izizawi* had already left.

AM's grandfather told him this and his great, great grandfather went through this war.

JB-PL: In the spring every year people came to the lake for fish. Two men came to where JB now lives.

ND's mother's father was one of these men. They came across a band of *Sai*. They went back to this side of Sutcliffe (High Rock) where the Indians were camped. They reported the enemy band but no one paid any attention to them. These two stayed with the rest of the people. The Pit River camped along the lake west of the Paiutes. Early in the morning about sun-up the *Sai* attacked the Paiutes who had made no defense. The Paiutes were massacred. ND's grandfather was not killed. Some had hidden and he was one of these. He was shot over the eye with an arrow. The doctor took the arrow out. He hid in a crevice. The massacre lasted only one day. The Pit River used buckskin armor. They wove willows into the armor. It was big enough so they could duck in back of it. It was covered with elkskin, and comes half way to the knees. They lifted it up with their shoulders to protect their faces from arrows. The Paiutes had no armor or shields. Some of the Paiutes got into crevices and the Pit Rivers threw burning sage brush on them. This burned them. The Pit Rivers got about forty women and children. Two women got away before the Pit Rivers left Sutcliffe and they [the women] went to Nixon. They told them about the fight. Only ten men came out. They caught up with the Pit Rivers at the water tank twelve miles west of Sutcliffe.[37] They had only a few arrows and they were outnumbered so they had to turn back. Some escaped by diving into the water and swimming to the cave under water.

A *Sai* stood on the cliff and spoke in Paiute to all the people hidden. He told them that all the *Sai* had gone and it was safe to come out. A woman got in a hole with a baby and it cried. She killed it to keep it quiet. The Pit River tried to spear her by thrusting spears down the hole. She protected herself by holding a rock over her head. They threw hot coals on the people in the crevices. The people tried to shield themselves with buckskin, but it did not protect them very well.

The Pit Rivers camped about ten or twelve miles northwest of the lake after the massacre. They made a big circle and placed the captives in the center. The captors slept around the circle.

The chief had had his stomach cut open. He gathered up his intestines and sat there and told his people to hide.

Wunuka ab (*tubus*, 'lizard')[38] was an old man who had left the camp to fish before the massacre. He took his children with him. He saw the burning of the Paiutes at night.

---

[35] The "Willows" is located on the west side of Pyramid Lake, near the present site of Sutcliffe.

[36] This method of killing was also used against the *saiduka'a*, legendary enemies of the Paiute at Lovelock (see Stewart 1941:441), and Hopkins (1883).

[37] This is probably located in Winnemucca Valley, north of Reno.

[38] Why this term is added is not known. It seems to have little to do with the man's name as recorded—unless he is named for another species of lizard.

These *Sai* came from around Aden, Likely, Alturas and Fall River.[39]

A year later they had two scouts out southwest of the Lake. They let the *Sai* chase them but they kept a certain distance ahead of the Pit Rivers. They went through a ravine and found that the Pit Rivers were almost on them. They ran to the Paiute camp at Sutcliff. The fight took place in the ravine above Sutcliffe. A Paiute warrior shot both eyes out of the Pit River chief. When he was killed, the Pit Rivers gave way. The Paiute encircled them and drove them to the shore of the lake. All were killed and the bodies were thrown into the lake. Many arrows came to the surface where the bodies had been thrown in the water.

The dead were piled up in heaps. The chief's body was covered with rocks. He was the only one to get burial.[40] About 10 of the *Sai* got away. They met a Paiute woman gathering food. They asked her if there were men about when she told them there were not they threw her over a cliff.

BB-PL: Pit Rivers wiped out a whole camp of Paiutes at Sutcliffe. People from Schurz, Fallon, etc., went up between the two lakes hunting. One man was out hunting deer and he shot one. He was trailing it when he came upon the trail of a band of Pit Rivers. They had two scouts out who found the Pit River band and came back and reported to the main band. The Pit Rivers had one Paiute woman with them. They had captured her at Sutcliffe. She told her captors that only women were left in camp. Then they saw the two Paiute scouts and so they pushed her off a big rock several times until they killed her.[41]

There were some Digger Indians (*takoni*) with the Pit Rivers. When they saw the Paiute band they deserted the Pit Rivers and started home. Then the battle started. Two of the Paiutes were cut off from their band. They were trying to get the leader of the Pit Rivers who was all dressed in owl feathers. He had a shield and he always stayed behind the shield. One of them had a handful of pebbles in his shield and it sounded as if a bunch of arrows had struck it. The Pit River leader lowered the shield to shoot and then the other Paiute shot him right in the eye. Then the whole Pit River party started to flee but the Paiutes surrounded them and they shot them all down. They laid them in a row and covered them

with a mound of dirt. They put a rock there for a monument to the Pit River chief.

JB-PL: The Pit River and Paiute men went north to see the Bannocks.[42] Two Bannocks often came to visit Paiutes in Honey Lake Valley.

Two went out hunting with one Paiute and were overtaken by *Sai*. The Bannocks were killed and the Paiute sent word to the Bannocks to meet them in northern Nevada. Indians from Fallon, Walker River and Lovelock came. Paiutes then combined with Bannock forces. They sent four scouts each day. The *Sai* had scouts out also. The Paiute scouts usually brought in a scalp every day. They ran onto the *Sai* at Bog Valley west of Alturas. They found some Indians that had been captured at Sutcliffe. They fought these *Sai* and if they could talk Paiute they were spared; otherwise they would be killed. They brought all the children back and one who had been made captive at Sutcliffe. This was the last time that the Paiute had trouble with the *Sai*. They threw the scalps away. Even women and children from Fallon were found among the captives. *Saituka*, are the 'tule eaters' (Pit Rivers).[43]

BR-L, PL: One time they had trouble here (Pyramid Lake). The chief sent word all over, to Fallon, Walker River and Lovelock, to meet here. The men went from here and fought the Pit Rivers about a mile from Willows along the southwestern shore of Pyramid Lake. While they were waiting to start out they played football games. I do not know if they had a dance then. There was no dance after the battle. The only Pit Rivers who got away were about twelve who deserted when they saw the size of the Paiute band. This happened before the gold rush in '49. There were no whites here then. My father was a young man at the time. That was the last big fight that we had with the Pit Rivers.[44]

Trade

[Park's notes on trade are minimal and, with one exception, do not appear to derive from specific questioning on the topic. In addition to the brief data that follow, there are other suggestions of trade given under Bands,

---

[39] Sai, as in *saiduka'a*, is a term applied generally to enemies — most commonly the Pit River (Achumawi) people — but also to others, including the Umatilla in Oregon (see Stewart 1941:441).

[40] An account by JG-PL also states that the chief in this battle was buried. See also the account of BB-PL below.

[41] This part of the story was repeated by others as well.

[42] The visitors in this case may have been either from Idaho or Oregon, as the term Bannock seems to be used for various peoples in those districts.

[43] Liljeblad (1982) gives an etymology for *saiduka'a* as "under the tules" (e.g., tule mats). The term is usually applied to legendary enemy people in the Humboldt and Carson Sinks, of whom the Pit River (Achumawi) are said to be descendants (see also note 39).

[44] Again, the date may be in the early 1840s or late 1830s — if the genealogical comments are accurate. Post-contact disruption probably precluded much in the way of aboriginal warfare after that time.

chap. 1, and Subsistence, chap. 2. The use of beads as a medium of exchange is also treated under the section on Beads in chap. 5.]

ND-HL: Small univalve shells were gotten from the Maidu. The Paiutes exchanged buckskin and dried fish for the shells. The Paiutes never went to California to collect beads before the Whites came. The only time they went to the California coast was when the immigrants were coming through.[45]

HW-Y: In the old days, the Digger Indians from Sonora [Miwok] came to trade for salt. They were called *wa.wa'*. They would give two deerskins for a piece of salt 6 in. long by 4 or 5 in. thick.

JB-PL: The Paiutes got horses from people on the Snake River. They would go up there and buy horses. The trip would last a month or two.

JG-PL: After peace was made, not very long ago, people went everywhere and they could trade. Before that they could not go any place; it was dangerous. After they made peace, they could go to Honey Lake or up north where they could make trade. They could trade and they did with the people at Fallon, Walker River, etc. They traded moccasins, beads, dentalium shells, etc.

Before peace was made the whites captured three Indians here and took them over to California. When they had a Mexican war there then those three came back. They told the others about California and the shells there. They took people to California and they got shells. Before this they had bone beads. My grandfather's brother was captured and came back to tell about the shells. One time one whole camp went down there.[46]

HS-D: HS does not think there was much trading in the old days. When a man had a surplus of pinenuts he would take them to another camp and give them to friends. In return he would be given presents but he would not ask for anything.

GK-WR: Food such as seeds, meat, and nuts and skins were traded for beads. The beads were measured on the finger joints or from the tip of the forefinger to the wrist, elbow or shoulder.

RP-WR: If some people had no seeds or meat, they bought some with beads or other things from those who had a good supply. If they had nothing to trade for seeds or fish, they carried wood for those who had a supply of food. In this way, they got some food.

Visiting

JG-PL: When a visitor comes from another place such as Walker Lake he would start at the beginning of his journey and tell the people all the details of his trip—where he slept, where he turned aside to get water. The most minute details of the journey would be given in the proper sequence. One special man repeated after him the account of his journey. The visitor would say a few words and then the repeater said those words. He said only a few words at a time so he would not miss any of the account. When a visitor arrived, if the repeater was not present he had to be sent for, if he were not too far away, before the visitor talked to the assembled people. In the meantime the visitor was visiting individual families. He was only visiting with them. He did not tell them about the way he came until the repeater arrived. If the repeater were too far away someone else would be pressed into service so the people could hear about the visitor's journey. They always did this. They could not get along without someone's repeating. The repeater is a good man. He talks loudly so all the people sitting around the camps can hear what the visitor has said. The repeater is called *nu.nikwikiid*. This is the same as the interpreter or the repeater for a shaman when he is doctoring. When the shaman talks the repeater talks loudly so all the people can hear what the shaman said. The repeater functions only at a doctoring and when a visitor comes from another band [see Shamanism in Vol. 2].

When anyone went from Pyramid Lake to visit any other band those people would have a man to repeat and he would tell about his journey.

ND-HL: When a messenger comes from another band all the people who are around when the visitor arrives gather to hear the news from the other band or if the visitor has a message it is delivered to the assembled members of the band. The chief repeats or interprets the words of the visitor for the people sitting around in the meeting.

When a visitor or messenger arrives, he goes first to see the people in that band whom he knows. They pass the word around to other members of the band that a messenger or a visitor has arrived. As soon as he arrived the hosts gave him something to eat. If it is nearly time

---

[45] Various, but not all, of the people Park interviewed were of the opinion that shell beads were obtained directly on the coast only after White contact and the introduction of horses. A few felt that individuals did walk there in former times. None mentioned inter-tribal trade as a means of obtaining shell beads.

[46] Oral tradition recorded by Pancho and Pancho (n.d.) states that Truckee and Old Pancho went to California as emigrant guides, probably in 1845 or 1846. They are said to have gone willingly rather than by force. The records of the U.S. Army, California Battalion, Muster Rolls (1846–47) indicate that three Paiute men fought with John C. Fremont in the Mexican War: Jose Truckee, Philip Truckee, and Juan Truckee. Jose later took the name Pancho and was known as Old Pancho.

for the host's family to eat the visitor waits to eat with the host and his family.

When the visitor departs the host gives him food to eat on his journey home. The visitor announces that he is going the next day (*mu'amiakwə,* "I am going tomorrow.") Before the visitor leaves he goes around and says goodbye to all the people with whom he has visited (*nanikə,* "to say goodbye;" *nanitunago,* "to ask to go along.")

RP-WR: When visitors came, if they were from some other place, food was offered to them. All the neighbors brought food, no matter what time of the day the visitors arrived. The visitors ate with the family; then food was given them to take home. The children ate as usual with the family. Visitors do not knock, but enter without asking. They may be invited in. A visitor might bring a present of food when he goes to see a friend. In return he was given a present of some food to take back with him.

People at Walker River never went to Nixon and those people never came to the Walker River Reservation.[47] People at Fallon visited both Pyramid Lake and Walker Lake for fish. People at Walker River visited Fallon and Yerington. A few might go to Wadsworth or Nixon for a big dance.

PROPERTY

[Eight individuals gave Park data on concepts of property and ownership. All agreed that the most common type of property was family/individual ownership of pinyon trees. People at Walker River, Yerington, Lovelock, and Honey Lake specifically note such rights. The one individual from Pyramid Lake who spoke on this topic also noted such personal rights, but cited his own as being in the vicinity of Yerington, and coming from his father who resided there. Given that Pyramid Lake had little in the way of pinyon reserves—most trees occurring south of the Truckee River—it was perhaps not a common concept there. One individual from Walker River noted that rights to trap small mammals in one's pinyon area were also exclusive. Small mammal trapping grounds were also considered private property at Pyramid Lake (see Small Mammal Trapping in chap. 2)

Various individuals also told Park that rights to eagle nests were exclusive to the discoverer, and were inherited within the family (see also Other Birds in chap. 2). Rights to fishing stations and their associated platforms and gear were noted by men from Walker River and Pyramid Lake as were rights to trap antelope in partic-

ular canyons at Walker River (see Fishing and Large Game Hunting in chap. 2). Otherwise, exclusive rights to hunting and seed gathering areas were denied by all. Theft of private property was handled by individuals, or through intercession of the headman if the offender were known. If the person's identity were not known, the headman apparently sought an identity.]

GK-WR: Plots of land in the pinenut mountains were claimed by certain families. Each family had its own trees. The whole family owned the plot of trees. That family went to that place all the time. Sometimes permission was given to others to pick pinenuts on the family plot. When one member of the family died the rest of the family combined to claim the same trees.[48]

GK has an interest in a plot of pinenuts. His uncles, mother and grandparent all claimed pine trees in the same place but each immediate family had its own trees in the larger plot. When GK's mother died he had a share in the trees that belonged to her. His uncles also claimed a share in his mother's trees. The same was true when his grandfather died.[49]

A great deal of trapping was done in the pine trees. A man trapped among his own trees. No one else was supposed to trap there. Outside of the pine trees a man could trap anywhere he wanted. There were no hunting grounds that were privately owned. Men hunted any place where they could find game.[50]

Seeds were gathered wherever they grew. Places where seeds were gathered were not claimed as private property.[51] Women went out in groups to gather seeds. They could gather seeds where other women were already working.

---

[48] Inheritance of trees or rights to pick from certain trees seems to have followed slightly different patterns, but always the family was paramount. ND-HL indicated that rights to trees went to the family members: "If a son went away and married and lived with his wife's parents, he still retained a share in these family owned trees . The girls' husbands were also entitled to help harvest the crop from these trees."

[49] HW-Y: "These trees were inherited by the owner's family at his death. A boy, a girl, or a nephew would inherit the trees. It was like a man making a will. The owner told them who was going to have the trees when he died." Stewart (1941:374) received positive responses from all groups within the distribution of pinyon to family ownership of plots. But he states that "among none of these was it true ownership. One family might claim a plot, but anyone who wished could gather there." This does not seem to agree with the above by HW-Y, or with the other statements given to Park.

[50] Stewart (1941:407) got nearly universal positive response to the question of band ownership of hunting territory. He did not question as to private ownership of these grounds.

[51] Stewart (1941:407) received positive response to seed plot ownership by families only among the Fort McDermitt and Winnemucca groups.

---

[47] RP seems to be referring to the post-contact period, perhaps after the Pyramid Lake War of 1860. However, in post-reservation times, travel was also severely restricted.

RP-WR: Some families claimed certain canyons where there were pine trees. Every year they go to the same place. You must have permission to get nuts in another canyon. When the crop fails in one place the family would go elsewhere and ask permission to gather nuts there. A certain number of trees would be allotted to them.

People who own canyons give their own names to the canyons, the mountains surrounding them and to the springs or water holes around which they camped. An antelope corral must be made in a man's own canyon.[52]

JG-PL: Pine trees were owned privately. My father's father owned a group of pine trees on Pine Grove Mountain 18 or 20 mi from Yerington. When my grandfather died my father owned the pine trees. His brother did not share in the trees. My father was the oldest and he lived in that country most of the time. His brother lived at Stillwater. He owned some pine trees there.[53] When my father died I owned the pine trees. All the people down around Yerington and Walker Lake know that the trees belong to me. They tell me to come down and get some pinenuts. They say, "There are lots of pinenuts over at your place." I have five sisters. They own a share in the pine trees. There were two or three springs on this place. It was a large place about a mile long and about 500 yds wide.

Sometimes when the pinenuts were scarce a man watched his trees carefully so others would not come and pick his nuts. Sometimes the Indians got in fights over the pinenuts when someone tried to pick from another's trees. If someone tried to take pinenuts from trees owned by another family, the men of the family owning the pinenut trees would destroy the intruders' baskets and other things in their pinenut outfit and other property. The men would fight with sticks and fists. Bows and arrows would not be used. The owners would drive the others away and try to destroy all their personal property. Women would not take part in these fights.

The boundaries to the pine tree groves were not marked. Natural boundaries such as ridges and the trees in a little valley or gulch marked off the property.

When a man married and lived with his wife's parents he still returned and picked pinenuts from the family grove. When his father died, he retained rights to pick pinenuts there.

BR-L, PL: Families claimed the right to certain pine trees. These were kept in the family and when one died the others retained his share. When any members of the family moved away because of marriage they still retained the right to go back and harvest pinenuts from the family trees. I have a claim on pine trees from my father. It is east of Lovelock. I have another claim that was my mother's. That is near Stillwater. In the old days if anyone intruded and picked pinenuts from the trees claimed by a family there would be a fight. The arguments were decided between the individuals — the dispute was not taken to the chief. If the owners had sufficient nuts they would give other people permission to pick from their trees.

There were no fishing or hunting areas claimed by families or individuals.[54] Places to gather seeds were also not owned by individuals or families. People could hunt, fish or gather seeds anyplace they wanted to. People from other bands could not come to Pyramid Lake to fish, hunt and gather seeds.[55]

GK-WR: Eagle nests were claimed by individuals. When a man got young eagles from a nest he claimed that nest as his property. When he died the nest belonged to his family. If anyone else captured young eagles from that nest the owner would get angry. He would go to the man and say, "What do you want to do that for, taking the eagles that belong to me." Then the owner of the nest would take the eagles away from him. "That is the way it used to be."

When a man died who claimed an eagle nest as his property the nest belonged to his family. His wife, sons, and daughter all claimed the nest. It was just the same as the rights to the pinenut groves. It belonged to the man's family and no one could use it without his permission. "That is the way it used to be a long time ago."[56]

THEFT

BR-L, PL: If the thief was detected he was forced to return the stolen goods. A thief was not fined. When a man had something stolen from him he would go to the chief. The chief would attempt to find out who the thief was and force him to return the things that he had stolen.[57]

---

[52] What appears to be a type of "land ownership" was not reported to Park by others. In other areas, antelope traps were made in other settings and none of these traps seems to have been privately owned (see Antelope Hunting in chap. 2).

[53] In this statement we can see both inheritance and ease of habitual use entering into the property concept.

[54] Fishing stations (platforms, weirs, etc.) were said by others to be inherited. See Fishing in chap. 2.

[55] This again suggests some recognition of local group rights to resources (see Stewart 1941:407).

[56] RP-WR: "Eagle nests were considered private property. Five or six men sometimes held the right to share in a single nest. Disputes arose over division of the eagles and rights to a nest." Stewart (1941:407) received nearly universal positive responses to questions on ownership of eagle nests.

[57] The powers of the chief in these actions appear to have been more through persuasion than authority.

GK-WR: If the thief were known in the case of theft the man who was robbed and several of his relatives would go to the thief and tell him to return the stolen goods.

RP-WR: If a man accidentally hurt another he had to help the injured man. He furnished medicine to help the man get well. There was no fixed payment or no formal present to be given. It was simply felt that there was an obligation to help the injured person regardless of whether intention or carelessness was responsible for the injury.

References Cited

Angel, Myron (editor)
   1881   *History of Nevada, with Illustrations and Biograph-
           ical Sketches of Its Prominent Men and Pioneers.*
           Thompson and West, Oakland, Calif.

Barrett, Samuel A.
   1910   *The Material Culture of the Klamath Lake and Modoc
           Indians.* Publications in American Archaeology
           and Ethnology, vol. 5(4). University of Califor-
           nia, Berkeley.
   1916   [Notes on Material Culture Collections Made
           Among the Paiute of Nevada.] Data in catalog
           on file, Milwaukee Public Museum, Milwaukee.
   1917   The Washo Indians. *Bulletin of the Public Museum
           of the City of Milwaukee* 2:1–52.

Brooks, George R. (editor)
   1977   *The Southwest Expedition of Jedediah S. Smith: His
           Personal Account of the Journey to California, 1826–
           1827.* Arthur H. Clark Co., Glendale, Calif.

Brown, Merle
   1960   *Climates of the States: Nevada.* Climatography of
           the United States No. 60–26. U.S. Department
           of Commerce, Weather Bureau, Washington,
           D.C.

Clemmer, Richard O., and Omer C. Stewart
   1986   Treaties, Reservations and Claims. In *Great
           Basin*, ed. Warren L. d'Azevedo, pp. 525–57.
           Handbook of North American Indians, vol. 11.
           William C. Sturtevant, general editor. Smithson-
           ian Institution, Washington, D.C.

Clifford, James
   1986   Introduction: Partial Truths. In *Writing Culture:
           The Poetics and Politics of Ethnography*, ed. James
           Clifford and George E. Marcus, pp. 1–26. Uni-
           versity of California Press, Berkeley.

Cronquist, Arthur, Arthur H. Holmgren, Noel H.
   Holmgren, and James L. Reveal
   1972   *Intermountain Flora: Vascular Plants of the Inter-
           mountain West, U.S.A.*, vol. 1. The New York
           Botanical Garden, New York.

Curtis, Edward S.
   1926   *The North American Indian: Being a Series of Vol-
           umes Picturing and Describing the Indians of the United
           States, and Alaska*, vol. 15. Plimpton Press, Nor-
           wood, Mass. Reprinted 1970, Johnson Reprint,
           New York.

Davies, K. G. (editor)
   1961   *Peter Skene Ogden's Snake Country Journal, 1826–27.*
           Publications of the Hudson's Bay Record Soci-
           ety, vol. 23. London.

Davis, Emma Lou
   1965   An Ethnography of the Kuzedika Paiute of Mono

           Lake, Mono County, California. In *Miscella-
           neous Collected Papers 8–10*, pp. 1–55. Anthropo-
           logical Papers, No. 75. University of Utah, Salt
           Lake City.

d'Azevedo, Warren L.
   1986   Washoe. In *Great Basin*, ed. Warren L. d'Aze-
           vedo, pp. 466–98. Handbook of North Ameri-
           can Indians, vol. 11. William C. Sturtevant,
           general editor. Smithsonian Institution, Wash-
           ington, D.C.

de Angulo, Jaime, and L. S. Freeland
   1929   Notes on the Northern Paiute of California.
           Journal de la Société des Américanistes de Paris,
           21:313–35.

Dixon, Roland B.
   1905   The Northern Maidu. *Bulletin of the American
           Museum of Natural History* 17:119–346.

Downs, James F.
   1966   *The Two Worlds of the Washo, an Indian Tribe of
           California and Nevada.* Holt, Rinehart and
           Winston, New York.

Driver, Harold E., and William C. Massey
   1957   Comparative Studies of North American Indi-
           ans. *Transactions of the American Philosophical Soci-
           ety* n.s. 47:165–456. Philadelphia.

Egan, Farol
   1972   *Sand in a Whirlwind: The Paiute Indian War of 1860.*
           Doubleday, Garden City.

Essene, Frank
   1935   Paiute and Shoshone Plant Uses. Ms. 86A–B
           on file, University Archives, Bancroft Library,
           University of California, Berkeley.

Essig, Edward O.
   1934   The Value of Insects to the California Indians.
           Scientific Monthly 38:181–86.

Fenneman, Nevin M.
   1931   *Physiography of the Western United States.* McGraw-
           Hill Co., New York.

Follett, W. I.
   1982   An Analysis of Fish Remains from Ten Ar-
           chaeological Sites at Falcon Hill, Washoe
           County, Nevada, with Notes on Fishing Prac-
           tices of the Ethnographic Kuyuidikadi North-
           ern Paiute. In *The Archaeology of Falcon Hill,
           Winnemucca Lake, Washoe County, Nevada* by
           Eugene M. Hattori, pp. 181–203. Anthropolog-
           ical Papers, No. 18. Nevada State Museum,
           Carson City.

Fowler, Catherine S.
   1964–   Field Notes, Northern Paiute. 11 vols. in posses-
   1982   sion of author, University of Nevada, Reno.

Fowler, Catherine S., and Joyce E. Bath
1981   Pyramid Lake Northern Paiute Fishing: The Ethnographic Record. *Journal of California and Great Basin Anthropology* 3: 176-86.

Fowler, Catherine S., and Ives Goddard
1986   Synonymy [Northern Paiute]. In *Great Basin*, ed. Warren L. d'Azevedo, pp. 461-65. Handbook of North American Indians, vol. 11. William C. Sturtevant, general editor. Smithsonian Institution, Washington, D.C.

Fowler, Catherine S., and Joy Leland
1967   Some Northern Paiute Native Categories. *Ethnology* 6:381-404.

Fowler, Catherine S., and Sven Liljeblad
1986   Northern Paiute. In *Great Basin*, ed. Warren L. d'Azevedo, pp. 435-65. Handbook of North American Indians, vol. 11. William C. Sturtevant, general editor. Smithsonian Institution, Washington, D.C.

Fowler, Catherine S., and Nancy Peterson Walter
1985   Harvesting Pandora Moth Larvae with the Owens Valley Paiute. *Journal of California and Great Basin Anthropology*, 7:155-65.

Fowler, Don D., and Catherine S. Fowler
1981   The Uses of Ethnographic Museum Collections: Some Great Basin Examples. In The Research Potential of Anthropological Museum Collections, Anne-Marie Cantwell, James B. Griffin, and Nan A. Rothschild, pp. 177-99. *Annals of the New York Academy of Sciences*, vol. 376. New York.

Fremont, John C.
1845   *Report of the Exploring Expedition to the Rocky Mountains in the Year 1842 and to Oregon and Northern California in the Years 1843-1844.* Gales & Seaton, Printers, Washington, D.C.

Garth, T. R.
1978   Atsugewi. In *California*, ed. Robert F. Heizer, pp. 236-48. Handbook of North American Indians, vol. 8. William C. Sturtevant, general editor. Smithsonian Institution, Washington, D.C.

Grosscup, Gordon L.
1974   Northern Paiute Archaeology. In *Paiute Indians IV*, pp. 9-51. American Indian Ethnohistory: California and Basin-Plateau Indians. David Agee Horr, general editor. Garland Publishing, New York.

Harper, Kimball T.
1986   Historical Environments. In *Great Basin*, ed. Warren L. d'Azevedo, pp. 51-63. Handbook of North American Indians, vol. 11. William C. Sturtevant, general editor. Smithsonian Institution, Washington, D.C.

Harrington, Mark R.
1933   A Cat-tail Eater. *Masterkey* 7:147-49.

Heizer, Robert F.
1945   Honey Dew "Sugar" in Western North America. *Masterkey* 19:140-45.
1950   Kutsavi, A Great Basin Indian Food. *Kroeber Anthropological Society Papers* 2:35-41.

Heizer, Robert F., and Lewis K. Napton
1970   *Archaeology and the Prehistoric Great Basin Lacustrine Subsistence Regime as Seen From Lovelock Cave,* *Nevada.* Contributions, University of California Archaeological Research Facility No. 10. Berkeley.

Holmgren, Arthur H., and James L. Reveal
1966   *Checklist of the Vascular Plants of the Intermountain Region.* Research Paper INT-32, U.S. Forest Service, Ogden, Utah.

Hopkins, Sarah Winnemucca
1883   *Life Among the Paiutes: Their Wrongs and Claims.* Cupples, Upham, Boston.

Hughes, Richard E., and James A. Bennyhoff
1986   Early Trade. In *Great Basin*, ed. Warren L. d'Azevedo, pp. 238-55. Handbook of North American Indians, vol. 11. William C. Sturtevant, general editor. Smithsonian Institution, Washington, D.C.

Janetski, Joel C.
1979   Implications of Snare Bundles in the Great Basin and Southwest. *Journal of California and Great Basin Anthropology* 1:306-21.

Jennings, Jesse D.
1974   *Prehistory of North America.* 2d. ed. McGraw-Hill, New York.

Johnson, Edward C.
1975   *Walker River Paiutes: A Tribal History.* Walker River Tribe, Schurz, Nev.

Kelly, Isabel T.
1932   *Ethnography of the Surprise Valley Paiute.* Publications in American Archaeology and Ethnology, vol. 31(3). University of California, Berkeley.

Kluckhohn, Clyde
1967   *Navaho Witchcraft.* Reprinted. Beacon Press, Boston. Originally published 1944, Papers of the Peabody Museum of Archaeology and Ethnology, Harvard University 22(2). Cambridge, Mass.

Kroeber, Alfred L.
1907   *Shoshonean Dialects of California.* Publications in American Archaeology and Ethnology, vol. 4(3). University of California, Berkeley.
1925   *Handbook of the Indians of California.* Bulletin, Bureau of American Ethnology 78. Washington, D.C.

Lamb, Sydney M.
1958   Linguistic Prehistory in the Great Basin. *International Journal of American Linguistics* 24:95-100.

Lanner, Ronald M.
1981   *The Piñon Pine: A Natural and Cultural History.* University of Nevada Press, Reno.

LaRivers, Ira
1962   *Fishes and Fisheries of Nevada.* Nevada State Fish and Game Commission Publication 401. Carson City.

Layton, Thomas N.
1978   From Pottage to Portage: A Perspective on Aboriginal Horse Use in the Northern Great Basin Prior to 1850. *Nevada Historical Society Quarterly* 21:242-57.
1981   Traders and Raiders: Aspects of Trans-Basin and California-Plateau Commerce, 1800-1830. *Journal of California and Great Basin Anthropology* 3:127-37.

Leonard, Zenas

1839   *Narrative of the Adventures of Zenas Leonard, A Native of Clearfield County, Pa., Who Spent Five Years in Trapping for Furs, Trading with the Indians &c., &c., of the Rocky Mountains, Written by Himself.* D. W. Moore, Clearfield, Pa.

Liljeblad, Sven

1966   Northern Paiute Manual I: Grammatical Sketch of the Northern Dialects. Mimeo, Department of Anthropology, Idaho State University, Pocatello.

1982   Northern Paiute and Mono. Ms. on file, Special Collections Department, Getchell Library, University of Nevada, Reno.

Liljeblad, Sven, and Catherine S. Fowler

1986   Owens Valley Paiute. In *Great Basin*, ed. Warren L. d'Azevedo, pp. 412–34. Handbook of North American Indians, vol. 11. William C. Sturtevant, general editor. Smithsonian Institution, Washington, D. C.

Lott, Patricia, and John McCormick

n.d.   Plants of the Government Pasture, Greenhead Club, Fallon, Nevada. Mimeo, in possession of author.

Loud, L. L.

1929   Notes on the Northern Paiute. In *Lovelock Cave*, L. L. Loud and M. R. Harrington, pp. 152–65. Publications in American Archaeology and Ethnology, vol. 25(1). University of California, Berkeley.

Loud, L. L., and M. R. Harrington

1929   *Lovelock Cave.* Publications in American Archaeology and Ethnology, vol. 25(1). University of California, Berkeley.

Lowie, Robert H.

1909   *The Northern Shoshone.* Anthropological Papers, vol. 2(2). American Museum of Natural History, New York.

1924   *Notes on Shoshonean Ethnography.* Anthropological Papers, vol. 20(3). American Museum of Natural History, New York.

1939   *Ethnographic Notes on the Washo.* Publications in American Archaeology and Ethnology, vol. 36(5). University of California, Berkeley.

Mahar, James M.

1953   *Ethnobotany of the Oregon Paiutes of the Warm Springs Reservation.* Unpublished Bachelor of Arts thesis. Division of History and Social Sciences, Reed College, Portland, Ore.

Miller, Wick R.

1967   *Uto-Aztecan Cognate Sets.* Publications in Linguistics 48. University of California, Berkeley.

1972   *Newe Natekwinappeh: Shoshoni Stories and Dictionary.* Anthropological Papers, No. 94. University of Utah, Salt Lake City.

Morrison, Roger B.

1964   *Lake Lahontan: Geology of Southern Carson Desert, Nevada.* Professional Paper 401. U. S. Geological Survey, Washington, D.C.

Munz, Philip A., and David Keck

1963   *A California Flora.* University of California, Berkeley.

Murdock, George P.

1966   Willard Z. Park, 1906–1965. *American Anthropologist* 68:135–36.

Natches, Gilbert

1923   *Northern Paiute Verbs.* Publications in American Archaeology and Ethnology, vol. 20(14). University of California, Berkeley.

Orchard, William C.

1975   *Beads and Beadwork of the American Indians.* Contributions, vol. XI. Museum of the American Indian, Heye Foundation, New York.

Osborne, C. M., and H. S. Riddell, Jr.

1978   A Cache of Deer Snares from Owens Valley, California. *Journal of California Anthropology* 5:101–9.

Pancho, Herbert S., and Hastings Pancho

n.d.   A Short Brief History of Old Pancho and Trukee. Ms. in possession of author, University of Nevada, Reno.

Park, Susan

1986   *Sampson Grant, Atsuge Shaman.* Occasional Papers No. 3. Redding Museum and Art Center, Redding, Calif.

Park, Willard Z.

n.d.   [Selected Extracts from Field Notes.] Affidavit and testimony before the Indian Claims Commission, Docket No. 87. Ms. in possession of author.

1933–   [Ethnographic Field Notes, Northern Paiute of
1940   Western Nevada]. 22 notebooks in possession of author, University of Nevada, Reno.

1934   Paviotso Shamanism. *American Anthropologist* 36:98–113.

1937   Paviotso Polyandry. *American Anthropologist* 39:366–68.

1938a   *Shamanism in Western North America: A Study in Cultural Relationships.* Studies in the Social Sciences 2. Northwestern University, Evanston, Ill.

1938b   The Organization and Habitat of Paviotso Bands. In Tribal Distribution in the Great Basin, Willard Z. Park, et al., pp. 622–26. *American Anthropologist* 40:622–38.

1941   Cultural Succession in the Great Basin. In *Language, Culture and Personality: Essays in Memory of Edward Sapir*, ed. Leslie Spier, A. I. Hallowell, and Stanley S. Newman, pp. 180–203. Sapir Memorial Publication Fund, Menasha, Wisc.

1946   Tribes of the Sierra Nevada de Santa Marta, Colombia. *Handbook of South American Indians*, ed. Julian H. Steward, vol. 2:865–86. Bulletin 143. Bureau of American Ethnology, Washington, D.C.

Powell, John Wesley

1895   Stone Art in America. *American Anthropologist* o.s. 8:1–7.

Powell, John Wesley, and George W. Ingalls

1873   Report on the Condition of the Ute Indians of Utah; the Pai-Utes of Utah, Northern Arizona, Southern Nevada, and Southeastern California; the Go-si Utes of Utah and Nevada; the Northwestern Shoshones of Idaho and Utah; and the Western Shoshones of Nevada; and Report Concerning Claims of Settlers in the Mo-a-pa Valley (Southeastern Nevada). *Annual Report of the Commissioner of Indian Affairs for 1873*, pp. 41–73. Washington, D.C.

Price, John A.
   1962   *Washo Economy*. Anthropological Papers, No. 6. Nevada State Museum, Carson City.

Remy, Jules, and Julius Brenchley
   1861   *A Journey to Great-Salt-Lake City; with a Sketch of the History, Religion, and Customs of the Mormons, and an Introduction on the Religious Movement in the United States*. 2 vols. W. Jeffs, London.

Riddell, Francis A.
   1960   *Honey Lake Paiute Ethnography*. Anthropological Papers, No. 4. Nevada State Museum, Carson City.

Rusco, Mary K.
   1976   Fur Trappers in the Snake Country: An Ethnohistorical Approach to Recent Environmental Change. In *Holocene Environmental Change in the Great Basin*, ed. Robert Elston, pp. 152–73. Research Papers 8. Nevada Archaeological Survey, Reno.

Ryser, Fred A.
   1985   *Birds of the Great Basin*. University of Nevada Press, Reno.

Sapir, Edward
   1930–   The Southern Paiute Language. *Proceedings of*
   1931   *the American Academy of Arts and Sciences* 65(1–3). Boston.

Simpson, James H.
   1869   *The Shortest Route to California, Illustrated by a History of Explorations of the Great Basin of Utah with Its Topographical and Geographical Character and Some Account of the Indian Tribes*. J. B. Lippincott, Philadelphia.
   1876   *Report of Explorations Across the Great Basin of the Territory of Utah for a Direct Wagon-route from Camp Floyd to Genoa, in Carson Valley, in 1859*. U.S. Government Printing Office, Washington, D.C.

Smith, Timothy B.
   1913   Recollections of the Early History of Smith Valley. *Biennial Report of the Nevada Historical Society*, 3rd (1911–13). Carson City.

Snyder, John O.
   1917   *The Fishes of the Lahontan System of Nevada and Northeastern California*. Bulletin vol. 35:31–86. U.S. Bureau of Fisheries, Washington, D.C.

Speth, Lembi C.
   1969   Possible Fishing Cliques Among the Northern Paiute of the Walker River Reservation, Nevada. *Ethnohistory* 16:225–86.

Spier, Leslie
   1928   *Havasupai Ethnography*. Anthropological Papers, vol. 29(3). American Museum of Natural History, New York.
   1930   *Klamath Ethnography*. Publications in American Archaeology and Ethnology 30. University of California, Berkeley.

Steward, Julian H.
   1933   *Ethnography of the Owens Valley Paiute*. Publications in American Archaeology and Ethnology 33(3). University of California, Berkeley.
   1936   Shoshoni Polyandry. *American Anthropologist* 38:561–64.
   1937   Linguistic Distributions and Political Groups of the Great Basin Shoshoneans. *American Anthropologist* 39:625–34.
   1938   *Basin-Plateau Aboriginal Sociopolitical Groups*. Bulletin 120. Bureau of American Ethnology, Washington, D.C.
   1943   *Culture Element Distributions, XXIII: Northern and Gosiute Shoshoni*. Anthropological Records 8(3). University of California, Berkeley.
   1955   *Theory of Culture Change*. University of Illinois Press, Urbana.
   1970   The Foundations of Basin-Plateau Shoshonean Society. In *Languages and Cultures of Western North America: Essays in Honor of Sven S. Liljeblad*, ed. Earl H. Swanson, pp. 113–51. Idaho State University Press, Pocatello.

Steward, Julian H., and Erminie Wheeler-Voegelin
   1974   The Northern Paiute Indians. In *Paiute Indians III*, pp. 9–328. American Indian Ethnohistory: California and Basin-Plateau Tribes. David Agee Horr, general editor. Garland Publishing, New York.

Stewart, George R.
   1962   *The California Trail*. McGraw-Hill, New York.

Stewart, Omer C.
   1937   Northern Paiute Polyandry. *American Anthropologist* 39:368–69.
   1939   *The Northern Paiute Bands*. Anthropological Records 2(3). University of California, Berkeley.
   1941   *Culture Element Distributions, XIV: Northern Paiute*. Anthropological Records 6(4). University of California, Berkeley.
   1966   Tribal Distributions and Boundaries in the Great Basin. In *Current Status of Anthropological Research in the Great Basin: 1964*, ed. Warren L. d'Azevedo, Wilber A. Davis, Don D. Fowler, and Wayne Suttles, pp. 167–238. Social Sciences and Humanities Publications 1. Desert Research Institute, Reno.

Train, Percy, James R. Hendrichs, and W. Andrew Archer
   1933   *Medicinal Uses of Plants by Indian Tribes of Nevada*. Contributions Toward a Flora of Nevada, No. 33. The Division of Plant Exploration and Introduction, Bureau of Plant Industry. U.S. Department of Agriculture, Washington, D.C.

Underhill, Ruth
   1941   *The Northern Paiute Indians of California and Nevada*. Indian Life and Customs Pamphlets 1. U.S. Bureau of Indian Affairs, Lawrence, Kans.
   1953   *Pueblo Crafts*. U. S. Bureau of Indian Affairs, Washington, D.C.

U. S. Army California Battalion of Mounted Riflemen
   1846–   Muster Rolls of California Battalion. Ms. in
   1847   Bancroft Library C-A 126–27. Copied from records in the National Archives. University of California, Berkeley.

Wagner, W. F. (editor)
   1904   *Leonard's Narrative, The Adventures of Zenas Leonard,*

Fur Trader and Trapper, 1831–1836. The Burrows Co., Cleveland.

Wheat, Margaret M.
1967   *Survival Arts of the Primitive Paiutes*. University of Nevada Press, Reno.

Wissler, Clark
1910   *Material Culture of the Blackfoot Indians*. Anthropological Papers, vol 5(1). American Museum of Natural History, New York.

Appendix: Lexicon

The lexical items recorded by Park are a valuable resource for Northern Paiute linguistic and cultural historical studies. Given that Park started his ethnographic field studies with little to no linguistic training or familiarity with the Numic languages of the Great Basin, it is understandable that his early attempts at transcription of native terms met with varying degrees of success. In later years, after linguistic courses from Edward Sapir at Yale, and probably also as his own ear became better attuned, his recording improved significantly. In order not to break the flow of Park's manuscript material, but yet provide transcriptions in the generally accepted phonemic orthography for Northern Paiute (Liljeblad 1966), the lexicon that follows is added as an appendix.

In drawing these materials together, I consulted my own files as well as the far more extensive data base accumulated by Sven Liljeblad over the past forty years (now housed in the Special Collections Department, Getchell Library, University of Nevada, Reno). These consultations resulted in the ability to provide new transcriptions for roughly 70 percent of Park's terms and some hints at another 10 percent. If his entry is followed by a ?, this indicates that this form could not be verified in the files or could not be analyzed from existing data. For some of these, a suggestion is offered, but it should be taken as such (i.e., each of these requires independent field verification). Although it often was not possible to match lexical items elicited by Park with data from the same community of speakers, an attempt was made to match them by the major dialects (NP 1 and NP 2) as defined by Liljeblad (1966). Unless otherwise indicated (very few cases), the NP 1 and NP 2 designations that follow each entry cover original data from Pyramid Lake, Honey Lake, and Lovelock (NP 1) and Dayton, Fallon, Yerington, and Walker River (NP 2). Although there is some lexical variation between dialects, the major features of difference are in the somewhat systematic variation in lenis to fortis and fortis voiced stops and affricates. Given that stress is predictable (with few exceptions), it is not marked.

Several changes in Park's transcription system are observable when comparing the data recorded in 1933 with those from later years. For example, Park initially used *aw* to represent [ɔ]. He also used ' for [ʔ], *ng* for [ŋ], and *ə* or *ü* for what is now written as [i]. In later years, he used ɔ, ʔ and ŋ, but continued to use *ə* and *ü* as did many of his day. No effort has been made to standardize Park's system to a single one over his field years. Rather, the recordings are presented as they occur in the notes, with the exception, largely for printing convenience, that ɔ is rendered *o*. Park's transcriptions appear in italics at the beginning of the entries, followed by the retranscriptions where possible. Alphabetization is as in English, with *ə* following *a*, *ü* following *u*, *ŋ* following *n* and ' and ʔ occurring last. Abbreviations of grammatical elements are as follows:

class.	classifier
contin.	continuative
fut.	future
gen.	general
instru.	instrumental
interj.	interjection
intran.	intransitive
loc.	locative
nomin.	nominal
obj.	objective
partic.	participle
pass.	passive
per.	person
pl.	plural
poss.	possessive
poten.	potential
pres.	present
prog.	progressive
reflex.	reflexive
sg.	singular
subj.	subjective
subord.	subordinate
trans.	transitive
1st	first
2nd	second
3rd	third
4th	fourth

abi abi, plant species, alkali bulrush, *Scirpus maritimus* [NP 2]

abudza abuza, plant species, possibly Fremont goosefoot, *Chenopodium fremontii*; [NP 2]; see apəsa

abui'wi apuiʔwi [a-, 4th. pers. sing. poss. puiʔwi, gall bladder], gall bladder [NP 1]

abuyu ?, organ around the liver [NP 1]

ada   ada, American Crow, *Corvus brachyrhynchos* [NP 2]

ada.'   ?, bladder [NP 2]; but compare ad·akiponoʔo, kidney [NP 2]; see sinupi, bladder

adabuga   ?, but possibly adabigaʔyu [adabi cheek, jaw; -gaʔyu, to have]; ND's grandfather, said to mean 'jaw' [NP 1]

adino   ad·inoho [a-, 4th pers. sing. poss.; tinoho, roast], pit roast [NP 2]

adodəm   adidam·u [adi, bow; tam·u, sinew], sinew for bow backing [NP 1]

aduno   see adino.

aduponokiʔi   ?, place name, mountain near Hawthorne [NP 2]

adü   adi, bow, bow and arrows [NP 1]

agai   agai, trout, *Salmo clarki henshawi* [NP 1, 2]

agaibənuna, agaiBəuna   agaipaniin·adi, [agai, trout; paniin·adi, lake], Summit Lake [NP 2]

agaibo   agaiboo [agai, trout; poo, trail], Walker Lake trail [NP 2]

againuhukwa   agai nahuukʷa [agai, trout; nahuukʷa, flowing stream], Walker River [NP 2]

agaipanunawaitu   agaipaniin·awaitu [agai, trout; paniin·a-, lake; -kʷ/waitu, locative], Summit Lake [NP 1]

agaitukad   agaidikadi [agai, trout; -tikadi, eater], people at Walker Lake [NP 1, 2]

agaitükədə   see agaitukad

agaiwan   agaiwana [agai, trout; wana, net], trout net [NP 1]

agomobi   okomubi [oko, ?; mubi, nose, beak], bird species, Northern Shoveler, *Anas clypeata* [NP 1]

agwazukə   akʷasiki [a-, 4th pers. sing. poss.; kwasi-, to fry; -ki, benefactive], to roast on top of the coals [NP 1]

aha, naudut puni hada   ahaa, nii iditi pun·i, ada [ahaa, yes; nii, 1st pers. sing. subj.; iditi, be hot; pun·i, to see, appear; adaa, interj.]; Yes, it is hot ['Yes, I see it is hot'] [NP 1]

ahodəm   see adodəm

aku   aki, sunflower, *Wyethia mollis* [NP 1]

akukaib   akigaiba [aki, sunflower; kaiba, mountain], Peavine Mountain [NP 2]

akwatsi   akʷaci [a-, 4th pers. sing. poss.; -kʷaci, spleen], deer spleen [NP 1]

a.misusu   ?, frogs and toads [NP 2]

anabiwükodəp   anobiwikodapi [a-, 4th pers. sing. poss.; nobi, house; wikota-, house binding ring; -pi, classif.], ring at top of house frame [NP 1]

anabuiʔi   ?, young buck [NP 2]

anakapuin   ?, tumpline [NP 2]

ang   aaŋa, bird species; Pinyon Jay, *Gymnorhinus cyanocephalus* [NP 1]

angaque   ?, but perhaps aŋakʷi; fish trap [NP 1]

angaqui   ?, see angaque [NP 1]

aʔnina   aʔninabi, large black ant species [NP 2]

aŋi   aŋibi, small gnat species [NP 1]

apəsa   ?, probably apus·a [NP 1]; see abudza

asa   aca, plant species, *Descurainia pinnata*; but also *D. sophia* (intro.) [NP 1, 2]

asaka   ?, [aca-, red], place name, 'red tipped' [NP 2]

ata.ʔ   ?, glands close to bladder of badger; see ada.' [NP 2]

atsa   see asa [NP 2]

atsagwasob   atsagʷasobi, plant species, *Artemesia douglassiana*; *A. ludoviciana* [NP 2]

atsagwəda.da   acakʷidaadi [aca-, red; -kʷidaadi, to be colored], red glass beads, black centers [NP 1]

atsakua   acakia [aca-, red; kia, cicada] cicada species, *Okanagodes* sp. [NP 1]

atsakutagayu   acakutagaʔyu [aca-, red; kuta, neck; -k/gaʔyu, to have], duck species, Redhead, *Aythya americana* [NP 1]

atsakwita   acakʷita [aca- red; kʷita, feces], red mush [NP 1]

atsanazakodid   ?, plant species, possibly milkweed, *Asclepias cryptoceras* [NP 1]

atsapakodoba   acapakodoba [aca-, red; pakodoba, blackbird], bird species, Red-winged Blackbird, *Agelaius phoeniceus* [NP 1]

atühu   atuhu [a-, 4th pers. sing. poss.; tuhu, fat], fat from back of deer [NP 1]

atühunadamayüən   atuhu nadimayina [a-, 4th pers. sing. poss.; tuhu, fat; na-, reflex. timayina, to be mixed], dried meat/tallow mixture [NP 1]

a'waga, awago, awagu   aʔwago ~ aʔwaago, fish species, Tahoe sucker, *Catostomus tahoensis* [NP 1, 2]

awakoni   ?, plant species [NP 2]

awb   ?, possibly ohobi [ohobi, bone], place name, stone near Bridgeport [NP 2]

awhen   ?, frozen, of pinenut soup [NP 2]

ayagwi   ?, see angaque [NP 2]

əapə, əpə   iapi [ia-, to plant; -pi, class.], plant species, pigweed, *Chenopodium nevadense* [NP 2]

haba, ha.ba   haba, shade; also windbreak [NP 1]

hakinub   haakinubi, hemlock waterparsnip, *Sium suave* [NP 1, 2]

hanoʼyu ükima   haanooʔyu ikim·a [haanooʔyu, where; i-, 2nd pers. sing. obj. kim·a, to come], Where do you come from? [NP 1]

haomai   hoawaʔi, to hunt by stalking [NP 1]

haotata   hoatataʔa, grasshoppers [NP 1]

hapudəbo   ?, perhaps hapudipoo [hapidi-, place name; Humboldt Sink; poo, trail]; Humboldt Sink trail [NP 1]

hapuDtükəd   ?, see hapudəbo; [-tikadi, eater], group at Humboldt Sink [NP 1]

hatsa   ?, unidentified plant species [NP 2]

həng, hüngü   hiŋ·i, plant species, *Claytonia umbellata* [NP 1]

hi.wabi   hiiwobi, medicinal plant species, *Hermidium alpies* [NP 1]

honoka   ?, mountain near Tonopah [NP 2]

hu'a   hua, trap [NP 1]

huda   ?, plant species, possibly *Balsamorhiza hirsuta* [NP 2]

hubu, hu.bu   hubu [NP 1], hub·u [NP 2], elderberry, *Sambuicus racemosa* spp. *pubens*

huda   ?, cave near Lunning [NP 2]

hudsi   huci [NP 1], huʒ·i [NP 2], Sage Grouse, *Centrocercus urophasianus*

hugu'na   huguʔna, quiver [NP 2]

hukwəpato   hikʷapatoo [hikʷapa, wind; too, hole], place name; cave near Fort Churchill [NP 1]

huna, hu.na   huna, badger, *Taxidea taxus* [NP 2]

hunabi   hinabi, plant species, antelope bitterbrush, *Purshia tridentata* [NP 1]

hunásotü   hunacotia [huna, badger; cotia, hat], badger hat [NP 1]

hunibui   hunibui, plant species, bigseed lomatium, *Lomatium macrocarpum* [NP 1]

huninobi, hunino.bi   huninobi, circular windbreak, kitchen [NP 1]

hu.pə   huupi [river], river [NP 2]

hupi   huupi, stick [NP 1]

hupui   huupui, plant species, Anderson wolfberry, *Lycium andersonii* [NP 2]

husa, husa   ?, cry while driving antelope into trap [NP 1] *hu'unaqwi* ?, unidentified plant species [NP 1]

huvui see hupui

ibi ibɨ, white paint [NP 2]

ibiamaka ?, [i-, 1st pers. sing. poss.; pia, mother; maka, to give] used in prayers, "give me" [NP 1]

ica is·a, gray wolf, *Canis lupus* [NP 1]

ignyo igin·u, twined spoon [NP 2]

imudui, imuduyu imuduyu, bird species, American Wigeon, *Anas americana* [NP 1]

i.sha see ica [NP 1]

isikuyui isikuyui [isi-, gray; kuyui, cui-ui], place name, duck lake [Winnemucca Lake] [NP 1, 2]

isikuyui panünǝd isikuyui paniin·adɨ [isi-, gray; kuyui, cui-ui; paniin·adɨ, lake], place name, Winnemucca Lake [NP 1]

iwa'ab ?, skins tanned with hair remaining [NP 1]

iwa'ab kwasugaiyu ?, [kʷas·ɨ, tanned hide; -ga'yu, to have], man's jacket [NP 1]

iwaoab ?, small hide tanned with hair remaining [NP 1]

iwǝ'a mago ?, [mago'o, sack], sack to carry catch [NP 2]

iza'a iʒa'a, coyote, *Canis latrans* [NP 2]

iza'a dua'a iʒa'adua'a [iaʒ'a, coyote; tua'a, son, child], man's name, 'coyote's son' [NP 2]

iza' pij iʒapis·apɨ, [iʒa'a, coyote; pis·apɨ, paint], medicinal plant species, probably a fungus [NP 1]

iza·poku iʒa'a puku, [iʒa'a, coyote; puku, pet], old word for dog, *Canis familiaris* [NP 1]

izikua isikɨa [isi-, gray; kɨa, cicada], gray cicada, *Okanagodes* spp. [NP 1]

izikuyuipanünǝd isikuyui paniin·adɨ [isi-, gray; kuyui, sucker; paniin·adɨ, lake], Winnemucca Lake [NP 1, 2]

izipühü isipɨhɨ [isi-, gray; pɨhɨ, duck], bird species, Canvasback, *Aythya valisineria* [NP 1]

izizawi isis·awɨ, Pit River Indians [NP 1]

izükoda isikuda [isi-, gray; kuda, neck] bird species, Gadwall, *Anas strepera* [NP 1]

kadupiba ?, cave near Ione [NP 2]

kagwidǝ kagʷida, unidentified lizard species [NP 1]

kahu'u kahi'ɨ, bird species, Blue Grouse, *Dendragapus obscurus* [NP 1]

kaiba kaiba [kaiba, mountain], place name, Wassuk Range [NP 2]

kaibǝtuhida kaiba tihid·a [kaiba, mountain; tihid·a, deer], wild horse [NP 2]

kaidap kidapɨ, plant species, Cusick's sunflower, *Helianthus cusickii* [NP 1]

kaizopuhugayu kai copɨhiga'yu [kai, negative; copɨhi, head hair; -k/ga'yu, to have], bald [NP 2]

kamǝ kam·ɨ, blacktail jackrabbit, *Lepus californicus* [NP 1, 2]

kamǝna kam·inaa, [kam·ɨ, jackrabbit; naa, father], rabbit boss [NP 1]

kamǝpodiatu ?, possibly kam·ɨ pootiatu [kam·ɨ, jackrabbit; poo-, trail; tia, cache, pit, decoy; -tu, loc.] rabbit pitfall [NP 2]

kamǝpoŋos kam·ipoŋos·a [kam·ɨ, jackrabbit; poŋos·a, arrow], rabbit arrow [NP 1]

kamǝsigi, kamusigi kam·isigi [kam·ɨ, jackrabbit; sigi, intestines], plant species, *Glyptoplera marginata* [NP 1, 2]

kamǝtukǝdǝ kam·itikadɨ [kam·ɨ, jackrabbit; tikadɨ, eater], people of Winnemucca Valley [NP 1]

kamǝwana kam·iwana [kam·ɨ, jackrabbit; wana, net, trap], rabbit net [NP 1]

kamǝwiga, kamuwiga kam·iwiga [kam·ɨ, jackrabbit; wiga, blanket], rabbitskin blanket [NP 1, 2]

kamu see kamǝ

kamu nada noakwʼ ?, perhaps kam·ɨ nadanoakʷɨ [kam·ɨ, jackrabbit; na-, pass.; tanoa-, to run; related tanoomani-, to run, pl.;-kʷɨ, future], 'there will be a rabbit drive' [NP 2]

kamupoinabi kam·ɨ poinabi [kam·ɨ, jackrabbit; poinabi, leader], head of a rabbit drive [NP 1]

kamu tanoa, kamǝ tanoa ?, see kamu nada noakwʼ; rabbit drive [NP 1]

kamutukǝdǝ kam·itikadɨ [kam·ɨ, jackrabbit; -tikadɨ, eater], 'rabbit eaters', people in Winnemucca Valley [NP 1]

kani, kan.i kani, kahni, house [NP 1, 2]

kanituba kanitib·a, [kani, house; tib·a, mouth], smoke hole [NP 2]

kanitupa kanitipa, see kanituba [NP 1]

kangita, kanǝt kaŋiti, plant species, bitterroot, *Lewisia rediviva* [NP 1]

kangǝ, kangǝpǝ kaŋipi, plant species, shadscale, *Atriplex confertifolia* [NP 1]

kangǝnatusiwabi kaŋi natisuabi [?; natisuabi, medicine], plant species, possibly purple sage, *Salvia dorii* [NP 1]

kapipad kapipanadi, space opposite door of house [NP 1, 2]

kasimonad ?, interior of house [NP 1]

kasob kasobi, slow match [NP 1]

kawa, kawǝ kawa, desert woodrat, *Neotoma lepida* [NP 1, 2]

kawasiin kawasiin·a [kawa, woodrat; siin·a, urine], plant species, lichen, 'rat's urine' [NP 1]

kazutukad ?, [perhaps related kacun·ibɨ, weeds, in Bannock; -tikadɨ, eater], people near Likely, Calif. [NP 1]

kidapu see kaidap [NP 1]

kidutuka, kidütükǝdǝ kiditika'a, kiditikadɨ [kidɨ, yellowbelly marmot; -tika'a, -tikadɨ, eater], people of Surprise Valley, Calif., "groundhog eaters" [NP 1]

kidü, kedü kidɨ, yellowbelly marmot, *Marmota flaviventris* [NP 1, 2]

kjbu natuswabi kaiba natisuabi [kaiba, mountain; natisuabi, medicine], plant species, possibly *Angelica linearloba* [NP 2]

koǝp, koǝpǝ, koǝpu ?, antelope corral; see ko.du [NP 1]

kodǝgwadǝ kudagʷ·adɨ [kudagʷ·a, peak, point, range], place name, Mount Grant [NP 2]

kodǝgwǝ kudagʷ·a; see kodǝgwadǝ [NP 2]

ko.du kudia, antelope corral [NP 1, 2]

kodü ?, unidentified plant species [NP 2]

kogi kogi, plant species, sego lily, *Calochortus nuttallii* [NP 1]

kogiatanop kogi'adanapi, plant species, *Zigadenus venenosus; Z. paniculatus* [NP 1, 2]

kohi'i kohii, beaver, *Castor canadensis* [NP 1]

koipa koipa, desert bighorn, *Ovis canadensis* [NP 1, 2]

kongida kaŋid·a [NP 2]; see kangita

konodzǝ natüzw ?, [natisua, medicine], unidentified plant species [NP 1]

kosi ?, packrat [NP 1]

kosinohop ?, bread of cattail pollen [NP 2]

kosipa, ko.sipa kus·ipaa, kus·ipa'a [kus·ɨ, dust, ashes; paa, pa'a, water], place name, Allen River [NP 2]

ko.sipatükǝd kus·ipatikadɨ, [see kosipa; -tikadɨ, eaters], people at Carson Lake [NP 2]

kua, küa kɨa, cicada, *Okanagodes* spp. [NP 1]

kuba, kubǝ, kup kɨib·a, kɨipa, ground squirrel, *Citellus townsendi; C. beldingi* [NP 2, 1]

kuda kudaa, bird species, Mallard, *Anas platyrhynchos* [NP 1, 2]

kudagwavǝ ?, unidentified plant species [NP 2]

kudusi kudusi, open twined burden basket [NP 2]

kuha kuha, plant species, small blazing star, *Mentzelia albicaulis* [NP 1, 2]

kuna kuna, firewood [NP 1]

kunaitu, kuna'ita kuna'idɨ, bird species, California Gull, *Larus californicus* [NP 1]

kupidə, kupidu kupita, drive with fire [NP 1]

kusa kus·a, man's clothing, leggings [NP 2]

kusabi kucabi, larvae of brine fly, *Ephedra hyans* [NP 2]

kusatikədu kucadikadɨ [kuca-, larvae of brine fly; -tɨkadɨ, eaters], people at Mono Lake [NP 2]

kuyui kuyui, fish species, cui-ui, *Chasmistes cujus* [NP 1, 2]

kuyuihukwa kuyuihuuk^wa [kuyui, cui-ui; huuk^wa, stream, river], Truckee River [NP 1, 2]

kuyuipanünəd kuyui paniɨn·adɨ [kuyui, cui-ui; paniɨn·adɨ, lake], Pyramid Lake [NP 1, 2]

kuyuitükədə kuyuidikadɨ [kuyui, cui-ui; -tɨkadɨ, eaters], people at Pyramid Lake [NP 1]

kuzabi see kusabi

küdu ?, rasp used in antelope drive

küpa see kuba

kütunano ?, basket hat

kwasəb-nagwi, kwasü-nagwi k^was·ibɨnag^wi, k^was·ɨnag^wi, [k^was·ɨ, tanned hide; nag^wi, dress], buckskin dress [NP 2]

kwasəmoko, kwasamoko k^was·ɨmoko [k^was·ɨ, tanned hide; moko, footwear], moccasins [NP 1]

kwasəpə k^was·ipɨ [tanned hide], buckskin dress [NP 1]

kwasipagap ?, perhaps k^was·ipagapi [k^was·ɨ, tail; pagapi, stone-tipped arrow], complete arrow [NP 1]

kwasu, kwasü k^was·ɨ [tanned hide], shirt [NP 2]

kwasüb k^was·ibɨ, see kwasəpə [NP 2]

kwasünadudno k^was·ɨ natinoopɨ [k^was·ɨ, tanned hide; natinoopɨ, that which is carried on the back], saddle [originally pad saddle?] [NP 1]

kwasüsotiya k^was·icotia [k^was·ɨ. tanned hide; cotia hat], skin cap [NP 1]

kwatino, kwatinyo k^watin·u [k^wati-, to shoot; -n·u, instru.], harpoon, two-pronged fish spear [NP 1, 2]

kwibanobu k^wibanopɨ, plant species, slim stinging nettles, *Urtica dioica* [NP 1]

kwidagai k^widagaga'i, bird species, Blackbilled Magpie, *Pica pica* [NP 1]

kwidagainahu k^widagaga'i nahua [k^widagagai'i, magpie; nahua, trap], magpie trap [NP 1]

kwidamogus k^widamugus·u [k^wida-, feces; mugus·u, lizard], small lizard species, unidentified [NP 2]

kwidətunab k^widatinabi, plant species, *Heliotropium curvassicum* [NP 2]

kwinasunobi k^wi'naa'a siɨnobi [k^winaa'a, eagle; siɨ-, willow; nobi, house] cage for eagle [NP 1]

kwi'na' k^winaa'a, bird species, Golden Eagle, *Aquila chrysaetos* [NP 1]

magasa'a magaza'a, horned toad, *Phrynosoma* sp. [NP 2]

magu.tuhupi magutihuupi, plant species, Nevada dalea, *Dalea polyademia* [NP 1]

maimwa maimu'a, to hunt individually, to trail [NP 1, 2]

maiwoməsubi ?, [mai-, with the hands; siɨbi, willow], house frame [NP 2]

manəts ?, Washoe [NP 1]

mata mata, metate [NP 1, 2]

mawgoni mogo'ni, woman [NP 1]

moa moa, plant species, probably *Allium parvum* [NP 2]

moata ?, a yellow mineral poison [NP 2]

mogoni see mawgoni

mogutuhup see magu.tuhupi

moibi muibi, insect species, fly [NP 1, 2]

mokano, mo.kano mukan·u, mukanu, flaker [NP 1, 2]

moko moko, footwear, moccasin [NP 1, 2]

mudubui mudubui, plant species, common threesquare, *Scirpus pungens* [NP 1]

mugutuhupi see magu.tuhupi

muhu mihi, porcupine, *Erethizon dorsatum* [NP 2]

muip, muipə muipi, plant species, sacred datura, *Datura meteloides* [NP 1, 2]

mu.zanə ?, wood used for night fire [NP 1]

mühü see muhu

nabagia nabagi'a, bath [NP 2]

nabawits nabawici'i [draw lines], tattoo [NP 2]

nabizasi napis·asi [na-, reflex.; pis·a, red paint; -si, subord.], to be painted [NP 2]

naboni ? [but nabo'o; na-, nomin.; poo, po'o, line, trail; a design], marks made on face or body during doctoring [NP 2]

naboŋna ? [but nabo'o or naboo, picture, mark, design], colored stitches on baskets [NP 2]

nabu nabu, plant species, *Opuntia polyacantha* [NP 2]

nadakadu nadakadɨ, [na-, nomin.; -ta-, foot; -kati, to sit (sg.); -di, past part.], stirrup [NP 1]

nadzitənə nazito'o, cane [NP 1]

nagəna ?, antelope drive [NP 1]

nagoihisamapu nakohicam·api [na-, nomin.; kohi-, stomach; cam·a, to pull; -pi, class.], cinch [NP 1]

naguta nagita, bird species, Canada Goose, *Branta canadensis* [NP 1]

nagwasisaniga nag^was·icaniga'a [na-, nomin.; k^was·i, tail; caniga'a, guard], crupper [NP 1]

nagwi nag^wi, dress, skirt [NP 2]

nagwiba nag^wiba'a, nag^wiban·u, whip [NP 1]

nahapi ?, but nihacida [niha, ?; cida, cup, bowl], coiled serving basket [NP 2]

nahu nahua [na-, nomin.; hua, to trap], trap [NP 1]

nakwi nak^wi [NP 1]; see nagwi

namabüsugin ?, but possibly namabɨcugin·a [na-, nomin.; mabɨcu, twist, squeeze; -gin·a, prog.], twisting [NP 1]

namagəd ?, unidentified plant species [NP 1]

namahibi namahii, personal belongings [NP 2]

namaku namaku, money, beads [NP 2]

namaqwi ?, beads [NP 1]

namosain ?, [muusa, sweat house as Owens Valley Paiute term; saa-, to boil], sweat house [NP 1]

nanumow ?, fish line [NP 2]

napisapo ?, deerskin skirt [NP 1]; see napizapo.bə.

napizapo.bə napicapogapi, breech cloth [NP 1]

napizapogo see napizapo.bə [NP 1]

napizəpogo yəp see napizapo.bə [NP 1]

nasiu ?, dream for antelope [NP 2]

nati nati, belt [NP 1, 2]

natsa ?, unidentified plant species [NP 2]

natsəgwanəpə nacakun·api, door [NP 2]

natüswa natisua, medicine [NP 1]

nawizo.du.na ?, duck snare [NP 2]

nawotunohopi ?, place name, Deephole Valley [NP 1]

nazihidu nacihidi [na-, nomin.; cihi, to stick; -di, past part.] coiled basketry [NP 2]

nədənəgədiidə ?, one who repeats after a leader or shaman [NP 1]

nizu niis·u, niisu, Mormon cricket, *Anabrus simplex* [NP 1, 2] *nobi, no.bi* nobi, house [NP 1, 2]

noda nod·a, insect species, Yellowjacket, *Vespula* spp. [NP 2]

noho noho, egg [NP 1]

nubamaka nibamoko [niba, snow; moko, footwear], overshoes or snow boots [NP 2]

nuba nadzitonə niba naʒitoʔo [niba, snow; naʒitoʔo, cane], stick used to aid walking on snowshoes [NP 1]

nuba tonaʔa nibatonoʔo [niba, snow; tinoʔo, to carry], bird species, Oregon Junco [NP 2]

nubokoi.ba nabogoʔi [split seed game], nabogaʔizaga [basket dice], basket dice [NP 2]

nuhapi ?, possibly nihapi or nihapi [nihacida, fine-woven serving basket], fine coiled serving basket [NP 2]; see nahapi.

numa nimi, person, Indian [NP 1, 2]

nutamə natam·u [na-, nomin.; tam·u, sinew] sinew wrapping on arrow [NP 1]

nükodəp nakodapi [na-, nomin.; koda- to coil; -pi, class.], top hoop on house frame [NP 1]

oapi oapi, yellow paint, sunflower [NP 2]

obə ?, place name, Black Mountains, "many rocks" [NP 2]

obə ?, plant species, possibly miner's lettuce, *Montia perfoliata* [NP 2]

obugwazu baid n ?, [pukʷa, to lie down, pl.], place where man hides to hunt ducks [NP 1]

odzaza ?, but probably os·as·a [os·a, water jug; -s·a, noun suffix], unidentified animal [insect ?], said to aid in pitching water jugs [NP 2]

odzaza dukanogwa ?, but probably os·as·a tikan·ugʷa [os·as·a, animal species; tikan·ugʷa, food], "that which odzaza eats," leaves of mansanita, *Archtostaphylos* sp. [NP 2]

ohen ?, frozen [NP 2]; see awhen

ohosomibi ohocomibi [oho, bone; comibi, beads] bone beads [NP 1]

ohotudama, ohotutama ohotid·am·a [oho, bone; tid·am·a, fish-hook], fishhooks [NP 2] ohotidam·a, ohotitam·a [NP 1]

oituhawai katukwəʔ oi tihoawaikatikʷiti [oi, there; tihoawai-, to hunt; -kati, to sit, sg.; -kʷi, fut.; -ti, gen. active], to sit and wait to kill game [NP 2]

oŋabi oŋ·abi, salt [NP 2]

opo, opu opo, boiling basket [NP 2]

osaba osapaa [osa-, alkali; paa, water] place name, Double Springs [NP 2]

osokoə ?, scraping hides [NP 1]

owabi see oŋabi [NP 2]

pa'abi ?, but probably paʔabi, shaft and awl straightener, sharpener [NP 1]

pabagatüdü pabagatidi [paba-, big; kati, to sit; -di, agentive], place name, highest peak, west side of Pyramid Lake [Tule Peak] [NP 1]

paba hub pabahuubi [paba, big; huubi, stream, river], place name [NP 2]

pabasugu pabasuku [paba-, big; suku, robin] bird species, Robin, *Turdus migratorius* [NP 1]

paba tupodz pabatipoca [paba-, big; tipoca, lizard species], lizard species, probably chuckwalla, *Sauromalus obesus* [NP 1]

pabikatud see pabagatüdü [NP 1]

pabisa, pabisi pabiʒi, longtail weasel, *Mustela frenata* [NP 1, 2]

pabui wəyu'a ?, place name, range west of Ione [Paradise Range?] [NP 2]

padi.kwa ?, place name, mountain on east side of Pyramid Lake [NP 1]

padu, padü pad·u, mush stirrer [NP 2]

padüs padis·i, plant species, onion, *Allium biseptrum* [NP 2]

padwaʔa paduaʔa [father's sister], bear, *Ursa* sp. [NP 2]

pagagib, pagagibə pagabibi, plant species, false hellebore, *Veratrum californicum* [NP 1]

pagagiv, pagagiva see pagagib

pagagwi, pagakwi pagakʷi, bow strings [NP 1, 2]

paganabo ?, unidentified tribe with whom people at Pyramid Lake traded [NP 1]

pagapə pagapi, stone-tipped arrow [NP 1]

pagasi tutabino ?, sling [NP 1]

pagun pahagan·u, pestle [NP 1, 2]

pagupu see pagapə

paguts pagucu, buffalo [*Bison bison*] [NP 2]

pagwi pagʷi, small fish species; all fish [NP 2]

paha paha, mortar [NP 1, 2]

pahabə, pa.habə pahaba, paahaba [pa-, paa-, water; haba, shade], platform for fishing [NP 1]

pahaguna, pahaguno see pagun

pahava see pahabə

pahü paahi, plant species, *Helianthus annuus* [NP 2]

paiaqwa ?, woven sections of weir [NP 2]

paido' ?, perhaps padia [pa-, water; tia, decoy], duck decoy [NP 1]

paikani pakani [pa-, water; kani, shelter], bird blind [NP 2]

pakə, pakhu, pahü paaki, plant species, sunflower, *Helianthus annuus* [NP 1]

pakodəp, pakodoba pakodoba, pakodopa, Brewer's Blackbird, *Euphagus cyanocephalus* [NP 1]; pakodob·a [NP 2]

pakwi pakʷi, small fish species; all fish [NP 1]

pakwiwana pakʷiwana [pakʷi, fish; wana, net], dip net [NP 1]

pamagadsa pamagaʒaʔa, horned lizard, *Phrynosoma* spp. [NP 1, 2]

pamahabi, pamahab paamahabi, plant species, *Eleocharis palustris* [NP 1, 2]

pamahanagwi paamahanagʷi, [pamaha-, plant species; nagʷi, skirt], skirt of rushes [NP 2]

pamasibə pamasaibi, plant species, *Eleocharis palustris* [NP 1]

pamogo pam·ogo, frog [NP 2]

pamus pamus·i, beaver [muskrat, *Ondatra zibethica*] [NP 1]

panak panakʷati [pa-, water; -nakʷati, direction], Bannock [NP 1]

panosə paan·us·a, bird species, White Pelican, *Pelecanus erythrorhynchos* [NP 1]

panu.nədə paniin·adi [lake], place name, Walker Lake [NP 2]

pasiwanüna pasiawiniʔi, gila monster [NP 2]

pa.soni pas·oni, fishing platform; four-post shade [NP 1]

pasugu, patsugu pacug·u, river otter, *Lutra canadensis* [NP 2]

patakai, patakai'i patakaiʔi, raccoon, *Procyon lotor* [NP 1, 2]

patu patu, mush stirrer [NP 1]

patuhita patihid·a, patihiʔya, wapati (elk), *Cervus elaphus* [NP 2, 1]

patupa ?, probably padiba [pa-, water; tiba, pinenut], pinenuts used as beads [NP 2]

pawagabish, pawakapic pawakapis·a, plant species, sweet anise, *Osmorhiza occidentalis* [NP 1]

pawgwahowi ?, place name, canyon on south side of Walker Lake [Cottonwood Creek] [NP 2]

pawhuəp ?, probably pahuapi [pa-, water; huapi, trap], weir [NP 2]

pawia pawia, plant species, curly dock, *Rumex crispis* [NP 1]

payona, payuna payuna, mink, *Mustela vison* [NP 1]

pazaki ?, probably pasaki [pa-, water; saki boat] willow fish trap [NP 1] *pazia* pas·ia, Bald Eagle, *Haliaeetus leucocephalus* [NP 1]

pazitono paƷidono, bird species, Western Meadow Lark, *Sturnella neglecta* [NP 1]

paʔyu, paʔyü paʔyɨ [desert kangaroo rat, *Dipodomys* spp.], brown mouse [NP 1]

pezip ?, piece on small stomach of animal [NP 1]

piəg piagɨ, caterpillar, probably of white-lined sphinx moth, *Hyles lineata* [NP 1]

picigu picigu, nock on arrow [NP 2]

pidanu pidan·u, fireplace [NP 1]

pigahana, pi.gahan pigahan·aʔa, bat, *Myotis* spp. [NP 1]

pihabi pihabi, sugar [NP 1, 2]

pihatuhu pihatuhu [piha-, sweet; tuhu, plant species, broomrape], broomrape, *Orobanche crymbosa* [NP 2]

pihihukaP ?, [pihi-, down], eagle breast feather strips; men's headdress [NP 1]

pi.jəp pis·api, red paint [NP 1, 2]

pinuga kwasia ?, sagebrush-bark apron/breechclout [NP 2]

pipuz pipuuzi, stink bug, *Eleodes* sp. [NP 1]

piquid pikʷiidi, plant species, Hooker's balsamroot, *Balsamorhiza hookeri* [NP 1]

pitənagwətə pitan·agʷati [pita-, base, bottom, south; -nagʷati, direction], people near Bishop, Calif. [Owens Valley Paiute] [NP 2]

pitsa mogui ?, leggings [NP 2]

piwətamə ?, [tam·u, sinew], wrapping at bottom of fletching on arrow [NP 1]

pixəp see pi.jəp [NP 2]

pixump pizuʔma, obsidian [NP 1, 2]

pizəpi, pizəupi see pi.jəp

pizəsutu ?, bird species, Canvasback, *Aythya valisineria* [NP 1]

pizump, pizəmu see pixump

podanu, podano pidan·u [pestle], mortar [NP 2]

podiatu ?, perhaps poodiatu [poo-, trail; tia, cache, decoy; -tu, loc.] pit for trapping deer [NP 2]

podo podo, digging stick [NP 1, 2]

pogopisha pogopis·a, plant species, golden currant, *Ribes aureum* [NP 1]

poinabi, poinab poinabi, leader; shaman's interpreter [NP 2]

poinyo ?, perhaps pihiʔigin·u [pihi, fur; igin·u, tongue] rabbit call [NP 1]

poku puku, pet, dog, horse [NP 1]

pongadsi poŋaaƷi, mouse [NP 1]

poniʔa, ponicya poŋia, striped skunk, *Mephitis mephitis* [NP 1]

poniʔa sotüʔa poŋiacotia [ponia, skunk; cotia, hat], skunk-skin cap [NP 1]

ponosa poŋos·a, arrow [NP 2]

poo, pəo poo, trail, line [NP 1]

pota, potə, potu potu, shell beads, probably specifically *Olivella* [NP 2]

pugu, pugə pug·u, pet, dog, horse [NP 2]

puhagam, puhagəm puhagam·i, [puha-, power; -ka-, to have; -m·i, animate pl.], shaman [NP 1, 2]

puhutüa pihɨtia [pihi, duck; tia, decoy], duck decoy [NP 2]

puidwa puiduaʔa, abalone shell [NP 2]

puiʔwi see abuiʔwi [NP 1]

pühü pihɨ, duck [NP 1, 2]

pühühua pihɨhua, duck trapping [NP 1]

pühünaha pihinoho [pihi, duck ; noho, egg], duck eggs [NP 2]

pühüno pihino'o [pihi, fur, hair; -noʔo, to carry], carry deer or antelope into camp [NP 1]

pühüponos pihiponos·a [pihi, duck; ponos·a, arrow], duck arrow [NP 1]

püwhan ?, [pihi, fur, hair], scraping hair from hides [NP 1]

quibanup see kwibanobu

quiui see kuyui

sa.go caago, glue for sinew backing on bows [NP 1]

sagwəda cagʷidi, porcupine, *Erethizon dorsatum* [NP 1, 2]

sai sai, saidukaʔa [sai-, tule; -dukaʔa, under], Pit River people [NP 1]

saib, saibə saibi, tule, *Scirpus acutus* [NP 2]

saidöka saidikaʔa, saidukaʔa [sai-, tule; -dikaʔa, eaters; -dukaʔa, under], early occupants of the Humboldt Sink [NP 1]

sainaguta sainagita, bird species, Aleutian Canada Goose, *Branta canadensis leucopareia* [NP 1]

sain.nobi sainobi [sai-, tule; nobi, house, shelter], tule house [NP 1]

sainobinawat sainobi nawata [sai-, tule; nobi, house, shelter; nawata, pole], poles of house framework [NP 1]

sainunədu ?, possibly saipaniin·adɨ [sai-, tule; paniin·adɨ, lake], Washo Lake [NP 1]

saisaki saisaki [sai-, tule; saki, boat], tule boat [NP 1]

saituka see saidöka [NP 2]

saiwabi sawabi, plant species, big sagebrush, *Artemesia tridentata* [NP 1]

saiwabi wənanobi ?, possibly sawabi wininobi [sawabi, sagebrush; wini-, to stand, sg.; nobi, house], circular windbreak [NP 1]

saiyagabu sayakabi, plant species, eriastrum, *Eriastrum sparsiflorum* [NP 1]

saiyapühü sayapihi [saya, mudhen; pihi, fur, hair, skin], mudhen-skin dress [NP 1]

saiyatukəd sayatikadi [saya, mudhen; -tikadi, eater], place name, Mudhen Lake [NP 1, 2]

saki saki, tule balsa boat [NP 1, 2]

samuna, samu'nə, samu'no ?, fine winnowing tray [NP 1]

samund see samuna

sana ?, Honey Lake Indians as said at Pyramid Lake [NP 1]

sanapobi ?, possibly sanapobi [sana- pitch; po-, to be round; -bi, classif.], gum from pine trees [NP 2]

saniki san·akiʔi, bird species, Nuthatch, *Sitta* sp. [NP 1]

sasinub ?, breechclout [NP 2]

sassi ?, probably saas·i [saa-, to boil; -s·i, subord.], place name, hot springs in Reese River Valley [NP 2]

sawabi see saiwabi

sawabi nagwi sawabi nagʷi [sawabi, sagebrush; nagʷi, skirt, dress], sagebrush bark skirt [NP 2]

sawapon-naʔa sawabonoʔo, gall from sagebrush [NP 2]

sa.ya saya, bird species, American Coot, *Fulica americana* [locally called mudhen] [NP 1, 2]

sa'ya tuma'a saʔyadima [saʔya, to screen; tima, fine twined tray], basketry tray [NP 2]

shabui ?, unidentified plant species [NP 2]

si sii, plant species, onion, *Allium anceps* [NP 2]

siabi ciabi, ciabui [cia-, wild rose; -bi, classif.; -bui, seed, berry], plant species, wild rose, *Rosa woodsii* [NP 2]

si.capi ?, soup of fish air sacks [NP 2]

sida cida, basket cup, drinking bowl [NP 2]

si.duna cidun·a, bird species, Horned Lark, *Eremophila alpestris* [NP 1, 2]

sigica cigica, spear used in warfare [NP 1]

sigoab, sikoabu sigoabi, plant species, death camas, *Zigadenus venosus; Z. paniculatus* [NP 1]

sigosa saigos·a, bird species, White-fronted Goose, *Anser albifrons* [NP 1] *sigu*   cigu, seed beater [NP 1, 2]

sigupi   sigupi, plant species, rubber rabbitbrush, *Chrysothamnus nauseosus* [NP 1, 2]

sigusanakaʔa   sigusan·akoʔo [sigu-, rabbitbrush; san·akoʔo, gum], gum from rabbitbrush [NP 2]

sigwa, sigwatu   siigʷa, cattail house mat [NP 1, 2]

sikawabu   ?, possibly sigoabi [NP 2]; see sigoab

sikigi   sikigiʔi, bird species, Mountain Quail, *Oreortyx pictus* [NP 2]

si.ku   see sigu

sima   cima, cattail pollen [NP 1]

sinu.pa, si.nupi   sinupi, bladder [NP 1]

si.tu.dapu   citidapi, fringe [NP 1]

siwanobi   ?, possibly siigʷanobi [siigʷa, tule mat; nobi, house, shelter], tule-mat-covered house [NP 2]

sogoduish   sogoduis·i [sogo-, ground, old time; tuis·i, pet], old term for dog [NP 1]

sogomoko   sogomoko [sogo-, ground, old time; moko, footwear], moccasins [NP 2]

sogonuma   sogonimi [sogo-, ground, old time; nimi, person, Indian], man walking [NP 2]

sogopuku   sogopuku [sogo-, ground, old time; puku, pet, horse], dog [NP 2]

sogopühü   sogopihi [sogo-, ground, old time; pihi, duck], bird species, Cinnamon Teal, *Anas cyanoptera* [NP 1]

soko, sokoʔo   sokoʔo, spoon [NP 1]

soko.bə   sokobi, damp place to bury hides for tanning [NP 1]

somibi   comibi, beads, particularly of shell [NP 2]

soŋo   soŋo, soŋoʔo, lungs [NP 2]

soŋu.i   soŋoiʔi, bird species, Hummingbird, [NP 1]

sopi   ?, unidentified grass, possibly mannagrass, *Glyceria* sp. [NP 1]

sopiwahabü   ? [wahabi, Great Basin wildrye], unidentified grass [NP 1]

sotua, sotüa   cotia, hat, hairnet or other head covering [NP 2]

su   siibi, plant species, willow, *Salix* spp. [NP 1, 2]

subi   see su

subi nambüsugin   ?, possibly siibi namabisoma [siibi, willow; namabisoma, tumpline], tumpline of willow [NP 1]

su.bi pi.tukwə   siibi pitakʷa [siibi, willow; pitakʷa, root], willow roots [NP 1]

sudəpi   cudupi, plant species, *Ephedra nevadensis; E. viridis* [NP 1, 2]

suhu   siihuu [sii-, willow; huupi, river, stream], place names: 1. Long Valley Creek; 2. stream in Pinenut Hills [NP 2]

suigi   ?, clamshell disk bead [NP 2]

sukü, səkü   suku, snowshoes [NP 1]

suno, sunu, su.nu   sunu, plant species, *Atriplex argenta* [NP 1]

su.osa   siios·a [sii-, willow; os·a, water jug], water jug [NP 1]

susida, sü.zida, su.sida   siizida [sii-, willow; cida, cup, bowl], small round cup or bowl [NP 1]

sü.da.   ?, two pieces of tallow near bladder of beaver [NP 1]

süigi   ?, abalone shell pendant [NP 2]; see suigi

süku, səku   see sukü

taba   tabaa, whitetail antelope ground squirrel, *ammospermophilus leucurus* [NP 1, 2]

tabisiba   tabiciba, small unidentified lizard [NP 1]

tabuʔu   tabuʔu, mountain cottontail, *Sylvilagus nuttallii* [NP 1, 2]

tagü   tagi, plant species, *Lomatium nevadensis; L. ravenii* [NP 2]

tagwani   ?, place name, mountain near Wobuska [NP 2]

taka   taka, arrow point [NP 2]

takakudawa'   takakudakʷa [taka, stone arrow point; -kudakʷa, mountain, peak, range], place name, near Eagleville [NP 1]

takatubiʔi   ?, probably takatib·iʔi [taka, stone arrow point; tibi, rock, stone], place name, near Walker Lake, probably Mount Hicks [NP 2]

takawihi   takawihi [taka, stone; wihi, knife] stone knife [NP 2]

takoni, takuna   ?, people near Susanville [Maidu?] [NP 1]

tama agai   tamaʔagai [tama, spring; agai, trout]; spring trout, *Salmo clarki henshawi* [NP 1]

tamo   tam·u, sinew [NP 2]

tanbong   tiboŋi, Shoshoni [NP 1]

ta.noə   tanoapi [from tanoomani-, to run, pl.], antelope drive [NP 1]

tasno   caan·u, pinenut pole [NP 1]

tawtiokiʔi   ?, perhaps todigʷa [Common Poorwill, *Phalaenoptilus nuttallii*, bird species, Nightingale [NP 2]

təsiagatu (numu)   tasiigatu nimi [tasii, middle; -ga-, to have; -tu, locative; nimi, person, Indian], people of Winnemucca Valley [NP 1]

tətugap   ?, antelope corral [NP 2]

tobo   ?, dirt used to paralyze antelope [NP 1]

tobonig   see tanbong [NP 1]

todza   tooʒaʔa, plant species, *Lomatium dissectum* [NP 1]

toga   tooga, bird species, Clark's Nutcracker, *Nucifraga columbiana* [NP 1]

togabaidua   ?, to track deer [NP 1]

togako, togoko   togogʷa, rattlesnake [NP 2]

toha'ada   tohaʔada [toha-, white; ada, crow], bird species, California Gull, *Larus californicus* [NP 2]

tohasikwad   tohacakʷaadi, bird species, Canvasback, *Aythya valisineria* [NP 1, 2]

toi   toiʔi, plant species, cattail, *Typha latifolia* [NP 2]

toibo   toiboo [toi-, cattail; poo, trail], Carson Lake trail [NP 2]

toidə   ?, possibly toidina [toi-, cattail; tina, root], cattail root [NP 2]

toinahukwa   toi nahuukʷa [toi-, cattail; na-, nomin.; -huukʷa, stream, river] Carson River [NP 2]

toinobi   toinobi [toi-, cattail; nobi, shelter, house], cattail house [NP 2]

toisaki   toisaki [toi-, cattail; saki, boat, watercraft], cattail boat [NP 1]

toitsma, toi tsma   toicima [toi-, cattail; cima, cattail pollen], cattail pollen [NP 2]

toitükudə   toidikadi [toi-, cattail; -tikadi, eater], 'cattail eaters', people at Carson Sink [NP 2]

tokogwa   see togako [NP 2]

tomanoba   ?, but possibly taamanoba [taamano, to be spring; -ba, class.], season of spring [NP 2]

tomo agai   tomoʔagai [tomo, winter; agai, trout], 'winter trout', *Salmo clarki henshawi* [NP 1]

toniga   tonigaʔa, toniigaʔa, flower [NP 2]

tonobi   tonobi, plant species, greasewood, *Sarcobatus vermiculatus* [NP 2]

tonobi-duhaka   ?, possibly tonobikudakʷa [tonobi, greasewood; -kudakʷa, point, hill]; place name [NP 2]

tonokudz   tonokuza [tono-, greasewood; ?], fish spear [NP 1]

topada   topada, breechclout, apron [NP 1]

topə, topu   topi, shield [NP 2]

tosə, toza   see todza [NP 2]

toshab, toshəbui   toʔis·abui [toʔis·a, pipe; -bui, berry, seed], plant species, western chokecherry, *Prunus demissa* [NP 1, 2] *tositonig, tossitonigadu*   tocitoniga'a, tocitonigadɨ, [toci-, shiny; toniga'a, flower; -dɨ, pres. part.], plant species, possibly common yarrow, *Achillea millefolium* [NP 1]

tozitun'ab   ?, plant species, mint, *Mentha canadensis* [NP 2]

tsago   caago, glue [NP 2]

tsano   caan·u, pinenut pole [NP 2]

tsiabi   ciabi, ciabui, plant species, wild rose, *Rosa woodsii* [NP 2]

tsikü   ciku, seed beater [NP 1]

tsma   cima, inflorescence of cattail [NP 1]

tuba   tɨba, pinyon nut [NP 1, 2]

tubagoda'a   tɨbag^woda'a [tɨba-, pinyon; woda'a, chipmunk], Townsend's chipmunk, *Eutamias townsendii* [NP 2]

tubagogwa   tɨbag^woda'a [tɨba, pinyon; woda'a, chipmunk]; kangaroo rat, *Dipodomys* spp. [NP 2]

tubakǝwanǝ   tɨba kawono [tɨba, pinyon; ka-, cone; wono, open-twined burden basket], cone basket [NP 1]

tubapi, tubǝpi   tɨbapi, single-leaf pinyon, *Pinus monophylla* [NP 1, 2]

tubapongadsi   tɨbapoŋaazi [tɨba-, pinyon; poŋaazi, mouse], pinyon mouse, *Peromyscus truei* [NP 2]

tubasǝ, tǝbas   ?, bridle [NP 2]; see tubǝsǝniga

tubǝsǝniga   tɨb·acaniga'a [tɨb·a, mouth; caniga'a, to guard]; bridle, but given to Park as cinch [NP 1]

tubi   tuubi, plant species, mountain mahogany, *Cercocarpus ledifolius* [NP 2]

tubi   tɨb·i [rock]; cooking rocks [NP 2]

tubi nabagia, tupinabagiab   tɨb·i nabagia'a, tɨpi nabagiabɨ [tɨb·i (NP 2), tɨpi (NP 1), rock; nabagia'a, nabagiabɨ, to bathe], sweat bath [NP 2, 1]

tubi owabi   tɨb·i oŋaabi [tɨb·i, rock; oŋaabi, salt], salt [NP 2]

tubi ozabi   tɨb·i osabi [tɨb·i, rock; osabi, alkali], salt [NP 2]

tubisiginobu   tɨbis·igin·ubi, plant species, purple sage, *Salvia dorii* [NP 2]

tubo   ?, possibly tɨboo [tɨ-, intrans.; poo, trail; lit. 'to mark'], ferrous material used to dye basket materials [NP 1]

tuboipihabi   tɨbapihabi [tɨba, pinyon; pihabi, sugar], pine sap [NP 2]

tubongǝ, tubonig   see tanbong [NP 1]

tubotsa, tubudza   tɨb·oca, large black lizard [NP 2]

tubus, tubuz, tubuzi   tɨb·us·i, plant species, *Cyperus esculentus* [NP 2]

tud.ama   tɨdam·a [-tɨ, nomin.; tam·a, tooth, teeth], fish hooks [NP 2]

tudaŋanotuna   ?, shuttle [NP 1]

tudǝmahuad   ?, but likely tɨdam·ahuadɨ [tɨ-, trans.; tam·a, tooth, teeth; hua-, trap; -dɨ, agentive], line with fish hooks [NP 2]

tudokwidǝnu   tok^widan·u, basket type, for pitting chokecherries, other berries [NP 1]

tugaisin   ?, people over the Sierra, perhaps Miwok [NP 1]

tugasawa   ?, but likely tɨkas·awa [tɨ-, intrans.; kas·a, feather, wing; -wa, class.], feathers on arrow, to feather an arrow [NP 1]

tugwicǝ, tukwicipi   tɨg^wis·i, tɨk^wis·ipi, to twine, twined baskets [NP 2, 1]

tuhagwǝda.da   tohag^witaadi [toha-, white; k^witaadɨ, to be colored], white beads [NP 2]

tuhida kwasü   tɨhid·a k^was·ɨ [tɨhid·a, deer; k^was·ɨ, shirt], deerskin shirt [NP 2]

tuhiwi   tɨhiwi [-tɨ, nomin.; hiwi, dig], hole, pit [NP 1]

tuhu   tuhu, plant species, broomrape, *Orobanche fasiculata* [NP 2]

tuhugwǝda.da   tuug^widaadi [tuu-, black; -k^widaadi, to be colored], black (beads) [NP 2]

tuhut   tɨhi'ya, deer [see tühita] [NP 1]

tuhuya, tuhu'ya   see tuhut [NP 1]

tuhu', tuhuu   tuhu'u, bobcat, *Lynx rufus* [NP 1]

tuipakwi   tuipak^wi [pak^wi, fish], fish species, tui chub, *Gila bicolor obesus* [NP 1]

tuka'wa   tuukawa [tuu-, black; kawa, packrat] bushy-tailed wood rat, *Neotoma cinerea* [NP 1]

tu'kiwǝnugwino   ?, perhaps tɨɨk^wiwinig^wino, [tɨɨk^wi-, to recite; -winɨ, contin.; -g^wino, aspect], antelope charming rasp (used to call antelope) [NP 1]

tukwiboin   ?, sling [NP 1]

tuma, tuma'a, tüma   tima, tɨɨma, close twined winnowing tray [NP 1, 2]

tumad   tɨmaadi, plant species, *Stanleya pinnata* [NP 2]

tumǝ'a kwina'a   ? [? k^winaa'a, eagle], mountain on east side of Walker River Reservation, said to mean 'eagle rivals' [NP 2]

tumuhabuno, tumuhabǝn   ?, high mountains on west side of Pyramid Lake; Virginia Range [NP 1]

tuna   tin·a, pronghorn, *Antilocapra americana* [NP 2]

tuna mahutwa   ?, perhaps tin·a mahitua [tin·a, antelope; mahi, to drive game; -tua, poten.]; antelope drive [NP 1]

tunabǝ   tɨɨnabi [tɨɨna, tina, root; -bi, classif.], ryegrass hairbrush [NP 2]

tunabonigǝ   ?, drivers of game [NP 1]

tunagadu   ?, probably tin·agadɨ [tin·a, antelope; -ga-, to have; -dɨ, pres. part.], antelope drive [NP 2]

tunagapi, tunagoap   ?, probably tin·agapi [tin·a, antelope; -ga-, to have; -pi, classif.] antelope drive [NP 1]

tunakwiba   ?, possibly tin·ak^wiba [tin·a, antelope; k^wiba, to hit], player of antelope rasp [NP 1]

tunanobi   tin·anobi [tin·a, antelope; nobi, house, shelter], circular brush shelter [NP 2]

tunanuga   tin·anika [tin·a, antelope; nika, to dance], antelope dance [NP 1]

tunapiw   tin·apiwɨ [tin·a, antelope; piwɨ, heart], place name, antelope's heart, a knoll 10 mi. west of Deep Hole [NP 1]

tunupi   ?, black paint [NP 1]

tunuyutukad   ?, probably tunuyutikadɨ [tunuyu, a biscuit root species, *Lomatium* sp.; -tikadɨ, eaters], people near Surprise Valley ?? [NP 1]

tunu'u kwina'a   ?, see tumǝ'a kwina'a [NP 2]

tupadǝpi   ?, arrow shaft [NP 1]

tupaz natuswǝ   tɨpoca natisua [tɨpoca, lizard; natisua, medicine], plant species *Crotaphytus* sp. [NP 1]

tu.pǝzibu   ?, probably tɨpas·ibi, plant species, possibly *Penstemon deustus* [NP 1]

tupi, tubi   ?, unidentified plant species (vine with red berries) [NP 1, 2]

tuponi   ?, unidentified plant species [NP 2]

tusano   tus·un·u [tus·u, to grind; -n·u, instru.], mano or muller [NP 2]

tusihi   ?, perhaps tɨcihi [tɨ-, intrans.; cihi, to stick], coiling, sewing [NP 1]

tusikwusab   tɨcik^wis·aba, mole [NP 1]

tusu, tǝsu   tus·u, usually tus·un·u [tus·u, to grind; -n·u, instru.], mano, muller [NP 1, 2]

tusuni'i   ?, unidentified small bird species [NP 1]

tutabino   tɨtabin·u, pestle [NP 1]

tutaigǝp   ?, probably tɨtaigapi [tɨ-, intrans.; tai- to die; -ga-, to have; -pi, past part.], paint, poison [NP 2] *tutamə* tɨdam·a, fishhook [NP 2]

tutubi tuutɨb·ɨ [tuu-, black; tɨb·ɨ, rock, stone], obsidian [probably basalt] [NP 2]

tuwonuga ?, probably tɨwooniga [tɨ-, intrans.; woo-, hair; nɨga, dance], scalp or war dance [NP 2]

tuwopi ?, possibly tɨwoopɨ [tɨ, intrans.; woo-, hair; -pɨ, class.], scalp [NP 1]

tuzikwituinyo ?, hot rock lifter [NP 2]

tu.zino.bi tɨcinobi [tici, small; nobi, house, shelter], sweat house [NP 1]

tüa tɨʔa, cache for duck decoys [NP 1]

tüa tɨʔaa [tɨ-, intrans.? ; ʔaa, horns; lit. 'put on the horns'], to stalk large game [NP 1]

tüa tia, tɨʔaa, duck decoy [NP 1, 2]

tü.abi tiabɨ, tiabui [-bi, class.; -bui, berry, seed], plant species, serviceberry, *Almenchier alnifolia* [NP 1]

tühita tɨhɨʔya, tɨhid·a, mule deer, *Odocoileus hemionus* [NP 1, NP 2]

tühu ?, probably tuhu, ['fat, meat'], place name, near Hawthorne, "back fat" [NP 2]

tühunadamayüən tuhu nadɨmayaina [tuhu, fat, meat; nadɨmaya-, to mix], mixture of meat and fat [NP 1]

tükəd tɨkadɨ, eater [designation of people of an area] [NP 1, 2]

tünü tuhuʔu, lynx, *Lynx rufus* [NP 1]

tüsono'ya tɨsunuʔya, to tan hides [NP 1]

ubishas ipis·as·ɨ, [ɨ-, 2nd per. sing.; pis·a, to paint; -s·ɨ, subord.], paint yourself [NP 2]

u.du idɨɨ, hot! [NP 2]

uduhu'u udɨhuʔu [udɨ, long; huʔu, to flow, 'long flowing'], place name, Pine Grove, "long stream" [NP 2]

udutnabagino idɨtɨ nabagiaʔa, nabagian·u, [idɨtɨ, hot; nabagiaʔa, bath; -n·u, instru.], sweat house [NP 1]

uninobi huninobi, brush shelter [NP 2]

üapa iapɨ, [iapɨ, to plant], plant species, *Chenopodium nevadense* [NP 1]

ü.ds iɨʒɨ, plant species, onion, *Allium nevadense* [NP 2]

üdüta hada idɨtɨ, adaa, [idɨtɨ, hot; adaa, exclam.], "It is hot!" [NP 1]

üino ?, perhaps iin·u [-n·u, instru.], wooden platter [NP 2]

wa.bo, wabü wapo, wab·o, deadfall trap [NP 1, 2]

wa.da, wadə wada, plant species, *Suaeda depressa* [NP 1]

wadanunədu ?, probably wadapaniin·adɨ [wada, seed species; paniin·adɨ, lake], Honey Lake [NP 1]

wadatükədə wadadɨkadɨ [wada, plant species; -tɨkadɨ, eater], people of Honey Lake Valley [NP 1]

wadə goəp ?, [wad·a, pole], deer corral [NP 2]

wadəgwaməpə wad·agᵂamapɨ [wad·a, pole; wama, framework, weir; -pɨ, class.], frame for house [NP 2]

wadoduina matonuin·u, drill [NP 1]

wagadu ?, possibly waagadɨ [waa-, two; katɨ, to sit, sg.], 'two sit', or wakɨdɨ [wakɨ, to work; -dɨ, agent], hunters who wait for deer [NP 1]

wagapi wogopi, plant species, *Pinus jeffreyi*, Jeffrey pine; or *P. lambertiana*, sugar pine [NP 2]

wagapihabi wogopihabɨ [wogo-, sugar pine; pihabɨ, sweet], candy of sugar pine sap [NP 2]

wagatsa wagaʒaʔa, frog species [NP 2]

wahabi habi ?, possibly wahapinabɨ [waha-, grass; pihabɨ, sweet], sugar [NP 1]

wahapəbi wahapuibɨ [waha-, juniper; puibɨ, berry], juniper berries [NP 2]

wahapi wahapɨ, waʔapɨ, waapɨ, plant species, *Juniperus osteosperma*; *J. communis* [NP 2]

wahitə wohita, bird species, Tundra Swan, *Cygnus columbianus* [NP 1]

waisidupə ?, [waʔici, old man; ?], "old man," post of antelope corral [NP 1]

waiyaba wayabɨ, plant species, *Elymus cinereus*; roots used for hairbrush [NP 1]

wakatədə waakatidɨ, [waa-, juniper; katidɨ, sitter], Fox Mountain, north of Pyramid Lake

wakokobə wokokobi, plant species, *Phragmites australis* [NP 1]

wamə waʔma, wam·a, fish weir [probably also 'framework'] [NP 2]

wana, wanə wono, burden basket [NP 2]

wana wana, net [NP 2]

wanaduna ?, shuttle [NP 1]

wanic waŋici [waŋi-, red fox; -ci, dimin.] red fox, *Vulpes vulpes* [NP 2]

wangi'i waŋiʔi, animal species, red fox, *Vulpes vulpes* [NP 2]

wangikudəgwaʔ see waŋigodəgwa

wanigodəgwa waŋigudakᵂa [waŋi-, red fox; -kudakᵂa, point, range], place name, Stillwater Range [NP 2]

wanihai' ? [waŋi-, fox; ?], place name, highest peak in Stillwater Range [NP 2]

wapi waapɨ, plant species, juniper, *Juniperus occidentalis* [NP 2]

wapui waapui, juniper berries [NP 1]

wa.sa was·a, bird species, Great Blue Heron, *Ardea herodias* [NP 1]

washu waasiuʔu, Washoe [NP 1]

wasiba waciibɨ, fire torch, slow match [NP 1]

wasidəgəp waciidigapɨ [wacii-, sagebrush bark; tigapɨ, rope], tumpline of sagebrush bark [NP 1]

wasimoko, watsimoku waciimoko [wacii-, sagebrush bark; moko, footwear], sagebrush-bark moccasins [NP 1]

wata see wa.da

watə, wa.ta wata, pole, for boats, houses; [NP 1]; see wa.da

wato.sai ?, two-pole drying rack

watsi waciibɨ, sagebrush bark [NP 2]

watsi ?, long grey organ on stomach of animals [NP 1]; see akwatsi

watsi mogo' waciimogoʔo [wacii-, sagebrush bark; mogoʔo, bag], sagebrush-bark bag [NP 1]

watsi nagwi waciinagᵂi [wacii-, sagebrush bark; nagᵂi, dress], skirt [NP 2]

watsi tasub waciitasobɨ [wacii-, sagebrush bark; tasobɨ, sock]; sagebush sack [NP 2]

watsia wociaʔa, kit fox, *Vulpes macrotis* [NP 1]

watsotaya ?, possibly woocotia [woo- hair; cotia, head covering]; deerskin head band [NP 2]

wa.wa' wawaʔa [wawaʔa, stranger], Digger Indians [Miwok?] [NP 2]

wa'adu waaʔadɨ [waa-, juniper; adɨ, bow], bow [NP 1]

wa'i waʔi, fire drill [NP 2]

wədəkatəd ?, possibly wɨdakatidɨ [wɨda, bear; katɨ, sit; -dɨ, past part.] place name, Granite Mountain [NP 1]

wənadso winazo, hairbrush [NP 1]

wənənumid winɨn·imidɨ ['move about while standing'; grazing animal], deer, antelope, mountain sheep [NP 1]

wəsia'a wociaʔa, kit fox, *Vulpes macrotis* [NP 2]

whatata hoatataʔa; see haotata [NP 2]

who'siabi ?, possibly huu-, 'arrow', plus ʔ; or huci-, bird; feathers on an arrow [NP 2] *whuwaits* ?, mineral used to paralyze antelope [NP 1]

wia wia, acorns, from California black oak, *Quercus kelloggii* [NP 1]

wiadu wiaʔadɨ [wia, oak; adɨ, bow], oak bow [NP 1]

wiapui, wiˑpui wiyɨpui, plant species, *Shepherdia argentea* [NP 2]

wiˑgwasi, wiˑgwaz wigʷasˑi, bird species, Pintail, *Anas acuta* [NP 1]

wiha wiha, string [NP 1, 2]

wihabi, wihab wihabi, line of string; fish line [NP 2]

wihi wihi, knife [NP 2]

wisa wukagaʔa see wisa wüpuguʔaga [NP 1]

wisa wüpuguʔaga wica wɨpagaʔa [wica, calf of leg; wɨpagaʔa, to wrap], leggings [NP 1]

wisi-puku wisˑipugu, small dog [NP 2]

witə, witu witɨ, awl [NP 1]

witsasahuma ?, [wica, calf of leg; ?], leg wrapping [NP 2]

witsawupuganu wica wɨpaganˑa [wica, calf of leg; wɨpaga-, to wrap; -nˑa, nomin.], leg wrappings [NP 2]

wizipugu see wisi-puku

wodaʔa wodaʔa, chipmunk, *Eutamias* spp. [NP 1]

wogotaba wogotabaa [wogo-, Jeffrey pine; tabaa, ground squirrel], western gray squirrel, *Sciurus griseus* [NP 1]

wokobihabi wokobihabi [woko-, cane; pihabi, sweet], cane sugar [NP 1]

wokokob wokokobɨ, plant species, cane, *Phragmites australis* [NP 1]

wo'siabi ?, feathers on an arrow [NP 2]

wunadzo see wənadso [NP 2]

wunuka ab ?, man's name [NP 1]

wupa'aga wɨpaʔaga, wrapping [NP 1]

wünüpida ?, probably winɨpida [wini-, to stand; pida, fire]; signal fire [NP 1]

wy wai, plant species, *Oryzopsis hymenoides* [NP 1, 2]

yada, yadu yadˑa, open twined parching tray [NP 2]

yadubi yadubi, powder [specular iron] [NP 2]

yamosəbo yamusˑuboo [yamusˑu, bend in river, semicircular valley; poo, trail], "big bend," Fort Bidwell trail [NP 1]

yamoswait yamusˑuwaitu [yamusˑu, bend in river; semicircular valley; -waitu, place], Fort Bidwell [NP 1]

yani yani, fishnet [NP 2]

yani ?, place name, Limbo Mountain [NP 1]

yapa, yapah, yap yapa, yabˑa, plant species, yampa, *Perideridia bolanderi* [NP 1, 2]

yata yata [NP 1]; see yada

yohi yohi, skin skirt/apron [NP 1]

za'abupijə coʔapapisˑa [coʔapa, butterfly; ghost; pisˑa, paint], plant species puffball, *Battarrea phalloides* [NP 1]

zaputukada ? [?; tɨkadɨ, eater], people at Likely, Calif. [Achumawi] [NP 1]

zowəpaga cowɨpagaʔa [co-, head; wɨpagaʔa, wrap, tie], headband [NP 1]

zeapuigwa wana ? [wana, net], a bag-type fishnet [NP 1]